Frommer's W9-CDL-570

Newfoundland & Labrador

2nd Edition

by Andrew Hempstead

Here's what the critics say about Frommer's:

"Amazingly easy to use. Very portable, very complete."
—*Booklist*

"Detailed, accurate, and easy-to-read information for all price ranges."
—*Glamour Magazine*

"Hotel information is close to encyclopedic."
—*Des Moines Sunday Register*

"Frommer's Guides have a way of giving you a real feel for a place."
—*Knight Ridder Newspapers*

WILEY

John Wiley & Sons Canada, Ltd.

Published by:

John Wiley & Sons Canada, Ltd

6045 Freemont Blvd.
Mississauga, ON L5R 4J3

Library and Archives Canada Cataloguing in Publication Data

Hempstead, Andrew
    Frommer's Newfoundland & Labrador / Andrew Hempstead. — 2nd ed.

First ed. published under title: Frommer's Newfoundland and Labrador / by
    Dawn Chafe & Doreen Pendgracs.
Includes index.
ISBN-13 978-0-470-83738-2
ISBN-10 0-470-83738-1

    1. Newfoundland and Labrador—Guidebooks. I. Chafe, Dawn, 1968–
Frommer's Newfoundland and Labrador. II. Title. III. Title: Frommer's Newfoundland
and Labrador

FC2157.H44 2006   917.1804'5   C2006-901012-9

Editor: Robert Hickey
Project Manager: Elizabeth McCurdy
Project Coordinator: Pamela Vokey
Cartographer: Mapping Specialists
Publishing Services Director: Karen Bryan
Publishing Services Manager: Ian Koo
Production by Wiley Indianapolis Composition Services

Front cover photo: Rose Blanche Lighthouse, Newfoundland
Back cover photo: Boat and boathouse, Atlantic Canada

Special Sales

For reseller information, including discounts and premium sales, please call our sales department: Tel. 416-646-7992. For press review copies, author interviews, or other publicity information, please contact our marketing department: Tel. 416-646-4584; Fax: 416-236-4448.
Manufactured in Canada

2   3   4   5   TRI   10   09   08   07   06

Contents

9 Labrador   199

Appendix: Newfoundland & Labrador in Depth   219

Index   232

List of Maps

An Invitation to the Reader

In researching this book, we discovered many wonderful places—hotels, restaurants, shops, and more. We're sure you'll find others. Please tell us about them, so we can share the information with your fellow travelers in upcoming editions. If you were disappointed with a recommendation, we'd love to know that, too. Please write to:

Frommer's Newfoundland & Labrador, 2nd Edition
John Wiley & Sons Canada, Ltd. • 6045 Freemont Blvd. • Mississuaga, ON
L5R 4J3

An Additional Note

Please be advised that travel information is subject to change at any time—and this is especially true of prices. We therefore suggest that you write or call ahead for confirmation when making your travel plans. The authors, editors, and publisher cannot be held responsible for the experiences of readers while traveling. Your safety is important to us, however, so we encourage you to stay alert and be aware of your surroundings. Keep a close eye on cameras, purses, and wallets, all favorite targets of thieves and pickpockets.

About the Author

Andrew Hempstead is a travel writer and photographer who has traveled widely throughout Canada from his home in Banff, Alberta. His research trip for the second edition of this book took him to every corner of the Maritimes, and along the way he found himself searching for fossils along the Bay of Fundy, wine-tasting in Nova Scotia, and golfing the fairways of Prince Edward Island.

In addition to this book, Hempstead has authored guidebooks to Alberta, British Columbia, the Canadian Rockies, and Vancouver, and has co-authored guidebooks to Atlantic Canada, Australia, and New Zealand. His writing and photography has also appeared in many national and international publications.

Frommer's Star Ratings, Icons & Abbreviations

Every hotel, restaurant, and attraction listing in this guide has been ranked for quality, value, service, amenities, and special features using a **star-rating system.** In country, state, and regional guides, we also rate towns and regions to help you narrow down your choices and budget your time accordingly. Hotels and restaurants are rated on a scale of zero (recommended) to three stars (exceptional). Attractions, shopping, nightlife, towns, and regions are rated according to the following scale: zero stars (recommended), one star (highly recommended), two stars (very highly recommended), and three stars (must-see).

In addition to the star-rating system, we also use **seven feature icons** that point you to the great deals, in-the-know advice, and unique experiences that separate travelers from tourists. Throughout the book, look for:

Finds	Special finds—those places only insiders know about
Fun Fact	Fun facts—details that make travelers more informed and their trips more fun
Kids	Best bets for kids and advice for the whole family
Moments	Special moments—those experiences that memories are made of
Overrated	Places or experiences not worth your time or money
Tips	Insider tips—great ways to save time and money
Value	Great values—where to get the best deals

The following **abbreviations** are used for credit cards:

AE	American Express	DISC	Discover	V	Visa
DC	Diners Club	MC	MasterCard		

Frommers.com

Now that you have the guidebook to a great trip, visit our website at **www.frommers.com** for travel information on more than 3,000 destinations. With features updated regularly, we give you instant access to the most current trip-planning information available. At Frommers.com, you'll also find the best prices on airfares, accommodations, and car rentals—and you can even book travel online through our travel booking partners. At Frommers.com, you'll also find the following:

- Online updates to our most popular guidebooks
- Vacation sweepstakes and contest giveaways
- Newsletter highlighting the hottest travel trends
- Online travel message boards with featured travel discussions

What's New in Newfoundland & Labrador

Things change slowly in Newfoundland and Labrador, but they do change. This section details recent goings-on.

The economy of Newfoundland and Labrador continues to hum along. The driving force is natural resources. In 2005, a third offshore oil-drilling operation (White Rose) commenced production and the first phase of construction at Voisey Bay, the world's largest known nickel deposit, was completed.

Back in 2001, the province officially changed its name to **Newfoundland and Labrador** (from Newfoundland). One year later, federal bureaucracy caught up with the new name by changing the provincial symbol from NF to **NL**. What hasn't yet changed are domain extensions—so be careful to type **.nf.ca** into your browser, not nl.ca (the provincial government website, www.gov.nl.ca, is the only exception).

PLANNING YOUR TRIP On a practical level for visitors, you'll find accommodations, restaurants, and attractions becoming more tourist-friendly as they discover value in providing services visitors are accustomed to enjoying in other destinations. Simple things like toll-free numbers for lodging reservations, acceptance of credit cards, and the use of websites are becoming more widespread. Don't get me wrong, the province is no Disneyland—many accommodations only open in summer, high-speed Internet is not widely available, and beyond St. John's cellphone coverage is still scant.

Getting to Newfoundland and Labrador has been made easier with additional **Air Canada** (© 888/247-2262; www.air canada.com) flights to St. John's and the expansion of **WestJet** (© 877/952-4638; www.westjet.com) and **CanJet** (© 800/809-7777; www.canjet.com) networks.

The new URL for **Newfoundland and Labrador Tourism** is www.newfoundland andlabradortourism.com. It's longer than the previous one, but easier to remember. Phone contacts remain the same (© 800/563-6353 or 709/729-2830).

ST. JOHN'S There has been little change in local lodging options, although prices have been creeping up for downtown rooms (although they still remain well below the national average). Connected travelers will be pleased to know high-speed Internet access is now provided in almost all city accommodations, including bed-and-breakfasts.

On the restaurant scene, you can now take to the harbor with **Atlantic Ocean Dinner Cruises** (© 877/834-6663 or 709/834-6663). Back on land, **Blue on Water,** 319 Water St. (© 709/754-2583), opened to rave reviews for its creative cooking and **Spirit's Pub & Thai Room,** at 390 Duckworth St. (© 709/722-0911), opened in a converted theater building. Closures include one of the city's most innovative kitchens (Bread

Pig) and a perennial favorite for fish and chips (Chucky's).

The biggest recent news in the capital was the opening of **The Rooms** (p. 89) in 2005. This magnificent building, styled on old-fashioned "fishing rooms," is home to the provincial museum, art gallery, and archives. It's the one attraction you won't want to miss in the capital.

AVALON PENINSULA While the Avalon Convention & Visitors Bureau changed its name to **Destination St. John's,** the organization's focus on the peninsula remains the same, as does the contact information (© **877/739-8899** or 709/739-8899; www.canadasfareast.com).

As word gets out about the interesting archaeological dig at Ferryland, visitor services continue to expand. The latest addition is **Lighthouse Picnics** (© **709/363-7456**), where you can order a picnic lunch at the local lighthouse.

EASTERN REGION While nothing much has changed in Trinity for over 200 years (and that's a good thing for this super-scenic village), up the road in Bonavista, **Elizabeth J. Cottages** (© **866/468-5035** or 709/468-5035; www.elizabethjcottages.com) reflect the demand for upscale lodging in faraway places.

CENTRAL REGION The website www.centralnewfoundland.com brings together tourism-related businesses across the region.

If you're planning on ferry travel along the south coast, be aware that schedules have been tweaked and information in some places (not this book, of course) is outdated. For more information, check the government website www.tw.gov.nl.ca/ferryservices.

WESTERN   NEWFOUNDLAND Expansion of Deer Lake Airport (www.deerlakeairport.com) will take place throughout 2006 and into 2007. Meanwhile, the number of flights in and out of this western hub continues to increase, with the most recent addition (2005) being Air Canada flights between Montreal and Deer Lake.

LABRADOR The big news in Labrador is political. In 2005, the Inuit ratified a land claim agreement with provincial and federal governments for self-government within a large chunk of Labrador known as **Nunatsiavut.** Elections are scheduled to take place in 2006. Part of the agreement was the creation of **Torngat Mountains National Park,** protecting a remote and ancient mountain range in the far north of the province.

Many maps still show ferry routes between Lewisporte (Central Region) and Cartwright and St. Anthony (Western Newfoundland) and Red Bay. Both these services were suspended after completion of an extension of Route 510 from Red Bay to Cartwright in 2002. The completion date for a continuation of Route 510, finally linking the Labrador Straits to Happy Valley–Goose Bay, is 2009.

The Best of Newfoundland & Labrador

You've done the Florida sun, the European tour, the Caribbean cruise, and the all-inclusive resort, but what you really want is something different. You want to experience something natural and untamed, to relax and rejuvenate without resorting to laziness. You want to create your own vacation memories, not re-enact someone else's itinerary. You yearn for a place unlike any other, somewhere that hasn't been sanitized and packaged for official tourist consumption. Well, now you've found it: Newfoundland and Labrador, the Far East of the Western world.

Here, in Canada's youngest and most easterly province, untold adventure awaits your discovery. What's around the next bend in the highway? Could it be a picturesque fishing village? A breaching humpback? A glistening iceberg? A beaming lighthouse? There's no script or schedule here, so you never know what you'll find when you start to explore. The key word here is "explore"—some of your most treasured memories will be found on the roads less traveled.

The rustic majesty that is Newfoundland and Labrador can be summed up in two words: "people" and "place." Both are unforgettable. The inhabitants of this isolated locale are as real as it gets. They are unpretentious, thoughtful, and witty. They'll charm you with their accents and their generous spirit. Though their lifestyle is neither opulent nor lavish, they will never hesitate to help a person in need. It comes from living in a harsh environment where a helping hand can make the difference between survival and some other, ugly, alternative.

Newfoundland and Labrador's landscape and its animal inhabitants are equally remarkable. There are fjords and mountain vistas of stunning beauty. Places where sky meets horizon in blazing color, and where stands of spruce flow in an evergreen sea. Here, salmon launch themselves against the current and traffic slows for road-hopping rabbits. It is a place where howling winds have blown trains off their track and arctic air chills your backbone. As any local will tell you, this is the most blessedly cursed union of land, sea, air, and sky on creation. Come here once, and you'll have a perpetual longing to return.

Up until the last decade, Newfoundland was virtually undiscovered as a tourist destination. Even most Canadians hadn't been to "the Rock." But over the past 10 years, the province has put great effort into promoting itself throughout North America and on the global stage. Newfoundland and Labrador has revealed itself to the world as an exciting, unique, and even trendy destination.

So be patient as you make your way throughout Newfoundland and Labrador, understanding that tourism is a new industry for the province and that services are not as abundant as they are in certain other locales. And really, isn't that why you're coming here in the first place?

Moments A Contagious Spirit

This is a true story about the potent influence of the Newfoundland character. While traveling on a Toronto subway, a family of four were chatting among themselves. Their lilting Irish-English accents signaled that they were obviously from Newfoundland, as did their friendly smiles and greetings to fellow commuters. Surprisingly, that jaded throng of usually sullen subway riders smiled back. Some even nodded in return. It wasn't long before someone asked if they were from Newfoundland. The affirmative response encouraged the stranger to ask if they were on vacation, and if they had yet seen a Toronto Blue Jays baseball game. Hearing that they hadn't, he explained that his company had season tickets set aside for its employees. He said no one was using the tickets for the next day's game, and offered them to the Newfoundland family because they had brightened up his day. He then gave them his business card so they could arrange to pick up the tickets later that evening. A whole subway car full of people actually took the time to acknowledge each other as individuals, one of them even extending his hand in a spontaneous act of generosity, all because a small group of Newfoundlanders had followed their natural instinct to greet their fellow travelers.

Note: The following pages are designed to give you a quick overview of the best Newfoundland and Labrador has to offer. Wherever possible, I have included at least one attraction per category for every region of the province.

1 The Best Travel Experiences

- **Walk the streets of downtown St. John's:** St. John's is one of the most interesting and visually exciting cities I've ever been to. The city is relatively small, and many of the top sights can be found within a four-block radius of the harbor. See chapter 4.

- **Stand on top of Signal Hill:** You literally have a city at your feet when you stand at the base of Cabot Tower (walk around the tower to the other side and you'll be gazing down at the broad expanse of the Atlantic Ocean). It's one of those must-see pilgrimages for any visitor to the capital city, and even for a good many local residents. See chapter 4, p. 90.

- **Watch the sun come up at Cape Spear:** On this, the most easterly point in North America, a spectacular sunrise, swirling surf, and picturesque

lighthouse make Cape Spear the perfect location for an unforgettable marriage proposal. Find your inner romantic; see chapter 4, p. 92.

- **Put the wind in your sails on board the *Scademia*:** Head out through the Narrows of St. John's harbor on a 27m (90-ft.), full-rigged schooner. If that doesn't have you feeling like a true Newfoundlander, the "screech-in" ceremony ought to do the trick. See chapter 4, p. 97.

- **Dance the night away on George Street:** With the most pubs per capita in North America, the fun continues long after the sun has set in St. John's. There's something for everyone on George Street (rap, jazz, traditional, contemporary, and more). Find your favorite nighttime hot spot in section 9, "St. John's After Dark," in chapter 4.

- **Get sprayed by the Spout:** A natural geyser that shoots saltwater more than 60m (197 ft.) into the air. You'll be wet, cold, and tired by the time you get there . . . and you won't even notice. You'll be too awestruck by every step along the spectacular East Coast Trail. For directions, see chapter 5, p. 104.

- **Experience an active archaeological dig at the Colony of Avalon:** Walk the oldest cobblestone street in North America and see artifacts from a 16th-century settlement. You'll learn about ancient battles for property ownership, and skirmishes with marauding privateers. See chapter 5, p. 110.

- **Enjoy a bird's-eye view of Bird Rock:** After a short walk through a coastal meadow, you'll feel like you've reached the end of the world on that cliff overlooking Bird Rock at **Cape St. Mary's Ecological Reserve.** Imagine gazing into the eyes of thousands of squawking gannets nearly within arm's reach! See chapter 5, p. 116.

- **Dig into history at Bell Island:** It's just a 30-minute boat ride from Portugal Cove, but a giant step back in time when you explore the abandoned iron-ore mines of Bell Island. Or step back even further with a scuba diving expedition to the wreckage of sunken ships that surround the island's perimeter. Find out how you can organize your own Bell Island adventure in chapter 5, p. 122.

- **Get carried away by Rising Tide:** Here's professional theater in both indoor and outdoor venues, in the heart of Newfoundland's most visually historical community. Whether it's the comedic characters of the Trinity Pageant, or the haunting tragedy of a more serious dramatic production, you're sure to be impressed by the Rising Tide theater company. Not to be missed! To reserve your seats, see chapter 6, p. 132.

- **Paddle into the sunset with Mag-Ami Kayaking:** Even if you've never paddled before, expert guides will make you feel at ease, and they know all the best spots for seeing seabirds, icebergs, caves, and whales. And, even though you'll feel like you could paddle forever, you'll be only mildly disappointed when it's time to stop for a break. That's when everyone takes part in a traditional Newfoundland beach boil-up. See chapter 6, p. 133.

- **Light up your day with a trip to the Cape Bonavista Lighthouse:** This step back in time is informative, introspective, and breathtakingly beautiful. Inside, you'll be greeted by costumed interpreters and a realistic portrayal of life as it once was for the lighthouse keeper and his family. Outside, you'll be equally enraptured by the rocky coastline and flowing seascape. See chapter 6, p. 135.

- **Chart a course for the North Atlantic Aviation Museum:** Experience the history of Gander's love affair with flight, as depicted through storyboards, scale model displays, and restored aircraft. And if you've ever dreamed of becoming a pilot, you can move a step closer to that dream when you park yourself in the cockpit of a DC-38. See chapter 7, p. 156.

- **Cruise the South Coast:** Visit the most isolated communities on the island portion of the province. These gems of outport perfection are accessible only by ferry. They might not have pavement, but they're also free of traffic jams and road rage. A trip to the South Coast is the best way to get up close and personal with the best (people) and worst (isolation) of rural Newfoundland. See chapter 7, p. 163.

- **Set sail on a Viking adventure:** Take your place at the oar on board a replica Viking *knarr* with Viking Boat Tours. It's a full-fledged Viking-style oceangoing adventure: you can even dress in traditional garb for a more authentic experience. Still, I doubt the Vikings would have approved—only good, clean fun is allowed on this ship. For information on how to book your Nordic adventure, see chapter 8, p. 190.

- **Cruise the fjords of Gros Morne:** A tour boat excursion across **Western Brook Pond** in Gros Morne National Park will be a highlight of your trip to Newfoundland and Labrador. You pass countless waterfalls, towering peaks, and feel at peace with nature. See chapter 8, p. 177.

- **Visit the province's last pocket of French settlement:** The **Port au Port Peninsula** is the only place in the province where French displaces English as the native language. *Ici, on parle français.* Language, however, is just one part of a larger cultural dynamic. Here you'll find a more overt Roman Catholic heritage, and a genuinely French *joie de vivre*—singularly unique in a society of primarily English and Irish descent. See chapter 8, p. 197.

- **Climb the lighthouse at Point Amour:** The rewards are well worth the effort. You'll get a spectacular view (including a bird's-eye view of some of the oldest fossils found in North America), and learn quite a bit about naval history and shipwrecks. Back at ground level, you can hike the Raleigh Trail when you're done. See chapter 9, p. 206.

2 The Best Spots for Observing Wildlife & Nature

- **The Fluvarium:** This interesting facility within St. John's city limits is easily accessible to those using public transport and very convenient to campers next door in Pippy Park. The Fluvarium offers a firsthand look at the underwater world of brook trout and other creatures that inhabit Newfoundland's many freshwater ponds. See chapter 4, p. 93.

- **See seals in action at the Ocean Sciences Centre:** It's the unofficial star of Logy Bay, an oceanfront research facility that has an outdoor seal tank (no set schedule, drop by anytime). You'll be entertained for hours by the comical antics of the resident seals as they splash and dive in their own private pool. If you're lucky, you may even see them interacting with Centre staff—and being rewarded for their efforts with a tasty fish. See chapter 4, p. 94.

- **Route 10, The Irish Loop:** Head south of St. John's and you'll find a number of the province's best nature attractions within close proximity.

Out at **Witless Bay Ecological Reserve** seabirds abound, numbering more than 2.5 million, including 500,000 Atlantic puffins. The waters are also full of playful humpback whales. The whales actually heave their massive bodies out of the water and snare mouthfuls of food during their descent. The reserve is accessible by boat tour. Meanwhile, back on land, a herd of caribou can often be seen from the highway near Trepassey, and if you're really lucky you may be able to watch the humpbacks feeding off the beach at St. Vincent's. See chapter 5, p. 106.

- **Visit with local wildlife at Salmonier Nature Park:** At this retirement/recovery home for aging and wounded animals, you'll see moose, fox, hare, lynx, and more in their natural environment (or almost natural—the holding areas are securely fenced enclosures). The Nature Park is a pleasant walk and education expedition combined with a rare opportunity to view reclusive animals. Best of all, no admission is charged. See chapter 5, p. 113.

- **Communicate with some of the biggest mammals on Earth with Ocean Contact Ltd.Tours:** Join Dr. Beamish and learn how to talk (or the next best thing) with the whales. You'll be spellbound watching Beamish maneuver his Zodiac in and around these graceful giants. To book your tour, see chapter 6, p. 134.

- **Watch salmon return to their spawning grounds at the Salmonid Interpretation Centre:** Here you'll get both a surface and an underwater view of these homeward-bound fish as they make their annual against-the-current pilgrimage. See chapter 7, p. 162.

- **White-water raft with Red Indian Adventures:** Your exhilarating ride through breathtaking scenery just might include passing a black bear or moose. You'll see the province in a way not possible from the highway. See chapter 7, p. 160.

- **Twillingate:** This is the place to be if you're thrilled by the sight of towering icebergs and gracious whales. Icebergs float by May through July (they seem to linger a bit longer in the bay near Twillingate than they do elsewhere around the province). Humpback whales are in abundance from June through September. See chapter 7, p. 158.

- **Northern Peninsula:** Anyone looking for a moose is bound to spot one here. This remote and rugged part of northwestern Newfoundland is home to many of the province's 150,000 big, brown, beautiful creatures. You'll often see them on or along the highway at dusk or dawn, especially during the fall. See chapter 8, p. 178.

- **Sail amid floating glacial castles with Northland Discovery Boat Tours:** You'll marvel at the cracks and colors in 10,000-year-old icebergs while traveling alongside playful dolphins, whales, and seabirds in their natural environment. To learn how you can get a taste of Northland Discovery's unique eco-tourism adventure (not to mention the purest water on Earth), see chapter 8, p. 187.

- **Tablelands:** Students of geology already know that there's no better place to be than Newfoundland and Labrador, commonly known as the Rock. And there's no more spectacular example of the world's natural geological forces than this UNESCO World Heritage Site where tremendous forces deep below the Earth's crust pushed upward 470 million years See chapter 8, p. 176.

- **Gros Morne Adventures:** Guided sea kayaking tours through the sheltered waters of Bonne Bay give you a sea-level view of bald eagles, terns, and other wildlife. You'll be gliding through one of the most scenic areas of the province: mountains, fjords, and glacial deposits are just a few of the features you'll encounter along your paddling adventure. See chapter 8, p. 178.

- **Pinware River Provincial Park:** Most of the Labrador Straits area is open, barren land with just a few stands of tuckamore for color. Not here. In Pinware Park you'll find a verdant spruce carpet in a sheltered valley, as well as abundant freshwater fish and extreme kayaking conditions (for experts only!). To learn more about the park, see chapter 9, p. 207.

3 The Best Scenic Drives

- **Cape Spear Road:** Just a 15-minute drive south of St. John's, Cape Spear is the most easterly point in North America, a National Historic Site, and site of the Cape Spear Lighthouse. Be sure to bring a sweater, as Cape Spear is often windy and considerably colder than the city of St. John's. If you're enjoying the drive, continue a little farther south toward the scenic fishing village of Petty Harbour. It won't take you more than an hour to drive the complete circle from St. John's to Cape Spear–Petty Harbour–Goulds–Kilbride and back to St. John's. See section 5, "Exploring St. John's," in chapter 4.

- **Middle Cove to Pouch Cove** (pronounced "pooch cove"): In the opposite direction from Cape Spear and Petty Harbour are the close-knit communities of Logy Bay–Middle Cove–Outer Cove, Torbay, Flat Rock, and Pouch Cove (follow routes 30 and 20). There's an interesting contrast along the drive: nestled in between the farmland and obviously rural lifestyle are some of the most prestigious properties on the island, evidence of the growing prosperity in this part of the province. See chapter 4.

- **Irish Loop:** A 4-hour round-trip drive through the heart of Newfoundland's Irish heritage and caribou country. Along the way you'll see beautiful coastal communities along a panorama of rugged shore and outport loveliness. Follow Route 10 south of St. John's. If you stay on the same route (the name changes to Rte. 90 about halfway), you'll be carried back to the capital city. See section 2, "Irish Loop," in chapter 5.

- **Baccalieu Trail:** The tiny outport communities that line the shores of this finger of the Avalon Peninsula

between Trinity and Conception bays are simply beautiful. Routes 80 and 70 will take you to inviting communities such as Heart's Delight, Heart's Content, and Harbour Grace. But remember to get off the highway and drive right into the villages in order to truly enjoy the beauty. See section 4, "Baccalieu Trail," in chapter 5.

- **Route 230 to Bonavista:** Beautiful in any season, this stunning stretch of highway is especially breathtaking when cloaked in early fall foliage. You'll find yourself wanting to pull over at every bend in the road so you can really appreciate the incredible views. The shining stars of the journey are the towns of Trinity and Bonavista and the sweeping ocean panorama seen from the end of the road at Cape Bonavista. See chapter 6.

- **The foot of the Heritage Run:** If you look at the Burin Peninsula on a map, you'll notice it resembles a leg with a foot on the end. The long "leg" of the Heritage Run has some memorable moments, though for the main it doesn't qualify as a scenic drive. But the loop journey from the ankle to the toe and back (routes 222, 220, and 213) is a different story. Here you'll follow a coastal trail with an obvious maritime theme. Highlights of the trip are the lobster pots, fishing boats, and immaculate wharf facilities you'll spot along the side of the road. See chapter 6.

- **Kittiwake Coast:** It's a long drive from Gambo through the assorted towns and villages along the north coast (routes 320–330) before heading back to the Trans-Canada at Gander, but it's so worth the effort. En route are picture-perfect picnic spots, a sandy beach (rare in this part of the world), and the community known as the "Venice of Newfoundland." See chapter 7.

- **Route 430 up the Northern Peninsula:** At Deer Lake, Route 430 spurs north along the western side of the Northern Peninsula. You'll pass through Gros Morne National Park, Port au Choix National Historic Site, L'Anse aux Meadows National Historic Site, and the town of St. Anthony, where you're likely to see an iceberg or two. In between all the official highlights, the road passes through some handsomely rugged and remote countryside. See chapter 8.

- **Port au Port Peninsula:** Just west of Stephenville on the west coast of Newfoundland is the last pocket of predominantly French settlement on the island. Here you'll see religious icons and ancient war relics, as well as the largest wooden structure and the highest mountain in the province. See chapter 8.

- **Labrador Coastal Drive:** Route 510 takes you from the ferry at Blanc Sablon, Quebec, to the captivating outport of Red Bay, Labrador. It's a paved road (one of the few in Labrador, so take advantage of it) and gives you a chance to tour the interesting communities and many historical attractions found on the Labrador Straits. Highlights include sunken Spanish galleons, a 7,500-year-old burial mound, and Atlantic Canada's tallest lighthouse. See chapter 9.

4 The Most Picturesque Villages

- **Quidi Vidi** (St. John's): Pronounced "kiddee viddee," this historical fishing village has managed to stop time in its tracks. You're not more than 5 minutes' drive from the traffic of downtown St. John's, yet Quidi Vidi has the oldest cottage in North America, horses grazing on the cliffs overlooking the peaceful lake, and timeless fishing sheds snuggling up to the granite cliffs that guard its sheltered harbor. See chapter 4, p. 91.

- **Petty Harbour** (St. John's): Just 15 minutes south of St. John's, this peaceful and quaint fishing village has been the backdrop for a number of films. With its aging fishing sheds, wooden slipways, and cliff-hugging houses tucked within a protective hillside embrace, its attraction as a movie set is readily apparent. It's amazing to find such a picturesque and well-preserved piece of traditional Newfoundland culture just minutes from the capital city. See chapter 4, p. 92.

- **Ferryland** (Avalon Peninsula): Aside from the unique lure of its ongoing archaeological dig (impressive as that is), the town of Ferryland is a strikingly attractive community. It flows down from the hills in graceful descent to sea level, layers of green grass and rocky knolls sprinkled amid stubborn settlement. On the small peninsula extending out from Ferryland Harbour is a lighthouse, its blinking eye a haunting reminder of the tragedy that can befall unwary sailors. To plan your visit to Ferryland, see chapter 5, p. 108.

- **Brigus** (Avalon Peninsula): You'll see lots of beautiful flowers and overhanging trees lining the narrow streets that lead to the harbor of this historic fishing village, and an abundance of heritage-style homes that give the place a real step-back-in-time feel. If you're looking to make the modern world go away for a while, Brigus is the perfect retreat. See chapter 5, p. 116.

- **Dildo** (Avalon Peninsula): If the name alone isn't enough to spark your curiosity, you might be attracted by this historical fishing village's proud seafaring history. And then there's its aesthetic beauty: it was named one of Canada's prettiest towns, and you're sure to agree when looking at the wonderful view of Trinity Bay. Green space and simple wooden fences add to Dildo's rustic charm. See chapter 5, p. 119.

- **Trinity** (Eastern Region): Time seems to have stood still for this quaint fishing village that has preserved many of its 19th-century buildings. Or, if it hasn't stood still, there's certainly a concerted community effort to turn back the clock. If you climb the hill from Courthouse Road behind the Royal Bank just before sunset, you'll get one of the most beautiful views available anywhere. See chapter 6, p. 128.

- **Twillingate** (Central Region): Here is a community perfectly positioned for optimum iceberg viewing. With such impressive floating monoliths frequenting the shore every spring and early summer, you'll be forgiven if your attention wanders from the man-made beauty in and around the town. But rest assured, Twillingate is indeed a complementary composition of raw landscape and human construction. You'll find it at the northern end of Route 340. See chapter 7, p. 158.

- **Francois** (Central Region): At the opposite end of the compass from Twillingate is an isolated outport village, accessible only by ferry. It has neither paved road nor hotel, but that doesn't put Francois at a disadvantage. Majestic cliffs ring the little community, and wooden boardwalks serve as the local land highway (the real highway is the ocean). You'll have to work to find it, as it's hidden from view on a narrow strip of land at the head of a fjord. See chapter 7, p. 164.

- **Port aux Basques** (Western Newfoundland): An often underappreciated community, Port aux Basques is more than a relay station for the Newfoundland–Nova Scotia ferry. It has both traditional architectural beauty and an impressive blasted-rock harbor entrance. It takes on a romantic ambience in the twilight hours thanks to the guidelights used to illuminate the ferry terminal. See chapter 8, p. 194.

- **Battle Harbour** (Labrador): Accessible only by boat, this one-time capital of Labrador was abandoned in the 1960s. Now restored, century-old buildings and a simple beauty create a haunting yet memorable destination. Escape the hustle and bustle of the modern world, whether for a day trip or overnight stay in the nostalgic Battle Harbour Inn. See chapter 9, p. 209.

Getting to Know Salvage

On the western edge of the Eastern Region, following Route 310 east of Glovertown, is one of the most picturesque (and most photographed!) fishing communities in the province. Salvage (pronounced "sal-*vage*") is a visual treat of stages, wharves, sheds, and slipways nestled in and around a granite shore. This, plus the never-ending ocean serenade and houses built in the unlikeliest of places, make Salvage an unforgettable destination.

5 The Best Hikes & Walking Tours

- **St. John's Haunted Hike** (St. John's): Looking for something different? Try this after-dark stroll through downtown St. John's with the Rev. Thos. Wyckham Jarvis, Esq. He'll take you on a rather eerie walk through some of the oldest graveyards in the city, and add quite a bit of theatrics along the way to keep your adrenaline pumping. See chapter 4, p. 98.

- **Signal Hill–Battery Trail** (St. John's): Not for the faint of heart! This walk starts at a pinnacle height towering over the capital city and follows a thigh-burning descent along a dizzying path less than 3m (10 ft.) from the edge of a 61m (200-ft.) drop to the Atlantic Ocean. Those brave enough to attempt it are rewarded with the most spectacular scenery in the city. See chapter 4, p. 90.

- **East Coast Trail** (Avalon Peninsula): This fantastic trail system is easily accessible from St. John's and takes you along the beautiful coastline of the Avalon Peninsula. You can see whales and seabirds close to shore and parts of the trail are easy enough for the beginner. It's divided into sections so you can do as much or as little as you like, tailoring your hike(s) to your time frame and skill level. See chapter 5, p. 103.

- **Discovery Trail** (Eastern Region): Similar to the East Coast Trail, this is also organized into sections of varying difficulty. Choose your hiking route based on what you want to see (sea stacks? abandoned communities? rocky outcrops?) as well as the level of difficulty. See chapter 6, p. 126.

- **Edible Trail** (Eastern Region): Ever wonder what you would live on if you were lost in the woods? You'll know the answer after you take part in this guided interpretive walk through Terra Nova National Park. Equally important, you'll know which plants to avoid! See chapter 6, p. 149.

- **Gros Morne National Park:** It's impossible to select one particular trail from this park as the best; they're all very dynamic, and you can easily find one that meets your own abilities or interests. If you're an experienced hiker and enjoy the challenges of a difficult climb, you'll find that **Gros Morne Trail,** the trail that leads to the peak of Gros Morne Mountain, offers the most spectacular scenery. See chapter 8, p. 170.

- **Port au Choix National Historic Site** (Western Newfoundland): Two connected hiking trails, each with its own attributes, crisscross this historically important site halfway up the Northern Peninsula. The **Phillips Garden Coastal Trail** stands out for the opportunity of watching archaeologists at work. See chapter 8, p. 180.

- **Raleigh Trail:** On this coastal hike at Point Amour, Labrador, you can marvel at 500-million-year-old fossils, search out a shipwreck, photograph a waterfall, and pick mouthwatering berries, all without having to go too far off the beaten track. The trail begins at Atlantic Canada's tallest lighthouse. See chapter 9, p. 206.

6 The Best Family Activities

- **Johnson Geo Centre** (St. John's): An underground geological display that's fun for the whole family. Adults will appreciate the educational interpretive program, while teenagers will be impressed by the oversize exhibits (and cool audiovisual presentation with simulated rain and volcanic eruptions). Younger children will entertain themselves for hours just squirting water at the exposed rock wall. See chapter 4, p. 90.

- **Fluvarium** (St. John's): A first-class interpretation facility where visitors can go beneath the surface to see trout and underwater species (the building boasts a glass-walled viewing area). Try to time your visit for the day's scheduled feeding. See chapter 4, p. 93.

- **Avondale Railway Station Museum** (Avalon Peninsula): For over a century, trains played a vital role in moving people and goods across Newfoundland. You can see just how important they were at the Avondale Railway Station Museum, the province's oldest railway station. There are decommissioned cars on display, and during the summer children can go for a ride on one of the museum's small rail cars. See chapter 5, p. 118.

- **Wilderness Newfoundland Adventures** (Avalon Peninsula): Kayaking is fun for the young and the young-at-heart. Wilderness Newfoundland Adventures has specially designed kayaks so children too young to paddle on their own can ride with mom or dad. And, for beginners, there's expert on-shore instruction before heading out onto the water. See chapter 5, p. 104.

- **Terra Nova Golf Resort** (Eastern Region): Golfing, nature hikes, minigolf, tennis, basketball, swimming, a comprehensive children's program . . . what more could you possibly want? There's something for every vacationer at Terra Nova Golf Resort. See chapter 6, p. 146.

- **Trinity Loop** (Eastern Region): This amusement/activity park features a working miniature train. The train does a loop around the park, overlooking the pond with its water-recreation facilities (paddle boats, kayaks, canoes, and rowboats) as well as the playground and Ferris wheel. See chapter 6, p. 131.

- **Frenchman's Cove Provincial Park** (Eastern Region): This Burin Peninsula park offers a pebble beach, playground, and freshwater pond for outdoor swimming. Don't worry, the adults won't find themselves at loose ends—they can walk the fairways of a 9-hole golf course. See chapter 6, p. 141.

- **Terra Nova National Park**: Terra Nova gets high marks for its family activities. The park has an excellent interpretive program, nice campgrounds, a sandy beach for watersports and swimming, campfire concert series, great hands-on displays at the Marine Interpretation Centre, easy walking trails, and boat tours of Newman Sound. See chapter 6.

- **Splash-n-Putt Resort** (Eastern Region): The largest water park in the province, with a 91m-long (300-ft.) waterslide. Comes complete with bumper cars, go-karts, and minigolf. See chapter 6, p. 150.

- **Newfoundland Insectarium** (Western Newfoundland): What kid doesn't like bugs or butterflies? This is a really neat facility where kids have a great time watching honeybees buzzing about, stretching out their hands to catch a butterfly, getting some bug-related souvenirs to take home, and having an ice cream when they're done. See chapter 8, p. 169.

- **Marble Mountain** (Western Newfoundland): Winter fun for the whole family. The 34 named runs have something for everyone, with snowboarders gravitating to the half pipe and terrain park. For the younger set, there's certified ski instruction and a supervised play program, which means both parents and children get to enjoy the resort on their own terms. See chapter 8, p. 193.

- **Norstead** (Western Newfoundland): This re-enactment village depicts the everyday life of Norsemen—and women—from 1000 A.D. Norstead's wonderful Discovery Program for kids offers a hands-on opportunity to participate in the various activities that would have been carried on in the settlement. Even the teens will be shocked out of their chronic boredom by the clanging swords and hand-to-hand combat of the mock battles. See chapter 8, p. 189.

7 The Best Places to Discover Local History & Culture

- **The Rooms** (St. John's): Constructed to resemble "fishing rooms," where families would process their catch, this imposing complex combines the provincial museum, art gallery, and archives. Far from your typical stuffy museum, it features a distinct contemporary ambience as the story of the province's human and natural history unfolds as you move from room to room. See chapter 4, p. 89.

- **Signal Hill** (St. John's): Just a short drive from downtown, this National Historic Site offers the best view of St. John's and the harbor. It was here that Guglielmo Marconi received the first wireless transatlantic signal, using a kite to catch the faint transmission from Poldhu, England. For the full effect, time your visit to take in the Signal Hill Military Tattoo. See chapter 4, p. 90.

- **Basilica of St. John the Baptist** (St. John's): For years the largest and most imposing structure on the St. John's skyline, the Basilica was one of the few buildings to survive the Great Fires that devastated the capital city during the early part of the 20th century. A highlight of your visit will be a viewing of the Veiled Virgin statue. See chapter 4, p. 89.

- **Quidi Vidi Battery** (St. John's): In the early battles for control of the colony of St. John's, heavy fortifications were constructed at strategic locations throughout the city. This quiet hill overlooking Quidi Vidi Harbour was one of them. Today, costumed interpreters explain the purpose of the installation and the people who resided there. See chapter 4, p. 91.

- **Colony of Avalon** (Avalon Peninsula): Make your first stop at this independently run National Historic Site south of St. John's the Interpretation Centre. From this point, it's a short stroll through the village of Ferryland to the dig site where archaeologists are continuing to uncover remnants of the first successful planned colony in Newfoundland. See chapter 5, p. 110.

- **Hawthorne Cottage** (Avalon Peninsula): The former home of famous Arctic explorer Captain Bob Bartlett includes intriguing insights into the life and times of the man and his family, as well as the struggles he faced on his expeditions. See chapter 5, p. 119.

- **Dildo Interpretation Centre:** This is a fascinating facility if you're interested in the workings of a fish hatchery and want to learn more about the way of life for Newfoundlanders of the not-so-distant past as well as the Native peoples who once inhabited the region. Plus, it comes with a replica of a giant squid that was caught in the area! See chapter 5, p. 119.

- **Trinity Historical Properties** (Eastern Region): While the entire community of Trinity is a living museum, with residents embracing their past as

Exploring St. John's Art Galleries

Artists are acknowledged mediums for the ideas and attitudes of their cultural generations. You can see (and buy) the work of some of the most talented artists in the province through one of several downtown art galleries: Christina Parker, Emma Butler, and Lane. See chapter 4, p. 100.

the route to future prosperity, a few buildings are open as tourist attractions. These include the Lester-Garland Premises, Hiscock House, Trinity Museum, Court House, and Green Family Forge. See chapter 6, p. 131.

- **Ryan Premises National Historic Site** (Eastern Region): This cluster of 19th-century harborfront buildings is a restoration of the merchant premises that served as the hub of a once-thriving fishing community. The Interpretive Centre has an excellent display about changes that have affected the province's fishery. Also check out the replica in the harbor of the *Matthew,* the three-masted 15th-century vessel sailed by John Cabot to Newfoundland in 1497. See chapter 6, p. 136.

- **Burin Heritage Museum** (Eastern Region): The communities of Grand Bank and Fortune are among the closest in the world to the infamous fishing grounds of the Grand Banks. Through interpretive panels and traveling exhibits, this museum pays tribute to that heritage. See chapter 6, p. 141.

- **Barbour Living Heritage Village** (Central Region): Similar to the Ryan Premises, but on a larger scale. It's not just a restored commercial property, but a series of reconstructed buildings typical of a fishing village (ca. 1900). They're more than just historical monuments, however: these multipurpose buildings also serve as the local museum, theater, and art gallery. See chapter 7, p. 157.

- **Boyd's Cove Beothuk Interpretation Centre** (Central Region): With all the hype about John Cabot discovering Newfoundland, and even the Vikings arriving a millennium ago, it's easy to forget that there were permanent residents here long before the Europeans arrived. Boyd's Cove is one of those sites that helps us remember. Although little is known about Newfoundland's now-extinct Beothuk, Boyd's Cove sheds some light on who they were and how they adapted to Newfoundland's harsh environment. See chapter 7, p. 157.

- **Dorset Soapstone Quarry** (Central Region): Even before the Beothuk, there were Dorset people living on the island of Newfoundland. Proof of their existence can be found in the province's earliest known mine, where the Dorset mined soapstone for use as bowls and cooking pots. See chapter 7, p. 163.

- **Port au Choix National Historic Site** (Western Newfoundland): What is it about Port au Choix that has made it the location of choice for five different Native populations over the last 4,500 years? Archaeologists are still trying to puzzle the answer from the clues left behind from past civilizations (including the Maritime Archaics, the Groswater, and the Dorset-Paleoeskimo). See chapter 8, p. 180.

- **Grenfell Interpretation Centre** (Western Newfoundland): This is a recommended stop for anyone interested in the early medical history of northern Newfoundland and Labrador. Learn about Sir Wilfred Thomason Grenfell, the English doctor who became a local hero to the Inuit and early settlers of the region. See chapter 8, p. 186.

- **L'Anse aux Meadows National Historic Site** (Western Newfoundland): Make your first stop the visitor center to learn about the Vikings who landed at the tip of the Northern Peninsula around A.D. 1000. Then you'll walk among the sunken foundations of their village. Plus, there is a re-created Viking village, with re-enactors on hand to demonstrate how these early settlers might have interacted with each other. See chapter 8, p. 189.

- **Red Bay National Historic Site** (Labrador): Once the whaling capital of the world, the name Red Bay came from the color of the water, which was supposedly so bright with whales'

blood that it flowed red. Inside the interpretive center is a reproduction of a wooden whaling boat, surrounded by the mandible (jawbone) of a bowhead whale. The area wasn't treacherous just to whales, however; at least three Spanish galleons are known to have gone down in the waters of Red Bay. For more information, see chapter 9, p. 209.

- **Battle Harbour** (Labrador): One of my favorite places in all of Newfoundland and Labrador, this community, once the hub of Labrador, was abandoned in the 1960s, but thanks to enterprising locals many buildings have been restored and you can visit for a day or even stay overnight. Access is by boat in summer only. See chapter 9, p. 209.

8 The Best Festivals & Special Events

- **Newfoundland & Labrador Folk Festival** (St. John's): This is an absolute must for lovers of traditional music. The 3-day event takes place in downtown St. John's during the first weekend of August and provides a good variety of music that includes folk, country, bluegrass, and Celtic. See chapter 4, p. 95.

- **Royal St. John's Regatta** (St. John's): This is the biggest event of the year for St. John's; its importance is recognized by its status as a municipal holiday. The oldest continuous sporting event in North America offers a day of fixed-seat rowing races and lots of fun for the whole family at Quidi Vidi Lake. See chapter 4, p. 95.

- **George Street Festival** (St. John's): You'll enjoy the George Street Festival if you're young (or at the very least young-at-heart) and don't mind loud music and crowds. During the 6-day event, a 2-block stretch of the downtown street is closed off, and bars open up their doors and bring in a

lineup of terrific entertainment. See chapter 4, p. 94.

- **Shamrock Festival** (Avalon Peninsula): Traditional Irish-Newfoundland music mingles with some modern material in this popular late-July event held outdoors in the community of Ferryland. Many of the province's best-known performers are from this part of the province, so the lineup is always guaranteed to impress. See chapter 5, p. 108.

- **Princess Sheila NaGeira Theatre** (Avalon Peninsula): Newfoundland is famous for its high-quality, informal, community theatrical productions. If the thought of sitting in a beautiful seaside setting and being entertained appeals to you, you're quite likely to enjoy this theater company's festival held in Carbonear each summer. See chapter 5, p. 120.

- **Brigus Blueberry Festival** (Avalon Peninsula): Arrive early, because there's always a crowd in Brigus for this popular event. It's an excellent venue for buying locally made products such as knitted goods, quilts, and, of course, blueberry products. See chapter 5, p. 116.

- **Summer in the Bight** (Eastern Region): Each year between June and October, the **Rising Tide Theatre** puts on a number of professional shows that give poignant life to the Newfoundland character and lifestyle. Staged at both indoor and outdoor venues, Summer in the Bight includes the renowned **Trinity Pageant.** See chapter 6, p. 132.

- **The Fish, Fun & Folk Festival** (Central Region): One of the largest and longest-running folk festivals in Newfoundland, this event is held the last full weekend of July in Twillingate. If you want to have a great time with the family and gain deeper insight into what makes Newfoundlanders tick, plan to take in this event. See chapter 7, p. 159.

- **Exploits Valley Salmon Festival** (Central Region): A 5-day family

event and salmon celebration held mid-July in Grand Falls–Windsor. Take time to enjoy a performance at the highly regarded **Summer Theatre Festival.** See chapter 7, p. 161 and p. 162.

- **Gros Morne Theatre Festival** (Western Newfoundland): Treat yourself to a dinner theater production of excellent regional music, comedy, and drama while in the area of Gros Morne National Park between June and September. The festival is held in the northern part of the park. Twice weekly, you'll have the chance to enjoy a theatrical performance as well as taste some of the best pan-fried cod found anywhere. See chapter 8, p. 174.

- **Bakeapple Folk Festival** (Labrador): Time your visit to the Labrador Straits for the second weekend of August, when the bakeapple berries are ripe and the biggest summer event of the year is taking place. You'll get four days of fun, music, and merriment. See chapter 9, p. 207.

9 The Best Hotels & Resorts

- **Fairmont Newfoundland** (115 Cavendish Sq., St. John's; ⓒ **800/ 257-7544** or 709/726-4980; www. fairmont.com/newfoundland): The best-known full-service property in the province. Although it lacks an outwardly Newfoundland style because of its size and branding, you will still find the unique island character in the personality of the caring and professional staff. See chapter 4, p. 77.

- **Murray Premises Hotel** (5 Beck's Cove, St. John's; ⓒ **866/738-7773** or 709-738-7773; www.murraypremises hotel.com): You simply can't beat the attention to detail at this beautifully decorated boutique hotel that was once a waterfront warehouse. The staff and management are top-notch, and although the hotel does not offer

the full range of services you'll find at the Fairmont, everything they do offer—most notably an exceptional standard of service—will ensure your stay is enjoyable. See chapter 4, p. 78.

- **Celtic Rendezvous Cottages By The Sea** (Rte. 10 to Bauline East; ⓒ **866/ 334-3341** or 709/334-3341; www. celticrendezvouscottages.com): Don't pick this lodging if a long list of amenities is important to you. But if you're looking for a place where you can hear the surf pounding from inside your cabin or while sitting on the porch overlooking the rugged coastline, this is a great choice. The cabins provide a retreat-style atmosphere within 45 minutes' drive of St. John's. See chapter 5, p. 107.

- **The Wilds at Salmonier River** (Rte. 90, Salmonier Line; ✆ **709/229-5444;** www.thewilds.ca): Even Fido is welcome at this terrific family resort. The Wilds has self-contained cabins as well as hotel-style rooms in the main building. One of the province's finest golf courses is on-site, and you're just minutes from Salmonier Nature Park. See chapter 5, p. 113.

- **Bird Island Resort** (Main Rd., St. Bride's; ✆ **709/337-2450;** www.birdislandresort.com): Fully equipped efficiency units ideal for traveling families. All-ages fun includes minigolf, horseshoe pits, and fitness center. This is the closest accommodations to Cape St. Mary's Ecological Reserve. See chapter 5, p. 115.

- **Kilmory Resort** (Rte. 210, Swift Current; ✆ **888/884-2460** or 709/549-2410; www.kilmory.nf.ca): If you were to imagine the perfect location for a cottage, you'd probably conjure up a location with privacy, alongside a pond or lake with timber-studded hills rising in the background. That's exactly what you'll find at Kilmory, along with a pool, playground, and rustic-luxe facilities. See chapter 6, p. 140.

- **Terra Nova Golf Resort** (Port Blandford; ✆ **709/543-2525;** www.terranovagolf.com): This full-service family resort offers a great kids' program, an outdoor swimming pool, tennis, a challenging 27-hole golf course, in-house dining, and is ideally situated for day trips into Terra Nova National Park. See chapter 6, p. 146.

- **BlueWater Lodge & Retreat** (Trans-Canada Hwy. near Gander; ✆ **709/535-3004;** www.relax-at-bluewater.ca): A wonderful place to stay while touring Notre Dame Bay and other points in the Central Region, the lodge has a private, serene setting on a small lake, making it a perfect retreat for anyone really wanting to get away from it all. See chapter 7, p. 152.

- **Sugar Hill Inn** (Norris Point Rd., Norris Point; ✆ **888/299-2147** or 709/458-2147; www.sugarhillinn.nf.ca): After a long day of hiking in Gros Morne National Park, this little slice of luxury will be much appreciated. The six guest rooms are warm and inviting, and the food top-notch. See chapter 8, p. 174.

- **Marble Inn** (Dogwood Dr., Steady Brook; ✆ **877/497-5673** or 709/634-2237; www.explorenewfoundland.com): It doesn't have the exclusive ambience of the official Marble Mountain Resort, and that's a good thing. I find these cabins are actually cozier and more inviting than their more expensive counterparts. The ample on-site amenities (sauna, fitness facility, canoe rentals, playground) add even more value to the package. See chapter 8, p. 192.

- **Strawberry Hill Resort** (Exit 10 off Rte. 1 to Little Rapids; ✆ **877/434-0066** or 709/634-0066; www.strawberryhill.net): When previous guests include a former prime minister and royalty, you know it has to be exceptional. And it is. Outside the luxury of the rooms, guests gravitate to the adjacent salmon river and scenic walking trails. See chapter 8, p. 192.

10 The Best Bed & Breakfasts & Heritage Inns

- **Bluestone Inn** (34 Queen's Rd., St. John's; ✆ **877/754-9876** or 709/754-7544; www.thebluestoneinn.com): Modern chic blends effortlessly with classic architectural design for a one-of-a-kind B&B. This place has it all: splendid downtown location, an interesting history, superlative food, and spacious guest rooms. See chapter 4, p. 79.

- **Winterholme Heritage Inn** (79 Rennies Mill Rd., St. John's; ✆ 800/599-7829 or 709/739-7979; www.winterholmeheritageinn.com): Bring your neck brace—you'll need it from constantly staring upward at the ornately carved woodwork. If you're a real romantic, reserve one of the suites with a jetted tub and fireplace. See chapter 4, p. 81.

- **Dogberry Hill B&B** (St. Phillip's; ✆ 709/895-6353; www.dogberryhill.com): Just 15 minutes' drive from St. John's, this beautifully designed B&B offers the finest linens and haute cuisine. If you don't mind paying a little more for that extra level of service and amenities, you'll really enjoy a stay at the Dogberry. See chapter 5, p. 121.

- **Inn By The Bay** (78 Front Rd., Dildo; ✆ 888/339-7829 or 709/582-3170; www.innbythebaydildo.com): Who can resist staying in one of "Canada's 10 Prettiest Towns"? This lovely B&B has an attentive owner and a waterfront location, and it's right in the heart of Dildo, an odd-sounding but very beautiful fishing village. See chapter 5, p. 117.

- **Campbell House** (High St., Trinity; ✆ 877/464-7700 or 709/464-3377; www.trinityvacations.com): This is a wonderful B&B in the scenic village of Trinity. Gover House is one of the buildings that make up Campbell House—and my favorite because of its large deck overlooking Trinity Bay. See chapter 6, p. 128.

- **Fishers' Loft Inn** (Mill Rd., Port Rexton; ✆ 877/464-3240 or 709/464-3240; www.fishersloft.com): A short drive from Trinity, this remote property with an ethereal atmosphere is perfect for anyone seeking peace, tranquillity, and fine food. See chapter 6, p. 129.

- **Elizabeth J. Cottages** (Harris St., Bonavista; ✆ 866/468-5035 or 709/468-5035; www.elizabethjcottages.com): One of the finest cottage accommodations in all of Newfoundland and Labrador—think fine cotton sheets on an oversize bed, plush bathrobes, a modern entertainment system, polished hardwood floors, and a private deck with gas barbecue. See chapter 6, p. 134.

- **Quirpon Lighthouse Inn** (boat transfer from Quirpon; ✆ 877/254-6586; www.linkumtours.com): This isolated island retreat is the perfect escape from techno-society. Amenities include hearty home-cooked meals, endless waves, iceberg views, and conversations with whales. It's just you and your thoughts for company. See chapter 8, p. 188.

- **Humberview Bed & Breakfast** (11 Humberview Dr., Deer Lake; ✆ 888/635-4818 or 709/635-4818; www.thehumberview.com): This B&B offers unparalleled modern luxury in an executive-style home, replete with Grecian columns and four-poster bed in the master suite. You'll wish you could pack it in your suitcase to take home with you. See chapter 8, p. 168.

- **Cape Anguille Lighthouse Inn** (Cape Anguille; ✆ 877/254-6586 or 709/634-2285; www.linkumtours.com): Experience life as a lightkeeper at this unique accommodations high above the Gulf of St. Lawrence. Aside from gracious hospitality and magnificent scenery, bird-watchers will love the diversity of species present in the area. See chapter 8, p. 195.

- **Battle Harbour Inn** (Battle Island, Labrador; ✆ 709/921-6325 or 709/921-6216; www.battleharbour.com): Looking to step back in time? This small inn will enable you to do just that. It has wood stoves and oil lamps, and the setting is in the oldest intact salt-fish community in the province. See chapter 9, p. 210.

11 The Best Restaurants

- **Cabot Club** (Fairmont Newfoundland, St. John's; ✆ **709/726-4980**): Upscale and old-world, the Cabot Club is the province's only semiformal restaurant. The food is exquisite (how does grilled caribou brushed with a partridgeberry and molasses demiglaze sound?) and the harbor view just as memorable. See chapter 4, p. 83.
- **Blue on Water** (319 Water St.; St. John's; ✆ **709/754-2583**): In the heart of historical downtown St. John's, this slick dining room features a bright blue-and-white interior and a kitchen that combines local game with modern cooking styles. See chapter 4, p. 82.
- **Magnum & Steins** (284 Duckworth St., St. John's; ✆ **709/576-6500**): Fine dining in eclectic, funky surroundings. A masterpiece of contemporary gastronomical delights—not to be missed! See chapter 4, p. 83.
- **Nautical Nellies** (201 Water St., St. John's; ✆ **709/738-1120**): Great food, big portions, and reasonable prices in cozy pub surroundings—that's what you'll find at Nautical Nellies. It's both small and very popular, making it hard to get a table. See chapter 4, p. 86.
- **Colony Café** (Rte. 10, Ferryland; ✆ **709/432-3030**; www.ferryland. com/colonycafe): A professional French chef waits to tempt your taste buds with succulent seafood and rich desserts. Situated next to the Colony of Avalon archaeological dig in Ferryland. See chapter 5, p. 109.
- **Skipper's Café** (42 Campbell St., Bonavista; ✆ **709/468-7150**): After touring the historical sites in Bonavista and taking in the views at Cape Bonavista, it's worth searching out this lovely waterfront restaurant if you like seafood and don't want to pay big prices. You'll find terrific seafood chowder, cod au gratin, and other delectable dishes. See chapter 6, p. 135.
- **Norseman Restaurant** (Rte. 436, L'Anse aux Meadows; ✆ **877/623-2018**): Located at the extreme northern tip of the Northern Peninsula, this restaurant is a fantastic surprise. The waterfront setting is a delight, the food is as creative and well-presented as the best restaurants in St. John's, and the service professional. See chapter 8, p. 187.
- **Thirteen West** (13 West St., Corner Brook; ✆ **709/634-1300**): Nouvelle cuisine that would be just as much at home in Montreal as it is in Newfoundland's smallest city. See chapter 8, p. 193.
- **Water's Edge Restaurant** (Spruce Pine Acres Country Inn, Front Rd., Port au Port West; ✆ **709/648-9273**): Overlooking the ocean west of Stephenville, this delightfully welcoming dining room features a seasonal menu of local specialties. Thankfully, the raspberry cheesecake is always in season. See chapter 8, p. 197.
- **Anchor Café** (Main St., Port au Choix; ✆ **709/861-3665**). Beyond the ship-shaped entrance is a simple

dining room with a wide-ranging menu of inexpensive seafood. My favorite combo is seafood chowder followed by a shrimp burger. See chapter 8, p. 179.

- **Whaler's Restaurant** (Red Bay, Labrador; © **709/920-2156**): Want the best fish and chips in Labrador? Then plan on trying the Chalupa fish and chips at Whaler's. They're tasty, tangy, and value-priced. And the restaurant is located in historic Red Bay, where you can finally find the answer to the riddle, What is a chalupa? See chapter 9, p. 208.

2

Planning Your Trip to Newfoundland & Labrador

Newfoundland and Labrador is the official name for the province, which combines two very distinct regions. Newfoundland is an island, whereas Labrador is part of the mainland, adjacent to Quebec. The official abbreviation for the province is NL. A mere 3,050km (1,895 miles) from Ireland, Newfoundland is the closest point in North America to Europe. By comparison, the capital city of St. John's is double that distance from Victoria, the capital of Canada's most westerly province, British Columbia.

A visit to Canada's most easterly province takes planning, but your efforts will be amply rewarded. You'll be taken with the warmth of the people, always quick with a smile and a friendly greeting. You'll enjoy spontaneous walks off the beaten path as you go exploring for migratory birds and follow the sounds of unseen waterfalls. But first you have to get here. The information on the following pages is designed to make your travel planning as informed as possible.

1 Visitor Information

Contact **Newfoundland & Labrador Tourism** to request a free *Travel Guide, Hunting and Fishing Guide,* or *Highway Map.* Reach them by mail at P.O. Box 8700, St. John's, NL A1B 4J6; call ✆ **800/ 563-6353** or 709/729-2830; or find them on the Web at www.newfoundland andlabradortourism.com. This Frommer's guidebook will give you a more richly detailed, first-person perspective of travel throughout Newfoundland and Labrador. And because this guidebook follows the same regional divisions as the provincial *Travel Guide,* you can easily cross-reference the two.

2 Entry Requirements & Customs

For information on how to get a passport, contact your local Passport Canada location or visit them at **www.ppt.gc.ca** to obtain downloadable passport applications as well as the current fees for processing passport applications. For an up-to-date country-by-country listing of passport requirements around the world, go to the "International Travel" Web page of the U.S. State Department at http:// travel.state.gov.

ENTRY REQUIREMENTS

Like just about every jurisdiction in our world post–September 11, 2001, strict security surrounds entry into Canada. Photo identification is required, especially if traveling by air. Keep it on your person at all times so you can show it to authorities upon request.

U.S. citizens, who used to be able to come into Canada with just a photo ID and either a birth certificate or proof of

Destination Newfoundland & Labrador: Red Alert Checklist

- Are you carrying a current, government-issued ID, such as a driver's license or passport?
- Do you have the address and phone number of your country's embassy or consulate with you?
- Do any lodging, restaurant, or travel reservations need to be booked in advance?
- If you purchased traveler's checks, have you recorded the check numbers, and stored the documentation separately from the checks?
- Did you stop the newspaper and mail delivery, and leave a set of keys with someone reliable?
- Did you pack your camera and an extra set of camera batteries?
- Do you have a safe, accessible place to store money?
- Did you bring your ID cards that could entitle you to discounts, such as AAA and AARP cards, student IDs, and so on?
- Did you bring emergency drug prescriptions and extra glasses and/or contact lenses?
- Did you find out your daily ATM withdrawal limit?
- Do you have your credit card PIN? If you have a 5- or 6-digit PIN, did you obtain a 4-digit number from your bank?
- Did you leave a copy of your itinerary with someone at home?

citizenship, are now advised to bring passports.

As of January 1, 2007, a passport *will* be required by U.S. citizens reentering the United States from Canada by air or sea. As of January 1, 2008, a passport will be required by U.S. citizens reentering the United States via land borders. At press time, the U.S. government was developing alternatives to the traditional passport. For current information, visit http://travel.state.gov/travel. For entry requirements to Canada, check the **Citizenship and Immigration Canada** website at www.cic.gc.ca.

If you're driving into Canada, bring along your vehicle registration papers. Permanent U.S. residents who are not U.S. citizens must carry their Alien Registration Cards (green cards).

CUSTOMS
WHAT YOU CAN BRING INTO CANADA

Customs regulations are fairly flexible with respect to most goods, provided they do not endanger the health of Canadian citizens, their industry, or their environment.

All guns must be declared. If you are a hunter bringing your own firearm, you should make advance arrangements with a local guide so you can provide proof of your intentions to Customs officials (see **Tourism Newfoundland & Labrador's** *Hunting & Fishing Guide* for a list of outfitters).

Household pets can be brought into the province accompanied by proof of rabies vaccinations within the previous 36 months. For more information concerning animals entering Canada, contact the Animal Health and Production Division

Atlantic Canada

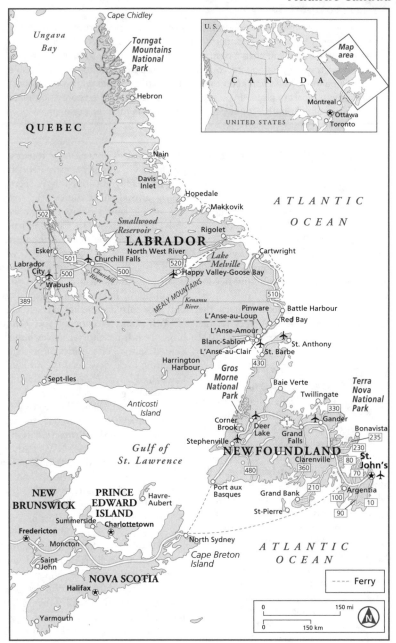

Tips Passport Savvy

Allow plenty of time before your trip to apply for a passport; processing normally takes 3 weeks but can take longer during busy periods (especially spring). And keep in mind that if you need a passport in a hurry, you'll pay a higher processing fee. When traveling, safeguard your passport in an inconspicuous, inaccessible place like a money belt and keep a copy of the critical pages with your passport number in a separate place. If you lose your passport, visit the nearest consulate or embassy of your native country as soon as possible for a replacement.

---

of the Canadian Food Inspection Agency (www.inspection.gc.ca).

The legal age for alcohol consumption is 19, so anyone aged 19 and over can bring in 1.14 liters (40 oz.) of wine or liquor or 24 (12-oz.) bottles/cans of beer.

You are also allowed to bring in 200 cigarettes or 50 cigars without paying any tax or duty. You are permitted to bring gifts valuing C$60 (US$52) duty-free for Canadian residents.

For more information, contact the **Canada Border Services Agency** on the Web at www.cbsa-asfc.gc.ca or call © **204/983-3500.**

WHAT YOU CAN TAKE HOME FROM CANADA

Returning **U.S. citizens** who have been away for at least 48 hours are allowed to bring back, once every 30 days, US$800 worth of merchandise duty-free. You'll pay a flat rate of duty on the next US$1,000 worth of purchases. Any dollar amount beyond that is subject to duties at whatever rates apply. On mailed gifts, the duty-free limit is US$200. Be sure to keep your receipts or purchases accessible to expedite the declaration process. *Note:* If you owe duty, you are required to pay on your arrival in the United States—either by cash, personal check, government or traveler's check, or money order (and, in some locations, a Visa or MasterCard).

To avoid paying duty on foreign-made personal items you owned before your trip, bring along a bill of sale, insurance policy, jeweler's appraisal, or receipts of purchase. Or you can register items that can be readily identified by a permanently affixed serial number or marking—think laptop computers, cameras, and CD players—with Customs before you leave. Take the items to the nearest Customs office or register them with Customs at the airport from which you're departing. You'll receive, at no cost, a Certificate of Registration, which allows duty-free entry for the life of the item.

With some exceptions, you cannot bring fresh fruits and vegetables into the United States. For specifics on what you can bring back, download the invaluable free pamphlet *Know Before You Go* online at **www.cbp.gov**. (Click on "Travel," and then click on "Know Before You Go! Online Brochure.") Or contact the **U.S. Customs & Border Protection (CBP),** 1300 Pennsylvania Ave., NW, Washington, DC 20229 (© **877/287-8667;** www.customs.gov) and request the pamphlet.

Citizens of the U.K. returning from Canada have a customs allowance of: 200 cigarettes; 50 cigars; 250 grams of smoking tobacco; 2 liters of still table wine; 1 liter of spirits or strong liqueurs (over 22% volume); 2 liters of fortified wine, sparkling wine, or other liqueurs; 60cc (ml) perfume; 250cc (ml) of toilet water; and £145 worth of all other goods, including gifts and souvenirs. People under 17 cannot have the tobacco or alcohol allowance. For more information, contact HM Customs & Excise at ☏ **0845/ 010-9000** (from outside the U.K., 020/ 8929-0152), or consult their website at www.hmce.gov.uk.

The duty-free allowance in **Australia** is A$400 or, for those under 18, A$200. Citizens can bring in 250 cigarettes or 250 grams of loose tobacco, and 1,125 milliliters of alcohol. If you're returning with valuables you already own, such as foreign-made cameras, you should file form B263. A helpful brochure available from Australian consulates or Customs offices is *Know Before You Go.* For more information, call the **Australian Customs Service** at ☏ **1300/363-263,** or log on to www.customs.gov.au.

The duty-free allowance for **New Zealand** is NZ$700. Citizens over 17 can bring in 200 cigarettes, 50 cigars, or 250 grams of tobacco (or a mixture of all three if their combined weight doesn't exceed 250g); plus 4.5 liters of wine and beer, or 1.125 liters of liquor. New Zealand currency does not carry import or export restrictions. Fill out a certificate of export, listing the valuables you are taking out of the country; that way, you can bring them back without paying duty. Most questions are answered in a free pamphlet available at New Zealand consulates and Customs offices: *New Zealand Customs Guide for Travellers, Notice no. 4.* For more information, contact **New Zealand Customs,** The Customhouse, 17–21 Whitmore St., Box 2218, Wellington (☏ **04/473-6099** or 0800/ 428-786; www.customs.govt.nz).

3 Money

CURRENCY

At the time of writing, the conversion rate between the U.S. and Canadian dollar had US$1 equal to C$1.17.

To convert Canadian prices to U.S. dollars, use a conversion ratio of approximately 0.8589, meaning an item you see for C$1 will cost approximately $.85U.S.

Although many places accept American dollars, it's better to arrive with Canadian currency. This is especially true if you are coming from a country other than the U.S., as Newfoundland and Labrador has no foreign currency house.

See the universal currency converter at www.xe.com/ucc for the most current conversions on global currencies.

Canada uses both paper money and coins. Paper bills start at $5 and go up from there to $10, $20, $50, and $100. Coins include denominations from the penny up to the two-toned $2 toonie. The $1 coin (called the loonie) is slightly smaller and is brass colored.

The prices of most goods in Newfoundland and Labrador are similar to those in the U.S. Canadian prices are higher for liquor and cigarettes, but you'll find prices for meals, accommodations, souvenirs, and clothing comparable to those in the U.S.

ATMs

The easiest and best way to get cash away from home is from an ATM (automated teller machine). The **Cirrus** (☏ **800/424-7787;** www.mastercard.com) and **PLUS** (☏ **800/843-7587;** www.visa.com) networks span the globe; look at the back of

---

Tips **Go for Small Change**

When converting money into Canadian dollars, you'd be wise to request mostly $20 bills. Some businesses (especially corner stores and service stations) won't accept $50 or $100 denominations because of problems with counterfeiters.

Tips **Small Change**

When you change money, ask for some small bills or loose change. Petty cash will come in handy for tipping and public transportation. Consider keeping the change separate from your larger bills, so that it's readily accessible and you'll be less of a target for theft.

---

your bank card to see which network you're on, then call or check online for ATM locations at your destination. Be sure you know your personal identification number (PIN) and daily withdrawal limit before you depart. *Note:* Remember that many banks impose a fee every time you use a card at another bank's ATM, and that fee can be higher for international transactions (up to C$5/US$4.30 or more) than for domestic ones (where they're rarely more than C$2/US$1.75). In addition, the bank from which you withdraw cash may charge its own fee. To compare banks' ATM fees within the U.S., use **www.bankrate.com**. For international withdrawal fees, ask your bank.

You can use your credit card to receive cash advances at ATMs. Keep in mind that credit card companies protect themselves from theft by limiting maximum withdrawals outside their home country, so call your credit card company before you leave home. And keep in mind that you'll pay interest from the moment of your withdrawal, even if you pay your monthly bills on time.

CREDIT CARDS

Credit cards are another safe way to carry money. Visa and MasterCard are widely accepted across Newfoundland and Labrador. Other credit cards, such as American Express and Diners Club, are less widely accepted, especially at smaller businesses such as bed-and-breakfasts.

Credit cards provide a convenient record of all your expenses, and they generally offer relatively good exchange rates. You can also withdraw cash advances from your credit cards at banks or ATMs, provided you know your PIN. If you don't know yours, call the number on the back of your credit card and ask the bank to send it to you. It usually takes 5 to 7 business days, though some banks will provide the number over the phone if you tell them your mother's maiden name or some other personal information.

Keep in mind that many banks now assess a 1%–3% "transaction fee" on **all** charges you incur abroad (whether you're using the local currency or U.S. dollars). But credit cards still may be the smart way to go when you factor in things like exorbitant ATM fees and the higher exchange rates and service fees you'll pay with traveler's checks.

For tips and telephone numbers to call if your wallet is stolen or lost, go to "Lost & Found" in the "Fast Facts: Newfoundland & Labrador" section of this chapter.

TRAVELER'S CHECKS

Traveler's checks are something of an anachronism from the days before the ATM made cash accessible at any time. Given the fees you'll pay for ATM use at banks other than your own, however, you might be better off with traveler's checks if you're withdrawing money often.

You can buy traveler's checks at most banks. **American Express** offers denominations of US$20, US$50, US$100, US$500, and (for cardholders only) US$1,000. You'll pay a service charge ranging from 1% to 4%. **Visa** offers traveler's checks at Citibank locations across the United States, as well as at several other banks. The service charge ranges between 1.5% and 2%; checks come in the same denominations as American Express. Call ✆ **800/732-1322** for information. AAA members can obtain Visa checks for a US$9.95 fee (for checks totaling up to US$1,500) at most AAA offices or by calling ✆ **866/339-3378. Master-Card** also offers traveler's checks. Call ✆ **800/223-9920** for a location near you.

Buying traveler's checks in Canadian dollars is useful if you're traveling beyond the major tourist areas and staying at locations such as bed-and-breakfasts. **American Express, Thomas Cook, Visa,** and **MasterCard** offer Canadian dollar traveler's checks. You'll pay the rate of exchange at the time of your purchase (so it's a good idea to monitor the rate before you buy), and most companies charge a transaction fee per order (and a shipping fee if you order online).

If you do choose to carry traveler's checks, keep a record of their serial numbers separate from your checks in the event that they are stolen or lost. You'll get a refund faster if you know the numbers.

TIPS & TAXES

Tips of 15% are the norm in the cities and tourist centers. Ten percent is still acceptable in some of the smaller, more rural regions.

Newfoundland and Labrador has a harmonized sales tax (HST) of 15%, which represents a combined 8% provincial tax and 7% federal goods and services tax (GST). The HST applies to most goods and services. Note that in the city of St. John's, an additional 3% hotel tax brings the tax on your hotel room to a total of 18%. Nonresidents can apply for a HST rebate on items they are taking out of Canada, in addition to a rebate on taxes paid on accommodations totaling at least C$50 through the **Tax Rebate Program**. You will need to keep all receipts and request a Proof of Export stamp when leaving Canada.

Call the **Canada Revenue Agency** (✆ **800/668-4748** or 902/432-5608; www. cra-arc.gc.ca/tax/nonresidents for more information.

4 When to Go

WEATHER

As they say locally, "If you don't like the weather, just wait five minutes—it'll change." So pack accordingly. Layered clothing and an oversize backpack or bag to carry your umbrella, rain gear, and an extra sweater are recommended.

You're apt to get the most stable weather, best whale-watching, and greatest variety of special events during July and August, but you'll also hit the highest prices and tightest availability for accommodations. Some of the most-visited places—such as St. John's and Trinity—book up well in advance during the summer, and especially in St. John's during the first week of August. That's when you'll find the Royal St. John's Regatta, the Newfoundland &

Tips **Dear Visa: I'm Off to Killarney!**

Some credit card companies recommend that you notify them of any impending trip abroad so that they don't become suspicious of foreign transactions and block your charges. If you don't call your credit card company in advance, you can still call the card's toll-free emergency number if a charge is refused—provided you remember to carry the phone number with you. Perhaps the most important lesson here is to carry more than one card, so you have a backup.

What Things Cost in Newfoundland & Labrador

Taxi from the airport to downtown St. John's	C$20/US$17
Taxi across town in St. John's	C$10/US$8.50
Metrobus within St. John's (no service to/from airport)	C$2/US$1.75
Local telephone call	C$35¢/US$30¢
Liter of gasoline	C95¢/US80¢
Pint of beer	C$5/US$4.30
Can of cola	C$1/US86¢
Cup of coffee or tea	C$2/US$1.75
Movie in St. John's (Mon–Thurs)	C$8/US$7
Movie in St. John's (Fri–Sun)	C$12/US$10.50
Double room at the Fairmont Newfoundland (expensive)	C$320/US$275
Double room at the Guv'nor Inn (moderate)	C$105/US$90
Dinner for one at Blue on Water (expensive)*	C$65/US$56
Dinner for one at Spirit's Pub & Thai Room (moderate)*	C$35/US$30

*Includes tax and tip, but not wine

Labrador Folk Festival, and the George Street Festival happening simultaneously.

If you're especially keen on seeing icebergs, June is the best time to visit. You'll see a few stragglers along the Northern Peninsula as late as the end of July, but you're nearly guaranteed a few sightings if you visit earlier in the season.

The island of Newfoundland has a temperate marine climate, with winters offering an average norm of 32° Fahrenheit (0° Celsius) and summer temperatures with an average of 61°F (16°C).

Labrador has a harsher winter climate, but its summer temperatures regularly hit upward of 77°F (25°C)—albeit for shorter periods.

The following chart provides the temperature ranges and precipitation rates for the capital city, as well as for St. Anthony on the Northern Peninsula. For temperature ranges in other locations throughout the province, visit the **Environment Canada** website at www.weatheroffice.ec.gc.ca.

St. John's Average Temperatures (°C/°F) & Precipitation (mm/inches)

	Jan	Feb	Mar	Apr	May	June	July	Aug	Sept	Oct	Nov	Dec
Avg. High	-1/34	-2/31	1/34	5/41	11/52	16/61	20/69	20/68	16/61	11/51	6/43	1/43
Avg. Low	-9/16	-9/15	-6/21	-2/28	2/35	6/43	11/51	11/51	8/46	3/38	-1/31	-6/22
Precip.	140/5.5	131/5.2	120/4.7	108/4.3	95/3.7	91/3.6	85/3.3	102/4	112/4.4	139/5.5	154/6.1	146/5.8

St. Anthony's Average Temperatures (°C/°F) & Precipitation (mm/inches)

	Jan	Feb	Mar	Apr	May	June	July	Aug	Sept	Oct	Nov	Dec
Avg. High	19/-7	18/-8	26/-3	34/1	33/6	54/12	62/17	62/17	54/12	43/6	34/1	25/-4
Avg. Low	3/-16	4/-16	12/-11	23/-5	31/-1	37/3	46/8	47/8	41/5	32/0	24/-5	12/-11
Precip.	4.2/107	3.5/90	4.0/101	3.4/87	3.5/89	4.5/114	4.1/104	4.7/120	5.0/126	4.6/117	4.7/119	4.9/124

HOLIDAYS

Newfoundland and Labrador respects all national statutory holidays, including New Year's Day, Good Friday, Easter Monday, Victoria Day (third Mon in May), Canada Day (July 1), Labour Day (first Mon in Sept), Thanksgiving (second Mon in Oct), Remembrance/Armistice Day (Nov 11), Christmas Day (Dec 25), and Boxing Day (Dec 26).

Holidays specific to Newfoundland and Labrador include St. Patrick's Day (Mar 17—usually just government offices and banks are closed), St. George's Day (fourth Wed in Apr), Discovery Day (fourth Tues in June), Orangeman's Day (second Sat in June), and Regatta Day (in St. John's, the first Wed in Aug, weather permitting).

Warning: Sunday shopping is not a given in Newfoundland and Labrador. You will find most shops open on Sunday afternoons in the larger centers, but many retail establishments in the smaller communities are not open at all on Sundays.

CALENDAR OF EVENTS

February

Conception Bay South Winterfest, Conception Bay South, Route 60 (Avalon Peninsula). Break out of hibernation and into a sweat with free swims at the local swimming pool, free skating, and a hockey tournament. Mid-February. Call ℭ **709/834-6534** or visit www.conceptionbaysouth.ca.

Frosty Festival, Mount Pearl, St. John's. The community comes alive for 10 days of fun for all ages: dances, choral demonstrations, a co-ed personality pageant, dart competitions, and basketball tournaments. Mid-February. Call ℭ **709/748-1008** or visit www.mtpearl.nf.ca.

Winterlude, Grand Falls–Windsor, Route 1 (Central Region). Warm up your winter by taking part in one of these lively events. Includes a hockey tournament, figure skating competition, teen dances, snow sculpting, a bowling tournament, cross-country skiing, and more. Mid-February. Call ℭ **709/489-0450.**

Grand Bank Winter Carnival, Grand Bank, Route 220 (Eastern Region). Ten days of winter fun for all ages including talent night, seniors' night, winter photography contest, a scavenger hunt, torchlight parade, snow sculpturing, snowman contest, a beard growing competition, cross-country skiing, and traditional Newfoundland music and food. Late February. Call ℭ **709/832-2617.**

March

Newfoundland (All-Breed) Kennel Club Championship, St. John's. A panel of experts judges more than 100 dogs representing 50 different breeds. Early March. Call ℭ **709/781-8855** or visit www.nkc.n3.net.

April

Smokey Mountain Annual Slush Cup, Labrador City, Route 500 (Labrador). Hosted by the local downhill ski resort, this wacky event commemorates the end of the winter season. Includes a ski run across open

---

Tips Quick ID

Tie a colorful ribbon or piece of yarn around your luggage handle, or slap a distinctive sticker on the side of your bag. This makes it less likely that someone will mistakenly appropriate it. And if your luggage gets lost, it will be easier to find.

shallow water. Mid-April. Call ℂ **709/944-2129.**

May

Labrador City Polar Bear Dip, Labrador City, Route 500 (Labrador). Are you brave enough to take the dip into the frigid waters of Northern Lake? Late May. Call ℂ **709/944-3602** or visit www.labcity.nf.ca.

June

Discovery Celebrations, Bonavista, Route 230 (Eastern Region). Commemorate the discovery of Newfoundland in 1497 by Italian explorer Giovanni Caboto (aka John Cabot). There's a parade, lots of childrens' activities, interesting food selections (moose burgers!), and a free tour of a Cabot ship replica. Late June. Call ℂ **877/468-1497** or 709/468-1493, or visit www.matthewlegacy.com.

National Aboriginal Day. This event is celebrated across the country, with local events held at Terra Nova National Park, North West River, and Nain. If sailing up the coast of Labrador is on your agenda, time your visit to coincide with this wonderful event in Nain and you'll be able to participate in Inuit games and enjoy traditional foods. June 21. Go to www.ainc-inac.gc.ca/nad for a schedule of events.

Franco-Fest, St. John's. *Parlez-vous* fun? Enjoy this weekend celebration of francophone culture. Late June. Call ℂ **877/407-1055** or 709/726-4900.

Cow Head Lobster Festival, Cow Head, Route 430 (Western Newfoundland). Daily lobster suppers, an assortment of local crafts, family entertainment, and fireworks. This town hosts the Gros Morne Theatre Festival throughout summer, with extra shows scheduled throughout the festival. First weekend of July. Call ℂ **709/243-2471** or visit www.cowhead.ca/festival.

July

Bird Island Puffin Festival, Elliston, Route 238 (Eastern Region). This festival features live local entertainment and one of the largest Jiggs Dinners held in the province—prepared with vegetables from the town's historical root cellars. Mid-July. Call ℂ **709/468-7117** or see www.rootcellars.com.

Tri-Fest, Corner Brook, Route 1 (Western Newfoundland). This festival coincides with the Corner Brook Marathon, one of only two triathlons sanctioned by the International Triathlon Union (www.triathlon.org). Not only does Corner Brook claim to host the only triathlon festival in the world, it also claims to have the toughest course in the world. Late July. Call ℂ **877/874-6353** or 709/639-2000, or see www.triourworld.com.

Labrador West Regatta, Wabush, Route 503 (Labrador). A smaller version of the St. John's Regatta, since 1973 this competition has offered a series of Olympic-style rowing races combined with a fun day of games, food, and music. Late July. Call ℂ **709/944-5780.**

August

Newfoundland & Labrador Folk Festival, St. John's. The year's foremost celebration of traditional Newfoundland music, performed by some of the province's best-known musicians. First weekend in August. Call ℂ **866/576-8508** or 709/576-8508, or visit www.sjfac.nf.net.

Royal St. John's Regatta, St. John's. North America's oldest continuous sporting event. Join more than 20,000 spectators along the shore of Quidi Vidi Lake for the capital's biggest event of the year. Enjoy a full day of fixed-seat rowing competition in addition to games of chance, pony rides, and live music. Second Wednesday in August, weather permitting. Call ✆ **709/576-8921** or see www.stjohnsregatta.org.

George Street Festival, St. John's. Serious partygoers will need to bank some zzz's in preparation for this event. Six days of live music, two dozen bars, a closed street, and as much liquid refreshment as your wallet allows. Not to be missed! Early August. Call ✆ **709/576-5990.**

Bakeapple Folk Festival, Forteau, Route 510 (Labrador). A 4-day, mouthwatering celebration of the bakeapple (a wild berry found in only two places in the world: this province and Norway). In addition to irresistible desserts, this event includes folk music, knitted crafts, embroidered goods, games of chance, and children's activities. Early August. Call ✆ **709/931-2545.**

September

Festival of Colors, Corner Brook, Route 1 (Western Newfoundland). This celebration of fall's rich foliage includes craft fairs, storytelling, visual and performing arts, food fairs, dinner theater, and traditional music. Mid-September through mid-October. Call ✆ **709/637-1584** or see www.cornerbrook.com.

October

Red Maple Festival, Grand Falls–Windsor, Route 1 (Central Region). Enjoy this 10-day community festival topped by a huge bonfire and fireworks display. Late October/early November. Call ✆ **709/489-0450** or see www.grandfallswindsor.com.

November

West Coast Craft Fair, Corner Brook, Route 1 (Western Newfoundland). The biggest and longest-running Christmas craft fair on Newfoundland's west coast has much to offer visitors, including demonstrations of crafting techniques. Early November. Call ✆ **709/753-2749** or see www.craftcouncil.nf.ca.

December

Bay Roberts Festival of Lights, Bay Roberts, Route 70 (Avalon Peninsula). A month-long event that kicks off with a tree-lighting ceremony and continues with community caroling, mummering (see "Any Mummers Allowed In?" below), and more. December 1 through early January. Call ✆ **709/786-2126** or see www.bayroberts.com.

New Year's Eve Celebration, St. John's. Dress warmly and prepare for an abundance of goodwill smooches from complete strangers. St. John's is the first city in North America to ring in the New Year (it's 30 min. ahead of Atlantic time). To commemorate that fact, the city hosts a terrifically popular midnight fireworks display from a barge floating in the middle of St. John's Harbour. December 31. Call ✆ **709/754-2489.** For street closure schedules see www.stjohns.ca.

⎛Fun Fact Any Mummers Allowed In?

If you happen to be visiting the province during the Christmas season, don't be alarmed by a loud pounding on the door and the muffled cry of "Any mummers allowed in?" Mummering is a traditional working-class Christmas pastime. A group of people disguise themselves in outlandish costumes and visit various homes throughout the community, entertaining their delighted hosts with comic antics, energetic dancing, and music. The hosts join in the game by trying to guess the identity of their mysterious visitors. Mummers are often rewarded for their efforts with a drink of rum, and then they're off to the next house to continue the fun.

5 Travel Insurance

Like all provinces in Canada, Newfoundland and Labrador has its own provincial medical plan. Wise travelers will obtain sufficient medical insurance before leaving home. Even though prices for health care in Canada are significantly lower than in the U.S., they are still costly for those not covered by the provincial plan.

Check your existing insurance policies and credit card coverage before you buy travel insurance. You may already be covered for lost luggage, canceled tickets, or medical expenses.

The cost of travel insurance varies widely, depending on the cost and length of your trip, your age and health, and the type of trip you're taking.

TRIP-CANCELLATION INSURANCE Trip-cancellation insurance will help retrieve your money if you have to back out of a trip or depart early, or if your travel supplier goes bankrupt. Permissible reasons for trip cancellation can range from sickness to natural disasters to the State Department declaring a destination unsafe for travel. (Insurers usually won't cover vague fears, though, as many travelers discovered when they tried to cancel their trips in Oct 2001.) In this unstable world, trip-cancellation insurance is a good buy if you're purchasing tickets well in advance—who knows what the state of the world, or of your airline, will be in 9 months? Insurance policy details vary, so read the fine print—and make sure that your airline or cruise line is on the list of carriers covered in case of bankruptcy.

For more information, contact one of the following recommended insurers: **Access America** (© 866/807-3982; www.accessamerica.com); **Travel Guard International** (© 800/826-4919; www.travelguard.com); **Travel Insured International** (© 800/243-3174; www.travelinsured.com); and **Travelex Insurance**

Services (© 888/457-4602; www.travelex-insurance.com).

MEDICAL INSURANCE BlueCross BlueShield is the most popular form of medical insurance in Canada and widely accepted at most, if not all, hospitals. Call © 800/810-2583 or find them on the Web at www.bluecares.com.

Most U.S. health plans (including Medicare and Medicaid) do not provide coverage for travel to Canada, and the ones that do often require you to pay for services upfront and reimburse you only after you return home. Even if your plan does cover overseas treatment, most out-of-country hospitals make you pay your bills upfront, and send you a refund only after you've returned home and filed the necessary paperwork with your insurance company. As a safety net, you may want to buy travel medical insurance, particularly if you're traveling to a remote area where emergency evacuation is a possible scenario. If you require additional medical insurance, try **MEDEX Assistance** (© 410/453-6300; www.medexassist.com) or **Travel Assistance International** (© 800/821-2828; www.travelassistance.com; for general information on services, call the company's Worldwide Assistance Services, Inc., at © 800/777-8710).

LOST-LUGGAGE INSURANCE On domestic flights, checked baggage is covered up to US$2,800 per ticketed passenger. On international flights (including to Canada), baggage coverage is limited to US$9.07 per pound. If you plan to check items more valuable than what's covered by the standard liability, see if your homeowner's policy covers your valuables, get baggage insurance as part of your comprehensive travel-insurance package, or buy Travel Guard's "BagTrak" product. Don't buy insurance at the airport, where it's usually overpriced. Be sure to take any valuables or irreplaceable items with you in your carry-on luggage, because many valuables (including books, money, and electronics) aren't covered by airline policies.

If your luggage is lost, immediately file a lost-luggage claim at the airport, detailing the luggage contents. Most airlines require that you report delayed, damaged, or lost baggage within 4 hours of arrival. The airlines are required to deliver luggage, once found, directly to your house or destination free of charge.

6 Health

GENERAL AVAILABILITY OF HEALTH CARE

Most larger communities in the province have hospitals and full medical service. Travelers who have a preexisting medical condition may wish to stay in a community offering full medical services; the more remote regions may be too far from emergency care.

WHAT TO DO IF YOU GET SICK AWAY FROM HOME

If you get sick, consider asking your hotel concierge to recommend a local doctor—even his or her own. You can also try the emergency room at a local hospital. Many hospitals also have walk-in clinics for emergency cases that are not life-threatening; you may not get immediate attention, but you won't pay the high price of an emergency room visit.

If you suffer from a chronic illness, consult your doctor before your departure. For conditions like epilepsy, diabetes, or heart problems, wear a **MedicAlert identification tag** (© 888/ 633-4298; www.medicalert.org), which will immediately alert doctors to your condition and give them access to your records through MedicAlert's 24-hour hot line.

Pack **prescription medications** in your carry-on luggage, and carry prescription medications in their original containers, with pharmacy labels—otherwise they won't make it through airport security. Also carry copies of your prescriptions in case you lose your pills or run out. Don't forget an extra pair of contact lenses or prescription glasses.

Carry the generic name of prescription medicines, in case a local pharmacist is unfamiliar with the brand name.

COMMON AILMENTS

GIARDIA   Best known as "beaver fever," *Giardiasis* has been reported in Newfoundland and Labrador, with occasional boil-water advisories applying to those drinking even town water. Mostly, the concern is for those drinking water from sources such as ponds or rivers. The simplest preventive measure is to boil all water for at least 10 minutes.

Giardia is caused by an intestinal parasite that lives in freshwater. Once swallowed, its effects can be dramatic; severe diarrhea, cramps, and nausea are the most common.

WEATHER EXPOSURE   Winter travel should not be undertaken lightly in Newfoundland and Labrador. Before setting out in a vehicle, check antifreeze levels, and always carry a spare tire and blankets or sleeping bags.

Dress for cold in layers, including a waterproof outer layer, and wear a warm wool cap or other headgear.

Frostbite is a major concern and sometimes deadly. Mild frostbite leaves a numbing, bruised sensation and the skin turns white. Exposed areas of skin (the nose and ears especially) are most susceptible.

Hypothermia occurs when the human body fails to produce heat as fast as it loses it. Exposure to cold weather, combined with fatigue and dampness, often leads to hypothermia. Warning signs include numbness, shivering, slurring of words, dizzy spells, and, in extreme cases,

Avoiding "Economy Class Syndrome"

Deep vein thrombosis, or as it's known in the world of flying, "economy-class syndrome," is a blood clot that develops in a deep vein. It's a potentially deadly condition that can be caused by sitting in cramped conditions—such as an airplane cabin—for too long. During a flight (especially a long-haul flight), get up, walk around, and stretch your legs every 60 to 90 minutes to keep your blood flowing. Other preventive measures include frequent flexing of the legs while sitting, drinking lots of water, and avoiding alcohol and sleeping pills. If you have a history of deep vein thrombosis, heart disease, or another condition that puts you at high risk, some experts recommend wearing compression stockings or taking anticoagulants when you fly; always ask your physician about the best course for you. Symptoms of deep vein thrombosis include leg pain or swelling, or even shortness of breath.

unconsciousness, and even death. The recommended treatment is to get the victim in a warm room, replace wet clothing with dry, and give hot liquids and sugary foods.

7 Specialized Travel Resources

TRAVELERS WITH DISABILITIES

Most disabilities shouldn't stop anyone from traveling. There are more options and resources out there than ever before.

Newfoundland and Labrador may be a step behind some of the more populated Canadian centers in terms of providing service for persons with disabilities, but it is making progress. But part of the charm of visiting Newfoundland and Labrador is having the opportunity to stay at Victorian-style privately run inns, and many, if not most, of them are not accessible to people with mobility problems. Some locations may be "wheelchair friendly" and offer a room or two on the main floor, but the second- and third-floor rooms with their beautiful winding staircases will not be accessible.

Many travel agencies offer customized tours and itineraries for travelers with disabilities. **Flying Wheels Travel** (© 507/451-5005; www.flyingwheelstravel.com) offers escorted tours and cruises that emphasize sports and private tours in minivans with lifts. **Access-Able Travel**

Source (© 303/232-2979; www.accessable.com) offers extensive access information and advice for traveling around the world with disabilities. **Accessible Journeys** (© 800/846-4537 or 610/521-0339; www.disabilitytravel.com) caters specifically to slow walkers and wheelchair travelers and their families and friends.

Organizations that offer assistance to disabled travelers include **MossRehab** (www.mossresourcenet.org), which provides a library of accessible-travel resources online; the **American Foundation for the Blind (AFB)** (© 800/232-5463; www.afb.org), a referral resource for the blind or visually impaired that includes information on traveling with Seeing Eye dogs; and **SATH** (Society for Accessible Travel & Hospitality) (© 212/447-7284; www.sath.org; annual membership fees: US$45 adults, US$30 seniors and students), which offers a wealth of travel resources for all types of disabilities and informed recommendations on destinations, access guides, travel agents, tour operators, vehicle rentals, and companion services. **AirAmbulanceCard.com** is now partnered with SATH and allows you to preselect top-notch hospitals in case of an emergency for US$195 a year (US$295 per family), among other benefits.

For more information specifically targeted to travelers with disabilities, the community website **iCan** (www.ican online.net/channels/travel) has destination guides and several regular columns on accessible travel. Also check out the quarterly magazine *Emerging Horizons* (www.emerginghorizons.com; US$14.95 per year, US$19.95 outside the U.S.); and *Open World* magazine, published by SATH (see above; subscription: US$13 per year, US$21 outside the U.S.).

The **Independent Living Resource Centre** (© **866/722-4031** or 709/722-4031; www.ilrc.nf.ca) is a good source of local information and the website has a wealth of helpful links. The **Canadian Paraplegic Association** (www.canparaplegic. org) is another source of information for travelers with disabilities. The telephone number for their St. John's office is © **709/ 753-5901. Eastern Medical Supplies** (© **709/754-7711**) at 95 Military Road in St. John's rents battery-operated wheelchairs for about C$100 (US$86) and scooters for about C$120 (US$104) per month. Daily and weekly rentals are also available.

GAY & LESBIAN TRAVELERS

The gay lifestyle is fully accepted in Newfoundland. So much so that the province is developing a reputation as a destination for health-conscious same-sex couples. St. John's is gaining status as the San Francisco of the Eastern seaboard with its Victorian architecture, fresh climate, hilly terrain, and the welcoming acceptance of local residents.

Curious, in Holdsworth Court, George St. (© **709/722-6999**) is the only dedicated gay nightclub in St. John's, although gay/straight **Liquid Ice,** at

186B Water St. © **709/754-2190,** attracts the larger crowds.

The **International Gay and Lesbian Travel Association (IGLTA)** (© **800/ 448-8550** or 954/776-2626; www.iglta. org) is the trade association for the gay and lesbian travel industry, and offers an online directory of gay- and lesbian-friendly travel businesses; go to their website and click on "Members."

Many agencies offer tours and travel itineraries specifically for gay and lesbian travelers. **Now, Voyager** (© **800/255-6951;** www.nowvoyager.com) is a well-known San Francisco–based, gay-owned and operated travel service. **Gay.com Travel** (© **800/929-2268** or 415/644-8044; www.gay.com/travel or www.out andabout.com) is an excellent online successor to the popular *Out & About* print magazine. It provides regularly updated information about gay-owned, gay-oriented, and gay-friendly lodging, dining, sightseeing, nightlife, and shopping establishments in Canada and elsewhere.

The following travel guides are available at many bookstores, or you can order them from any online bookseller: *Frommer's Gay & Lesbian Europe* (www.frommers. com), an excellent travel resource to the top European cities and resorts; *Spartacus International Gay Guide* (Bruno Gmünder Verlag; www.spartacusworld.com/ gayguide) and *Odysseus: The International Gay Travel Planner* (Odysseus Enterprises Ltd.), both good, annual, English-language guidebooks focused on gay men; and the *Damron* guides (www. damron.com), with separate, annual books for gay men and lesbians.

SENIOR TRAVEL

Recognizing the importance of mature travelers to the tourism industry, most establishments will reward seniors' patronage with a special discount. However, just who qualifies for a seniors' discount is determined by each provider.

Some companies offer seniors' rates to anyone over 50. For others, you must be 65. If you are 50 or older, don't hesitate to ask if you are eligible for a discount—it could add up to substantial savings.

Members of **AARP** (formerly known as the American Association of Retired Persons), 601 E St. NW, Washington, DC 20049 (© **888/687-2277;** www. aarp.org), get discounts on hotels, airfares, and car rentals. AARP offers members a wide range of benefits, including *AARP: The Magazine* and a monthly newsletter. Anyone over 50 can join.

Many reliable agencies and organizations target the 50-plus market. **Elderhostel** (© **877/426-8056;** www.elderhostel.org) arranges study programs for those aged 55 and over (and a spouse or companion of any age) across Newfoundland and Labrador and around the world. Most courses last 5 to 7 days, and many include airfare, accommodations in university dormitories or modest inns, meals, and tuition.

Recommended publications offering travel resources and discounts for seniors include: the quarterly magazine *Travel 50 & Beyond* (www.travel50andbeyond. com); *Travel Unlimited: Uncommon Adventures for the Mature Traveler* (Avalon); *101 Tips for Mature Travelers,* available from Grand Circle Travel (© **800/ 221-2610** or 617/350-7500; www.gct. com); and *Unbelievably Good Deals and Great Adventures That You Absolutely Can't Get Unless You're Over 50* (McGraw-Hill), by Joann Rattner Heilman.

FAMILY TRAVEL

If you have enough trouble getting your kids out of the house in the morning, dragging them thousands of miles away may seem like an insurmountable challenge. But family travel can be immensely rewarding, giving you new ways of seeing the world through the eyes of children.

Vacationing with a family does require advance planning, especially to Newfoundland and Labrador, where you will spend long hours on the road and not all accommodations are suited to children, especially younger ones. An ideal scenario from St. John's is to limit your travels to the eastern half of the island, making the **Splash-n-Putt Resort** (p. 150) your turnaround point. In the vicinity is **Terra Nova Golf Resort** (p. 146), one of the province's most kid-friendly lodgings, and **Terra Nova National Park**, with an excellent summer activity program.

To locate accommodations, restaurants, and attractions that are particularly kid-friendly, refer to the "Kids" icon throughout this guide.

Recommended family travel websites include **Family Travel Forum** (www.family travelforum.com), a comprehensive site that offers customized trip planning; **Family Travel Network** (www.family travelnetwork.com), an award-winning site that offers travel features, deals, and tips; **Traveling Internationally with Your Kids** (www.travelwithyourkids.com), a comprehensive site offering sound advice for long-distance and international travel with children; and **Family Travel Files** (www.thefamilytravelfiles.com), which offers an online magazine and a directory of off-the-beaten-path tours that includes Newfoundland and Labrador.

8 Planning Your Trip Online

Newfoundland and Labrador is not considered a major international destination, so it is unlikely you will encounter any big sales or super deals to help get you here.

Unless you are extremely savvy with respect to online bookings, you're best off putting your planning in the hands of a knowledgeable travel counselor or service that can help you with the logistics of getting to and around this deceivingly expansive and varied province. Plus, a travel agent can save you money by alerting you to special, unadvertised deals (such as vacancies on charter flights).

But if you've got a few online bookings under your belt and you have the time to thoroughly research the transportation segments that will be necessary in planning your trip, go for it! Here are a few resources that may help.

SURFING FOR AIRFARES

The "big three" online travel agencies, **Expedia.com, Travelocity.com,** and **Orbitz.com,** sell most of the air tickets bought on the Internet. (Canadian travelers should try expedia.ca and Travelocity.ca; U.K. residents can go for expedia.co.uk and opodo.co.uk.). **Kayak.com** is also gaining popularity and uses a sophisticated search engine (developed at MIT). Each has different business deals with the airlines and may offer different fares on the same flights, so it's wise to shop around. Expedia, Kayak, and Travelocity will also send you **e-mail notification** when a cheap fare becomes available to your favorite destination. Of the smaller travel-agency websites, **SideStep** (www.sidestep.com) has gotten the best reviews from Frommer's authors. The website (with optional browser add-on) purports to "search 140 sites at once," but in reality only beats competitors' fares as often as other sites do.

Also remember to check **airline websites. Air Canada** (www.aircanada.com) has an easy-to-use site with the option to search by fare or schedule. The other two major Canadian airlines flying into Newfoundland and Labrador are **CanJet** (www.canjet.com) and **WestJet** (www.westjet.com), and their fares are always competitive but often missing from the online travel agency websites. Even with major airlines, you can often shave a few

bucks from a fare by booking directly through the airline and avoiding a travel agency's transaction fee. But you'll get these discounts only by **booking online:** most airlines now offer online-only fares that even their phone agents know nothing about.

Last-minute deals are available through free weekly e-mail services provided directly by the airlines. Most of these are announced on Tuesday or Wednesday and must be purchased online. Most are only valid for travel that weekend, but some (such as Southwest's) can be booked weeks or months in advance. Sign up for weekly e-mail alerts at airline websites or check mega-sites that compile comprehensive lists of last-minute specials, such as **Smarter Travel** (www.smartertravel.com). For last-minute trips, **site59.com** and **lastminutetravel.com** in the U.S. and **lastminute.com** in Europe often have better air-and-hotel package deals than the major-label sites.

If you're willing to give up some control over your flight details, use what is called an **"opaque" fare service** like **Priceline** (www.priceline.com; www.priceline.co.uk for Europeans) or its smaller competitor **Hotwire** (www.hotwire.com). Both offer rock-bottom prices in exchange for travel on a "mystery airline" at a mysterious time of day, often with a mysterious change of planes en route. The mystery airlines are all major, well-known carriers—and the possibility of being sent from Philadelphia to Chicago via Tampa is remote; the airlines' routing computers have gotten a lot better than they used to be. Your chances of getting a 6am or 11pm flight, however, are still pretty high. Hotwire tells you flight prices before you buy; Priceline usually has better deals than Hotwire, but you have to play their "Name Your Own Price" game. If you're new at this, the helpful folks at **BiddingForTravel** (www.biddingfortravel.com) do a good job of demystifying Priceline's prices and strategies. Priceline and Hotwire are great for flights within North America and between the U.S. and Europe.

SURFING FOR HOTELS

Most Newfoundland and Labrador accommodations have websites. The larger hotels and motels have the tools for making online reservations, while for smaller properties, such as bed-and-breakfasts, you'll need to send off an e-mail to reserve a room. Privately operated bed-and-breakfasts and smaller inns generally don't offer discounts, and so the following information is aimed at those planning on staying at chain hotels and motels, which are located in St. John's and other major centers along the Trans-Canada Highway through the province.

Shopping online for hotels is generally done one of two ways: by booking through the hotel's own website or through an independent booking agency. These Internet hotel agencies have multiplied in mind-boggling numbers of late, competing for the business of millions of consumers surfing for accommodations around the world. This competitiveness can be a boon to consumers who have the patience and time to shop and compare the online sites for good deals—but shop they must, for prices can vary considerably from site to site. And keep in mind that hotels at the top of a site's listing may be there for no other reason than that they paid money to get the placement.

Of the "big three" sites, **Expedia** offers a long list of special deals and "virtual tours" or photos of available rooms so you can see what you're paying for (a feature that helps counter the claims that the best rooms are often held back from bargain-booking websites). **Travelocity** posts unvarnished customer reviews and ranks its properties according to the AAA rating system. **Trip Advisor** (www.tripadvisor.com) is another excellent source of unbiased user reviews of

hotels around the world. While even the finest hotels can inspire a misleadingly poor review from picky or crabby travelers, the body of user opinions, when taken as a whole, is usually a reliable indicator.)

Other reliable online booking agencies include **Hotels.com** and **Quikbook.com**. An excellent free program, **TravelAxe** (www.travelaxe.net), can help you search multiple hotel sites at once, even ones you may never have heard of—and conveniently lists the total price of the room, including the taxes and service charges. Be aware that more than once, travelers have arrived at the hotel, only to be told that they have no reservation. To be fair, many of the major sites are undergoing improvements in service and ease of use, and Expedia will soon be able to plug directly into the reservations systems of many hotel chains—none of which can be bad news for consumers. In the meantime, it's a good idea to **get a confirmation number** and **make a printout** of any online booking transaction.

SURFING FOR RENTAL CARS

For booking rental cars online, the best deals are usually found at rental-car company websites, although all the major online travel agencies also offer rental-car reservations services. Priceline and Hotwire work well for rental cars, too; the only "mystery" is which major rental company you get, and for most travelers the difference between Hertz, Avis, and Budget is negligible.

You'll find many travel websites, and each has an upper hand in certain aspects of service. Your first stop should be www.frommers.com (check out the online newsletter). Another site, www.smartertravel.com, offers weekly e-mail notification of special fares from your chosen city. As most flights to St. John's originate out of Toronto or Halifax, you're wise to subscribe to this service for those two cities. The only drawback is that you usually

Frommers.com: The Complete Travel Resource

For an excellent travel-planning resource, we highly recommend **Frommers. com** (www.frommers.com), voted Best Travel Site by *PC Magazine*. We're a little biased, of course, but we guarantee that you'll find the travel tips, reviews, monthly vacation giveaways, bookstore, and online-booking capabilities thoroughly indispensable. Among the special features are our popular **Destinations** section, where you'll get expert travel tips, hotel and dining recommendations, and advice on the sights to see for more than 3,500 destinations around the globe; the **Frommers.com Newsletter,** with the latest deals, travel trends, and money-saving secrets; our **Community** area featuring **Message Boards,** where Frommer's readers post queries and share advice (sometimes even our authors show up to answer questions); and our **Photo Center,** where you can post and share vacation tips. When your research is finished, the **Online Reservations System** (www.frommers. com/book_a_trip) takes you to Frommer's preferred online partners for booking your vacation at affordable prices.

have to travel the same week as the posting, and last-minute travel doesn't work well in the summer when availability of accommodations is at a premium. Another great site is www.expedia.com (or www.expedia.ca, the Canadian version), which offers e-mail notification if a sale to your chosen destination becomes available.

9 The 21st-Century Traveler

INTERNET ACCESS AWAY FROM HOME

Travelers have any number of ways to check their e-mail and access the Internet on the road. Of course, using your own laptop—or even a PDA (personal digital assistant) or electronic organizer with a modem—gives you the most flexibility. But even if you don't have a computer, you can still access your e-mail and even your office computer from cybercafes.

WITHOUT YOUR OWN COMPUTER

Newfoundland and Labrador is well connected, with public libraries across the province offering free Internet access. For locations and hours contact **Newfoundland and Labrador Public Libraries** at ℂ **709/643-0900,** or visit www.nlpublic libraries.ca. But the best resource by far is

the **Community Access Program (CAP),** a government initiative that is represented in over 150 Newfoundland and Labrador communities. Usually a room in a local community hall, access centers have computers hooked up to the Internet, as well as scanners and printers. The cost of getting online is minimal or free. For hours and locations call ℂ **877/929-1829** or 709/729-1828, or visit www.nf cap.nf.ca.

To retrieve your e-mail, ask your **Internet Service Provider (ISP)** if it has a Web-based interface tied to your existing e-mail account. If your ISP doesn't have such an interface, you can use the free **mail2web** service (www.mail2web.com) to view and reply to your home e-mail. For more flexibility, you may want to open a free, Web-based e-mail account with **Yahoo! Mail** (http://mail.yahoo. com). (Microsoft's Hotmail is another popular option, but Hotmail has severe spam problems.) Your home ISP may be able to forward your e-mail to the Web-based account automatically.

If you need to access files on your office computer, look into a service called **GoToMyPC** (www.gotomypc.com). The service provides a Web-based interface for you to access and manipulate a distant PC from anywhere—even a cybercafe—provided your "target" PC is on and has an always-on connection to the Internet (as with Road Runner cable). The service offers top-quality security, but if you're worried about hackers, use your own laptop rather than a cybercafe computer to access the GoToMyPC system.

WITH YOUR OWN COMPUTER

Newfoundland and Labrador has very few Wi-Fi (wireless fidelity) "hotspots," from where you can get high-speed Internet connection without cable wires or a phone line, but this is sure to change quickly. At the time of writing, St. John's International Airport, the Marine Atlantic ferries from Nova Scotia, and the Fairmont Newfoundland (St. John's) have Wi-Fi service.

Many Newfoundland and Labrador accommodations offer dataports for laptop modems. **Call the lodging in advance** to see what your options are. In addition, major Internet Service Providers (ISPs) have **local access numbers** around the world, allowing you to go online by placing a local call. Check your ISP's website or call its toll-free number and ask how you can use your current account away from home, and how much it will cost.

The **iPass** network also has dial-up numbers around the world. You'll have to sign up with an iPass provider, who will then tell you how to set up your computer for your destination(s). For a list of iPass providers, go to www.ipass.com and click on "Individuals Buy Now." One solid provider is **i2roam** (www.i2roam. com; © **866/811-6209** or 920/235-0475).

Wherever you go, bring a **connection kit** of the right power and phone adapters, a spare phone cord, and a spare Ethernet network cable—or find out whether your accommodations supplies them to guests.

USING A CELLPHONE

Just because your cellphone works at home doesn't mean it'll work in Newfoundland and Labrador. It's a good bet that your phone will work in St. John's, and other cities like Gander and Corner Brook, but beyond these population centers, coverage is almost nonexistent.

The three letters that define much of the world's **wireless capabilities** are GSM (Global System for Mobiles), a big, seamless network that makes for easy cross-border cellphone use throughout Europe and dozens of other countries worldwide. In the U.S., T-Mobile, AT&T Wireless, and Cingular use this quasi-universal system; in Canada, Microcell and some Rogers customers are GSM, and all Europeans and most Australians use GSM.

If your cellphone is on a GSM system, and you have a world-capable multiband phone such as many Sony Ericsson, Motorola, or Samsung models, you can make and receive calls across civilized areas around much of the globe, from Andorra to Uganda. Just call your wireless operator and ask for "international roaming" to be activated on your account. Unfortunately, per-minute charges can be high—usually C$1 (US85¢) to C$1.50 (US$1.25) in Canada. That's why it's important to buy an "unlocked" world phone from the get-go. Many cellphone operators sell "locked" phones that restrict you from using any other removable computer memory phone chip (called a **SIM card**) card than the ones they supply. Having an unlocked phone allows you to install a cheap, prepaid SIM card (found at a local retailer) in Canada. (Show your phone to the salesperson; not all phones work on all networks.) You'll get a local phone number—and much, much lower calling rates. Unlocking an already locked phone can be complicated, but it can be done; just call your cellular operator and say you'll be going abroad for several months and want to use the phone with a local provider.

Two good wireless rental companies are **InTouch USA** (© **800/872-7626;** www.intouchglobal.com) and **RoadPost** (© **888/290-1606** or 905/272-5665; www.roadpost.com). Give them your itinerary, and they'll tell you what wireless products you need. InTouch will also, for free, advise you on whether your existing phone will work overseas; simply call © **703/222-7161** between 9am and 4pm EST, or go to http://intouchglobal.com/travel.htm.

For trips of more than a few weeks, **buying a phone** becomes economically attractive, as Canada has a cheap, no-questions-asked prepaid phone system. Stop by Rogers, at 193 LeMarchant Rd., St. John's (© **709/739-9751;** www.rogers.ca) and ask about Pay As You Go packages; you'll pay less than C$100 (US$86) for a phone and a starter calling card.

SATELLITE PHONES

If you need to stay in touch at a destination where you know your phone won't work, consider renting a **satellite phone ("satphone"),** which is different from a cellphone in that it connects to satellites rather than ground-based towers. A satphone is more costly than a cellphone but works in the absence of cellular signal and towers. Contact **RoadPost** (© **888/290-1606** or 905/272-5665; www.roadpost.com;) or **InTouch USA** (© **800/872-7626;** www.intouchglobal.com). Per-minute call

---

Online Traveler's Toolbox

Veteran travelers usually carry some essential items to make their trips easier. Following is a selection of handy online tools to bookmark and use.

- **Airplane Seating and Food.** Find out which seats to reserve and which to avoid (and more) on all major airlines at www.seatguru.com. And check out the type of meal (with photos) you'll likely be served on airlines around the world at www.airlinemeals.net.
- **Environment Canada** (www.weatheroffice.ec.gc.ca). Gives weather forecasts for over 50 cities and towns across Newfoundland and Labrador.
- **Mapquest** (www.mapquest.com). This best of the mapping sites lets you choose a specific address or destination and, in seconds, returns a map and detailed directions.
- **Time and Date** (www.timeanddate.com). See what time (and day) it is anywhere in the world.
- **Universal Currency Converter** (www.xe.com/ucc). See what over 100 different currencies are worth against the Canadian dollar.
- **Visa ATM Locator** (www.visa.com), for locations of PLUS ATMs worldwide, or **MasterCard ATM Locator** (www.mastercard.com), for locations of Cirrus ATMs worldwide.

charges can be even cheaper than roaming charges with a regular cellphone, but the phone itself is more expensive (up to US$150 a week to rent), and depending on the service you choose, people calling you may incur high long-distance charges. As of this writing, satphones were outrageously expensive to buy, so don't even think about it.

10 Getting There

More than a thousand years ago, Leif Eriksson—acting on the rumored sighting of an unknown westward land—stocked the Viking-era equivalent of a cargo ship with provisions, cattle, and tools. With only the most rudimentary navigational aids (a notched bearing dial, a sunstone, and the stars), Eiriksson set out from Greenland. He and his crew braved the uncertain temper of the North Atlantic in an open longboat for almost 3 weeks before reaching their destination. Proof of their landing can be found in L'Anse aux Meadows, on Newfoundland's Northern Peninsula. Fortunately for today's travelers, while the destination is just as enticing as it was for Eiriksson, you no longer have to row your way across the Atlantic (unless you want to).

BY PLANE

Air Canada is the biggest player in Canada, offering two flight options: Air Canada's regular air service and its regional carrier Jazz. Between the two, you'll find connections from destinations around the world to St. John's, Gander, Deer Lake, and Happy Valley–Goose Bay. Call **Air Canada** at ℂ **888/247-2262** or visit them on the Web at www.aircanada.com.

CanJet is a low-fare, no-frills (not a huge sacrifice; none of the airlines offer many amenities anymore) carrier providing direct flights to St. John's from Toronto, Moncton, and Halifax, with connections through these three cities as far south as Florida and as far west as Vancouver. CanJet also flies between Halifax and Deer Lake. Call ℂ **800/809-7777** or 506/544-7230, or visit their website at www.canjet.com.

WestJet is a low-fare airline from Western Canada that flies into St. John's from Halifax, with connections from there across the country. To compare prices, see www.westjet.com, or call ℂ **888/937-8538** or 403/250/5839.

Conquest Vacations offers reasonably priced flights to St. John's from Toronto via Skyservice. Call ℂ **866/232-4722** or visit them on the Web at www.flyconquest.com.

In summer only, **Air Transat** flies to St. John's. Call ℂ **866/847-1112** or visit their website at www.airtransat.com for details on their seasonally adjusted flight schedules.

Provincial Airlines offers service from St. John's and Halifax to many of the smaller communities throughout Newfoundland and Labrador. For reservations, call ℂ **800/563-2800** or visit them on the Web at www.provair.com. The customer service number is ℂ **709/576-3091.**

Air Labrador is an intraprovincial airline with connections from Montreal and Sept Îles to 18 Labrador and western Newfoundland communities. Call ℂ **800/563-3042** or 709/758-0002, or visit them online at www.airlabrador.com.

GETTING THROUGH THE AIRPORT

Airport security in Canada is taken as seriously as it is in the United States. Generally, you'll be fine if you arrive at the airport **1 hour** before a domestic flight and **2 hours** before an international flight, the same as applies at U.S. airports.

Bring a **current, government-issued photo ID** such as a driver's license or passport. Keep your ID at the ready to present at check-in, the security checkpoint, and

⌐Tips⌐ Don't Stow It—Ship It

If ease of travel is your main concern, and money is no object, consider shipping your luggage and sports equipment with one of the growing number of luggage-service companies that pick up, track, and deliver travel bags (often through couriers such as Federal Express). Traveling luggage-free, however convenient, isn't cheap: One-way overnight shipping can cost from US$100 to US$200, depending on what you're sending. Still, for some people, especially the elderly or the infirm, it's a sensible option. Specialists in door-to-door luggage delivery include **Luggage Express** (www.usxpluggageexpress.com), and **Sports Express** (www.sportsexpress.com), both of which deliver to Canada from the United States.

sometimes even the gate. Passengers with e-tickets, which have made paper tickets nearly obsolete, can beat the ticket-counter lines by using airport **electronic kiosks** or even **online check-in** from their home computers. Online check-in involves logging on to your airline's website, accessing your reservation, and printing out your boarding pass—and the airline may even offer you bonus miles to do so! **Air Canada** (www.aircanada.com) offers Web check-in for all flights originating in Canada, as well as those departing major U.S. airports. If you're using a kiosk at the airport, bring the credit card you used to book the ticket or your frequent-flier card. Print out your boarding pass from the kiosk and simply proceed to the security checkpoint with your pass and a photo ID. If you're checking bags or looking to snag an exit-row seat, you will be able to do so using most airline kiosks.

Security checkpoint lines are getting shorter than they were a few years back, but high passenger volume can still make for a long wait. *Tip:* If you have trouble standing for long periods of time, tell an airline employee; the airline will provide a wheelchair. Speed up security by **not wearing metal objects** such as big belt buckles. If you've got metallic body parts, a note from your doctor can prevent a long chat with the security screeners. Keep in mind that only **ticketed passengers** are

allowed past security, except for people escorting disabled passengers or children.

Know **what you can carry on** and **what you can't.** The general rule is that sharp things are out, nail clippers are okay, and food and beverages must pass through the X-ray machine—but security screeners can't make you drink from your coffee cup. Bring food in your carry-on rather than checking it, as explosive-detection machines used on checked luggage have been known to mistake food (especially chocolate, for some reason) for bombs. Air travelers in Canada and the U.S. are allowed one carry-on bag, plus a "personal item" such as a purse, briefcase, or laptop bag. Carry-on hoarders can stuff all sorts of things into a laptop bag; as long as it has a laptop in it, it's still considered a personal item. The Transportation Security Administration (TSA) has issued a list of restricted items for U.S. airlines; check its website (www.tsa.gov/public/index.jsp) for details.

Airport screeners may decide that your checked luggage warrants a hand search. You can now purchase luggage locks that allow screeners to open and relock a checked bag if hand searching is necessary. Luggage inspectors can open these TSA-approved locks with a special code or key—rather than having to cut them off the suitcase, as they normally do to conduct a hand search. Look for Travel

Sentry certified locks at luggage or travel shops worldwide; for store locations, visit www.travelsentry.org.

FLYING FOR LESS: TIPS FOR GETTING THE BEST AIRFARE

Passengers sharing the same airplane cabin rarely pay the same fare. Travelers who need to purchase tickets at the last minute, change their itinerary at a moment's notice, or fly one-way often get stuck paying the premium rate. Here are some ways to keep your airfare costs down.

- Passengers who can book their ticket either **long in advance or at the last minute,** or who **fly midweek** or **at less-trafficked hours** may pay a fraction of the full fare. If your schedule is flexible, say so, and ask if you can secure a cheaper fare by changing your flight plans.
- Search **the Internet** for cheap fares (see "Planning Your Trip Online" earlier in this chapter).
- Keep an eye on local newspapers for **promotional specials** or **fare wars,** when airlines lower prices on their most popular routes. You rarely see fare wars offered for peak travel times, but if you can travel in the off-months, you may snag a bargain.
- **Consolidators,** also known as bucket shops, are great sources for international tickets, although they usually can't beat Internet fares within North America. Start by looking in Sunday newspaper travel sections; U.S. travelers should focus on the *New York Times, Los Angeles Times,* and *Miami Herald. Beware:* Bucket shop tickets are usually nonrefundable or rigged with stiff cancellation penalties, often as high as 50% to 75% of the ticket price, and some put you on charter airlines, which may leave at inconvenient times and experience delays. Several reliable consolidators are worldwide and available online. **STA Travel** has been the world's lead consolidator for students since purchasing Council Travel, but their fares are competitive for travelers of all ages. **ELTExpress (Flights.com)** (*©* 800/ TRAV-800; www.eltexpress.com) has excellent fares worldwide, with "departure" websites in 18 countries. **Air Tickets Direct** (*©* 800/778-3447; www.airticketsdirect.com) is based in Montreal and leverages the Canadian dollar for low fares.

- Join **frequent-flier programs.** Frequent-flier membership doesn't cost a cent, but it does entitle you to better seats, faster response to phone inquiries, and prompter service if your luggage is stolen or your flight is canceled or delayed, or if you want to change your seat. And you don't have to fly to earn points; **frequent-flier credit cards** can earn you thousands of miles for doing your everyday shopping. With more than 70 mileage awards programs on the market, consumers have never had more options, but the system has never been more complicated—what with major airlines folding, new budget carriers emerging, and alliances forming (allowing you to earn points on partner airlines). Investigate the program details of your favorite airlines before you sink points into any one. Consider which airlines have hubs in the airport nearest you, and, of those carriers, which have the most advantageous alliances, given your most common routes? **Aeroplan** (www. aeroplan.com), Air Canada's frequent-flier program, has one of the better programs and is affiliated with a number of international airlines and hotel partners. To play the frequent-flier game to your best advantage, consult Randy Petersen's **Inside Flyer** (www. insideflyer.com). Petersen and friends review all the programs in detail and post regular updates on changes in policies and trends. Petersen will also field direct questions (via e-mail) if a partner airline refuses to redeem points, for instance, or if you're still not sure after researching the various programs which one is right for you. It's well worth the US$12 online subscription fee, good for one year. **Flyer Talk.com** is the world's busiest forum for frequent flyers.

BY SEA
ARRIVING BY FERRY

Marine Atlantic offers service between North Sydney, Nova Scotia, and two points in Newfoundland. Shorter of the two is the 6-hour journey to Port aux Basques. Ferry service on this route operates year-round, with one-way fares of C$27 (US$23) adults, C$14 (US$12) children, and C$77 (US$66) and up for vehicles. Extras include dorm beds (C$16/US$14) and cabins (C$99/US$85).

If your primary destination is St. John's, you can take the approximately 14-hour sailing to Argentia, which is a 1½-hour drive to the capital city. This is a seasonal service that operates from mid-June to mid-September. One-way fares include C$76 (US$65) adults, C$14 (US$12) children, and C$157 (US$135) and up for vehicles. A dorm bed is C$28 (US$24) and cabins start at C$138 (US$118).

Give serious consideration to the additional cost for a cabin on the ferry, as fog and high winds can easily extend those 14 hours into 16 or 18 very long hours at sea. The more moderately priced cots are not a good choice for those who like their privacy or are even mildly claustrophobic.

Advance reservations are recommended for all sailings, and a C$25 (US$22) deposit, payable through a major credit card, is required for reservations booked more than 48 hours prior to departure.

Contact Marine Atlantic at ✆ **800/341-7981** or 902/794-5700, or visit the website at www.marine-atlantic.ca.

ARRIVING BY PRIVATE VESSEL

If you're planning on sailing your own yacht to Newfoundland and Labrador, you should contact the **Canadian Coast Guard** (Search & Rescue) at www.ccg-gcc.gc.ca.

The volunteer **Canadian Coast Guard Auxiliary (CCGA)** offers information on boating safety and regulations you need to know while sailing Canadian waters. Visit them on the Web at www.ccga-gcac.com/home/home_e.asp for an online version of their *Safe Boating Guide*. The Newfoundland chapter of the CCGA can be reached by phone at ✆ **709/772-4074.**

BY RAIL

The island of Newfoundland is not accessible by train, nor does it have an internal

---

Travel in the Age of Bankruptcy

Airlines go bankrupt, so protect yourself by **buying your tickets with a credit card**, as the Fair Credit Billing Act guarantees that you can get your money back from the credit card company if a travel supplier goes under (and if you request the refund within 60 days of the bankruptcy). **Travel insurance** can also help, but make sure it covers against "carrier default" for your specific travel provider. And be aware that if a U.S. airline goes bust mid-trip, a federal law requires other carriers to take you to your destination (albeit on a space-available basis) for a fee of no more than US$25, provided you rebook within 60 days of the cancellation.

rail service. Limited rail service is available in western Labrador.

You can travel by train between Sept-Îles, Quebec, and Labrador on the Quebec North Shore & Labrador Railway. The trip takes 7 hours. For information, contact **Quebec North Shore & Labrador Railway** at © **800/463-4123** or 418/968-1350.

11 Packages for the Independent Traveler

Before you start your search for the lowest airfare, you may want to consider booking your flight as part of a travel package. Package tours are not the same thing as escorted tours. Package tours are simply a way to buy the airfare, accommodations, and other elements of your trip (such as car rentals, airport transfers, and sometimes even activities) at the same time and often at discounted prices—kind of like one-stop shopping. Packages are sold in bulk to tour operators—who resell them to the public at a cost that usually undercuts standard rates.

Package tours can vary by leaps and bounds. Some offer a better class of hotels than others. Some offer the same hotels for lower prices. Some offer flights on scheduled airlines, while others book charters. Some limit your choice of accommodations and travel days. You are often required to make a large payment upfront. On the plus side, packages can save you money, offering group prices but allowing for independent travel. Some even let you add on a few guided excursions or escorted day trips (also at prices lower than if you booked them yourself) without booking an entirely escorted tour.

Before you invest in a package tour, get some answers. Ask about the **accommodations choices** and prices for each. Then look up the hotels' reviews in a Frommer's guide and check their rates online for your specific dates of travel. Finally, look for **hidden expenses.** Ask whether airport departure fees and taxes, for example, are included in the total cost.

One good source of package deals is the airlines themselves. You can book hotels and rental cars through the **Air Canada** website (www.aircanada.com), or through this airline's online travel agency, **Destina.ca**. You can also use the websites of Canada's other two major airlines, **WestJet** (www.westjet.com) and **CanJet** (www.canjet.com) to book rooms and cars in conjunction with your flight to Newfoundland and Labrador.

Many accommodations bundle rooms with local activities. **Delta St. John's** (www.deltahotels.com; p. 77) has some excellent deals, even in mid-summer. Also in the capital, check the **Fairmont Newfoundland** website (www.fairmont.com; p. 77). Packages offered by smaller lodgings are usually more about convenience than getting a great deal. Two standouts are the **Village Inn,** at Trinity (www.oceancontact.com; p. 130), which offers multi-night whale-watching and hiking packages; and **Marble Inn,** in Western Newfoundland (www.marbleinn.com; p. 192), which bundles summer or winter activities with accommodations.

12 Escorted Tours

Escorted tours are structured group tours, with a group leader. The price usually includes everything from airfare to hotels, meals, tours, admission costs, and local transportation. One of the best choices of local tours is offered by **Ambassatours,** part of the Grayline tour company. Their 13-day Circle Newfoundland and Labrador tour starts and ends in Halifax, and takes advantage of both ferry services to cross the island without backtracking. The cost of C\$3,750 (US\$3,221) includes hotel accommodations and all meals. The 8-day Viking Trail tour costs C$2,370 (US$2,036) and concentrates on western Newfoundland highlights such as Gros Morne National Park and L'Anse aux Meadows, and also includes the Labrador Straits. Contact Ambassatours at © 800/565-7173 or 902/423-6242, or visit www.ambassatours.com. **Collette Vacations** (© 800/340-5158; www.collettetours.com) runs an 11-day Maritime Wonders & Newfoundland tour that begins in Halifax and ends in St. John's. The cost is C$2,000 (US$1,718).

Tour operators offering Newfoundland and Labrador packages are listed on the province's tourism website: www.newfoundlandandlabradortourism.com.

One company, **Maxxim Vacations,** has 15 years' experience in packaging theme trips to Newfoundland and Labrador that include visiting local movie sites; taking in a Viking Trail experience; immersing yourself in the traditional culture; visiting the offshore French islands; or participating in road races, golf, or skiing. Call © 800/567-6666 to request their brochure, or visit www.maxximvacations.com.

Elderhostel, the not-for-profit organization dedicated to providing learning adventures for people 55 and over, offers a good variety of inexpensively priced Newfoundland and Labrador experiences. Visit www.elderhostel.org or call toll-free © 877/426-8056 to receive a copy of their catalog.

Despite the fact that escorted tours require big deposits and predetermine hotels, restaurants, and itineraries, many people derive security and peace of mind from the structure they offer. Escorted tours—whether they're navigated by bus or boat—let travelers sit back and enjoy the trip without having to drive or worry about details. They take you to the maximum number of sights in the minimum amount of time with the least amount of hassle. They're particularly convenient for people with limited mobility and they can be a great way to make new friends.

On the downside, you'll have little opportunity for serendipitous interactions with locals. The tours can be jam-packed with activities, leaving little room for individual sightseeing, whim, or adventure—plus they also often focus on the heavily touristed sites, so you miss out many a lesser-known gem.

Before you invest in an escorted tour, request a complete **schedule** of the trip to find out how much sightseeing is planned and whether you'll have enough time to relax or have an adventure of your own. Also ask about the **cancellation policy:** Is a deposit required? Can they cancel the trip if enough people don't sign up? Do you get a refund if they cancel? If *you* cancel? How late can you cancel if you are unable to go? When must you pay in full? If you choose an escorted tour, think strongly about purchasing trip-cancellation insurance, especially if the tour operator asks you to pay in advance. See the section on "Travel Insurance," p. 32. If you plan to travel alone, find out if they'll charge a **single supplement** or whether they can pair you with a roommate.

The **size** of the group is also important to know upfront. Generally, the smaller the group, the more flexible the itinerary, and the less time you'll spend waiting for people to get on and off the bus. Find out the **demographics** of the group as well. What is the age range? What is the gender breakdown? Is this mostly a trip for couples or singles?

Discuss what is included in the **price.** You may have to pay for transportation to and from the airport. A box lunch may be included in an excursion, but drinks might cost extra. Tips may not be included. Find out if you will be charged if you decide to opt out of certain activities or meals.

Before you invest in a package tour, get some answers. Ask about the **accommodations choices** and prices for each.

Then look up the hotels' reviews in a Frommer's guide and check their rates online for your specific dates of travel. You'll also want to find out what **type of room** you get. If you need a certain type of room, ask for it; don't take whatever is thrown your way. Request a nonsmoking room, a quiet room, a room with a view, or whatever you fancy.

SPECIAL-INTEREST TRIPS

Peregrine Adventures (© 888/456-3522; www.peregrineadventures.com) offers a compelling 9-day expedition aboard a small ship that tours many of the top spots around the island, with an emphasis on national parks and historical sites. You'll sail around the southern end of the island from St. John's to Gros Morne National Park, then on to Cape Breton

Island in Nova Scotia. On the return journey, you get to visit the remote island community of Ramea and the nearby French islands of St. Pierre and Miquelon. The final stop before heading back to St. John's is the wonderful Cape St. Mary's. This is a fantastic itinerary well worth the price tag of C$1,990 (US$1,710). **Adventure Canada** offers a similar itinerary, but one that circumnavigates the entire island of Newfoundland. The prices are higher, probably because of the high-profile tour guides (they regularly include celebrity biologists, top photographers, and distinguished chefs). You'll pay at least C$3,800 (US$3,264) for a cabin on a 10-day voyage that begins and ends in St. John's. If you're interested, call Adventure Canada at © **800/363-7566** or visit them online at www.adventurecanada.com.

13 Getting Around Newfoundland & Labrador

BY AIR

Traveling by air is the best option if your time is limited. One suggestion would be to fly into St. John's, spend a few days touring the Avalon Peninsula and then fly across to Deer Lake and pick up another rental car for exploring Gros Morne National Park.

In addition to Air Canada flights between St. John's, Gander, Deer Lake, and Goose Bay, **Provincial Airlines** (© **800/563-2800;** www.provair.com) and **Air Labrador** (© **800/563-3042** or 709/758-0002; www.airlabrador.com) combine to fly throughout the province, including as far north as Nain.

Air Saint Pierre (© **902/873-3566;** www.airsaintpierre.com) charges C$260 (US$224) for a round-trip between St. John's and the islands of St. Pierre and Miquelon.

BY CAR

The **Trans-Canada Highway** (also known as Hwy. 1) starts in St. John's and heads west 905km (562 miles) across the

province to Channel-Port-aux-Basques (about a 12-hr. drive), where you can hop the ferry to Nova Scotia. It is paved, but just two lanes wide most of the way.

You'll have the most fun—and meet the most interesting people—if you get off the Trans-Canada and take the smaller arteries into the coastal communities. *Tip:* You have to know ahead of time what each community offers, and search out the ones that appeal to your specific interests. Otherwise it would take months to visit them all.

Note: Other than the Trans-Canada Highway (Rte. 1), which has speeds of 90 or 100kmph (around 55–62 mph), the smaller regional routes have a maximum speed of 80kmph (around 50 mph), with speed limits being reduced to 50kmph (31 mph) once you enter many communities.

Warning: The island of Newfoundland is home to more than 150,000 moose. Extreme caution and reduced speeds are recommended when traveling any time between sunset and sunrise, as

Newfoundland & Labrador

Ferry

0   150 mi
0   150 km

Cape Chidley

Ungava Bay

Torngat Mountains
National Park

Labrador Sea

Hebron

QUEBEC

Nain

Davis
Inlet

Hopedale

Makkovik

ATLANTIC

OCEAN

*Smallwood
Reservoir*

Rigolet

LABRADOR

North West River

Esker

501 Churchill Falls

Labrador
City 500

Wabush

502

389

*Churchill
River*

500

520

*Lake
Melville*

Cartwright

Happy Valley-Goose Bay

MEALY MOUNTAINS

*Kenamu
River*

Port Hope Simpson

Pinware

Battle Harbour

L'Anse-au-Loup

Red Bay

L'Anse-Amour

Blanc-Sablon

St. Anthony

L'Anse-au-Clair

St. Barbe

Roddickton

430

Sept-Iles

Havre-
St.-Pierre

Harrington
Harbour

Daniel's
Harbour

Baie
Verte

*Terra
Nova
National
Park*

Natashquan

La Scie

Twillingate

*Gros Morne
National Park*

Springdale 330

*Anticosti
Island*

Corner
Brook

Gander

Bonavista

Deer
Lake

1

Grand
Falls

Trinity

Stephenville

NEWFOUNDLAND

*Gulf of
St. Lawrence*

Clarenville

**St.
John's**

St. George's Bay

480

360

Port aux
Basques

Harbour
Breton

210

Argentia

Havre-
Aubert

Grand Bank

100

Ferryland

St-Pierre

Tips **Winter Driving Survival Kit**

Include a scraper and brush; a shovel; booster cables; traction pads, sand, salt, or kitty litter (for traction on ice); a flashlight; flares; extra fuses, radiator hoses, and fan belts; blankets, sleeping bags, and extra winter clothing and footwear; a tow line or chain; an axe or hatchet; a supply of nonperishable foods; and a first–aid kit. As an added precaution, make sure someone knows where you are traveling and when you expect to arrive at your destination.

that's when the massive animals are most likely to be about.

Warning: Driving conditions can be severely hampered by the weather. Fog and heavy rains can happen unexpectedly, and roads are fairly narrow, leaving little room for error. Call © **900/451-3300** for road conditions anywhere in the province or © **709/729-7669** for road conditions in St. John's or the Avalon Peninsula. See www.roads.gov.nl.ca for local road conditions.

Note: If you're adventuring into more remote areas, you'll find fewer gas stations (and any you encounter may not necessarily be open), so always check your tank, oil, tires, and windshield wipers before leaving a populated area.

On road trips, remember to wear your seat belt or risk facing a hefty fine. Motorcyclists are legally required to wear helmets. And the use of radar detectors is prohibited.

RENTING A CAR

You'll find that most of the popular rental companies have counters at the St. John's airport. If you're coming in peak season (July–Aug), be sure to book your rental as far in advance as possible.

If you're doing a cross-province trek, you'll need to find a rental company that will permit pickup in St. John's and drop-off at the Deer Lake airport. National Car Rental, which charges a drop-off fee of C$100 (US$86), is the least expensive option. National is also a good company to choose if you're looking for a rental in

some of the smaller communities, such as St. Anthony.

Most rental companies offer unlimited kilometers for rentals originating in St. John's and returned to the same location. Elsewhere in the province, you're generally looking at a rental price subject to a daily limit on kilometers driven. Deals change from time to time, so your best bet is to check the websites below.

Major companies and their contacts are: **Avis** (© **800/879-2847;** www.avis.com), **Budget** (© **800/268-8900;** www.budget.com) **Hertz** (© **800/263-0600;** www.hertz.com), and **National** (© **800/227-7368;** www.nationalcar.com).

BY BUS

DRL Coachlines offers scheduled bus service along the Trans-Canada Highway from St. John's west across the province. Stops include Gander, Grand Falls–Windsor, Deer Lake, Corner Brook, and Channel-Port-aux-Basques. Call © **888/263-1852** or 709/738-8088 for details. You'll also find them online at www.drlgroup.com. DRL buses offer comfortable seats, air-conditioning, and onboard washroom facilities.

BY FERRY

The **Provincial Ferry Service** (www.tw.gov.nl.ca/ferryservices) operates along 16 different routes. Some are short hops—in the case of Portugal Cove to Bell Island, an enjoyable day trip from St. John's.

For more extensive travel, there are three sailings you should be aware of.

Between May and early January, daily ferry service crosses the Strait of Belle Isle from St. Barbe (Western Newfoundland) to Blanc Sablon (Quebec), from where Route 510 winds up the southern Labrador coast. The one-way fare is C$11 (US$9) for adults, C$5.50 (US$4.75) for children, and C$22 (US$19) per vehicle. From the end of Route 510, 405km (252 miles) north of Blanc Sablon, a ferry service operates from May to October between Cartwright and Happy Valley–Goose Bay. The one-way fare is C$46 (US$40) for adults, C$23 (US$20) for children, and C$75 (US$65) for vehicles. Also in Labrador, through summer a passenger and freight ferry departs Happy Valley–Goose

Bay, calling at some 20 isolated villages as far north as Nain, Labrador. The one-way trip takes 2 days each way.

Reservations are recommended for all three routes by calling ⓒ **866/535-2567;** check schedules at www.tw.gov.nl.ca/ ferryservices.

If your destination is the French islands of St. Pierre and Miquelon, you'll need to catch the ferry from the town of Fortune on the Burin Peninsula. **St. Pierre Tours Ltd.** offers walk-on passenger service only (no vehicles) to this little bit of France right off the southern coast of Newfoundland. It costs C$85 (US$73) round-trip per adult. Call ⓒ **800/563-2006** or 709/832-0429 for reservations or more information.

14 Tips on Accommodations

St. John's has the wide range of accommodations you'd expect in a major city— the major chains you know, upscale heritage inns, bed-and-breakfasts, moderately priced roadside motels, budget lodging in the local university. Outside of the capital, there are many fine accommodations, but searching them out takes some effort. Through the travel chapters of this book, I've included the very best in all price ranges and styles. In this section, I give an overview of what to expect.

HOTELS, MOTELS, AND RESORTS

Big hotels are limited to St. John's and other large towns like Gander and Corner Brook. You'll find chain properties like Holiday Inn and Best Western, as well as upscale Fairmont and Delta, represented in St. John's.

HERITAGE INNS

You should stay in at least one heritage inn while visiting Newfoundland and Labrador. St. John's is unique for its incredible number of inns, but you will find others scattered across the province.

Facilities and standards vary greatly, so it's important to know in advance not only what you're paying for, but also that the lodging has what you need to be comfortable. You can do this by reading the reviews in this book, or by talking to the owners directly when making reservations.

Most of the historic lodgings in St. John's are more expensive than elsewhere in the province. The average price for one of the nicer ones is well over C$100 (US$86) per night, but keep in mind you usually get a cooked breakfast.

BED & BREAKFASTS

This is the most common type of accommodations in Newfoundland and Labrador. It is also the most varied, in terms of both price and what you get for your money. The simplest are often described as "hospitality homes" (see below), while in St. John's you can pay up to C$200 (US$172) for a room with its own fireplace and jetted tub. What they do have in common is that, as the name suggests, rates include breakfast, and you can expect personal service, knowledgeable hosts, and conversation with travelers from around the world.

Many people (myself included) do not especially like to share a bathroom with other travelers—or even with the owner of the home. In St. John's, you don't really have to worry about this as virtually all B&Bs offer private bathrooms. Elsewhere in the province, accommodations with a shared bathroom become a reality. Those with mobility problems should also ask questions, as bed-and-breakfasts don't have an elevator to get you up the stairs.

The best way to make reservations is directly with the bed-and-breakfast, either by phone or e-mail. My favorites are detailed in this book, or check the *Travel Guide* available from Newfoundland and Labrador Tourism for details of all the properties. You can also browse some of the better options and make reservations online through **Select Inns of Atlantic Canada** at www.selectinns.ca. Bed and Breakfast Online (www.bbcanada.com) doesn't take bookings, but has tools to help find bed-and-breakfasts suited to your needs and budget.

Tip: To prevent surprises, ask the following two questions before reserving a room at a bed-and-breakfast: will I be getting a private bathroom or is it shared with other guests, and do you accept credit cards. *Warning:* Bed-and-breakfasts are not usually suited to families with young children. Of course there are exceptions, and these are noted through this guidebook.

HOSPITALITY HOMES

Hospitality homes are common in smaller communities and in coastal villages. A hospitality home brings back the simple roots of what B&Bs originally were: a basic bedroom in someone's house and breakfast for a reasonable price. In general, expect to get less (that is, usually no in-room phone or private bathroom) and pay less than you would in a commercial establishment. Properties having 3 rooms or fewer for rent are not subject

to the 15% combined provincial and federal tax (HST), saving you even more. Larger homes with more than three bedrooms for rent will generally fit under the bed-and-breakfast banner and are subject to the HST tax.

CAMPGROUNDS

Campgrounds are scattered across the province. The season is short, with campgrounds usually opening sometime in June, and then closing for the season by the end of September. All campgrounds are detailed in the annual *Travel Guide.* For a free copy, contact **Newfoundland and Labrador Tourism** at © **800/563-6353** or 709/729-2830, or order online at www.newfoundlandandlabradortourism.com.

NATIONAL PARKS

Newfoundland and Labrador has two national parks with auto-accessible camping—Terra Nova, a few hours' drive west of St. John's, and Gros Morne, in Western Newfoundland. Both have multiple campgrounds, with at least one offering washroom facilities with hot showers. In general, campsites are private and each has its own picnic table and firepit. Firewood is C$6 (5.15) per bundle. Overnight fees range from C$17 (US$15) to C$26 (US$23).

In 2005, Parks Canada established a reservation system for national park campgrounds. To ensure a spot on the most popular weekends, contact the **Parks Canada Campground Reservation Service** (© **877/737-3783;** www.pccamping.ca). The cost is C$11 (US$9.50) per reservation. For information on specific parks, click through the links at www.pc.gc.ca.

PROVINCIAL PARKS

Thirteen provincial parks have campgrounds. They are described as **Fully Serviced** (showers, flush toilets, laundry facilities, powered campsites) for C$20 (US$17) per night; **Partially Serviced**

Fun Fact What's "Dressing"?

Don't be surprised if you're asked if you want dressing and gravy with your fries. Just as Montrealers love their fries dipped in mayonnaise, many locals wouldn't want their fries unless they were smothered in dressing and gravy. As it relates to food, "dressing" in Newfoundland and Labrador usually means one thing: bread crumbs mixed with chopped onion, savory, and melted butter. Some people add diced celery as well. In addition to its use as a side dish for french fries, it's also the stuffing of choice for roast turkey and chicken.

(washrooms with hot showers and flush toilets) for C$13 (US$11); and **Unserviced** (pit toilets, drinking water) for C$10 (US$8.50). Bonuses at the larger facilities include convenience stores, minigolf, bike rentals, and more. For details go to www.env.gov.nl.ca/parks.

15 Tips on Dining

Traditional Newfoundland and Labrador cuisine revolves around simple cooking of locally available produce, game, and seafood—a style derived from the province's close ties with Great Britain. This unadorned style extends into most restaurants, where a full cooked breakfast may cost C$8 (US$7) and a roast beef dinner will rarely set you back more than C$12 (US$11).

Most seafood is deep-fried, even delicacies such as scallops. The exception is lobster (thankfully!), which is boiled and usually served with sides of melted butter, coleslaw, and a roast potato. Fish and chips is an inexpensive favorite with the locals. You will get sizable portions of battered cod served with french-fried potatoes. Just remember that you automatically get cod when you order fish unless it's otherwise specified. A local delicacy is cod tongues, which are usually deep-fried, but request them pan-fried for the full effect. Fish and brewis is a longtime favorite that dates to the days of pre-refrigeration—the "fish" is salted cod and "brewis" is heavy, doughy bread. Wild game is common on menus along the Northern Peninsula, in Labrador, and better restaurants in St. John's. Caribou and moose come baked, braised, and in burgers, and both have a distinctive "gamey" taste.

The restaurant scene in St. John's is a little different to the one described above. Here, you'll find all manner of cooking styles, ranging from traditional to Thai. Prices in the city are also higher, with mains as high as C$30 (US$26).

Warning: While the province boasts many fine dining restaurants, Newfoundlanders have traditionally enjoyed simple—often deep-fried—cooking. Therefore, a local's answer to your query about favorite restaurants may lead you to a local fish-and-chip shop as opposed to an elegant Italian eatery.

16 Recommended Books & Films

Many books have been written about this colorful land that is rich in history, culture, and natural resources. Several of these volumes have even been turned into movies for the large and small screen. To make the most of your visit, I'd recommend reading at least a couple of the gems listed below.

Note: Some of these titles may be unavailable from your favorite local or Internet bookseller because of their limited distribution. If this the case, try Wordplay (© **800/563-9100** or 709/726-9193; www.wordplay.com) for new and out-of-print titles or the Downhomer (© **888/588-6353** or 709/722-2970; www.shopdownhome.com) for new books. Both of these outlets are located in St. John's and carry an exceptional variety of Newfoundland titles.

Of the many non-fictional accounts of Newfoundland and Labrador's history, none are more readable than *As Near to Heaven by Sea,* by Kevin Major (Penguin Canada). Major does an admirable job of describing the many people and events that have contributed to the current-day personality of Newfoundland and Labrador—in under 500 pages.

Literally hundreds of books bring Newfoundland's history to life in a sympathetic and enduring form. One of the most recent is *River Thieves,* by Michael Crummey (Anchor Canada). This haunting tale set in Newfoundland at the turn of the 19th century depicts the uneasy relations between the Peyton family and the Beothuk Indians. Set in a similar era, *Curse of the Red Cross Ring,* by Earl B. Pilgrim (Flanker Press), is an enjoyable novel giving an insight into what it was like to be a Newfoundland fisherman in the late 19th and early 20th centuries. *Voyage of the Matthew—John Cabot and the Discovery of North America,* by Peter Firstbrook (McClelland & Stewart), is a detailed account of Cabot's history-making voyage more than 500 years ago to Bonavista, Newfoundland. *In the Hand of the Living God,* by Lilliane Bouzane (Turnstone Press), is a story about John Cabot's wife and the letters that were exchanged between her and her explorer husband.

Much has been written about Joey Smallwood, the politician who brought Newfoundland into Confederation in 1949. One of the more readable tomes is *Smallwood: The Unlikely Revolutionary,* by Richard Gwyn (McClelland & Stewart). Better known is *The Colony of Unrequited Dreams,* by Wayne Johnston (Vintage Canada), a fantastic historical novel written by a Newfoundlander about the life and times of this Newfoundland hero, and the land he so loved.

A great book for those interested in contemporary Newfoundland culture and Canadian politics is *All in Good Time,* by Brian Tobin (Penguin Group [Canada]): Tobin, one of Canada's most colorful politicians, was premier of Newfoundland and Labrador from 1996 to 1999 and also had a successful career in federal politics before resigning in 2002, the year this book was published. *No Holds Barred,* by John C. Crosbie (McClelland & Stewart), is the political memoirs of another colorful Newfoundland politician, a former federal cabinet minister who came close to winning the leadership of the Progressive Conservative Party of Canada—and the top job in the country.

The Labradorians: Voices from the Land of Cain, by Lynne D. Fitzhugh (Breakwater Books), describes the challenges of settling the rugged untamed frontier; the book tells the story of mixed-race settlers and their battle to survive Labrador's harsh conditions. *The Danger Tree: Memory, War, and the Search for a Family's Past,* by David Macfarlane (Vintage Canada), is a memoir about a contemporary Newfoundland family and how current events have had an impact on their lives. Claire Mowat's *The Outport People* (Key Porter), originally published in 1983 but reprinted in 2005, tells of life in a remote fishing village, but from the perspective of an outsider. (The author is the wife of famed Canadian writer Farley Mowat.)

Newfoundland & Labrador: Insiders' Perspectives, by James Tuck and Douglas

House (Johnson Family Foundation): This compilation of 24 short essays is written by a variety of experts who call Newfoundland and Labrador home, including Dr. Tuck, an archaeologist from the Colony of Avalon. Learn more about the province's history, politics, economics, people, culture, music, food, and natural history from people who work in the field. Because the book is in a compact format, it's also suitable for travelers to take with them. The book is also available in French under the name *Terre-Neuve et la Labrador: Perspectives locales,* and in German under the name *Neufundland und Labrador: Insider berichen. The Day the World Came to Town: 9/11 in Gander, Newfoundland,* by Jim DeFede (Regan Books): Stories of kindness and humanity in the face of the worst act of terrorism in United States history. A close-knit Newfoundland community opens its hearts and homes to stranded airline passengers.

The province of Newfoundland and Labrador stars as itself in many movies based on books. Read or watch any of the following and you'll get a great feel for the province. Best known is *The Shipping News,* by E. Annie Proulx (Pocket Books), which tells the contemporary story about a troubled man coming home to his Newfoundland roots. The book was made into a movie starring Kevin Spacey that is now available on DVD. *Rare Birds,* by Edward Riche (Doubleday Canada), is the humorous story about a man struggling to make a go with an unsuccessful restaurant in a Newfoundland outport. A 2002 movie based on the book and starring William Hurt was filmed in around St. John's and nearby Petty Harbour.

Random Passage, by Bernice Morgan (Breakwater Books), is an enthralling novel about a young Irishwoman's 19th-century journey from England to Random Passage, a remote Newfoundland outport (you can visit the film set just south of Trinity). The book was made into a mini-series by CBC television and is now available on DVD at tourist shops in St. John's or online at www.shopdownhome.com.

FAST FACTS: Newfoundland & Labrador

Area Codes All of Newfoundland and Labrador uses the **709** area code.

ATMs See "Money," earlier in this chapter.

Automobile Clubs The Canadian equivalent of AAA is the **CAA** (Canadian Automobile Association), which does not have an office in Newfoundland and Labrador. If you are a **CAA** or **AAA** member, call 🕻 **800/222-4357** for emergency road assistance. Call 🕻 **800/947-0770** for emergency roadside service if you are a member of the **Good Sam Club**. (If you're not a member but would like to join, call 🕻 **800/842-5351**.) Both clubs' operators will connect you with appropriate local service providers.

Car Rentals See "Getting Around Newfoundland & Labrador," earlier in this chapter.

Climate See "When to Go," earlier in this chapter.

Currency See "Money," earlier in this chapter.

Documents See "Entry Requirements & Customs," earlier in this chapter.

Driving Rules See "Getting Around Newfoundland & Labrador," earlier in this chapter.

Drugstores These are more commonly referred to as "pharmacies" in Canada. Many of the larger grocery chains fill prescriptions. Be sure to bring a copy of any prescriptions along with you in case you lose your medication and need to have the prescription refilled.

Electricity Electrical and phone outlets are the same as in the U.S.: 110–115 volts, AC, 60 cycles. No special adapters are necessary.

Embassies & Consulates All embassies within Canada are located in Ottawa, Ontario, the national capital. The **U.S. embassy** is situated at 90 Sussex Dr., Ottawa, ON K1M 1M8 (✆ 613/238-5335). You can find a **U.S. consulate** in Halifax, Nova Scotia, at 2000 Barrington St., Suite 910, Scotia Square (✆ 902/429-2485). The **British consulate** can be found at 1 Canal St., Dartmouth, NS (✆ 902/461-1381).

Emergencies Call ✆ 911 in case of emergency to reach police, ambulance, or in case of a fire.

Liquor Laws The legal drinking age is 19. Don't drink and drive, as Canadian laws are tough if you are caught impaired behind the wheel, and you will be charged under the Criminal Code.

Mail It currently costs C51¢ to mail a letter or card (weighing 30g or less) within Canada. It costs C89¢ to mail that same letter or card to the U.S.

Newspapers & Magazines The major newspaper in St. John's is the *Telegram*. There are also many community newspapers throughout the province. See www.thepaperboy.com for a full listing. The province's major lifestyle/nostalgia magazine is *The Downhomer.*

Religion Many religions are practiced throughout Newfoundland and Labrador. Check the phone book of the communities you are visiting for locations of your chosen house of worship.

Safety Whether you're gay, elderly, of a visible minority, or a woman traveling alone, you will feel secure in Newfoundland and Labrador. Street crimes are rare, but you still need to practice common sense. Lock your vehicle, don't leave your purse or backpack unattended, and be aware of your surroundings.

Taxes & Tipping You will pay 15% tax on most purchases. Tips of 15% are expected in larger cities such as St. John's, with 10%–15% being more common in smaller centers. See "Money," earlier in this chapter.

Telephones Pay phones cost C35¢ for local calls. You can purchase prepaid calling cards from local retailers if you find that your calling card from home doesn't work. You're unlikely to get digital cellphone service while in Newfoundland and Labrador, but analog service will work in many places. Here's a local tip: If your cellphone doesn't work in one of the smaller coastal communities (which are all generally at sea level), you may be able to get service just a kilometer or two up the road if you head for higher ground.

Time Zones Newfoundland has its own time zone, **Newfoundland time zone,** which runs a half-hour ahead of the rest of Atlantic Canada. Most of Labrador is in the Atlantic time zone, so be sure to check the time upon your arrival in Labradorian communities apart from the Labrador Straits, as chances are they're on Atlantic time. Daylight saving time is practiced throughout the province in summer.

Tobacco Laws You must be at least 16 years of age to legally purchase cigarettes. Smoking is not allowed in most St. John's restaurants, but you can smoke and eat in liquor lounges. Outside of St. John's, most restaurants provide designated smoking areas. However, many of the smaller inns do not allow smoking at all. If you are a smoker, be sure to check with the establishment before making a booking or reservation.

3

Suggested Newfoundland & Labrador Itineraries

The first thing you need to realize is that Newfoundland and Labrador is big—very big—compared to the rest of Atlantic Canada. The island of Newfoundland alone stretches for 111,390 sq. km—(43,442 sq. miles)—it's nearly as large as the three maritime provinces of Nova Scotia, New Brunswick, and Prince Edward Island combined. Add in the vast territory of Labrador at 294,330 sq. km (114,789 sq. miles) and the provincial total becomes a massive 405,720 sq. km (158,231 sq. miles).

To see highlights of the entire province, you'll likely need at least 2 weeks. If you can't afford the time or resources for a lengthy visit, however, choose the first itinerary, which concentrates on the eastern portion of Newfoundland. This itinerary, like the other 5, requires a rental vehicle. Driving is really the only way to get beyond St. John's, but you should read "By Car" under "Getting Around Newfoundland & Labrador" in chapter 2 for more information.

Always keep one thing in mind when planning your trip—the wonderfully slower pace of Newfoundland and Labrador is best enjoyed if you don't have to rush through it.

1 Newfoundland & Labrador in 1 Week

It is simply impossible to see all of Newfoundland and Labrador in 1 week. But you can get a taste of the province by following this itinerary, which starts and ends in St. John's, but also takes in all the main points of interest within easy driving distance of the capital. For this itinerary, I assume you will be renting a vehicle at St. John's International Airport.

Day ❶: Getting Oriented in St. John's

Make your way to **Signal Hill** ✸✸✸ (p. 90). Not only is the summit panorama a good way to get oriented with the city's layout, but from this single vantage point you'll be able to search out the Atlantic Ocean for icebergs, look down across the busy working harbor, and see out over downtown. Squeeze in a visit to the **Johnson Geo Centre** ✸✸ (p. 90) on the way down the hill. Opened in 2005,

The Rooms ✸✸✸ (p. 89) is not your usual stuffy museum, and well worth a couple of hours for its interesting approach to telling the story of the province's natural and human history. Monday through Thursday, I highly recommend joining a **St. John's Haunted Hike** (p. 98).

Day ❷: Irish Loop

Leaving St. John's behind via the road to North America's most easterly point,

Notre Dame Bay

Twillingate

0   50 mi
0   50 km

Terra Nova National Park

Bonavista Bay

Bonavista

ATLANTIC OCEAN

Trinity

Trinity Bay

Conception Bay

NEWFOUNDLAND

St. John's
START AND END HERE

Dildo

Salmonier

Fortune Bay

Witless Bay Ecological Reserve

Placentia Bay

Cape St. Mary's

Cape Spear ✹✹ (p. 92), you're soon surrounded by the wildly rugged scenery Newfoundland and Labrador is famous for. Continuing down the coast is **Ferryland,** where a 1621 settlement known as the **Colony of Avalon** (p. 110) is carefully being unearthed by archaeologists. For something a little different, walk up to Ferryland's lighthouse where **Lighthouse Picnics** ✹✹✹ (p. 109) will fill a basket of local goodies for you to enjoy on the surrounding grassy hillside. Continue around the Irish Loop to **Salmonier Nature Park** ✹✹ (p. 113), which is home to many of the birds and animals you would probably have seen in the wild if you had more time.

Day ❸: Cape St. Mary's to Bonavista

Cape St. Mary's Ecological Reserve ✹✹✹ (p. 116) is foggy more than 200 days a year, but this somehow adds to the appeal of seeing thousands of seabirds nesting on and flying around a sea stack rising just a few meters from the cliff-top lookout. Spend the rest of the morning driving up the Trans-Canada Highway to Clarenville, and then traveling east along the Bonavista Peninsula. Explore the charmingly historic streets of **Trinity** ✹✹✹ (p. 128) before continuing north to Bonavista, where you get to soak up unequalled luxury at **Elizabeth J. Cottages** ✹✹ (p. 134).

Day ❹:

The morning is spent on an **Ocean Contact** ❊❊❊ (p. 134) whale-watching excursion led by one of the world's foremost whale experts, Dr. Peter Beamish. Drive across to **Terra Nova National Park** ❊❊ (p. 144) where you can choose between golfing, kayaking, hiking, or simply soaking up the surrounding wilderness. Continue west to **Twillingate** ❊❊ (p. 158) for an overnight stay.

Day ❺:

I recommended making the effort to reach Twillingate for one reason—icebergs. Nowhere else in the world are icebergs as accessible as in local waters. Reserve a spot with **Twillingate Island Boat Tours** ❊❊❊ (p. 160) to get out in heart of iceberg territory. On the way out of town, step back in time at **Boyd's Cove Beothuk Interpretation Centre** (p. 157). You could spend the night of your fifth day in an anonymous hotel along the Trans-Canada Highway, or continue on to the delightful **Inn By the Bay** ❊❊ (p. 117), overlooking Dildo Bay. *Tip:* Icebergs are not always present, so call ahead

before driving out to Twillingate. If you don't go, spend the extra time on the Bonavista Peninsula or hiking in Terra Nova National Park.

Day ❻:

The breakfast served at Inn By the Bay sets you up for a full day of sightseeing, starting with a drive along the Baccalieu Trail, passing coastal villages that are as charming as their names suggest (Heart's Content, Harbour Grace, Heart's Delight, Cupids). Then take Route 60 up the east side of Conception Bay to some surprisingly inviting beaches. If it's not beach weather, hop over to **Bell Island** (p. 122) for the afternoon. Spend your last night in Newfoundland and Labrador at **Dogberry Hill** ❊❊❊ (p. 121), an upscale bed-and-breakfast overlooking Conception Bay.

Day ❼: Tying up Loose Ends

Make one final trip into St. John's to do some souvenir shopping. You can easily spend a couple of hours browsing the interesting shops along Water Street, but those at the north end of Duckworth Street are also worth visiting.

2 Newfoundland & Labrador in 2 Weeks

This itinerary begins and ends in St. John's. I've organized it so you get the long trek across the province over and done with early, leaving you with 12 days to wind your way back to the capital.

Day ❶: Hit the Road

Arriving in St. John's the night before, you should rise early for the drive to Deer Lake, 640km (400 miles). Gander, halfway between the two, is a good lunch stop—and right on the highway is the **North Atlantic Aviation Museum** ❊ (p. 156), perfect for a leg stretch. From Deer Lake, it's less than 1 hour's drive to **Rocky Harbour,** where you find accommodations for all budgets (p. 172).

Day ❷: Gros Morne National Park ❊❊❊

A visit to the **Discovery Centre** ❊❊ (p. 176) will whet your appetite to get out and explore the park, so head to the **Tablelands** ❊ (p. 176) for a short walk through some of the oldest rocks on Earth. In the afternoon join a boat tour of **Western Brook Pond** ❊❊❊ (p. 177). It takes 40 minutes on foot to reach the dock, but once onboard you'll be rewarded with the panorama of impossibly steep mountains rising from the lake.

Continue to Cow Head and take in an evening performance of the **Gros Morne Theatre Festival** (p. 174).

Day ❸: Viking Trail

Route 430 up the Northern Peninsula is known as the Viking Trail, and when you reach the end of the road you'll find out why. Spend the afternoon at **L'Anse aux Meadows National Historic Site** 🎀🎀🎀 (p. 189) learning about the Vikings who once called this barren knob of land home. Dinner at the **Norseman Restaurant** 🎀🎀🎀 (p. 187) is a must.

Day ❹: Labrador

There's no hurry to get up this morning, as the ferry from St. Barbe to Blanc Sablon doesn't leave until the early afternoon. Still, I recommend making the effort to rise early so as to squeeze a visit to **Burnt Cape Ecological Reserve** 🎀🎀 (p. 190), underrated for its stark beauty. After the ferry ride, it's only a short drive up the Labrador Straits to **Lighthouse Cove B&B** 🎀🎀 (p. 205), your lodging in L'Anse Amour, so take your time, stopping at the **Gateway to Labrador Visitor Centre** 🎀🎀 (p. 203). After dinner walk out to **Point Amour Lighthouse** 🎀 (p. 206) in time to watch the last rays of light hit Atlantic Canada's tallest lighthouse.

Day ❺: More Labrador

Visit **Red Bay National Historic Site** 🎀🎀 (p. 209) to learn how three Spanish galleons finished at the bottom of the harbor. Drive to Mary's Harbour to catch the boat shuttle to **Battle Harbour** 🎀🎀🎀

(p. 209). Located on a rocky island seemingly at the end of the world, this once-abandoned fishing village has been brought back to life, with a range of visitor services allowing outsiders to get a glimpse of life in an "outport." Stay overnight on the island at **Battle Harbour Inn** ⨍ (p. 210).

Day ❻: Island to Island
Jump aboard the morning shuttle back to Mary's Harbour, drive to Blanc Sablon, and catch the ferry back across the Strait of Belle Isle. From St. Barbe, it's a 1-hour drive to Port au Choix. Here, **Port au Choix National Historic Site** ⨍⨍ (p. 180) protects an amazing 4,500 years of human history. The visitor center is interesting, but the **Phillips Garden Coastal Trail** ⨍⨍ (p. 180) gets you out into the field where you can watch archaeologists at work. Continue south, bypassing the roadside motels of Deer Lake to stay at **Humberview Bed & Breakfast** ⨍⨍ (p. 168).

Day ❼: Deer Lake to Twillingate
Two weeks in the province means you don't miss anything major. But it also gives you the opportunity to get off the main tourist trail, and that is what Day 7 on the **Baie Verte Peninsula** is about. The turnoff is less than 100km (63 miles) northeast of Deer Lake, and before you know it you'll be a world away from modern civilization. Official attractions aside—a miner's museum and the **Dorset Soapstone Quarry** ⨍ (p. 163), where you can see where and how the Dorset people mined soapstone—you'll be amazed at just how ruggedly remote this region is. Continue on to **Twillingate** ⨍⨍ (p. 158) for an evening cruise searching for icebergs with **Twillingate Island Boat Tours** ⨍⨍⨍ (p. 160).

Day ❽: Kittiwake Coast
It's a beautiful drive along the Kittiwake Coast to Gambo, and if you'd like to see how little the fishing villages dotting Route 330 have changed in the last century, plan on visiting **Barbour Living Heritage Village** ⨍ (p. 157) at Newtown. Spend the night at **Terra Nova National Park** ⨍⨍ (p. 144).

Day ❾: Terra Nova to Trinity
Go down to the park's waterfront interpretive center and join a kayaking trip on Newman Sound. Even if you've never kayaked before, the experienced guides at **Terra Nova Adventures** ⨍ (p. 150) will make you feel comfortable in the water. Back at the dock is the perfectly positioned **Starfish Eatery** (p. 147). Resist the temptation to order seconds of the delicious chowder and you'll feel up to walking a section of the **Coastal Trail** ⨍ (p. 149). Drive to **Trinity** ⨍⨍⨍ (p. 128) and settle in for a 2-night stay.

Day ❿: Bonavista Peninsula
In Trinity, there are a few historic buildings open to the public, but for the most part, you get the most enjoyment out of simply wandering through the streets. After lunch, drive to **Bonavista** ⨍⨍ (p. 134), a surprisingly large town at the tip of the Bonavista Peninsula. Be sure to visit the local **lighthouse** ⨍⨍ (p. 135) for the dramatic setting and **Paterson Woodworking** ⨍ (p. 137) for a locally crafted souvenir. Back in Trinity, the antics at the **Rising Tide Theatre** (p. 132) will have you in stitches.

Day ⓫: Avalon Peninsula
Head south on the Trans-Canada Highway to Dildo. Once you've finished sniggering at the name, you'll find a picturesque fishing village and the **Dildo Interpretation Centre** (p. 119), worth a stop for its portrayal of local history. Drive around the Baccalieu Trail to rejoin the Trans-Canada Highway near historic Brigus. Spend the night farther south at **Bird Island Resort** ⨍ (p. 115).

Day ⓬: Cape Shore and Irish Loop
Sure, you may have seen a moose on the Northern Peninsula and birds on your

boat tour from Twillingate, but today is devoted to nature on a much larger scale. Even if you're not a keen bird-watcher, the sheer number of birds at **Cape St. Mary's Ecological Reserve** ✹✹✹ (p. 116) will amaze you. A 1-hour drive north at **Salmonier Nature Park** ✹✹ (p. 113), it will be the variety of species to catch your attention. Meanwhile, on an afternoon boat tour through **Witless Bay Ecological Reserve** ✹✹✹ (p. 106), frolicking humpback whales are the attention getters. Spend this night in **Ferryland** (p. 108).

Day ⑬: St. John's
There are two places you won't want to miss in St. John's—**Signal Hill** ✹✹✹ (p. 90) for harbor and ocean views, and

The Rooms ✹✹✹ (p. 89) for its modern approach to displaying the province's long and colorful history. You've managed to fit a great deal into the last 2 weeks, so you deserve a treat. In this regard, spend an hour or two at **Spa at the Monastery** (p. 89) and then get dressed up for dinner at the **Cabot Club** ✹✹✹ (p. 83).

Day ⑭: Leaving Newfoundland
Fly out of St. John's Airport. If time allows, detour north to the **Ocean Sciences Centre** ✹ (p. 94), where admission to an outdoor pool of seals is free, and stop at the **Fluvarium** ✹✹ (p. 93), to catch a glimpse of the underwater world of a freshwater pond.

---

3 An Extended Weekend in St. John's

There are two scenarios that may have you looking for the best way to spend just a few days in St. John's—you have 2 weeks in Atlantic Canada, and don't want to miss Newfoundland, or you've been attending a conference or sporting event in the capital and want to experience more than the inside of a boardroom. If it's the latter, I'm sure the business hotel your boss put you up in had all the modern conveniences, but now is the time to pack your bags and move into one of the many heritage inns scattered through downtown.

Day ❶: Getting Acquainted with the City
Drive to the summit of **Signal Hill** ✹✹✹ (p. 90) for city views. Get even higher, by climbing the winding stairway of the Cabot Tower, for is a good way to get oriented with the capital's layout. On the way back down the hill, visit the **Johnson Geo Centre** ✹✹ (p. 90) to learn about the natural history of this ancient land. You will have spotted the distinctly shaped buildings of **The Rooms** ✹✹✹ (p. 89) from Signal Hill. After lunch and once inside, you'll be even more wowed by the ultra-modern displays of the provincial museum and gallery. The hub of evening entertainment is the lively **pubs of George Street** (p. 101), which

fill nightly with the sounds of foot-stomping Newfoundland music.

Day ❷: Scenic Touring
Ferryland, less than 100km (62 miles) south of the city, is a good turnaround point for a day trip from the capital. But not so quick—there's lots to see along the way. First up is **Cape Spear** ✹✹ (p. 92), where the ocean views may be spectacular, but a stop here allows you to tell the folks back home you've stood at the easternmost point of North America. A boat tour to **Witless Bay Ecological Reserve** ✹✹✹ (p. 106), with almost guaranteed sightings of humpback whales, should be next on your agenda. Order a picnic from **Lighthouse Picnics** ✹✹✹ (p. 109) before taking in Ferryland's **Colony of Avalon** ✹✹

An Extended Weekend in St. John's

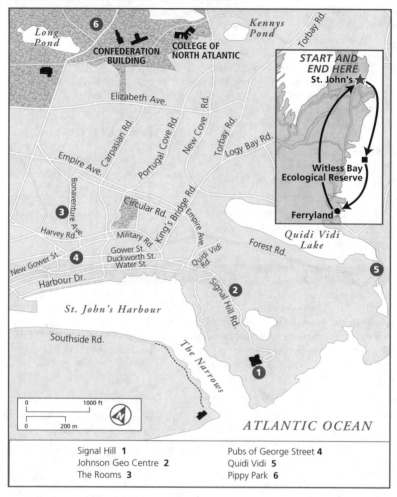

Signal Hill **1**
Johnson Geo Centre **2**
The Rooms **3**
Pubs of George Street **4**
Quidi Vidi **5**
Pippy Park **6**

(p. 110) archaeological dig. You should be back in St. John's in time for your dinner reservation at **Blue on Water** ✸✸✸ (p. 82).

Day ❸: Tying up Loose Ends

Take some time out from official attractions on your last morning in St. John's to admire residential streets like Gower and Cochrane, which are lined with colorful clapboard homes. Then head to charming **Quidi Vidi** ✸✸✸ (p. 91) to soak up the fishing village ambience. Back downtown, do your souvenir shopping on Water Street. If you have an afternoon flight, reserve a tee time at a local golf course; if golfing isn't your style, the walking trails of **Pippy Park** are a good leg stretcher.

4 Exploring the West & Labrador

The Northern Peninsula is one of my favorite places in all of Canada, so I couldn't help but include this itinerary. It includes places you have seen pictures of, fishing villages that are just as you imagine they should be, and out-of-the-way attractions you will never forget. What it doesn't have are fancy hotels or fast-food restaurants—simply because there are none. This itinerary assumes that you are flying in and out of Deer Lake, and have reserved a rental car at the airport.

Day ❶: Sunset over Lobster Cove Head

Chances are this day is spent in the air and changing planes to get to Deer Lake. But in summer the sun doesn't set over Rocky Harbour's **Lobster Cove Head Lighthouse** ✦ (p. 176) until late in the evening, so you can take advantage of the many scenic stops en route from the airport.

Day ❷: Gros Morne and Beyond

Take a morning boat tour on **Western Brook Pond** ✦✦✦ (p. 177), allowing time to hike in to the boat dock from Route 430. The drive north from Gros Morne to Port au Choix takes well under 2 hours, so you'll have plenty of time to explore **Port au Choix National Historic Site** ✦✦ (p. 178), where thousands of years of human history unravel themselves. The town itself is a good overnight stop, if only so you can dine on local seafood at the **Anchor Café** ✦ (p. 179).

Day ❸: Labrador Straits

The ferry trip across the Strait of Belle Isle takes just a couple of hours. Make your first stop across the other side at the **Gateway to Labrador Visitor Centre** ✦✦ (p. 203). At L'Anse Amour, walk to the top of **Point Amour Lighthouse** ✦ (p. 206) and spend a leisurely hour or so walking the Raleigh Trail. Catch the afternoon boat shuttle to **Battle Harbour** ✦✦✦ (p. 209), which would look like the dozens of other outports (remote fishing villages) abandoned in the last 40 years, except that enterprising locals have spruced the old wooden buildings, put up

interpretive panels, and operate a variety of visitor services. **Battle Harbour Inn** ✦ (p. 210) is where you stay overnight, taking advantage of being able to explore the village long after the day-trippers have left.

Day ❹: To St. Anthony

Catch the morning shuttle back to civilization and drive down the Labrador Straits to catch the ferry back across to Newfoundland. From St. Barbe, it's a 1-hour drive to St. Anthony. This town at the tip of the Northern Peninsula is filled with attractions related to Sir Wilfred Grenfell. Even if you're not familiar with the good doctor, you will marvel at his achievements in bringing health care and schooling to this remote part of the world through a visit to the **Grenfell Historic Properties** ✦✦ (p. 186).

Day ❺: L'Anse aux Meadows

Take the morning tour with **Northland Discovery Boat Tours** ✦✦ (p. 187) in search of whales and icebergs and you'll be out on the water before the wind comes up. At **L'Anse aux Meadows**, step into the world of Vikings at **L'Anse aux Meadows National Historic Site** ✦✦✦ (p. 189), where Vikings established a village over 1,000 years ago. Across the road is **Norstead** ✦✦ (p. 189), a re-created Viking village complementing the historic site perfectly. Dinner at the **Norseman Restaurant** ✦✦✦ (p. 187) will be a real treat; add to the experience by ordering lobster (you get to go across to the docks and pick your own).

Exploring the West & Labrador

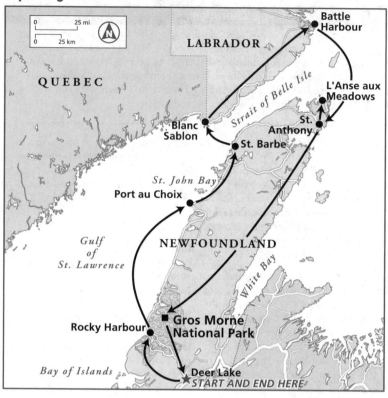

Day ⑥: South Along Route 430

Even if you don't rise early, you'll probably be one of the few visitors to **Burnt Cape Ecological Reserve** ✹✹ (p. 190). If you're interested in learning about the cape's ancient origins and many rare plant species, join a guided tour. On the drive back south along Route 430, you'll have plenty of time to stop at scenic fishing villages, ocean lookouts, and **Bird Cove Archaeological Dig** ✹ (p. 181). Plan on overnighting at Cow Head so you can take in a performance of the **Gros Morne Theatre Festival.**

Day ⑦: Gros Morne National Park ✹✹✹

The trail to the summit of **Gros Morne Mountain** (p. 170) takes most of the day, but summit views are phenomenal. If the difficulty of this hike is a little beyond you, there are many other options, such as combining a visit to the **Discovery Centre** ✹✹ (p. 176) with a walk through the moonlike **Tablelands** ✹ (p. 176). Allow an hour to drive from the park back down to Deer Lake Airport, plus another 90 minutes for check-in procedures.

5 Newfoundland & Labrador for Families

The golden rule for traveling families is not to try and fit too much into each day, which is why this itinerary, starting and ending in St. John's, keeps driving to a minimum. This itinerary is directed at families with preteens and teenaged children. I've made family-friendly lodging recommendations in this itinerary, but you should do your part, too—by making advance reservations.

Day ❶: Settling into St. John's

Regardless of whether you have children or not, your first stop in St. John's should be the same—**Signal Hill** ✿✿✿ (p. 90). The first to spot an iceberg wins a prize. Even if the children aren't captivated by the history of the hill, the silent cannons overlooking a harbor filled with ships make the visit worthwhile. On the way back into the city, plan on spending at least an hour at the **Johnson Geo Centre** ✿✿ (p. 90). The best downtown lodging for families is the **Quality Hotel Harbourview** ✿ (p. 78), where children under 18 stay free and the casual in-house restaurant has a menu with something for all ages.

Day ❷: Exploring the Capital

There's no way children—or most adults—will want to miss the opportunity to get up close and personal with seals, so start out this day by visiting the **Ocean Sciences Centre** ✿ (p. 94), where an outdoor pool is home to a half-dozen of these amusing mammals. Keep the nature theme going with a stop at the **Fluvarium** ✿✿ (p. 93), where you can watch pond life from the comfort of an underwater viewing chamber. If the weather is warm, head to **Bowring Park** (p. 96) for a swim in the outdoor pool or some fooling around on the adventure playground. It seems most children love trains, which makes the **Railway Coastal Museum** ✿ (p. 88) popular (the **Newfoundland Science Centre,** p. 88, is a better alternative in inclement weather).

Day ❸: Irish Loop to Salmonier

Take a family photo at North America's easternmost point, **Cape Spear** ✿✿ (p. 92) then continue down the Irish Loop for a boat cruise through the whale-rich waters of **Witless Bay Ecological Reserve** ✿✿✿ (p. 106). After lunch, make the short drive to **The Wilds at Salmonier River** (p. 113), a family-style resort with activities for everyone.

Day ❹: To Terra Nova

The province's only wildlife park is **Salmonier Nature Park** ✿✿ (p. 113). It should take well under 1 hour to walk the park's 3km (1.9-mile) loop trail, but with animals like lynx, moose, and foxes playing hard-to-spot, allow at least 2 hours to take it all in. Then drive to **Terra Nova Golf Resort** ✿✿ (p. 146) for a 2-night stay. Spend this first afternoon at your leisure—golfing, swimming, playing tennis, or simply doing nothing at all.

Day ❺: Terra Nova National Park ✿✿

Newman Sound is at its most peaceful in the morning, so plan on an early paddle with **Terra Nova Adventures** ✿ (p. 150). Those with younger children will prefer to let someone else lead the way, so plan on a boat trip with **Ocean Watch Tours** ✿ (p. 150). Spend the afternoon at **Splash-n-Putt Resort** (p. 150), which combines waterslides with bumper boats, go-karts, and more.

Day ❻: Return to St. John's

It will take a little over 2 hours for the drive back to St. John's, so stall for time by exploring the park's **Sandy Pond** (p. 149), where you can rent canoes, and **Avondale Railway Station** (p. 118), where mini-trains run along a section of narrow-gauge

Newfoundland & Labrador for Families

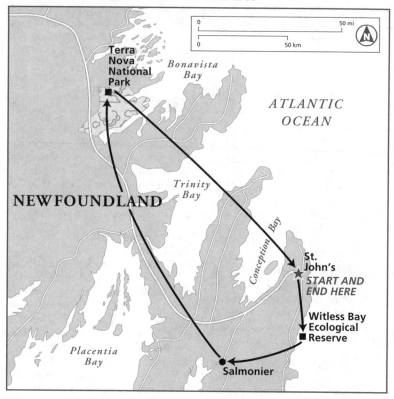

track. **Holiday Inn St. John's** ✈ (p. 78) is handy to the airport, and has plenty of activities to keep children busy, including a great outdoor pool, where grown-ups can relax on the surrounding deck chairs.

Day ❼: Leaving St. John's

If time allows, head downtown for some last-minute souvenir shopping. The **Downhomer Shoppe & Gallery** (p. 99) has the widest selection of gifts.

St. John's

St. John's, the capital of Newfoundland and Labrador, is one of my favorite cities. It's full of old-world charm, new-world finesse, and the fresh salt smell of the sea. The vistas and views in and around St. John's are spectacular. At the center of it all is the city's harbor. It was—and still is—the heart and soul of the city. Nothing has been more instrumental to its origin, growth, hard times, and return to prosperity than the city's connection to the sea. Downtown St. John's is concentrated along the harbor's western side, with steep streets lined by an enchanting mix of historic buildings and modern high-rises. An extension of the commercial core are residential streets where you'll be enchanted by the colorful row houses standing tall in various shades of red, brown, yellow, blue, and green.

St. John' mystique comes from the wealth of history that looks down on the city from the surrounding cliffs. To one side, **Signal Hill** (now a National Historic Site), with its rich military history, stands proud high atop the hill. Just across the Narrows (the protective entrance to the harbor), the 1810 lighthouse and World War II gun batteries at nearby **Fort Amherst** are reminders of past battles. And maritime history lives on in the fishermen and sailors who make their living much in the same way as their ancestors did over a century ago. Beyond these official attractions, you can immerse yourself in the past by staying at one of the city's delightful historic accommodations; spending time at The Rooms,

a magnificent provincial museum; or, as generations of sailors have done, by simply pulling up a stool at a downtown pub. The goal of this chapter is to provide you with the tools to make your visit to St. John's a fun and fulfilling one. Just be sure to allow yourself time to see it all—especially if you visit during July and August, when St. John's is at its peak at both the George Street Festival and the Royal St. John's Regatta.

The cultural and music scene in St. John's is unparalleled for a city this size. Indeed, many larger and supposedly more metropolitan centers would find it hard to compete with the range and quantity of its homegrown talent. At many places, you can catch free (or very inexpensively priced) live local entertainment of an excellent caliber.

St. John's is full of color. Not just in the buildings, but in its people, who seem to take time to greet everyone they meet on the street. In a small city of about 100,000 residents, it's a lot easier to get to know others than it would be in larger centers.

Yet the city's "townies"—the nickname for those who live in St. John's as opposed to the numerous outports throughout the province—are a special lot who seem to have treasured and preserved the art of knowing and caring about their neighbors more than many of us do.

Visitors are treated well in St. John's much like long-awaited friends. And you'll find your fill of good restaurants where the service is more than friendly and the food a treat for any palate. The wide range of choices for accommodations should please nearly every budget. And plenty of activities are available without going more than an hour from the city. As one of the oldest cities in North America, St. John's boasts a history bursting with stories of pirate treasure, restless ghosts, and military prowess. Visit the "City of Legends" once and I guarantee you'll find a way to return.

1 Essentials

GETTING THERE

St. John's is a 3-hour flight from Toronto or Boston, a 4-hour flight from New York, and a 5-hour flight from London, England. Air Canada has direct flights to St. John's from Halifax, Montreal, and Toronto, with connections from cities throughout the world made through the latter two hubs. Other Canadian airlines serving St. John's are WestJet from Halifax and CanJet from Halifax, Moncton, Toronto, and Montreal.

Continental has daily flights between St. John's and Newark. Local airlines include Air Labrador and Provincial Airlines, both providing reliable links between the capital and points throughout the province. Upon arrival in St. John's you'll be pleased to find a modern airport with desks for all major rental-car companies, a choice of eateries, currency exchange, gift shops, and an information booth. The airport is just minutes (6km/4 miles) and a relatively inexpensive cab ride (C$20/US$17 for one person, plus C$5/US$4.30 per extra person) to downtown.

Warning: If you're leaving St. John's on one of the early-bird flights (anywhere between 6–6:30am), you'll want to arrive at least 1½ to 2 hours before your scheduled departure. That's usually the busiest time of the day at the airport, and arriving early will save you from getting caught in congestion at the airport security counter. The latest you should arrive at the airport for any domestic flight is 1 hour prior to departure.

Taking the ferry from Nova Scotia to Newfoundland and Labrador is cheaper than flying, but it's a much more time-consuming endeavor. The routing that gets you closest to St. John's is a full 14-hour sailing from North Sydney to Argentia, followed by a 1½-hour drive to the city. But if you have the time, you can save a considerable chunk of change by sailing and driving your own car vs. flying and then renting a car on arrival. (Find more detail in section 10, "Getting There," in chapter 2.)

VISITOR INFORMATION

The marketing organization **Destination St. John's** (© **877/739-8899** or 709/739-8899; www.canadasfareast.com) has a visitor information booth open year-round daily 10am to midnight, conveniently located on the main floor of the airport by the car-rental counter. Here you can pick up regional travel brochures, maps, and information. Use the contacts above to order travel literature in advance of your arrival.

Downtown, the St. John's Visitor Information Centre is centrally located at 348 Water St. (© **709/576-8106;** www.stjohns.ca). It's open year-round Monday to Friday 9am to 4:30pm, with extended summer hours of daily 9am to 5pm.

Note: The Avalon Peninsula includes and surrounds St. John's and comprises about half the province's total population and many of its major attractions. The Avalon Peninsula outside of St. John's is covered in detail in chapter 5.

2 Getting Around

From as far back as the early 1500s, life in St. John's has centered on its harbor. Indeed, in its early days, the city owed its existence to the British, Spanish, French, Portuguese, and other fleets whose annual arrival signaled the beginning of another fishing season—usually for cod. Shops and local businesses seemed to spring from the water itself, so close were they to the city's teeming waterfront. Even today, most everything you'll want to see in St. John's will either be on, or just off, one of four streets.

Harbour Drive and Water, Duckworth, and George streets all run parallel to the waterfront. You'll find the boat tours, an opportunity to get close to all sorts of foreign ships, and most of the parking spaces in town along Harbour Drive, which runs adjacent to the harbor and is accessible off the Trans-Canada Highway (Rte. 1) leading into downtown from the west.

Most of the services (shops, financial institutions, post office, and so on) are on Water Street, the next street up from the waterfront, running the full length of the harbor. And you'll find the highest concentration of restaurants along Duckworth Street, one block farther up the hill. If you're looking for nightlife, about two dozen pubs can be found on George Street, a two-block stretch of excitement between Water Street and City Hall.

BY FOOT

The streets of St. John's are ideal for walking enthusiasts. Buildings throughout the downtown area (especially along Gower St.) have brightly colored, beautifully restored historical facades. It's a perfect area for wandering, the air is invigorating, and there are many interesting diversions along the way to wherever you're heading.

Warning: The city center is on a fairly steep incline, so if you have difficulty walking you may want to stick to Harbour Drive and Water Street, which are relatively flat. By the time you get up to Duckworth Street, the incline gets more difficult to navigate. Between Duckworth Street and LeMarchant Road, there are places where you'd be grateful for a ski lift.

Another reason you may want to walk the city is that it's tricky navigating your way around by vehicle. St. John's has many one-way streets, quite a few hidden intersections (the one turning on to Harbour Dr. from the Quality Hotel on **Hill O'Chips** is especially tricky), and some crazy intersections where you have to do a roundabout to get where you want to go (watch out for one of these by the Fairmont). Plus, you may be so absorbed by the wildly colored and intriguingly named buildings (such as the **Bread Pig**) that the driving should be left to someone else.

(Fun Fact Buried Treasure

Legend has it that in the 1940s, a dishonest bank employee stole tens of thousands of dollars and buried his loot in a laneway connecting New Gower and Water streets. The criminal was charged, found guilty, and spent 4 years in jail for the deed—only to be released and discover that the laneway had been covered over with concrete during his incarceration. The money has never been recovered.

Downtown St. John's

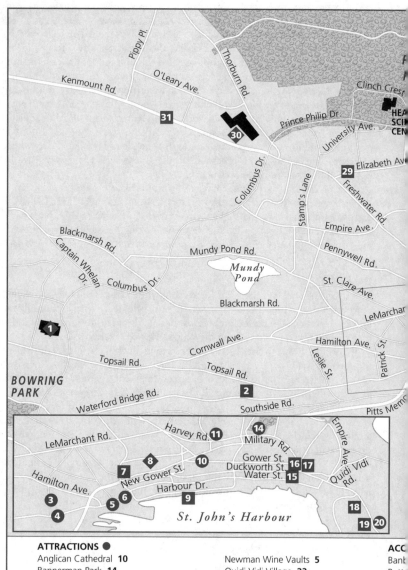

Pippy Pl
O'Leary Ave.
Thorburn Rd.
Kenmount Rd.
Clinch Crest
31
Prince Philip Dr.
HEA
30
University Ave.
SCI
CEN
Columbus Dr.
Elizabeth Av
29
Stamp's Lane
Freshwater Rd.
Blackmarsh Rd.
Empire Ave.
Captain Whelan Dr.
Mundy Pond Rd.
Pennywell Rd.
Columbus Dr.
Mundy Pond
St. Clare Ave.
Blackmarsh Rd.
LeMarchar
1
Cornwall Ave.
Hamilton Ave.
Patrick St.
Topsail Rd.
Topsail Rd.
Leslie St.
BOWRING PARK
2
Waterford Bridge Rd.
Southside Rd.
Pitts Mem
Harvey Rd. 11
14
LeMarchant Rd.
Military Rd
Empire Ave.
8
10
Gower St. 16 17
7
New Gower St.
Duckworth St.
Quidi Vidi Rd.
Hamilton Ave.
Harbour Dr.
Water St. 15
3
5 6
9
18
4
St. John's Harbour
19 20

ATTRACTIONS ●

Anglican Cathedral **10**
Bannerman Park **14**
Basilica of St. John the Baptist **11**
Fluvarium **27**
Fort Amherst **21**
James J. O'Mara Pharmacy Museum **6**
Johnson Geo Centre **20**

Newman Wine Vaults **5**
Quidi Vidi Village **23**
Railway Coastal Museum **4**
The Rooms **24**
Signal Hill National Historic Site **22**
Spa at the Monastery **3**

ACC
Banl
Batt
Best
Blue:
Delt
Fairr
Guv'

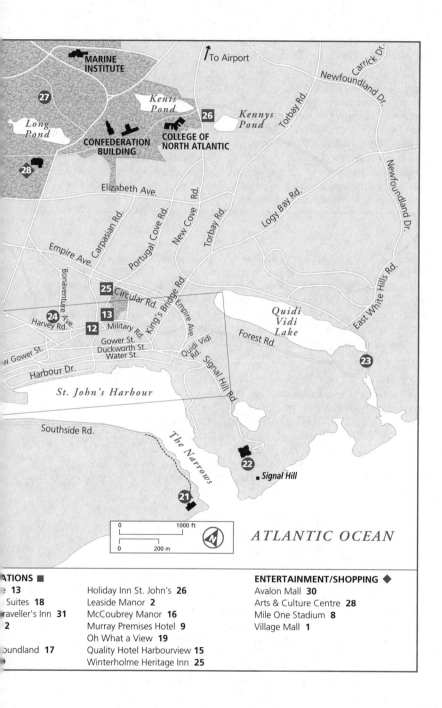

MARINE INSTITUTE

 27

Long Pond

Kents Pond

26

Kennys Pond

CONFEDERATION BUILDING

COLLEGE OF NORTH ATLANTIC

28

↑To Airport

Newfoundland Dr.

Carrick Dr.

Torbay Rd.

Elizabeth Ave.

Carpasian Rd.

Portugal Cove Rd.

New Cove Rd.

Torbay Rd.

Logy Bay Rd.

Newfoundland Dr.

Empire Ave.

Bonaventure Ave.

25 Circular Rd.

King's Bridge Rd.

Empire Ave.

24 Harvey Rd.

13

12 Military Rd.

Gower St.
Duckworth St.
Water St.

New Gower St.

Harbour Dr.

Quidi Vidi Rd.

Forest Rd.

Quidi Vidi Lake

East White Hills Rd.

23

Signal Hill Rd.

St. John's Harbour

Southside Rd.

The Narrows

22

■ Signal Hill

21

0   1000 ft
0   200 m

N

ATLANTIC OCEAN

73

ATIONS ■

e **13**

Suites **18**

aveller's Inn **31**

2

oundland **17**

Holiday Inn St. John's **26**

Leaside Manor **2**

McCoubrey Manor **16**

Murray Premises Hotel **9**

Oh What a View **19**

Quality Hotel Harbourview **15**

Winterholme Heritage Inn **25**

ENTERTAINMENT/SHOPPING ◆

Avalon Mall **30**

Arts & Culture Centre **28**

Mile One Stadium **8**

Village Mall **1**

Moments Unforgettable Stories

You'll find that, regardless of which company they work for, most taxi drivers are exceedingly friendly. Many of them have a delightful Irish brogue, a sure hint of a marvelous storyteller who needs just a little encouragement to get started. One driver, named Sean, noted the time a passenger—after a wee bit too much fun on George Street—stumbled into his cab and promptly fell asleep. On awakening the passenger to find out where he lived, the groggy man threw $20 on the seat, thanked Sean for the ride, and got out of the car right where he'd gotten in! It took some encouragement to get the man back in, and even more coaxing to find out where he lived, but Sean made sure his passenger was delivered safe at home.

BY CAB

Cabs in St. John's are fairly priced. Most rides about town will cost you under C$10 (US$8.50). The biggest company is **Bugden's Taxi** (© 709/726-4400). Others include **Co-op Taxi** (© 709/726-6666) and **Gulliver's City Wide Taxi** (© 709/722-0003). If you're planning to pay by credit card, be sure to call ahead before you get in the cab to verify that credit cards—and your particular card—are accepted. Similarly, if you require an infant car seat make sure you ask for one when you call for a cab—most taxi companies have at least a couple of vehicles equipped with that option.

BY BUS

As any experienced traveler knows, public transit is one of the cheapest and fastest ways to become acquainted with unfamiliar surroundings. St. John's doesn't have subways, streetcars, or passenger trains, but it does have an inexpensive public bus system, **Metrobus** (© 709/570-2020; www.metrobus.com). Adults (including seniors) ride for C$2 (US$1.75). Children ages 3 to 18 pay C$1.50 (US$1.25). Under age 3 is free. You may find one of the 10-ride passes (C$18/US$16 adults, C$14/US$12 children) to be a bit more economical if you're planning to use the bus a lot.

Warning: Metrobus operates with an exact–cash fare policy. Drivers do not carry change.

BY CAR

Get yourself a detailed city map and have your navigator guide you along the way, as driving in St. John's—despite the fact that it's a compact city—isn't the easiest. A lot of the streets in the capital city, as well as in most other communities throughout the province, are in desperate need of repair. According to some expert tellers of tall tales, there are potholes so big you could get lost in them. Unfortunately, after a few days driving around the municipal obstacle course, you start to believe them.

Warning: Beware of the multitude of one-way streets, hidden and roundabout intersections, and the fact that streets change names at whim from one block to the next. The good thing is that it's not that difficult to find your way back on track even if you do get lost or turned around, as the city isn't very large and traffic volumes are generally not a problem. Also, be aware that you may find a shortage of downtown parking during business hours and when there are special events taking place at Mile One Stadium.

FAST FACTS: **St. John's**

ATMs You'll find a number of financial institutions along **Water Street** in downtown St. John's. Check the phone book for other bank locations.

Business Hours See the "Holidays" section in Chapter 2 for a detailed listing of days that stores would be closed. Most shops in the city are open weekdays for business from around 10am until 6pm, but individual store hours may vary. Malls are open 10am to10pm. The malls and some shops are open Sundays from noon to 5pm. Banks are generally open weekdays 10am to 4pm, although some close at 3pm while others are open until 5pm.

Car Rentals All the major players have rental booths at the St. John's airport. Check the phone book for other locations.

Climate St. John's has a temperate marine climate. See the "When to Go: Weather" section of chapter 2 for further details. Call ✆ 709/772-5534 for local updates or check out the Environment Canada Web site www.weatheroffice.ec.gc.ca.

Emergencies Call ✆ **911** in case of emergency to reach police, ambulance, or the fire department.

Internet Access All major hotels and most bed-and-breakfasts have in-room Internet access. The only true Internet/cybercafe in St. John's is located in the **Wordplay Bookstore,** 221 Duckworth St. (✆ **709/726-9193**). **Starbucks/Chapters** at 70 Kenmount Rd. (✆ **709/726-0375**) also offers Internet access. As well, free Internet service is available at the following public libraries: **A. C. Hunter Library,** at the Arts and Culture Centre, Allandale Road (✆ **709/737-2348**); **Marjorie Mews Library,** 18 Highland Dr. (✆ **709/737-3020**); and **Michael Donovan Library,** 655 Topsail Rd. (✆ **709/737-2621**).

Libraries See "Internet Access," above or check out the Web site www.nlpub libraries.ca.

Newspapers The major newspaper in St. John's is the *Telegram.* Their online version (www.thetelegram.com) offers many useful local links.

Post Office The main **Canada Post** outlet is at 354 Water St. (✆ **709/758-1003**). You can also find postal outlets in most **Shoppers Drug Mart** stores, for example at 430 Topsail Rd. in the Village Shopping Centre (✆ **709/368-6084**) and 141 Torbay Rd. (✆ **709/722-6270**).

Safety Whether you're gay, elderly, of a visible minority, or a woman traveling alone, you should feel secure walking the streets of St. John's. Street crimes are relatively rare. *Warning:* Be aware that because so many pubs are on George Street, the area can get quite rowdy late in the evening and is best avoided if you're not a pub-goer. (If you are, it can be a lot of fun!) Be sensible and lock your vehicle when unattended anywhere in the city. Don't leave your purse or daypack unattended, and be alert to your surroundings as you would when visiting anywhere.

Taxes An HST (harmonized federal and provincial sales tax) of **15%** is applicable to most purchases. St. John's has an **additional 3% tax on accommodations** within the city limits. See the "Tips & Taxes" section in chapter 2 for info on tax rebates.

Telephone It costs **C35¢** to make a local call from a pay phone. If you have a cellphone, you'll have no difficulty getting service while in St. John's. Call ⓒ **411** for directory assistance.

Water St. John's tap water is fine for drinking. Bottled water is provided in many hotels and is available for purchase throughout the city.

3 Where to Stay

St. John's offers a rich choice of accommodations, everything from a modest room in a local resident's home to upscale chain hotels. When it comes to historic lodgings, St. John's really shines. Not only are many of the best within walking distance of downtown, but prices are reasonable and the atmosphere always unstuffy and welcoming.

During peak season, which is generally late July to mid-August, the city books to capacity. This is when the Folk Festival, the George Street Festival, and the Royal St. John's Regatta all take place. If you like excitement, it's the best time to visit St. John's, but it can also be the most difficult time to secure accommodations. So plan well ahead whenever possible.

The listings in this guidebook include properties that stand out for a particular reason. For example, one is located next to the Folk Festival grounds; another is an aesthetic treat with its beautiful stained glass; and yet another is best known as a favorite hideaway for honeymooners. And to get away from strictly material amenities, one listing offers the friendliest hosts in the city. You get the picture.

If you're staying in St. John's for more than a few days, you may want to consider staying at more than one type of accommodations—say, a hotel and at least one heritage inn or B&B—to get a fuller flavor of the city's interesting range of offerings.

Type of accommodations may be more relevant in your decision-making process than strictly price, so I've grouped accommodations by type rather than price. I've used two broad categories to cover standard accommodations: **Hotels/Motels** and **Heritage Inns/B&Bs**. Depending on your individual preference, you can choose a particular property from within that category based on the price you want to pay and the amenities offered.

HOTELS & MOTELS

Battery Hotel & Suites ⚐   An all-white, sentinel-like structure, the Battery at night appears to be an almost spectral image suspended above the city. Located on the way up to Signal Hill and a 5-minute walk from the Geo Centre, the Battery has unparalleled harbor views. And while the location is superb, it follows the standard impersonal script found in the majority of midrange hotels. The most striking amenities are the view, the natural Newfoundland courtesy of hotel staff, and a restaurant where you can soak up the harbor lights over baked salmon glazed with strawberries and cream.

There's ample free parking, and a business center in the lobby with free computer use (except for modest online charges) that's available to all guests. There is no air-conditioning in the guest rooms but the windows do open. Some rooms have whirlpool baths and suites are fully equipped with kitchenettes.

100 Signal Hill Rd., St. John's. ⓒ 800/563-8181 or 709/576-0040. Fax 709/576-6943. www.batteryhotel.com. 125 units. C$109–C$189 (US$94–US$163) double. AE, DC, MC, V. Pets welcome. **Amenities:** Restaurant; bar; indoor pool; sauna; whirlpool; laundry and dry-cleaning services; walking trails. *In room:* TV w/pay movies, coffeemaker, hair dryer, iron.

Best Western Traveller's Inn   Moderately priced, reliably clean, and uncomplicated accommodations that are perfect for the business traveler or the budget-conscious visitor. Because it's situated on one of the busiest streets in St. John's, you'll want to ask for a room at the back of the building where the noise of passing traffic is less likely to keep you awake at night. The guest rooms are bright, spacious, and comfortably appointed. It also has one of the province's few outdoor pools, and as a bonus for families, children 18 and under stay free and those 12 and under eat free.

199 Kenmount Rd., St. John's. (℅) **800/261-5540** or 709/722-5540. Fax 709/722-1025. www.bestwestern.com. 88 units. C$89–C$119 (US$77–US$103) double. AE, DC, MC, V. Free parking. **Amenities:** Restaurant; lounge; heated outdoor pool; billiard room; laundry service. *In room:* TV w/pay movies, coffeemaker, hair dryer, iron, free local calls.

Delta St. John's Hotel & Conference Centre ✦   Adjacent to the convention center and Mile One Stadium, the Delta is an ideal choice for the business or individual traveler attending a function at any of these venues. It's also one of the closest accommodations to downtown shopping and nightlife, so you can shop 'til you drop, bring your parcels to your room, and be back in action within minutes. Part of an upscale Canadian chain, it's a modern hostelry, easily recognized by the harbor-facing glass-walled exterior. Inside, you find midsize rooms filled with all the amenities needed for a comfortable stay, including in-house dining, a modern fitness facility, and an indoor pool. Of special note for those who like a little extra luxury are the Signature Club rooms, which come with niceties like bathrobes, CD players, as well as thoughtful touches like complimentary umbrellas.

120 New Gower St., St. John's. (℅) **877/814-7706** or 709/739-6404. Fax 709/570-1622. www.deltahotels.com. 276 units. C$185–C$345 (US$159–US$297) double. AE, DC, DISC, MC, V. Underground, valet parking available for C$8/US$7 additional/day. **Amenities:** Restaurant; indoor pool; fitness center; children's program and babysitting; concierge; laundry/dry cleaning. *In room:* A/C, TV w/pay movies, minibar, coffeemaker, hair dryer, iron.

Fairmont Newfoundland ✦✦   Still referred to as the "Hotel Newfoundland" among locals because of its longtime history under that name, the Fairmont Newfoundland stands alone as the best full-service hotel in town. Positives include everything from one of the city's best restaurants (see the "Where to Dine" section later in this chapter for a review); a spa and fitness center; art gallery; gold-level service floor, complete with no-wait check-in, on-floor concierge, and lounge with computer for guest use; and wonderful water views from most rooms. The only negatives are its lack of traditional charm and windows that don't open to provide you with a whiff of that fresh sea air.

With more than 300 guest rooms on 7 floors, the Fairmont is where royalty and other dignitaries stay while in St. John's. If you can spare the C$800 (US$687) it costs for a night, go for the lavish Admiral Suite and you can say you slept in the same room as the queen of England. End-of-the-hall rooms with numbers ending in 00 offer the best panoramic views. The Junior Suites offer extra space and large porthole-style windows for only slightly more than standard rooms. For these and other rooms, check the Fairmont website for specials, especially on weekends and outside of summer.

115 Cavendish Sq., St. John's. (℅) **800/257-7544** or 709/726-4980. Fax 709/726-2025. www.fairmont.com/newfoundland. 315 units. C$320–C$800 (US$275–US$687) double. AE, DC, DISC, MC, V. Pets allowed for additional C$25 (US$22)/night. **Amenities:** 2 restaurants; lounge; indoor pool and fitness center; day spa; business center; babysitting; concierge; 24-hr. room service. *In room:* A/C, TV w/pay movies and PlayStation, minibar, coffeemaker, hair dryer, iron, bathrobes, daily newspaper.

Guv'nor Inn ✦   You'd miss the Guv'nor on a quick drive-by because of its modest exterior, but this isn't one of those hotels you visit for its ambience. Its strongest feature is its location: minutes from Memorial University and within walking distance of the General Hospital Health Sciences Centre. The rooms are super spacious, although the furnishings are unremarkable. *Note:* The inn has no elevator, so anyone with heavy luggage or bad knees may have trouble with the stairs.

389 Elizabeth Ave., St. John's. (C) 800/961-0092 or 709/726-0092. Fax 709/726-5921. www.guvnor-inn.com. 37 units. C$85–C$105 (US$73–US$90) double; extra person C$8 (US$7). AE, DC, MC, V. **Amenities:** Restaurant; pub. *In room:* A/C, TV, dataport, coffeemaker, hair dryer, iron.

Holiday Inn St. John's *Kids*   With its own outdoor heated pool surrounded by deck chairs, as well as two walking trails, a playground, and the best 18-hole minigolf course in the city (Sir Admiral John's Green) all within a 5-minute walk, this hotel is the perfect accommodations for traveling families. If you request one of the motel-style rooms, you'll have the added bonus of being able to park your vehicle directly outside your door (great when small children fall asleep on the drive—you can carry them straight to bed). You also don't need to go searching for somewhere to eat—the in-house family-style Italian restaurant is open long hours.

180 Portugal Cove Rd., St. John's. (C) 888/465-4329 or 709/722-0506. Fax 709/722-9756. www.holidayinnstjohns.com. 252 units. C$135–C$200 (US$116–US$172) double. AE, DC, DISC, MC, V. **Amenities:** Restaurant; lounge; outdoor heated pool (open July–Aug only); fitness room; salon; babysitting. *In room:* A/C, TV w/pay movies, dataport, minibar, coffeemaker, hair dryer, iron, daily newspaper.

Murray Premises Hotel *Finds*   A boutique hotel that gets top marks for its excellent service and distinctive character. Constructed as a waterfront warehouse in 1846, the building has been completely transformed, with luxurious rooms filling the top two floors, complete with luxuries such as towel warmers, fireplaces, and marble bathrooms with jetted tubs. The original beamed ceilings, columns, and timber-slanted roofs add a rustic, cozy feeling to the otherwise contemporary rooms.

If you can pull yourself away from the custom-made maple beds with gorgeous duvets and top-quality linens, you should take the time to discover the other businesses conveniently located under the same roof, including eating establishments, the province's best-stocked wine boutique, and art galleries. The hotel is accessible from Water Street and Harbour Drive, which means you have both the downtown shopping district and the waterfront on your doorstep.

5 Beck's Cove, St. John's. (C) 866/738-7773 or 709-738-7773. Fax 709/738-7775. 28 units. www.murraypremises hotel.com. C$129–C$189 (US$111–US$163) double. AE, DC, MC, V. **Amenities:** 2 restaurants; limited room service; all nonsmoking guest rooms. *In room:* A/C, TV, dataport, fridge, coffeemaker, hair dryer, iron, bathrobe, daily newspaper.

Quality Hotel Harbourview   Located as it is on Hill O'Chips, you'd think this hotel would be well known for its food—and you'd be right! Its lobby restaurant, Rumpelstiltskin's, has a casual atmosphere with well-prepared meals and reasonable prices (see the review in the "Where to Dine" section below). The hotel itself is less memorable, although its harborside rooms offer a picturesque view of the Narrows.

Fun Fact **Remember When**

The original Hotel Newfoundland opened in 1926. With its steam heating, ballroom, and luxury accommodations, it was heralded in the news of the day as the ultimate in "artistic taste." Rooms cost $18/night for double occupancy; running water cost an extra $7.

Because it's part of the Choice Hotels chain, you know what to expect before you arrive. Which means it doesn't have the personality of a boutique hotel, but at the same time you know you can depend on it for reliable service as well as clean and comfortable rooms. Its 42 Business Class rooms furnished with full-size desks and ergonomic chairs make it a popular choice with corporate travelers.

2 Hill O'Chips, St. John's. (C) **800/228-5151** or 709/754-7788. Fax 709/754-5209. www.choicehotels.ca. 160 units. C$154–C$189 (US$133–US$163) double; kids under 18 stay free with an adult. AE, DC, DISC, MC, V. **Amenities:** Restaurant; lounge. *In room:* A/C, TV w/pay movies, dataport, fridge in some rooms, coffeemaker, hair dryer, iron.

HERITAGE INNS & BED & BREAKFASTS

Banberry House 🕂🕂   One of the best things about Banberry House is Annie, the cook. She loves to be creative, and is bound to please and surprise you with such local breakfast delicacies as *toutons* (fried bread dough that tastes much better than it sounds, especially topped with molasses), salt cod cakes, and bread-stuffed bologna. Everything is made on-site, and guests are guaranteed not to get the same breakfast twice if they're staying for a week or less, as a different specialty is featured each morning.

Another great thing about this property is its location. When staying here, just a stone's throw from Bannerman Park where the Folk Festival is held each summer, you can actually sit on the patio amid the potted plants and enjoy the music without ever leaving the yard—or getting too far from Annie's delights. Built in 1892, immediately following the Great Fire, Banberry House boasts wonderful stained glass by the same craftsman whose work adorns the nearby Catholic Basilica of St. John the Baptist.

The guest rooms at the Banberry exhibit carefully preserved historical authenticity. One of the rooms has an old-style four-poster bed and wood-burning fireplace. Some have the old-fashioned footed tubs as well as shower stalls. The main-floor "Labrador Room" has an especially rugged feel to it, as well as views across the private garden. With your room rate, you get a complimentary gourmet breakfast and off-street parking.

116 Military Rd., St. John's. (C) **877/579-8226** or 709/579-8006. Fax 709/579-3443. www.banberryhouse.com. 6 units. C$139–C$169 (US$120–US$145) double; off-season rates from C$99 (US$85). AE, DC, MC, V. **Amenities:** Non-smoking rooms. *In room:* TV, en-suite bathroom, dataport, free local calls.

Bluestone Inn 🕂🕂 *(Finds)*   This funky yet classic inn in downtown St. John's is tastefully decorated with a wonderful selection of original art mingled with historical embellishments. It took owner Neil Oates a year and a half to dig out the original stone wall, which adds an old-world atmosphere to "Excess Baggage," the name he's given this wonderful meeting/conference room.

The original building dates back more than 250 years, and is reported to be the oldest stone structure in the city. The location is fantastic—by foot, it's within minutes of downtown restaurants and shopping, yet you're a 10-minute drive from St. John's International Airport.

For breakfast, you can enjoy local specialties such as partridgeberry pancakes. The lower-level breakfast nook doubles as a bar for guests later in the day and evening. To unwind at the end of the day, you can enjoy a glass of wine and share stories with fellow travelers here or out on the lovely street-front patio.

The guest rooms are spacious and above average in every way. High-quality bedding is used throughout. Room no. 1 is magnificent, with dark wood and more of a masculine feel. Some of the other rooms have a softer touch. All have Jacuzzis and many other amenities such as high-speed Internet and a hotel-style telephone system. Self-contained units are available for longer stays. For an additional charge, the owner can even arrange unique float-plane excursions.

34 Queen's Rd., St. John's. ℭ **877/754-9876** or 709/754-7544. Fax 709/722-8626. www.thebluestoneinn.com. 4 units. C$139–C$299 (US$120–US$257) double; ask about off-season rates. AE, DC, MC, V. **Amenities:** Lounge; non-smoking rooms; group-use space available. *In room:* TV, dataport.

Leaside Manor ★★   A charming Tudor mansion situated in a quiet suburban location a 20-minute walk from downtown, Leaside Manor provides a peaceful and serene place to lay your head. The grounds are lovely, with gardens in full bloom if you're fortunate enough to visit during summer or early fall.

The most important thing to note about Leaside Manor is that the rooms vary considerably, both in rates and amenities. The Parker Suite is gorgeous, with a bedside Jacuzzi. The spacious Signal Hill apartment is also nice, with full kitchen, a Jacuzzi, and lovely furnishings. The Confederation Room, although nicely furnished and equipped with plenty of reading material as well as a VCR, has a phone booth–size shower stall that doesn't meet the standards of the rest of the inn.

All rooms include a complimentary full breakfast and parking. Tour planning assistance is offered and fully equipped apartments are available for long-term stays at two additional locations.

39 Topsail Rd., St. John's. ℭ **877/807-7245** or 709/722-0387. Fax 709/739-1835. www.leaside.nf.ca. 7 units. C$109–C$229 (US$94–US$197) double. AE, DC, MC, V. **Amenities:** *In room:* TV/VCR, dataport.

McCoubrey Manor ★★   Across the road from the Fairmont Newfoundland, McCoubrey Manor is a gracious Queen Anne–style home built in 1904. Now converted to an inn, it is quaintly nostalgic with black-and-white photos of the original owners throughout the home. Antique furnishings and log-burning fireplaces make this a cozy choice—especially during the colder months. The warm colors used to decorate McCoubrey Manor provide a comfortable ambience for the complimentary evening wine-and-cheese get-togethers hosted by the owners, Jill and Roy Knoechel. Some of the guest rooms have a view of the harbor; "Catherine's Haven" offers the romantic luxury of a double Jacuzzi as well as a fireplace. Rates include a terrific breakfast of fresh fruit salad, muffins, loaves, homemade jams, and a choice of two hot entrees.

6–8 Ordnance St., St. John's. ℭ **888/753-7577** or 709/722-7577. Fax 709/579-7577. www.mccoubrey.com. 6 units. C$139–C$199 (US$120–US$170) double. AE, DC, MC, V. **Amenities:** Laundry facilities; nonsmoking rooms. *In room:* A/C, TV/VCR, CD player.

Oh What a View *(Finds)*   A simple Newfoundland home has been converted to this welcoming bed-and-breakfast central to everything, including the attractions of Signal Hill and the restaurants you find within the Battery Hotel and Fairmont Newfoundland. A full breakfast is included and the most expensive room has harbor views. The same owners rent out the nearby Harbour View Cottage, a two-bedroom home with full kitchen, for C$150 (US$129).

184 Signal Hill Rd., St. John's. ℭ **709/576-7063**. Fax 709/753-6934. www.ohwhataview.com. 4 units. C$75–C$150 (US$65–US$129) double. MC, V. Open April–Nov. **Amenities:** Internet access; nonsmoking rooms. *In room:* TV/DVD.

Points East   It takes around 20 minutes to reach Points East from St. John's International Airport, or a little longer from downtown. But friendly host Elke Dettmer will pick you up from either location, so for those without transport the distance is not an issue. Upon arrival, you'll find a trim fisherman's home that has been given a fresh coat of paint and transformed into good-value accommodations. Perched on an oceanfront lot, the setting is nothing less than stunning, with a good chance of spotting icebergs in spring and whales in summer. The three guest rooms are simple, yet clean and comfortable. Outside, you find plenty of spots to sit and soak up the view, or if you're feeling energetic, have Elke set up day hikes along the northernmost section of the East Coast Trail (p. 103). Meals are offered with advance notice.

34 Sullivan's Loop, Pouch Cove. ⓒ **709/335-8315**. www.trailconnections.ca. 3 units. C$50–C$75 (US$43–US$65) double. MC, V. **Amenities:** Communal kitchen; lounge. *In room:* Shared bathrooms.

Winterholme Heritage Inn ⓕⓕⓕ   Anyone who appreciates fine craftsmanship and has a sense of history would enjoy staying at Winterholme, built in 1905 for the delightfully named Marmaduke Winter, who was a wealthy merchant. Sitting across the road from Bannerman Park, the property is now designated a National Historic Site—a wonderful example of Queen Anne Revival architecture, which was popular in Canadian house construction from the 1880s until about 1914, and truly breathtaking inside and out. The intricate woodwork, the lovely stained glass, and the spacious double-Jacuzzi rooms are all special touches, but it's the English oak staircase—appraised at C$250,000/US$214,725!—that will leave you in awe. It's a piece of artwork in itself. Every guest room is different and offers its own charm, but all are extremely spacious and equipped with luxuries such as a double Jacuzzi and fireplace. A delicious full breakfast and parking are included in the rates.

79 Rennies Mill Rd., St. John's. ⓒ **800/599-7829** or 709/739-7979. Fax 709/753-9411. www.winterholme.com. 12 units. C$129–C$199 (US$111–US$170). AE, DC, MC, V, Interac. **Amenities:** Laundry facilities; fax machine; computer and printer; microwave. *In room:* Cable TV, dataport, coffeemaker, hair dryer.

HOSTELS AND CAMPING

Butter Pot Provincial Park ⓕ   Along the Trans-Canada Highway 36km (23 miles) south of town, this beautiful tract of wilderness is just a taste of what you'll find throughout the province. "Butter pot" is the local name for a rounded hill; the summit of the most prominent of these within the park is reached by a trail that takes around 2 hours round-trip. Hikers are rewarded with sweeping views across the forested park. Add to the mix swimming, fishing, three playgrounds, and a summer interpretive program and you'll find it hard to drag the family into the nearby city.

36km (23 miles) south of town beside the Trans-Canada Hwy. ⓒ **709/458-2417**. www.env.gov.nl.ca/parks/parks/p_bup. 126 sites. C$14 (US$12) for unserviced sites. MC, V, Interac. Open mid-June to mid-Sept. **Amenities:** Shower and washroom facilities; drinking water; kitchen shelter; dump station; picnic tables; firewood (C$5/US$4.30 per bundle); playgrounds; hiking.

Memorial University Campus ⓥ*alue*   All budget-conscious travelers should know about the inexpensive accommodations available from May to August through the Conference Office at Memorial University. Rooms are standard dormitory issue (single and twin rooms, all with linen supplied but no in-room TV or phone) with communal, gender-specific bathrooms. University residences are linked to the campus fitness facility, which has an indoor running track and Olympic-size swimming pool, and a restaurant open weekdays for three buffet-style meals. The university is also on a main bus route and across the road from Pippy Park. All this in a quiet, parklike setting with mature trees and the added protection of campus security.

Register at the Conference Office, Room 316C, Hatcher House, Prince Philip Dr., St. John's. ⓒ **709/737-7657**. Fax 709/737-6705. www.housing.mun.ca/conf. C$39 (US$34) senior double; C$56 (US$49) non-students, twin room. MC, V. **Amenities:** Cafeteria-style restaurant; fitness facility with pool; coin-operated laundry facilities; shared bathrooms; TV room; pay phones.

Pippy Park Trailer Park   Whether you're camping in a tent or a fancy RV, Pippy Park provides a wonderfully treed setting close to Memorial University and within minutes of downtown St. John's. Across the road is the Fluvarium, well worth investigating for its underwater angle on local pond life, while walking trails lead on in various directions including one that encircles Long Pond. The campground comprises 94 fully serviced, 38 semi-serviced, and 26 unserviced sites, and an overflow area needed for the busiest summer nights.

Nagle's Place, St. John's. ℰ 877/477-3655, 709/737-3669, or 709/737-3655 off-season. Fax 709/737-3303. www.pippypark.com/trailer.shtml. C$25 (US$22) full service, C$22 (US$19) semi-serviced, C$20 (US$17) unserviced. MC, V. May 1–Sept 30 subject to weather conditions. **Amenities:** Dumping station; electrical, sewer, and water hookup; hiking; pets allowed; playground; fully accessible shower and washroom facilities.

4 Where to Dine

For such a small city, St. John's has some wonderful restaurants and a great variety of culinary adventures to choose from: traditional "Newfie" meals, wild game, expertly prepared seafood, Asian favorites, slick contemporary cooking—the list goes on. The most sophisticated independent eating establishments are on Duckworth or Water streets, but surprisingly several of the hotels also have great food.

Regardless of where you venture for finer dining, you have to have fish and chips at least a couple of times while in Newfoundland. St. John's has some excellent places that specialize in *fi and chi* (pronounced "fee and chee"; that's waiter-speak for fish and chips), with a concentration of casual places along Freshwater Road. The most famous is **Ches's**, at 9 Freshwater Rd. (ℰ **709/722-4083**), but **Johnny's**, at 11 Freshwater Rd. (ℰ **709/739-1810**), and **Leo's**, at 27 Freshwater Rd. (ℰ **709/726-2658**), are also recommended. You'll find Newfoundlanders are definite connoisseurs of this particular dish, judging each establishment by the texture of the batter and the crispness of the fries. *Note:* Smoking is banned in all public places, including restaurants and bars.

EXPENSIVE

AQUA Restaurant & Bar ✦✦ FUSION   Owners Kevin and Kim Parker have put together a rather exotic seasonal menu for this stylish downtown restaurant with an interesting selection of black-and-white photography on the walls and fresh flowers adorning the bar. Specialties of the house include pistachio-encrusted goat cheese (made locally) served on mixed greens with a mango chipotle sauce and garlic crostini and curry and mango chicken wings; both are listed as starters, but combined they make a perfect and affordable meal. I went for the grilled caribou brushed with blueberry port reduction, which was absolutely divine. Be sure to try the flatbread coated with sea salt served at your table. Save room for dessert. Everything is made on-site and is fantastic, including the rich and creamy crème brûleé and the sour cream and coconut ice creams. Come at lunch and enjoy the same creative cooking at half the price. For example, pan-seared salmon on a bed of sushi rice with tamari sauce is just C$14 (US$12).

310 Water St. ℰ **709/576-2782.** www.aquarestaurant.ca. Reservations recommended, especially during summer weekends. Main courses C$18–C$31 (US$16–US$27). AE, DC, MC, V. Mon–Fri noon–2pm; Sun–Thurs 5:30–10pm; Fri–Sat 5:30–10:30pm.

Blue on Water ✦✦✦ MODERN/SEAFOOD   A little bit of the Mediterranean along the main shopping and restaurant strip. This stylish space is decorated in blue and white, with well-spaced tables extending from the large street-front window to a stylish bar along the back wall. I came for breakfast and had the smoked salmon eggs Benedict, which were excellent, and then came back for lunch with local company that swore by the seafood bouillabaisse. Dinner is a more elaborate affair. You could

---

Tips Dining Money Matters

You'll find a 15% harmonized sales tax added to your bill before tip, so at better establishments you're looking at 30% (for tip and taxes) on top of the base price of your bill.

Most of the better downtown restaurants have mains in the C$20 to C$30 (US$17–US$26) price range. If that's a bit steep for your budget, you can order a soup or salad followed by an appetizer as your entree, a more economical—yet satisfying—way to try the best restaurants without breaking the bank. Or you may want to save some of the more expensive places for lunch rather than dinner; many of these establishments offer basically the same menu at lunch, but for less money.

Another tip: To try as many restaurants as possible when you're on a limited schedule, why not restaurant hop? Ordering a soup or salad with a glass of wine in one restaurant and then heading to another for a hot appetizer or entree (and another glass of wine!), and maybe a third for dessert and coffee is a terrific way to try the offerings of a greater number of places. This works especially well on Duckworth Street, where you'll find several very good—yet varied—restaurants close together.

Warning: Wine prices in the capital tend to be higher than elsewhere in the province. It's not uncommon to pay C$8 to C$10 (US$7–US$8.50) for a good glass of wine with dinner. Another somewhat more adventurous alternative is to go with the house wine, which can be as much as C$3 (US$2.60) cheaper per glass.

---

start by ordering lobster salad drizzled with warm garlic mayonnaise and then get serious with salmon stuffed with roasted red peppers and spinach for a main. A thoughtful wine list rounds out one of the city's premier dining experiences.

319 Water St. ℂ **709/754-2583.** www.blueonwater.com. Reservations recommended. Main courses C$20–C$29 (US$17–US$25). AE, MC, V. Mon–Fri 7:30am–9:30am and noon–2:30pm; daily 5:30–9:30pm.

Cabot Club ✿✿✿ CONTINENTAL   The harbor view in itself is worth the hefty prices you'll pay in this magnificent dining room at the Fairmont Newfoundland. Is it any wonder that the most elegant hotel in the city should be home to St. John's only four-diamond restaurant (so named by AAA/CAA)? You can be assured that the quality of service matches the impeccable quality of the food served at the Cabot Club. Menu selection includes everything from grilled caribou brushed with a partridge-berry and molasses demiglaze to a wonderful offering of Atlantic lobster in garam Marsala aioli served with a squash and lentil stew. The desserts are so decadent that the locals order them to take home. If you're a chocolate lover, try the chocolate Italiano. It's truly magnifico!

115 Cavendish Sq. ℂ **709/726-4980.** Reservations recommended. AE, DC, DISC, MC, V. Main courses C$24–C$37 (US$21–US$32). Daily 6–10pm.

Magnum & Steins ✿✿ *Finds* CONTEMPORARY   It's one of those rare establishments that actually lives up to its promotional persona: Magnum & Steins bills itself as a creative dining experience. And it is. From your first glimpse of its audacious sidewalk presentation (oversize metal signage, floor-to-ceiling windows) you immediately recognize that this restaurant is dramatically different from anything else in the city. The bold metallic accents continue inside, where a steel-plated winding staircase invites you to the upstairs dining room. But regardless of the artistic merit of your surroundings, they are no more (and no less!) than the perfect setting for the *pièce de résistance:* the food. Each dish is a masterful creation, blending layers of subtle flavor with complementary colors and extraordinary plate arrangement. The result is gourmet. The menu reflects modern trends extending from Toronto to California. Brie, leek, and apple in phyllo pastry sparkles as a starter while for a main, choices run from roast rack of lamb to cedar-planked maple salmon.

284 Duckworth St. ⓒ **709/576-6500**. Reservations recommended. Main courses C$21–C$34 (US$18–US$29). AE, DC, MC, V. Mon–Fri noon–2pm; daily 6–10pm.

MODERATE

Bonavista CANADIAN   This informal dining room at the Fairmont Newfoundland is bright and cheery, and offers a more relaxed setting than its formal counterpart, the Cabot Club (see above). The Bonavista is highly regarded among locals for its terrific "Newfoundland buffet," served every Thursday night. The daily breakfast buffet is particularly good value while the Monday-to-Friday lunch buffet attracts a mix of local businesspeople and visitors. Friday and Saturday nights there is a special menu revolving around juicy prime rib. The one thing I didn't like about the layout of this eating area is that it isn't fully enclosed, so that other people in the hotel can watch you eat as they walk past.

Fairmont Newfoundland, 115 Cavendish Sq. ⓒ **709/726-4944**. Reservations not required. AE, DC, DISC, MC, V. Breakfast buffet C$14 (US$12); lunch buffet C$16 (US$14); dinner main courses C$13–C$24 (US$11–US$21). Mon–Fri 6:30am–10pm; Sat–Sun 7:30am–10pm.

Oliver's 𝕮𝕮 NORTH AMERICAN   Here you'll find classic dishes served in Mediterranean-style comfort with cozy booths that are large enough for a group of friends and intimate enough for a romantic duo (although there are a couple of tables

---

Harbor Cruising

Without a doubt, the best views of the city are from the tables offered by **Atlantic Ocean Dinner Cruises** (ⓒ **877/834-6663** or 709/834-6663; www.atlanticoceandinnercruises.com), which offers lunch and dinner aboard their covered vessel that slowly makes its way around the harbor. Departures are from Pier 7 along Harbour Drive. The pace is leisurely and the ambience casual yet professional. Menus change weekly, with dinner a three-course affair that may include choices such as baked cod or stuffed pork tenderloin.

Lunch cruises last two hours and depart May to October at noon. The cost is C$37 (US$32) adults, C$19 (US$17) children. Dinner cruises depart year-round daily at 7pm and last between 3 and 4 hours. For this trip, all ages pay C$68 (US$59), but the cruise is best suited for adults.

that are too close to their neighbor for comfort). The Cajun jambalaya pasta is a deliciously spiced medley of shrimp and chicken, served over perfect al dente linguine. And the jumbo scallops marinara is a low-fat menu choice so sinfully tasty that you won't feel the least bit deprived. But my personal favorite is the salmon baked in a citrus-flavored herb crust. Their wine list also deserves some attention. Oliver's stocks more than 500 wines, and selects several different varieties to feature as their house wine of the day.

160 Water St. ✆ 709/754-6444. www.olivers-cafe.com. Dinner reservations recommended. Main courses C$14–C$27 (US$12–US$23). AE, DC, MC, V. Sun–Wed 10am–10pm; Thurs–Fri 10:30am–11pm; Sat 9:30am–11pm.

Pepper Mill ⚔ NOUVELLE   Owner Eric Collins says his restaurant offers "Haute cuisine without the haute attitude." He's right! It's a casual, comfortable place, yet the food is second to none. The Pepper Mill specializes in soups and generally has five to choose from each day. Other healthy choices include a good assortment of salads (which come in two sizes). Try the scallops sautéed in white wine and garlic for a starter. The daily dinner specials include such delicacies as arctic char (farmed locally and served trout-style with a citrus sauce). If you come here in the winter, request a table in the back of the restaurant. Patrons closest to the door are apt to feel the draft.

178 Water St. ✆ 709/726-7585. Reservations recommended. Main courses C$14–C$27 (US$12–US$27). AE, DC, MC, V. Daily noon–2pm and 5–9:30pm.

Rumpelstiltskin's CANADIAN   A casual and informal atmosphere, with harbor views from some tables. Typical of hotel dining, the multi-page menu has something for everyone: teriyaki chicken, creamy shrimp and scallop pasta, prime rib of beef, single-serve pizza, and more, lots more. Save room for one of their excellent desserts. A personal favorite is the Very Berry Cheesecake, a truly decadent creation topped with raspberry mousse.

Quality Hotel, 2 Hill O'Chips. ✆ 709/579-6000. Reservations not necessary. Main courses C$6.95–C$20 (US$5.95–US$17). AE, DC, MC, V. Sun–Thurs 7am–10pm; Fri–Sat 7am–10:30pm.

Spirit's Pub & Thai Room ⚔⚔ THAI   A traditional pub where you can choose from over 80 beers on tap while poring over a menu of fresh and innovative Thai cooking. The usual favorites, such as pad Thai, are all there, along with dishes that take advantage of local seafood, such as the cod, pan-fried in a spicy coconut cream sauce. Other highlights include the mango and water chestnut salad, and peanut and sesame-crusted beef tenderloin. On Tuesday between 8 and 10pm, it costs just C$10 (US$8.50) to taste five beers, order a full pint of your favorite, and have an accompanying appetizer.

390 Duckworth St. ✆ 709/722-0911. Reservations recommended on weekends. Main courses C$10–C$26 (US$8.50–US$23). AE, MC, V. Daily 11am–10pm.

Velma's NEWFOUNDLAND   Locals swear by Velma's for its traditional cooking, while many of the folk from elsewhere in the province swear it's the only place they'll eat when visiting the capital. And while Newfies may find Velma's well within their comfort zone, outsiders may be a little put off by a menu filled with deep-fried cooking that, in my humble opinion, is no better or worse than you can find in any small-town restaurant across the province. But it is what it is—a friendly spot with moderately priced seafood. A hearty starter is the pea soup filled with salted beef, or stick with seafood and order cod cakes. For a main, a couple of platter-type combos provide the opportunity to try a little of everything, including cod tongues.

264 Water St. ✆ 709/576-2264. Reservations not necessary. Main courses C$8–C$16 (US$7–US$14). MC, V, Interac. Daily 8am–9:30pm.

Fun Fact **A Local Delicacy**

Boiled corned beef and cabbage, along with potatoes, carrots, parsnip, turnip, and peas pudding (made from dried, split peas) was a dietary staple in Newfoundland in the days before modern refrigeration. It was also the favorite meal for Mr. Jiggs, a character in an American comic strip. Hence the nickname Jiggs Dinner.

INEXPENSIVE

Green Sleeves Pub, Lounge & Restaurant ⊛ BAR AND GRILL   It's like having three restaurants in one, all offering the same menu but completely different dining experiences. The main floor is a pub—complete with boisterous patrons, video lottery terminals, and smoking. Upstairs is a more subdued, civilized environment with table linens and no smoking. Outside is a multilevel open-air deck; the preferred choice for midday relaxation on a sunny afternoon. If you're in the mood for finger food, try the wings. They're the best chicken wings in the city, with a secret dry-spice mix that's zesty on its own, or you can boost the zing with a mild, medium, or hot dipping sauce. For a more substantial main course, choose the chicken savoyarde (tender chicken breast with mushrooms and onions in a sour cream and bacon sauce, tossed with linguine). It's a house specialty.

14 George St. ℂ **709/579-1070.** Main courses C$6.95–C$14 (US$5.95–US$12). AE, DC, MC, V. Sun 10am–10pm; Mon 11am–10pm; Tues–Fri 11am–9:30pm; Sat 10am–9:30pm.

Guv'nor Pub & Eatery ⊛ PUB FARE   You'll want to come here for the atmosphere of this very English-style pub. Although it can be moderately boisterous if a bunch of students are on hand (it's close to Memorial University), the comfortable booths give you enough space and privacy to still enjoy your meal. The lasagna (served with garlic toast) is exceptionally good for pub fare. And the soup of the day (a turkey-, chicken-, or beef-vegetable variation) has a tasty broth that'll have you swiping the bowl with your dinner roll. Menu selection is very broad, including local specialties such as rabbit and caribou potpies. The Guv'nor also has a location downtown at 210 Water St., in the McMurdo Building (ℂ **709/738-3018**), but it lacks the ambience of the Elizabeth Avenue location.

389 Elizabeth Ave. ℂ **709/726-3053.** Reservations not necessary. Main courses C$8–C$16 (US$7–US$14). AE, DC, MC, V. Sun–Mon 9am–11pm; Tues–Sat 9am–midnight.

Moo Moo's Ice Cream ICE CREAM   If it's a warm day, you'll find hordes of locals gravitating to Moo Moo's. Housed in a building boldly painted to look like a black-and-white Holstein cow, Moo Moo's has excellent homemade ice cream. The orange-pineapple flavor is especially refreshing.

88 King's Rd. ℂ **709/753-0999.** No reservations. Single scoop C$4.50 (US$4). MC, V. Daily 9am–11pm.

Nautical Nellies ⊛⊛ *Value* PUB FARE   From the road, this pub looks rather nondescript, but once inside, your eyes will quickly become accustomed to the dim lighting and the friendly bar staff will quickly welcome you with a choice draft beers and a menu of traditional Newfoundland cooking. It's always crowded—especially from the start of Friday happy hour until closing. And, as you can tell from a quick conversation with any of those with Scottish, British, or Australian accents seated at the bar, it's the preferred hangout of visiting oil industry personnel. Why? Because it's the ideal place to have an ale and unwind, a true pub where staff know their regulars by name and drink preference. The food is excellently prepared and generously portioned(even at lunch, where one meal is probably enough for two people. Their pan-fried cod with sides of pork scruncheons and rice is delicious. The crab spring roll appetizers are similarly exceptional.

201 Water St. (C) 709/738-1120. No reservations. Main courses C$12–C$18 (US$11–US$16). AE, DC, MC, V. Sun 11am–3pm; Mon–Thurs 11:30am–3pm and 5–9pm; Fri 11:30am–3pm; Sat 11:30am–3pm and 5–9pm.

5 Exploring St. John's

Many of the capital city's most well-known attractions are within walking distance of downtown lodgings, while a few others such as Fort Amherst, Signal Hill, Cape Spear, and Quidi Vidi require some sort of transportation to access. Unless you have mobility problems, the best way to explore the downtown area is on foot. In general, local motorists are courteous (they have to be, because pedestrians have a tendency to just walk into traffic(especially downtown), so you don't have to worry about taking your life in your hands when you step off the curb. Another great thing is that walking doesn't cost anything, and many of the buildings you'll want to see or stop at have either no—or a very small—admission. So take your time and enjoy what's around you.

Warning: Downtown parking meters are strictly monitored, so you're best off parking in a lot if you're unsure of the amount of time you'll need. The maximum amount of time you can buy on a meter is 2 hours. Parking meters are free on weekends and after 6pm weekdays.

DOWNTOWN ATTRACTIONS

Anglican Cathedral of St. John the Baptist   This National Historic Site was built between 1843 and 1885, with some reconstruction necessary following the Great Fire of 1892. The massive cathedral's Gothic architecture gives it a somewhat eerie presence, making the church an excellent meeting point for participants of the St. John's Haunted Hike, held late on summer evenings. (See more about this attraction in the "Walking Tours" section later in this chapter.) A small museum is on-site. During July and August, you can include a stop for tea weekday afternoons (2:30–4:30pm) at the Cathedral Crypt Tea Room (ℭ **709/726-1999**) for C$7 (US$6).

22 Church Hill (at Gower St.). (C) 709/726-5677. Free tours June–Sept daily 10am–5pm.

Up In Smoke

St. John's has been the victim of three "Great Fires." According to history, the first was actually a combination of two fires that took place in November 1817 (on the 7th and 21st). Together, they caused about $4 million in damage and destroyed almost 400 homes. The second major conflagration happened in June 1946, again causing $4 million in damage. But these were just sparks compared to the biggest fire of them all: the Great Fire of 1892. From a dropped pipe in a hay stable, the flames grew to nightmarish proportions. At its height, the heat was so intense it melted glass from windows throughout the city, most notably the Anglican Cathedral. When the smoke cleared, one-third of the city's population (10,000 people) were homeless.

Government House   Completed in 1831 for the Governor of Newfoundland (the island was an independent democracy until it joined Canadian Confederation in 1949), Government House is one of the city's few architectural treasures to have survived the Great Fire of 1892. Built of locally quarried sandstone, it has a number of intriguing features, including a surrounding ditch that allows the basement to fill with natural light. The magnificent property reportedly cost four times more to complete than the U.S. White House (built the same year). Today, Government House is the official residence of Newfoundland and Labrador's lieutenant governor. The lovely grounds feature flower gardens and a place to have a relaxing stroll.

Military Rd. at King's Bridge Rd. Ⓒ **709/729-4494.** www.mun.ca/govhouse. Free admission. Grounds daily 9am–dusk.

James J. O'Mara Pharmacy Museum   This Provincial Heritage Site is a good spot to visit if you've always been fascinated by pharmacies and the dispensing of prescription medicines. This heritage drug store was built in 1895 and is particularly interesting because of its Art Nouveau/Art Deco amalgam design. Inside, you can see a set of original drugstore fixtures made in England in 1879 that found its way to St. John's, and an assortment of antique apothecary bottles.

488 Water St. (at Brennan St.). Ⓒ **709/753-5877.** Free admission. June to late Aug daily 10am–5pm; by appointment only the rest of the year.

Newfoundland Science Centre *Kids*   Contagiously enthusiastic scientific presentations that will motivate kids to experiment with all kinds of gross, goofy stuff. Here, they can walk like a dinosaur, build a castle, try out the "astronaut toilet," or even race with a bubble. A small section is dedicated to insects, fossil digs, and the telephone. And the interactive Space Odyssey display is way cool (with the magic of computer simulation, you, too, can blast off to Mars!). Just don't use the dreaded "e" word (educational). The Newfoundland Science Centre is very much a learning experience, but what the kids don't know won't hurt them.

Murray Premises, 5 Beck's Cove. Ⓒ **709/754-0823.** www.nlsciencecentre.com. Admission C$6 (US$5.15) adults, C$4.25 (US$3.65) students and seniors, free for children under 2, C$20 (US$17) family. Mon–Fri 10am–5pm; Sat 10am–6pm; Sun noon–6pm.

Newman Wine Vaults   These stone and brick vaults, constructed in the late 18th or very early part of the 19th century, were used by Newman & Co. (a British wine merchant) until at least 1893—possibly as late as 1914—to age their fine port. It started by accident in 1679, when a Newman's ship had been diverted to the island of Newfoundland to escape pirates and ended up storing its precious cargo in caves during that winter. When the crew returned to England with their port the following year, they discovered that its flavor had improved dramatically. Newman then began a cross-Atlantic custom of bringing its port to Newfoundland for aging in wine cellars, and eventually in these vaults, now a Provincial Historic Site. Allow yourself 20 minutes to explore.

436 Water St. (north side, just west of Springdale St.). Ⓒ **709/739-7870.** Free admission. Mid-June to Aug daily 10am–4:30pm.

Railway Coastal Museum *Kids*   There's something strangely compelling about trains. Whatever it is, the mystique carries over to this museum, which is contained within the former Newfoundland Railway Station, a grandiose stone structure that was once the province's main railway station. Meticulously renovated, displays within

Spa at the Monastery

If exploring the capital leaves you exhausted, let the **Spa at the Monastery** take you on a journey of renewal. The only facility of its kind in the province, this day spa has 40 well-trained staff eager to pamper you. The most popular treatments include the wonderful hydrotherapy (C$45/US$39) and the Ayurveda Bindi herbal body therapy (C$80/US$69), the spa's specialty. Reservations aren't just recommended, they're essential(unless you're lucky enough to step into a cancellation.

The spa is at 63 Patrick St. (© **709/754-5800**; www.monastery-spa.com). Follow Water Street out of downtown to Patrick. Hours are Monday to Saturday 10am to 9pm, Sunday 10am to 6pm. A boutique, salon, and cafe are on-site, where they make some dynamite strawberry smoothies.

the building tell the story of the narrow-gauge Newfoundland Railway, which operated between 1880 and 1988, and extended all the way from St. John's to Port-aux-Basques. Kids especially will be captivated by the 1940s passenger train diorama as well as the automated train model. All aboard!

495 Water St. W. © **866/600-7245** or 709/724-5929. www.railwaycoastalmuseum.ca. Admission C$5 (US$4.30) adults, C$4 (US$3.50) seniors and students, C$3 (US$2.60) children 5–17, free for under age 5, C$12 (US$11) family rate. June to mid-Oct Mon–Sat 10am–5pm, Sun noon–5pm; the rest of the year Tues–Sun noon–5pm.

Roman Catholic Basilica Parish of St. John the Baptist   The twin towers of the Basilica are a striking landmark in the city and can be seen rising high above its surroundings. You are free to tour this magnificent old stone church (a National Historic Site) of Romanesque design, built between 1841 and 1855, at any time other than during Mass, which is held Sunday at 10:30am, Tuesday at 7pm, Wednesday to Friday at 9:30am, and Saturday at 5pm. You are, of course, welcome to attend Mass.

The affiliated Basilica Cathedral Museum, in an adjacent residence, holds a treasured collection of books, oil paintings, sacred vessels, and a massive oak table dating to the late 1800s.

200 Military Rd. © **709/726-3660**. www.thebasilica.ca. Entry to the church is free; C$2 (US$1.75) for anyone over 12 to tour the Basilica Cathedral Museum. Mon–Sat 11am–4pm.

The Rooms ♠♠♠   This cultural oasis—combining the provincial museum, art gallery, and archives—is the one place you just must visit while in St. John's. Located on a hill above downtown, the design of The Rooms pays tribute to the traditional lifestyle of Newfoundland and Labrador. "Fishing rooms" were buildings along the shoreline where fish were processed and where nets and other fishing equipment were stored. While the design has historic connotations, the interior is contemporary and slick, with state-of-the-art technology used to tell the story of Newfoundland and Labrador's natural and human history. The main display area is Connections: This Place and its Early Peoples, which tells the story of human habitation that began as the last Ice Age ended 9,000 years ago. Another point of interest is that Fort Townshend, the site of The Rooms, is itself an archaeological treasure, as a late-18th-century strategic fortification and also once the residence and seat of early Newfoundland governors. An exhibit dedicated to the fort's history leads outside to the actual grounds.

A portion of The Rooms is devoted to the **Provincial Art Gallery,** which has the same hours as the main museum and is included in admission. It is the province's largest public gallery, housing more than 7,000 works on two floors. The emphasis is on contemporary Canadian art (but there's only a small sampling of this on display), including traditional and mixed media. The permanent collection features major works by nationally recognized artists as well as hooked mats made by women who live in the many outport communities throughout Newfoundland and Labrador.

9 Bonaventure Ave. ⓒ **709/757-8020.** www.therooms.ca. Admission C$5 (US$4.30) adults, C$4 (US$3.50) seniors and students, C$3 (US$2.60) children 6–16, free for under age 6 (free admission for everyone Wed 6–9pm and on the first Sat of every month). June to mid-Oct Mon–Sat 9am–5pm, Sun noon–5pm, with extended hours to 9pm Wed–Thurs; mid-Oct to May Tues–Sat 9am–5pm, Sun noon–5pm.

SIGNAL HILL

Take Duckworth Street east through downtown, pass below the imposing Fairmont Newfoundland, and you'll soon find yourself on Signal Hill Road, which leads to the following two attractions.

Johnson Geo Centre ✿✿ *Kids*   What better place than the Rock to have a world-class geology center? But this is much more than a rock exhibit. A glass-walled elevator carries you three stories underground to the floor of the main reception hall, where you are greeted by an oversize 3-D display of the solar system. Your next stop is the Geo Theatre for a dramatic presentation (with voiceover by actor Gordon Pinsent) on plate tectonics and continental formation. From there, it's impossible not to be intrigued by the exposed bedrock along one side of the cavernous room. Water bottles encourage you to spray the wall—thereby revealing the nuances of the 550-million-year-old granite. The main display areas are divided into four themes: Our Planet, describing how the Earth was formed; Our Province, telling the story of Newfoundland and Labrador's 4-billion-year natural history; Our People, dedicated to explaining human relationships to the natural world; and Our Future, which touches on subjects such as energy needs of generations to come. Allow a minimum of 1 hour to visit—more if anyone in your party has a fascination with the natural world.

175 Signal Hill Rd. ⓒ **866/868-7625** or 709/737-7880. www.geocentre.ca. Admission C$7.50 (US$6.50) adults, C$6 (US$5.15) seniors and students, C$3.50 (US$3) children and youth 5–17, free for children under 5, C$18 (US$16) family. Open Mon–Sat 9:30am–5pm, Sun 1–5pm; Oct 16–May 15, closed Mon.

Signal Hill National Historic Site ✿✿✿   Rising 183m (600 ft.) above the entrance to St. John's Harbour, this is the city's granite guardian. The harbor and city views alone make a drive to the top worthwhile, but as a National Historic Site it also has much significance as a lookout post. The military history of this site is well explained at the informative Interpretive Centre halfway up the hill. You'd be wise to stop here and learn about the site before you head to the next level. Between the Interpretive Centre and the top of Signal Hill you'll find a restored cannon battery pointed seaward, much as it was when it was necessary to protect the settlement from marauding pirates or warring nations.

At the top of the hill is Cabot Tower, a stone tower built in 1897 to commemorate the 400th anniversary of John Cabot's landing at St. John's. Inside, displays tell the story of the site, including that of Guglielmo Marconi, who received the first transatlantic wireless message from the hill in 1901. On the tower's second floor, ham radio enthusiasts operate a small station through summer. While visitors can access the roof of the Tower, it's not advisable on windy days—particularly not with children. The winds here can get very high and could literally pull a small child out of your arms.

Try to time your visit to take in the Signal Hill Military Tattoo, held below Cabot Tower 4 days a week during the summer (Wed, Thurs, Sat, and Sun), at 3pm and 7pm. The colorful artillery and military drumming display takes you back to the days when this site was of paramount importance to the safety of St. John's. It costs C$2 (US$1.75) for a close-up seat, or watch (and listen) from afar for free.

If you're feeling really energetic, and I mean *really* energetic, you can tackle the 896-step descent that skirts the seaward side of Signal Hill. The view from the trail is breathtakingly beautiful. But don't be deceived: it's also very dangerous. If you do the complete walk, there are sections where only 1.5m (5 ft.) of terra firma and an iron chain hammered into the rock separate you from a 61m (200-ft.) drop. Not recommended for children, pets, or acrophobics.

Signal Hill Rd. ✆ **709/772-5367**. Admission charge to tour the Interpretive Centre and Cabot Tower C$3.50 (US$3) adults, C$2.50 (US$2.15) seniors and children. May 15–Oct 15 10am–6pm daily.

QUIDI VIDI ✿✿✿

Pronounced "kiddee viddee," the historical fishing village of Quidi Vidi quite literally has something for everyone. Its namesake, Quidi Vidi Lake, is the site of the Royal St. John's Regatta (see more about this in the "Festivals & Special Events" section below).

A self-guided walking trail around Quidi Vidi Lake provides information about the local history and the opportunity to enjoy the outdoors. Plan to spend most of the day in Quidi Vidi Village. It's just minutes from the modern world of downtown St. John's, yet a historical world away. Across the tiny, picture-perfect harbor, your imagination will be captured by the sheds and stages seemingly suspended from the side of a cliff. They are accessible only by boat. (*Note:* The village has no inn, but the Stagehead Restaurant serves a fine lunch.)

Mallard Cottage Antiques and Collectibles   In the heart of the village, you'll find this character-filled shop ensconced in North America's oldest cottage. Here, you can purchase some lovely collectibles and antiques. If the door is locked when you arrive, just cross the street. The owner, Peg, lives there and will be pleased to open up for you.

2 Barrows Rd., Quidi Vidi. ✆ **709/576-2266**. Daily 10am–5pm.

Quidi Vidi Battery   At this Provincial Historic Site you can learn more about the military presence in old St. John's. The Battery was first erected in 1762 by the French. It was later rebuilt by the British and has been restored to around 1812. The knowledgeable interpretive guides in period costume make history come alive.

Cuckhold's Cove Rd., Quidi Vidi. ✆ **709/729-2977**. Admission C$3.50 (US$3) age 13 and up. Mid-June to early Sept daily 10am–4pm.

Quidi Vidi Brewery   If you're a beer drinker, consider a tour of Quidi Vidi Brewery, a microbrewery offering six great brews. The 1892 Dark Ale is fantastic, and the Honey Brown and Eric's Cream Ale are also very nice. The Northern Lager and Northern Light are pretty standard offerings. If you're looking for something really different, try the Kriek cherry beer. It's uniquely refreshing on a hot summer's day.

15 Barrows Rd. ✆ **800/738-0165** or 709/738-4040. www.newfoundlandbeer.com. Tour cost is C$3.50 (US$3) adults. Weekday tours are offered year-round and run hourly beginning at 1pm.

SOUTH SIDE OF THE HARBOR

Cape Spear 🖈🖈   Cape Spear is the most easterly point in North America and protected as a National Historic Site for its lighthouse, which was built in 1832. The lightkeeper's residence has been restored and allows a glimpse at daily life at this remote outpost in the mid-1800s. History aside, the cape is worth visiting for its naturally dramatic setting. You may be amazed at how different its weather can be from that in the city—it's situated just 15 minutes and 11km (7 miles) south of St. John's, but you may feel as much as a 59°F (15°C) temperature difference. Be sure to bring a sweater or jacket along with you. Allow at least 1½ hours to tour the visitor center, lighthouse, and gift shop, more if you'd like to linger and watch for whales along the coast.

Cape Spear Rd. (heading out of town, Water St. provides access to Cape Spear Rd.). 🅒 **709/772-5367.** Lighthouse tour C$4 (US$3.50) adults, C$3 (US$2.60) seniors and children. Grounds open year-round; guided tours May 15–Oct 15 daily 10am–6pm.

Fort Amherst   The former lightkeeper's house at the Fort Amherst light station has been privately restored and now houses a small museum, photo gallery, craft shop, and a lovely tearoom with breathtaking view. Local military, lighthouse, and community history is interpreted in each room. The original lighthouse at this spot was put into operation in 1813 and was the first on the island of Newfoundland. The current structure dates to 1952. Fort Amherst is across the Narrows from Signal Hill—a reminder of just how much protecting St. John's must have needed in its early days. It takes a bit of an effort to get there, but makes for a pleasant outing.

Step Back In Time at Petty Harbour/Maddox Cove

If you don't have the time or resources to tour the outlying regions of the province, try to make it to Petty Harbour/Maddox Cove. It's only a 15-minute drive to the capital city, and a favorite stop for visitors touring Cape Spear.

Petty Harbour is the most picturesque part of the community, a fact recognized by filmmakers, who have used the town as a backdrop for a number of feature films (*Orca, A Whale for the Killing, John and the Missus*). As you can tell from the number of boats around the harbor, as well as the old-time wooden wharves, this is a vibrant fishing community—and has been for more than 500 years. Even the name reflects its maritime heritage (Petty is derived from the French word "petite," meaning "small").

This is a great place to stay if you'd like to be near but out of the city, or if you're hiking along the East Coast Trail. Spend a night with Reg and Mil Carter at the **Orca Inn Bed & Breakfast.** Weather permitting, you can have breakfast on the deck, looking out on the harbor. Call 🅒 **877/747-9676** or 709/747-9676, or visit them on the Web at www.orcainn.nf.ca for more info. The village also has an interesting antiques and flea market shop by the town's bridge. Herbie's Olde Shoppe is a craft store worth visiting just so you can see its interior: until recently, it was a traditional, working, rural grocery.

To get to Petty Harbour/Maddox Cove, take Route 11 (Cape Spear Rd.) south from downtown.

Prosser's Rock Boat Basin. (Traffic to Fort Amherst is restricted because of the narrowness of the road and lack of parking. You can park at Prosser's Rock and walk the rest of the way. It's not a difficult walk, but be aware of it. To get there, go west on Water St. until you reach the turnoff for Cape Spear Dr., at the intersection of Leslie and Water sts. Turn left at the traffic light; go over the bridge, then turn left again. This will take you along the south side of the harbor and to Prosser's Rock.) ✆ **709/368-6102.** Admission C$2 (US$1.75). June–Sept Mon–Fri noon–8pm, Sat–Sun 10am–8pm.

ACADEMIA

Don't be put off by the heading—the local university holds something of interest for everyone. Established in 1925, the Memorial University of Newfoundland sprawls across a wide swath of land adjacent to Pippy Park on the north side of downtown. The student population is 17,000 and it employs over 3,000 full-time staff. Although no general campus tours are offered, each of the following departments operates its own visitor program.

Fluvarium ✮✮ (Kids) If you're interested in what's underwater in the local freshwater ponds, the Fluvarium is a great place to visit. Within this distinctive octagonal building, you'll learn about three distinct freshwater habitats and see a free-range fish habitat, a deepwater display of brown trout, and many interactive displays. You're looking through a glass wall at the underwater world outdoors, so it's best not to visit immediately after a rain as the water will be cloudier and visibility poorer. Allow no less than 1½ hours to visit, more if you'd like to enjoy the surrounding hiking trails. Feeding time is at 4pm, so it's best to arrive around 3pm.

Nagle's Place, off Allandale Rd. ✆ **709/754-3474.** www.fluvarium.ca. C$6 (US$5.15) adults, C$5 (US$4.30) seniors and students, C$4 (US$3.50) children 5 and older, free for children under 5, C$18 (US$15) family rate. Summer daily 9am–5pm; rest of year Mon–Sat 10am–4:30pm, Sun noon–4:30pm.

Institute for Ocean Technology ✮ (Finds) The free tours offered by the Institute for Ocean Technology are fantastic. Most visitors wouldn't think of St. John's as a locale boasting such advanced technology, but this facility does scale-model testing on boats and ships: everything from Coast Guard ice breakers to America's Cup yachts and oil platforms. The institute has three test tanks: a 90m-long (295-ft.) Ice Tank, which simulates an Arctic environment; a 200m-long (660-ft.) Tow Tank, where scaled models are pulled through simulated waves and wind scenarios; and the Offshore Engineering Basin, complete with waves and a simulated retractable beach! Just as with the Marine Institute (see the listing below), a full slate of activities may not be scheduled for the day you plan to visit, so when you phone ask what's going on that day.

Kerwin Place, Memorial University Campus. ✆ **709/772-4366.** http://iot-ito.nrc-cnrc.gc.ca. Reservations required for the free tours, conducted May–Aug Mon–Fri 9am–4:30pm. Children under 10 are not permitted.

Marine Institute Affiliated with the Memorial University of Newfoundland, the Marine Institute teaches everything from fishing techniques to sea rescue. You can see the world's largest flume tank where actual-size fishing gear is lowered: from the amphitheater observatory it's like looking into a huge aquarium. There's also a marine simulator room where captains are trained and tested. Computer screens at the institute can simulate various harbors from around the world, creating virtual storms and causing the floor to move while students navigate their way on the screens. Both rooms are extremely interesting if in use but not nearly as exciting if you happen to visit while nothing is scheduled.

155 Ridge Rd. ✆ **800/563-5799** or 709/778-0200. www.mi.mun.ca. Free tours conducted during the summer Mon–Fri 1:30 and 3pm. Call in advance for reservations or to see what's happening that day.

Finding Your Lucky Rock

While in the area of the Ocean Sciences Centre, be sure to stop in at **Middle Cove Beach** and look for your lucky rock! Many Newfoundlanders believe that finding a stone with a complete white line (the white line is calcite) around it will bring you good luck. And finding one with a double white line is said to bring you double the luck.

Memorial University Botanical Garden   If you're curious about the province's flora, you should make your way over to the 110-hectare (272-acre) Botanical Garden, linked to the main campus by walking trail and accessible by road via Nagle's Place. Plants are tastefully arranged by theme—one section is devoted to boreal species, another to wetlands. I found the barrens garden most interesting, and it made visiting the barrens at places like Burnt Cape Ecological Reserve (see "Northern Peninsula" in chapter 8) more meaningful. There are also walking trails that take you down to Oxen Pond. Give yourself a couple of hours to enjoy the setting. The on-site gift shop is filled with floral-themed arts and crafts with a cafe open daily for light snacks and afternoon tea.

306 Mt. Scio Rd. (C) **709/737-8590**. www.mun.ca/botgarden. Admission C$4 (US$3.50) adults, C$3 (US$2.60) seniors and students, C$1.50 (US$1.25) children ages 6–18, free for children under 5. May–Sept daily 10am–5pm; Oct–Apr daily 10am–4pm.

Ocean Sciences Centre ✿ *Finds* *Kids*   Just a short 5km (3-mile) drive from St. John's you'll find the Ocean Sciences Centre, an oceanfront research facility for studying ocean ecology, oceanography, and fisheries. The building itself is not open to the public (except by guided tour), as it is strictly a research facility, but outside you can see seals joyfully frolicking in large outdoor tanks and kids can examine whale bones and small ocean creatures in a touch tank—all for free. Plans are under way to construct an Ocean Sciences Research Aquarium, which will be on the shores of Logy Bay, adjacent to the Ocean Sciences Centre. Check their website for updates. Even if you don't arrange for a tour, the outdoor exhibits are still worth the drive.

Marine Lab Rd. (take Rte. 30 [Logy Bay Rd.] onto Marine Dr. to get to Marine Lab Rd.). (C) **709/737-3706**. www.osc.mun.ca. Tour cost C$4.50 (US$4) adults, C$3.50 (US$3) children. Tours June to early Sept every half-hour 10am–5pm.

6 Festivals & Special Events

The atmosphere in St. John's is festive year-round, but especially so during the first week of August, when you'll find the province's three largest events—the **Newfoundland & Labrador Folk Festival,** the **George Street Festival,** and the **Royal St. John's Regatta**—happening simultaneously.

George Street Festival   One word best describes the George Street Festival—*wild!* If you don't like crowds, loud music, and lots of noise, best not to visit George Street during the first week of August. That's when you'll find bands playing on the street and in the 20 pubs and clubs that occupy this two-block stretch of rowdydom. But if you *do* like great music—and standing shoulder-to-shoulder with your fellow enthusiasts—check it out!

Not just for the 19-to-25 crowd, over a 6-day period the George Street Festival provides cheap—but great—entertainment of most music types, from rock to bluegrass, country, and Celtic, and for all ages. And you're allowed to walk freely on the street—beer in hand—until 3am. But navigating your way down the street can be tough. Not just from the amount of beer you're likely to consume, but because it's difficult to find a place to walk. It's as crowded—and rowdy—as you'll find any evening on Bourbon Street in New Orleans (perhaps except during Mardi Gras). No advance tickets required. Just show up and politely nudge your way in. The street is closed off to traffic during the festival. Ticket booths are by Trapper John's (George St. at Bishop's Cove) and at the other end of George Street at Adelaide, by the Sundance Saloon and Kelly's Pub.

George St. (between Queen's Rd. and Bate's Hill). ℭ **709/685-9232** or 709/576-5990, or drop in to any George St. pub for a schedule of performers and additional info.

Newfoundland & Labrador Folk Festival   This festival is most rewarding because of its size. It's not like many larger festivals throughout North America where you're one very small part of a massive sea of fans, waving with excitement in the wind, but rather the crowds are smaller and the performances more personal.

The event takes place the first full weekend in August, beginning on the Friday night and concluding with singing of the **"Ode to Newfoundland"** on Sunday evening. The Ode was the national anthem of Newfoundland when it was an independent nation, and was written by Sir Cavendish Boyle while he was Britain's governor of Newfoundland between 1901 and 1904.

Most of the entertainment is top-notch local, and of a bluegrass or Celtic nature. There are booths where you can purchase the performers' music, as well as watch artisans blowing glass and turning woodcrafts. Others are selling pottery, jewelry, dyed silks, and T-shirts. Reasonably priced food can be purchased at booths on-site, and of course there's the expected beer tent, where you can purchase beer, wine, or coolers. You can't take your alcoholic beverage out of the beer tent, but you can see the stage and hear the music from the open-sided tent.

Bannerman Park (enter from Military Rd.). ℭ **709/576-8508.** www.sjfac.nf.net. Regular weekend pass C$40 (US$35) adults, C$20 (US$17) seniors and children 12–18; evening and afternoon sessions C$10 (US$8.50) adults, C$5 (US$4.30) seniors and children 12–18; free for children age 12 and under.

Royal St. John's Regatta   This is the event of all events in St. John's. And it's the only civic holiday in all of North America that's weather dependent! The Regatta started in 1825 and is the oldest continuous sporting event in North America. The excitement centers on a day of fixed-seat rowing races in six-man (or -woman) sculls. It's normally held on the first Wednesday of August—if you wake up that morning and the weather is windy or wet, the best thing to do is turn on the radio or TV to find out whether the Regatta has been postponed. If it's on, head down to Quidi Vidi Lake and have yourself a great time.

The action centers on teams of rowers challenging one another in a series of races. You'll also find dozens of food booths, games of chance, rides for the kids, and small items such as jewelry for sale. Moo Moo's homemade Newfoundland ice cream has a booth offering delicious treats. Another local favorite is the Hiscock's Wedge Fries truck from Grand Falls. Make sure to try the grilled shish kabob (marinated pork cubes skewered with onions). Where else can you get a country-fair atmosphere with free entertainment, free admission, and a day's worth of inexpensive family fun within 5-minutes' drive of a city's downtown?

Quidi Vidi Lake (take King's Bridge Rd. to Lakeview Ave.). ℭ **709/576-8921.** www.stjohnsregatta.org. Free admission. Parking can be a problem; be prepared for a long walk. 1st Wed of Aug, weather permitting. Races run continually from 8:30am–6pm.

7 Outdoor Activities

The city of St. John's is full of parks and a great place to enjoy the outdoors. Whether you just want to take a leisurely walk and smell the flowers or you're looking to be educated along the way, there are a number of good options from which to choose. The city is small, so seeing it on a big motorcoach tour should be a last resort. (That mode of travel is best reserved for touring other regions of the province and will be touched on in subsequent chapters.) To best enjoy the full flavor of St. John's, take a walk or a carriage ride and see the city slowly—as it should be seen.

If you're a golfer, you'll be pleased to learn that Newfoundland and Labrador has a number of fine courses and that some of them can be found right in St. John's. The best-groomed 18-hole course in the city is the Osprey (one of two courses at Clovelly), but if you want more of a challenge look to the Admiral's Green, located in Pippy Park. For a free copy of the province's *Golf Guide*, call ⓒ **866/563-4653** or visit www.golfnewfoundland.ca.

PARKS & GARDENS

Bowring Park   Bowring Park is the city's preeminent green space. It has a river and brook running through it, ducks swimming happily about, and pigeons doing their best to make a mess of the lovely bronze statues. There's a whimsical statue of Peter Pan (it's a replica of the same statue that stands in the Kensington Gardens of London) alongside the pond that, while beautiful to look at, has a melancholy history. It's actually a memorial for a little girl who had loved the park, but who, along with her father, had been tragically shipwrecked. The park also contains a tribute to St. John's military history, with a number of commemorative war plaques to read. Bowring Park also offers a large adventure playground, an outdoor swimming pool, tennis courts, picnic grounds, walking trails, and cross-country ski trails and tobogganing in the winter.

Southwest of downtown on Waterford Bridge Rd. ⓒ **709/576-6134**. Freeadmission to enter the park. Daily 9am–10pm.

Pippy Park   Northwest of downtown, adjacent to the Memorial University of Newfoundland, this park features a peaceful pond where you can rent canoes or kayaks. There's a playground and minigolf for the kids, two golf courses, camping, picnic grounds, hiking trails, a botanical garden, and the Fluvarium (see "Exploring St. John's," earlier in this chapter). Locals regard Long Pond as excellent for city birdwatching, and the occasional moose has even been sighted in the park. You'll pass the expansive park many times on your travels in and around the city.

Take Kenmount Rd. to Thorburn Rd. or Prince Philip Dr. ⓒ **709/737-3655**. www.pippypark.com. Free admission to enter the park. The grounds are open daily dawn–dusk.

WATERSPORTS

Swimming in the ocean off St. John's is definitely not recommended. Not only is the water bone-chillingly cold, but the seas are often rough and the coastline rocky. The water of Conception Bay, on the west side of the city, is slightly more tempting, and you'll often see locals splashing around on warmer days at sandy Chamberlains Beach (Conception Bay South) and Lance Cove (Bell Island). If these options don't sound too enticing, head to Bannerman Park Outdoor Pool, on Bannerman Road (ⓒ **709/ 576-7671**). It's open July and August daily 11am to 5pm.

Ocean Quest   If you can put up with the cold water, scuba diving in and around St. John's has lots going for it, including an abundance of shallow-water shipwrecks and extremely clear water. Based on the edge of Conception Bay, a 20-minute drive southwest of St. John's, Ocean Quest covers all bases. It takes certified divers on day trips to local wreck sites, has stylish waterfront accommodations, offers full rental packages, and even has its own dive school.

17 Stanley's Rd., Conception Bay South. (C) **866/623-2664** or 709/834-7234. www.oceanquestcharters.com. C$170 (US$146) for a full day boat diving, inclusive of gear rental and barbecue lunch; C$540 (US$464) for 2 days diving, 2 nights accommodations, and airport transfers.

Wilderness Newfoundland Adventures   Based at Cape Broyle, a 45-minute drive south of downtown, this company offers sea kayaking tours that take in an amazing number of natural attractions. The highlight is paddling around icebergs that occasionally come to rest near the shoreline. But even without icebergs, seeing whales, puffins, sea caves, and waterfalls will not disappoint. Tours include rental and basic instruction. A good source of information for kayakers heading to St. John's is the website www.kayakers.nf.ca.

Harbour Rd., Cape Broyle (a 45-min. drive south of St. John's on Rte. 10). (C) **888/747-6353**. www.wildnfld.com. C$49 (US$42) 2½-hr. tour, C$69 (US$60) 4-hr. tour, C$149 (US$128) full-day tour. Overnight options also offered. Transportation from St. John's extra.

CUSTOM TOURS

Scademia Adventure Tours   This 2-hour cruise aboard a 27m (90-ft.) refitted fishing schooner is a must for anyone who loves tall ships, traditional Newfoundland music, and Newfoundland dogs—and who wants to get screeched! You'll take in some great views of St. John's Harbour and the Narrows. As well, you'll have the opportunity to see a variety of seabirds—and some whales, if you're lucky. The fun-loving crew is knowledgeable and eager to please. And if you're not too shy, go ahead and get screeched. This involves reciting a silly limerick, tossing back a shot of Newfoundland rum (also known as screech), and then kissing a piece of salt cod. The screech straight up is pretty wicked stuff, but for your reward you'll be presented with a genuine Newfoundland Purity mint—to get the taste out of your mouth—and a certificate (making you an honorary Newfoundlander) to take home and put in your photo album.

Fog is common here, so good visibility can't be guaranteed, and there are often cold winds (even on a warm day), so be sure to bring along a jacket and a hat that won't get blown off.

Pier 7, Harbour Dr. (across from the Murray Premises). (C) **800/779-4253** or 709/726-5000. www.nfld.com/scademia. Fares C$40 (US$35) adults, C$25 (US$22) children ages 13 and under, free under age 4. DC, MC, V. Departures May–Sept daily at 10am, 1pm, 4pm, and 7pm (weather permitting). Wheelchair accessible.

St. John's Carriage Tours   A fun way to tour the city is to hire a horse-drawn carriage. Owner Derm Duggan has a small stable of horses that he pastures on a hill overlooking Quidi Vidi Lake. The carriage will take you along your selected course; you can choose either an hour or a half-hour tour of "Old Downtown" or the "Historic East." Both are lovely routes, but depending on the time of day you take the ride ask the driver which route is less busy, as the horse understandably gets somewhat agitated in times of heavier traffic.

The horse stops at Belbin's, the oldest grocery store in St. John's, where he/she will receive a tasty apple. (If you want to make a hit with the horse, bring along your own cut-up apple as a present to offer at the beginning or end of your journey.)

You'll find the carriage parked near the Fairmont Newfoundland. (C) **709/364-5120**. Tour prices are C$30 (US$26) for the half-hour tour and C$50 (US$43) for the 1-hr. tour. V. Summer daily 10am–midnight.

WALKING TOURS

Many companies offer reasonably priced walking tours in and around St. John's. Each service provider will appeal to a slightly different clientele, so take your pick and enjoy the walk.

- **Boyle's Walking Tours** (© 709/364-6845; www.boylestours.com); C$5 (US$4.30); Thursdays 7:30 to 9pm by reservation only: Smiling Michael Boyle is quite the character and claims to be a direct descendant of Sir Cavendish Boyle, who wrote the "Ode to Newfoundland." Boyle offers several different themes to his walking tours, including a pub tour of the old city.
- **St. John's Haunted Hike** (© 709/685-3444; www.hauntedhike.com); C$5 (US$4.30) cash per person; June to September, Monday to Thursday nights 9:30 to 10:45pm; no reservations required: Meet at the west entrance of the Anglican Cathedral on Church Hill. If you're not afraid to delve into the dark side and want to be spooked a little, take this evening hike with the very Rev. Thos. Wyckham Jarvis, Esq. *Note:* This hike isn't the ideal choice for children, as they may find it too scary and it runs late into the evening.
- **Vault into History Walking Tour** (© 709/739-7870); C$5 (US$4.30) cash per person; July through August daily at 2pm; departs from Newman Wine Vaults at 436 Water St.; no reservations necessary: Led by costumed interpreters, this walking tour delves into the history of downtown's west end, which was traditionally a center for local industry.

8 Shopping

St. John's has a lively shopping scene, with local arts and crafts that hold a seafaring theme always popular as souvenirs. Touristy shops line Water Street, but if you're looking for bargains you might have to venture away from downtown and into suburbia where the locals shop. One such suburb is called "The Goulds." This is where you'll find **Bidgood's,** one of the most comprehensive places in St. John's to shop for traditional food products (see below for more information).

Suburban malls are generally open Monday to Saturday from 10am until 9pm, Sunday noon to 5pm. Close to downtown is **Avalon Mall,** at 48 Kenmount Rd., which has more than 100 stores and services including movie theaters and a grocery store. Avalon Mall is accessible by Metro bus nos. 3, 4, 9, 14, and 15. **Village Shopping Centre** is at 430 Topsail Rd. and has 100 stores and services including Sears and Shoppers Drug Mart. The location is very accessible by bus if you don't have wheels. (Bus nos. 1, 2, 5, 7, 8, 11, 12, 21, 22, and 25 all stop at the mall.)

Bidgood's ⟨⟨ What will you find at Bidgood's? Just about everything! It's basically a family-run supermarket, but so much more. "Bidgood's Cottage Crafts" (at the back of the store) has a noteworthy collection of Newfoundland and Labrador crafts and books—and at very reasonable prices. "Bidgood's Cove" is a section of the store where you will find a vast array of traditional Newfoundland foods, all prepared on-site and of the same quality you'd find in the home of a Newfoundlander. You can buy (or just look at!) such local delicacies as seal flipper pie, cod heads, and caribou or rabbit pies.

On shelves throughout the store you'll also find many local products, such as Bidgood's wonderful own jams (try the bakeapple) and a huge selection of Purity products such as the mints you get on the *Scademia* and tasty ginger cookies. There's a lunch bar in the store, where you can grab a light bite to eat in or take out. There's even a playland for the kids to keep them amused while you shop. And the store is located in picturesque dairy farm country, only a 20-minute drive from downtown.

Rte. 10 (just off Old Bay Bulls Rd.), Goulds. ℂ **709/368-3125**. www.bidgoods.ca. Mon–Sat 9am–9pm; Sun 11am–5pm. MC, V.

Devon House Craft Centre   Probably the best-known craft shop in the city, Devon House offers a great selection of Newfoundland handicrafts at very reasonable prices (jewelry, sculpture, silk painting, hooked mats, model boats, and so on). It's a non-profit venture operated by the Newfoundland Crafts Development Association. Every product in the store has been vetted by the Association for its exceptional quality and artistic merit. Devon House is located behind the Fairmont Hotel on Duckworth Street. Don't overlook the upstairs showroom, where you'll find the larger and more eclectic pieces.

59 Duckworth St. (below the Fairmont Newfoundland). ℂ **709/753-2749**. www.craftcouncil.nf.ca. Mon–Wed and Sat 10am–5pm; Thurs–Fri 10am–9pm; Sun 1–5pm. AE, MC, V.

Downhomer Shoppe & Gallery   This is a one-stop shop where you can choose from a wide selection of videos, books, music, souvenirs, and gifts. They claim to have the world's largest collection of "Newfoundlandia," and after a few glances around the place, you'll likely agree. It's definitely worth a look. A unique offering is the *Household Almanac & Cookbook*, which provides a good assortment of traditional recipes in addition to household hints and home remedies.

303 Water St. ℂ **888/588-6353** or 709/722-2970. www.shopdownhome.com. Mon–Fri 9:30am–8:30pm; Sat 10am–6pm; Sun noon–5pm. AE, DC, MC, V.

Fred's Records   You can pick up recordings of Newfoundland music everywhere from gas stations to grocery stores, but Fred's is the place to search out the real thing. Here you'll find an amazing collection of new and used recordings, as well as the occasional live performance by local or touring musicians.

198 Duckworth St. ℂ **709/753-9191**. www.freds.nf.ca. Mon–Fri 9:30am–9pm; Sat 9:30am–6pm; Sun noon–5pm. MC, V.

Living Planet   The screen printing is done upstairs and the street-level shop down below sells the finished product. The bright artwork featured on some T-shirts is tasteful and eye-catching, while other designs are most definitely politically incorrect—making them all the more popular.

116 Duckworth St. ℂ **709/739-6810**. www.livingplanet.ca. Mon–Sat 9:30am–5:30pm. Closed Sun. MC, V.

Newfoundland Weavery   The Weavery has been open for business for more than 30 years and has continued to add to its offerings. Look for quality local art and crafts, including pottery, hand-knit sweaters, oilskin coats, silks, jewelry, and pewter.

177 Water St. (across from the Courthouse). ℂ **709/753-0496**. Mon–Wed 10am–6pm; Thurs–Fri 10am–9pm; Sat 10am–6pm; Sun 12:30–5pm. AE, MC, V.

Nonia Handicrafts   Nonia is a non-profit, volunteer-driven network founded by the Newfoundland Outport Nursing & Industrial Association (NONIA). Unique products include hand-knit baby bonnets, booties, tuques, mittens, and lots and lots of sweaters in all sorts of designs. Plus they'll do special orders on request.

286 Water St. (at George St.) ℂ **709/753-8062**. Mon–Sat 9:30am–5:30pm. Closed Sun. MC, V.

Outfitters   In the heart of downtown, this is a great place to get equipped for the wilderness of Newfoundland and Labrador. The store stocks a range of top-notch recreational clothing, climbing equipment, everything you need for a sea kayaking trip, camping gear such as tents and sleeping bags, as well as guides and maps. Tents, kayaks, and snow sports equipment are available to rent.

220 Water St. ✆ **709/579-4453.** Mon–Sat 10am–6pm; Sun 1–5pm. MC, V.

Wild Things   Looking for local items such as raw Labradorite (the provincial stone), Newfoundland pottery, or nature photography? Visit Wild Things, coordinator of the world humpback count. The store also stocks a good collection of travel books and field guides.

124 Water St. (near the War Memorial). ✆ **709/722-3123.** www.wildlands.com/wildthings. Mon–Sat 9am–6pm; Sun 10am–5pm. AE, MC, V.

Woof Design   This is the place to go if you want one of those great Newfoundland sweaters like Kevin Spacey wore in *The Shipping News.* Woof Design specializes in the design and production of mohair, wool, and angora sweaters and accessories. All of their sweaters are handcrafted in Newfoundland homes by independent craftspeople using domestic knitting machines; expect to pay around C$130 (US$112) each. The accessory items are hand-knit, hand-crocheted, or woven.

181 Water St. ✆ **709/722-7555.** www.woofdesign.com. Mon–Sat 9am–5:30pm. Closed Sun. AE, MC, V.

Wordplay   A must for book lovers is Wordplay, a centrally located independent bookstore offering more than 100,000 new, used, and rare books. Their specialty is books on Newfoundland and Labrador. For a small fee, Wordplay also offers public access to the Internet. Check out the James Baird Art Gallery upstairs, featuring a good selection of contemporary Canadian art. Give yourself plenty of time to browse—you'll need it.

221 Duckworth St. ✆ **800/563-9100** or 709/726-9193. www.wordplay.com. Mon–Sat 10am–6pm; Sun noon–5pm. MC, V.

GALLERIES

Christina Parker Gallery   Built in the 1930s and originally occupied as a canning factory, this somewhat funky gallery features an eclectic mix of visual art in an open, spacious environment. All the artists featured are contemporary artists from Newfoundland and Labrador. Highlights include landscape paintings by Cliff George, recycle art by Peter Drysdale, photographic art by Ned Pratt, and dyed silk art by Diana May Dabinett, who is responsible for the beautiful silk art hanging at the Fluvarium.

7 Plank Rd. ✆ **709/753-0580.** www.christinaparkergallery.com. Mon–Fri 10am–5:30pm; Sat 11am–5pm. MC, V.

Emma Butler Gallery   This is a more traditional gallery, with a wonderful selection of classic art. Blue-chip artists such as Christopher and Mary Pratt and David Blackwood—Canada's foremost printmaker—are well represented. Blackwood's etchings provide an excellent visual history of Newfoundland and Labrador. The gallery also handles several international artists from countries that include the U.S., France, and Russia. You will find many pieces by Jean-Claude Roy, a French artist who comes to Newfoundland and Labrador every year to paint. Emma will ship your purchases worldwide.

111 George St. W. (between Waldegrave and Springdale). ✆ **709/739-7111.** www.emmabutler.com. Free admission. Tues–Sat 11am–5pm and by appointment. MC, V.

Lane Gallery   If you're interested in photography, don't miss the Lane Gallery. Don Lane sells and exhibits strictly his own work, but don't think that's limiting. As a native of the city, he knows where—and how—to get the best shots. His photographs of icebergs are simply breathtaking. If you're looking for a photograph to hang on your wall that will always remind you of just how beautiful this province is, drop in to visit the Lane Gallery, situated on the main floor of the Fairmont. Prices range from C$100 (US$86) for smaller prints to C$1,000 (US$859) for larger pieces.

Fairmont Newfoundland, 115 Cavendish Sq. ℂ 877/366-5263 or 709/753-8946. www.lanegallery.com. Mon–Fri 9am–5pm; Sat 10am–5pm. Closed Sun. MC, V.

9 St. John's After Dark

St. John's may be the oldest European settlement in North America, but it has a very young population. The average age of a "townie" is 35 to 44. That translates into a very active nightlife. In fact, it's said that the city has the highest concentration of pubs per capita on the continent! You'll find great live music playing everywhere, as well as a good selection of dinner theaters and other cultural offerings. So don't wear yourself out during the day. You'll miss too much at night!

GEORGE STREET & SURROUNDS

This is where you want to be if you're looking for the local pub scene. Within a 2-block stretch, you'll find about 20 establishments eager to draw you a pint. Keep in mind that it gets wildly busy on weekends—especially during the academic year at Memorial University—so plan to arrive early if you want to get in to a certain place. *Note:* Lineups can be long on Thursday, Friday, and Saturday nights, so bring your umbrella, and in winter wear warm clothing and boots so you don't freeze. Once you get in, you're bound to have a great time no matter which of these establishments you choose.

Sundance, George Street at Adelaide (ℂ **709/753-7822**), is the largest facility and boasts Top 40 music nightly. It's especially popular on summer weekend afternoons when local bands play out in the large beer garden east of Montreal. Very welcoming to visitors is **Trapper John's** (2 George St.; ℂ **709/579-9630**) a pub well known for its "screeching-in" ceremony, which allows you to become an honorary Newfoundlander. **Turkey Joe's** (7 George St.; ℂ **709/722-5757**) is for the just-turned-19 (and barely dressed) set that's heavy into the latest music trends. **Bridie Molloy's** (5 George St.; ℂ **709/576-5990**) has a great outdoor patio and traditional Irish music. **Benders on George** (13 George St.; ℂ **709/738-3687**) is basically a dance bar with DJ music Wednesday to Saturday where you can also have a friendly game of billiards. **O'Reilly's Irish Pub** (15 George St.; ℂ **709/722-3735**) is an institution. It's the most popular Irish pub on the strip. The music will have you tapping your toes, but you can expect to have them squished on the minuscule dance floor. **Kelly's Pub** (25 George St.; ℂ **709/753-5300**) has live entertainment every weekend and no cover charge.

A couple of blocks north from George Street are two more good choices, both traditional and lively, but without the raucous crowds associated with their neighbors. **Nautical Nellies** (201 Water St.; ℂ **709/738-1120**) has a distinct maritime theme (including a scale model of the *Titanic*), a menu filled with local specialties, and friendly bar staff. Across the road is **Erin's Pub** (186 Water St.; ℂ **709/722-1916**), a very Irish drinking spot with Celtic artists performing most nights.

OTHER OPTIONS

If you're looking for a quieter, more relaxing atmosphere, try the **Windsock Lounge** (161 Water St.; ✆ **709/722-5001**), a downtown piano bar featuring local performers Thursday to Saturday. Similarly stylish is Narrows Lounge, within the Fairmont New-foundland (115 Cavendish Sq.; ✆ **709/726-4980**). Here, you can sip a cocktail over-looking the greenery of a cavernous atrium.

The **Ship Pub** on Solomon's Lane (access from 265 Duckworth St.; ✆ **709/753-3870**) is the most famous drinking establishment in the city. It's a rather dark but lively pub with a history that boasts many well-known writers and artists as frequent customers. The Ship Pub is known for hosting literary events such as book launches and readings, so you just never know what—or whom—you'll find when you drop in. Expect live jazz, blues, reggae, rock, or folk Thursday through Saturday and poetry readings on Monday.

Another unique and interesting option is the **Crow's Nest,** located next to the War Memorial (between Water St. E. and Duckworth St.; ✆ **709/753-6927;** www.crows nestnf.ca). Here, you'll find a periscope from a German World War II sub as part of the decor! The only drawback is that the Crow's Nest offers limited hours of opera-tion: Tuesday to Thursday 4:30 to 7:30pm; Friday, lunch is served from noon to 2pm and they remain open until 8pm; Saturday 2 to 8pm; and closed Sunday and Mon-day. In business since 1942, the Crow's Nest is a private officers' club, but visitors to the city are welcome to drop in. A "smart casual" dress code is in effect, with summers being a bit more flexible.

The **LSPU Hall** (3 Victoria St. at Duckworth St.; ✆ **709/753-4531**) shows good live comedy and alternative theater through the resident Resource Centre for the Arts. The building itself has been designated a registered heritage structure, and you'll find an art gallery downstairs. The LSPU Hall offers a good selection of imported beer and provides live entertainment Wednesday through Sunday during the summer.

If you like classical music, see if the **Newfoundland Symphony Orchestra** is play-ing while you're in town. Call ✆ **709/722-4441** or visit www.nso-music.com for an online schedule of performances and corresponding ticket prices. The season runs October through early April with most performances at either the Arts & Cultural Centre on Prince Philip Drive or Cook Recital Hall on the university campus.

5

Avalon Peninsula

If your visit to Newfoundland allows for a mere week or so, you really only have time to see one region of the province—the Avalon Peninsula.

The Avalon not only includes the capital, St. John's (see chapter 4), but also is home to half the entire provincial population, whom you'll find living in the many tiny coastal communities dotted throughout this charming and picturesque region. Using St. John's as a base you can plan day trips around the Avalon Peninsula or, better still, pack your bags for an overnight stay. Here, in the annual playground of more than 5,000 humpback and minke whales, you'll be entertained by a natural marine show unparalleled by any of the world's most talented trained mammals. You'll find yourself on the verge of flight, vicariously soaring with the most spectacular seabird colony in North America. And you'll be speechless when a majestic caribou herd emerges from the dissolving fog within arm's reach of the highway.

If you want to walk your cares away, you can't beat the beauty and solitude of the 220km (138-mile) East Coast Trail. Fortunately, you won't have to go the whole distance all at once; the trek is divided into convenient, manageable chunks.

You can paddle your way through a variety of sea kayak adventures, and dive for sunken treasure in the graveyard of the Atlantic. Or get into the swing of things on one of several top quality golf courses (where wayward moose and marauding fox join the challenge of sand traps and water hazards). And you'll really dig the way history comes alive at several active archaeological sites, in addition to breathtaking scenery. Yes, there's all that and more on the Avalon—if you know where to look (and you will, thanks to Frommer's).

Destination St. John's has information available at their booth in the St. John's airport, open from 10am to midnight, 7 days a week. You can contact the association at ⓒ 877/739-8899, or visit their website at www.canadasfareast.com.

1 Getting Around

EAST COAST TRAIL

For the avid hiker, the **East Coast Trail** will be the Avalon Peninsula's most magnetic attraction. The trail takes you 220km (138 miles) along North America's easternmost coastline. Some sections are difficult, requiring overnight excursions. Other parts are easy—and short—enough for someone in moderate shape.

The trail is open year-round and extends along the coast from Petty Cove in the north to Cappahayden in the south. A trail south from Cappahayden to Trepassey exists, but there is little or no signage. There is no fee for walking the East Coast Trail, nor do you need to book a time for your journey.

> **Tips Hiking Tips**
>
> Keep these suggestions in mind before setting out on the East Coast Trail (or anywhere in the province, for that matter):
>
> - When hiking in damp weather, be careful when stepping over logs, as they can be very slippery when wet.
> - Always bring rain gear along with you as the weather can—and does—change at whim. Also, layer your clothing so you can enjoy the sun's warmth when it comes out.
> - If you have a bad back or weak knees take along a walking stick, as it helps take some of the pressure off those areas.
> - Never hike alone. Always travel with at least one companion as well as an emergency pack with a flashlight and flares. And be sure to let someone know where you're going, and when you expect to return.

The most spectacular stretch is the **Spout Path,** an 18km (11-mile) expanse rated as difficult and strenuous. It begins at Bay Bulls, with the bonus being the chance to get close to the **Spout,** a wave-driven geyser that shoots saltwater 60m (197 ft.) into the air. You'll also have the opportunity to view sea stacks (stand-alone stone pillars rising from the sea), a cast-iron lighthouse, and a couple of abandoned settlements along the way.

Your best resource is the **East Coast Trail Association** (© 709/738-4453; www.eastcoasttrail.com). They can advise you about renting hiking equipment from any number of outfitters in the St. John's area if you don't want to bring (or don't have) your own. They also sell a comprehensive series of guidebooks on the East Coast Trail, including two volumes covering the northern part of the trail. Alternatively, for C$23.95 (US$20.50) you can purchase a set of 19 waterproof topographic maps—also available through the ECTA website.

Another good resource is **Trail Connections** (© 709/335-8315; www.trailconnections.ca), an association of accommodations and eco-tourism service providers for hikers. For a reasonable fee, a member of Trail Connections will pick you up at the airport, make bag lunches geared especially for hikers, provide bed-and-breakfast accommodations, and set you up with dinners if you desire. Daily rates for the Trail Connections service are C$75 (US$65) per person double, and C$120 (US$104) single. Five percent of their profits go toward maintenance of the East Coast Trail.

If you plan to hike the East Coast Trail and want to do a little kayaking at the same time, get in touch with Stan Cook at **Wilderness Newfoundland Adventures** (© 888/747-6353; www.wildnfld.ca), which is based out of a converted general store at Cape Broyle. One- and two-person kayaks are available; there are even special kayaks that can accommodate children too young to paddle. Experienced professionals ensure beginners get thorough on-shore instruction before they head out on the water, and the sheltered environment of the harbor makes it an ideal experimental paddling ground. *Note to parents:* There are few better cures for a chronically bored teen than an oceanside view of a surfacing humpback! Guided kayaking is C$50 (US$43) for 2½ hours, C$70 (US$60) for 4 hours, and C$110 (US$95) for a full day.

Avalon Peninsula

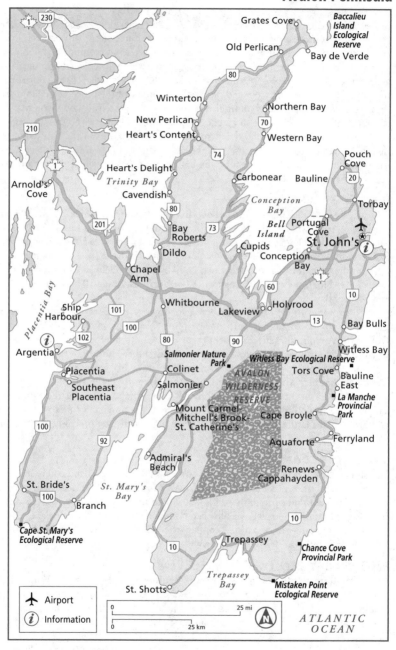

Grates Cove

Baccalieu Island Ecological Reserve

Old Perlican

Bay de Verde

80

Winterton

Northern Bay

New Perlican

70

Heart's Content

Western Bay

74

Pouch Cove

Heart's Delight

Carbonear

Bauline

20

Arnold's Cove

Trinity Bay

Cavendish

Torbay

210

80

Conception Bay

201

Bell Island

Portugal Cove

St. John's

Bay Roberts

73

Cupids

Conception Bay

Dildo

60

Chapel Arm

1

Placentia Bay

Whitbourne

Holyrood

10

Ship Harbour

101

Lakeview

13

100

Bay Bulls

Argentia

102

80

90

Witless Bay

Salmonier Nature Park

Witless Bay Ecological Reserve

Placentia

Colinet

AVALON

Tors Cove

Bauline East

Southeast Placentia

Salmonier

WILDERNESS

La Manche Provincial Park

100

RESERVE

Mount Carmel-Mitchell's Brook-St. Catherine's

Cape Broyle

92

Aquaforte

Ferryland

Admiral's Beach

Renews

Cappahayden

St. Bride's

St. Mary's Bay

100

Branch

10

Cape St. Mary's Ecological Reserve

10

Trepassey

Chance Cove Provincial Park

Trepassey Bay

St. Shotts

Mistaken Point Ecological Reserve

✈ Airport

ⓘ Information

0   25 mi

0   25 km

ATLANTIC OCEAN

2 Irish Loop

If your time is limited (an extra day in St. John's?), choose the Irish Loop for a day trip. Around 320km (200 miles) in total, the loop is a series of connected highways south of St. John's that pass the jumping-off point for whale-watching, an active archaeological dig, dozens of picturesque fishing villages, a wonderful golf course, and the opportunity to get up close and personal with many of the province's mammals.

As you stop at the various communities that comprise the Irish Loop, you may be surprised at the very strong Irish accent of the Newfoundlanders who call this region home. Most of the people who live here are direct descendants of the Irish who settled this area hundreds of years ago. And because many of the communities have been somewhat isolated until recent times, the Irish heritage has remained vibrant and the accent kept nicely intact.

GETTING THERE

To reach the 320km (200-mile) Irish Loop from St. John's, take Route 2 (Pitts Memorial Dr.) out of town, and then head south via Route 3, which will lead you to **Route 10,** which forms the first section of the Irish Loop. You can make a slight detour onto Route 11 and stop in at **Cape Spear** (p. 92) or **Petty Harbour** (p. 92) along the way.

From the west, you can access the Irish Loop by taking Highway 1 to Route 13 (the Witless Bay Line), and then heading east to hook up with Route 10 between Bay Bulls and Witless Bay.

Back on Route 10, **Bay Bulls,** northern gateway to Witless Bay Ecological Reserve, is reached 40km (25 miles) south of St. John's. Next up is **Ferryland,** site of the Colony of Avalon, an active archaeological dig. Continuing south, **Cape Race** is worth the detour if you're interested in shipwrecks and the history of the *Titanic.*

Around the coast, as the highway turns back north, you'll arrive at **St. Vincent's,** a seaside community whose waters are known as a favorite dining spot for humpback whales. At St. Vincent's, Route 10 becomes **Route 90** (also known as the Salmonier Line) and carries on to **Salmonier,** home to one of the province's finest golf courses and **Salmonier Nature Park,** home to a variety of animals you probably won't see in the wild.

VISITOR INFORMATION

You should have a detailed highway map and travel literature in hand before heading out from St. John's. Once you get into the smaller communities, services are more difficult to find and they operate shorter hours. There are, however, visitor centers offering localized information at Bay Bulls, Ferryland, and Salmonier Nature Park.

For trip planning information, contact the **Irish Loop Development Board** (© **888/438-2898** or 709/438-2898; www.irishloop.nf.ca).

WITLESS BAY ECOLOGICAL RESERVE ✦✦✦

Extending from **Bay Bulls** in the north to **Bauline East** in the south, Witless Bay Ecological Reserve was established to protect North America's largest puffin colony. In addition to 500,000 of the province's official bird, the reserve provides a home for over two million other seabirds, as well as humpback and minke whales. If you're visiting in spring, icebergs are a spectacular bonus. The actual reserve is offshore, protecting coastal water and four uninhabited islands. Access is by tour boat from the villages of Bay Bulls and Bauline East.

Heading south from St. John's, the village of Bay Bulls will probably be your first stop on your way round the Irish Loop. It's a vibrant community of striking contrasts—rural attitude and architecture stand side by side with a strong commercial and industrial base—but for you the visitor, it's the departure point for the ecological reserve.

WHERE TO STAY

Celtic Rendezvous Cottages By The Sea ☆☆ (Finds)
Immaculately clean and fully equipped cottages with a view that pays homage to the endless harmony of surf and sky. Truly a find and an incredible sanctuary, yet just a 45-minute drive from St. John's. Each of five cottages has a huge kitchen and dining table, large sitting area, and outdoor patio. The Luxury Cottage comes with its own bedside jetted tub. In addition to the free-standing cottages is a row of 12 motel-like rooms, all of which open to an ocean-facing deck. One unit is wheelchair accessible. There is room for 12 RVs. Sites have electrical hookups and great ocean views, but no privacy. The Lookout on-site convenience store sells groceries, ice, and beer, rents movies, and has a small cafe.

Main Rd., Bauline East. (C) **866/334-3341** or 709/334-3341. www.celticrendezvouscottages.com. 17 units. C$119–C$249 (US$103–US$214) double; C$16 (US$14) RV site. DC, MC, V. Pets allowed. **Amenities:** Playground; coin-operated laundry; barbecues; Internet access. *In room:* TV/VCR, kitchen, hair dryer, iron.

Elaine's B&B By The Sea ☆
If you like kids, kittens, warm welcomes, and hearty breakfasts, Elaine's is set on a charming seaside meadow, with 152m (500 ft.) of ocean frontage overlooking Bird Island and a panoramic view of Witless Bay Ecological Reserve. Late May and early June is the prime time for iceberg watching from the backyard swing. If you're really lucky, your morning view just might include a whale waving his tail in a friendly hello.

It's a modern home, with big windows to take advantage of the view. Modest though comfortably spacious guest rooms and firm mattresses work in conjunction with the invigorating power of sea-salt air to ensure one of the most restful sleeps imaginable. The owners offer their guests 90-minute whale-watching tours in a rigid-hulled Zodiac for C$45 (US$39).

Lower Loop Place, Witless Bay. (C) 709-334-2722. www.elainesbythesea.com. 4 units. C$65–C$80 (US$56–US$69) double including breakfast. V. **Amenities:** Kitchen available to guests; nonsmoking facility; beachside bonfires. *In room:* TV, en suite.

La Manche Provincial Park
For overnight and/or day use, La Manche Provincial Park offers hiking, canoeing, swimming, and bird-watching opportunities. The highlight for me is the abandoned fishing village of La Manche (destroyed by a winter storm in 1966), which is reached in around 30 minutes on foot from the campground (the trail begins by Site 59). Each of the 70 campsites has a picnic table, fireplace, garbage can, and parking. You will have to stock up on supplies before you arrive, as there is no convenience store on-site. Nor are there shower or laundry facilities.

Rte. 10 (53km/33 miles south of St. John's). (C) **800/563-6353** or 709/685-1823. www.env.gov.nl.ca/parks/parks/p_lm. Campsites C$10 (US$8.50). Open mid-May to mid-Sept. **Amenities:** Trout angling; day-use facilities; drinking taps and pit toilets located throughout the park; hiking trails; interpretation program; outdoor freshwater swimming; picnic sites; playground. Firewood is C$5 (US$4.30) per bundle.

EXPLORING WITLESS BAY ECOLOGICAL RESERVE

Each of the following operators is listed here because of certain unique characteristics, but others are around if the choices below are booked to capacity. Tours run from May to September and last around 2 hours. They are very weather dependent, so call before leaving St. John's to confirm that you'll be going.

For general information on the reserve, visit www.env.gov.nl.ca/parks/wer/r_wbe.

Gatherall's Puffin & Whale Watch (✆ **800/419-4253** or 709/334-2887; www. gatheralls.com) operates a high-speed catamaran that departs 1 to 6 times daily from Bay Bulls. Because the boat travels at high speed, you spend less time getting to and from the best viewing sites, and more time watching the whales and puffins. There's enough seating for 100 passengers in the heated cabin, but if you prefer the wind in your hair you can stand outside on the top deck. Gatherall's provides a shuttle service from St. John's for those without transportation. Cost is C$49 (US$42) adults, C$44 (US$38) seniors, C$36 (US$31) students, C$15 to C$21 (US$13–US$18) children.

Also departing from the Bay Bulls waterfront, **O'Brien's** (✆ **877/639-4253** or 709/753-4850; www.obriensboattours.com) is justifiably popular. It's like getting two events for the price of one: a world-class marine adventure and a heck of a party, too. The 2-hour tour takes you aboard a two-level passenger vessel where you'll hear—and sing along to—lively Irish Newfoundland folk music; drink screech; have lots of fun; and get to see whales, puffins, and icebergs. Prices are similar to Gatherall's. O'Brien's also offers a zippy 2-hour Zodiac trip that will get you close to the Spout, sea caves, sea stacks, and more. These trips are C$60 (US$52) per person. This trip is not recommended for really younger kids.

Colbert's Tours (✆ **709/334-3773**) is based at Bauline East, a 15-minute drive farther south than the two companies detailed above. It's also a smaller operation, less touristy, and closer to the action (meaning less travel time in the boat). The converted fishing boat leaves on demand throughout the summer season, and upon return Captain Colbert collects C$30 (US$26) from each passenger.

FERRYLAND

With almost 400 years of European settlement to its credit, **Ferryland,** 75km (47 miles) south of St. John's, is one of the oldest communities in North America. It's also the site of an ongoing excavation of a 17th-century settlement known as the Colony of Avalon. It's a unique archaeological dig in that local residents live in the midst of the pick-and-shovel activity.

The Sights & Sounds of Ireland

The **Southern Shore Folk Arts Council** (✆ **709/432-2052**; www.ssfac.com) provides a variety of entertainment from a restored building in downtown Ferryland that's been painted a nationalistic Irish green.

June through September, the association puts on a **dinner theater** Tuesday, Thursday, and Friday nights at 7pm. For C$35 (US$30), you get a three-course meal and entertainment that brings the village's Irish heritage to life.

The **Shamrock Festival** offers lively music with traditional Irish/Newfoundland flavor. It's held outdoors, right in the middle of town, with some of the biggest names in Newfoundland music taking to the stage over the 2 days of the fourth weekend of July. Entry costs C$10 (US$8.50) per day; those that don't want to pay fill the adjacent hillside with blankets and chairs—quite a sight!

WHERE TO STAY & DINE

Colony Café SEAFOOD   A dining experience with Continental flavor, overlooking the archaeological dig. The enterprise, in a building once occupied by a fish plant, began as a simple coffee shop. Customer demand forced those modest plans to be upgraded to a full-service restaurant, replete with attractive pine interior, custompainted historical mural, and the services of professional French chef Christian Houle. He specializes in seafood, with a particularly tender touch for cod (this mild fish is easily overpowered by excessive accouterments). A tantalizing whiff of a passing bowl of chowder will have you salivating for more. Give in to temptation. I guarantee you won't be disappointed.

Rte. 10, Ferryland. ℭ 709/432-3030. www.ferryland.com/colonycafe. Dinner reservations recommended. Lunch C$7–C$13 (US$6–US$11); main courses C$10–C$21 (US$8.50–US$18). MC, V. May–Sept Mon–Thurs 11am–8pm, Fri–Sun 10:30am–8:30pm.

Downs Inn   By the time you leave Downs Inn, you'll be wondering if owners Aiden and Dianne Costello are psychic—that's how good they are at anticipating their visitors' needs. You might even think they're getting divine direction from the former occupants of this well-maintained, Victorian-style, three-story waterfront property (it used to be a convent). But no, the full breakfasts, private bathrooms (shower only in some rooms), and laundry service aren't the work of supernatural advisors. Unobstructed ocean views make up for slightly dated in-room decor. Host Aiden is the local tourism development officer, and he's well versed in the little extras that can transform a comfortable stay into an unforgettable experience—like the cozy warmth of a fireplace, or a gift shop crammed with handmade crafts. And if you're not sure what else you'd like to see or do along the Irish Loop, don't be afraid to ask for Aiden's recommendations. He is, after all, the expert.

Rte. 10, Ferryland. ℭ 877/432-2808 or 709/432-2808. 4 units. C$55–C$75 (US$48–US$65) double; additional person C$10 (US$8.50). MC, V. Open mid-May to mid-Nov. **Amenities:** Tearoom; full breakfast; laundry service; nonsmoking; TV room.

Hagan's Hospitality Home B&B   The house isn't an architectural masterpiece, nor will the decorating scheme win any awards, but everything beyond that is extraordinary. Both in portion and flavor, the food epitomizes homemade perfection. And there's a standard of cleanliness here that would put an army barracks to shame. But even that pales in comparison to the warmth and friendliness of your host, the delightful Rita Hagan. Her perpetual smile and musical brogue more than make up for any splendor lacking from her listed amenities. With a mug of tea in your hand and one of her timeless stories in your ear, you'll feel as privileged as royalty.

Rte. 10, 8km (5 miles) southwest of Ferryland in Aquaforte. ℭ 709/363-2688. www.haganshospitality.com. 2 units. C$70 (US$60) double; 10% discount for seniors. Rate includes lunch and full breakfast. No credit cards. **Amenities:** Room service; laundry facilities; TV lounge.

Lighthouse Picnics LUNCH   From the archaeological dig, walk up onto the headland and Ferryland Lighthouse will soon come into view. Built in 1870, this classic red-and-white lighthouse was abandoned until 2004 when enterprising locals spruced up the exterior and began using it as a store providing picnic baskets for visitors—and they even supply blankets to lay out on the surrounding grassy headland. Although you can order goodies as simple or as gourmet as your taste and budget dictate, the strawberry shortcake is an absolute must.

Lighthouses

You'll find many lighthouses as you make your way around Newfoundland and Labrador. They have been protecting seafarers since 1813, when the first lighthouse was built and operated by volunteers at Fort Amherst at the mouth of St. John's Harbour. Other lighthouses were built after the formation of Newfoundland's Lighthouse Board in 1832. Most of those colorful lighthouses or their replacement structures still stand. The Cape Bonavista Lighthouse is of prime significance as the place where continental Europeans first landed in Newfoundland. And the Point Amour Lighthouse on the Labrador Straits, first illuminated in 1858, is the tallest in Atlantic Canada. It is now automated, as are most of the lighthouses in the province, but their history remains alive and of prime significance to residents and visitors hoping to gain a deeper understanding of this seafaring province.

Many lighthouses are open to the public, with exhibits related to the fishery, the naval history and shipwrecks, and the strong people who have built this land. Some lighthouses have been made even more appealing to visitors, including the 1871 **Ferryland Lighthouse** where you can order a picnic lunch to enjoy on the grassy headland. For something really unique, plan on an overnight stay at the **Quirpon Lighthouse Inn** (p. 188).

Ferryland Lighthouse, Ferryland. (C) **709/363-7456**. www.lighthousepicnics.ca. Picnic baskets C$10–C$25 (US$8.50–US$22). MC, V. Mid-June to early Sept daily 11am–6pm.

EXPLORING FERRYLAND

Colony of Avalon ⭐⭐   Give yourself a half-day to get immersed in the history of this living archaeological dig in the heart of Ferryland. The site comprises two parts—a modern interpretive center and the actual dig site. Start at the interpretation center. Watch the short documentary and then view artifacts from the first successful planned colony in Newfoundland, including everything from coins to cannonballs. Visitors are welcome to view the second-floor lab where the cataloging and reconstruction of artifacts takes place (weekdays only). An on-site gift shop sells local crafts and reproductions of 17th-century items from the colony. Outside is an interesting garden filled with the same herbs as the first settlers would have planted.

You're then ready to take a 1½-hour guided tour (or a more leisurely self-guided tour) of the village settled in 1621 by Sir George Calvert (who later became Lord Baltimore). On the guided tour, you'll learn about the world's first flushable toilet (we have clogs to thank for artifacts found in the "pipe") and walk on the oldest cobblestone street in British North America.

Rte. 10, Ferryland. (C) **877/326-5669** or 709/432-3200. www.heritage.nf.ca/avalon. Admission C$6 (US$5.15) adults, C$4 (US$3.50) seniors and students, C$12 (US$11) family. Mid-May to mid-Oct daily 8:30am–4:30pm.

TREPASSEY AND SURROUNDS

Midway round the Irish Loop, you'll come to the small fishing village of Trepassey, a good place to stop for the night if you find yourself at Mistaken Point late in the day.

The location is somewhat remote, but there are advantages to that: you're right in the heart of caribou country. **Warning:** Be aware that this area is prone to heavy fog, so be careful when driving, as the animals frequently cross the road. Trepassey's historic claim to fame is as the place where Amelia Earhart launched her cross-Atlantic flight in 1928. The town has a small museum with a commemorative display featuring photos of the famous aviator during her visit to the town, but the real highlights are the ecological reserve and the views from **Cape Race Lighthouse.**

WHERE TO STAY & DINE

Northwest Lodge Bed & Breakfast   Hosts Harold and Marie Pennell offer safe, clean, and economical accommodations in a family environment. Marie is noted for her homemade jams (and her cooking in general), while Harold has loads of stories about his days as a lighthouse keeper at nearby Cape Race. Although comfortable, the rooms alone won't lure you here (they're almost filled to capacity by a bureau and double bed). You'll be far more impressed by the leaping salmon in the nearby river, as well as the chance to get up close and personal with the resident caribou herd.

Rte. 10, Trepassey. ✆ **877/398-2888** or 709/438-2888. www.bbcanada.com/bbnorthwest. 4 units. C$60–C$65 (US$52–US$56) double; rollaway cot C$10 (US$8.50) extra. MC, V. **Amenities:** Nonsmoking; wheelchair accessible; barbecue pit. *In room:* TV.

Trepassey Motel & Restaurant   If all you need are clean sheets, a roof over your head, and a shower in the morning, this is an excellent choice roughly halfway around the Irish Loop. Treat yourself to breakfast in the motel restaurant. Not only is the food reasonably priced and well prepared, but the dining room's floor-to-ceiling windows provide a view that'll be the highlight of your stay.

111–113 Coarse Hill, Trepassey. ✆ **709/438-2934.** www.trepasseymotel.com. 10 units. C$75 (US$65) double. AE, MC, V, Interac. **Amenities:** Restaurant; laundry facilities; nonsmoking rooms. *In room:* TV, no phone.

TO CAPE RACE

From Trepassey, backtrack to Portugal Cove South and make the turn south to Cape Race. You'll pass Mistaken Point on the 30km (19-mile) drive to Cape Race.

⌜Fun Fact   Graveyard of the Atlantic

With its perpetual fog and rock-studded shore, it's no wonder the area of the southern Avalon around Cape Race is called the **"Graveyard of the Atlantic."** Records show 365 ships have gone down between Renews Harbour and Cape Pine. Cape Race is in the center between these two points. If you're interested in maritime history, be sure to visit the **Cape Race Lighthouse,** operating since 1856. It has the largest lighthouse lens in North America. You can tour the lighthouse and its museum for C$3 (US$2.60). In the museum, you'll find an extensive *Titanic* display, highlighting the Cape Race connection to the doomed ship (this is where the SOS. signal from the sinking luxury liner was received). Although the lighthouse is automated there is a lightkeeper in residence, and students provide interpretive services in the summer. To make advance arrangements for your trip to the lighthouse, call ✆ **709/438-2451.**

Mistaken Point Ecological Reserve This is the only place in the world where Precambrian animal fossils are so abundant that they cover exposed areas the size of tennis courts. If you're into fossils, you'll appreciate the area's key importance to paleontologists as the home of 560-million-year-old fossils. They are the world's oldest known multi-celled creatures, living in the ocean before animals had developed skeletons.

Allow around 25 minutes to drive from the Portugal Cove South turnoff and then a 40-minute walk from the parking lot to the fossil bed. The site has no signage, nor are guided tours offered, so you're on your own. *Note:* Fossil collecting is prohibited. *Warning:* The unpaved access road is rough and the parking lot for the fossil bed not well marked, so drive carefully and keep your eyes peeled for the small and faded sign.

Turn off Rte. 10 at Portugal Cove South. (℃ 709/635-4520. www.env.gov.nl.ca/parks/wer/r_mpe. Accessible year-round during daylight hours, weather permitting. Free admission.

ST. VINCENT'S

The tiny village of St. Vincent's, 38km (24 miles) west of Trepassey in the beautiful Peter's River Valley, is the place to be between June and August if you want to see humpback whales **lunge feeding.** The whales launch their bodies right out of the water—mouths wide open—and fill themselves with capelin (small fish similar to smelt, which are a favorite dinner for the whales). The whales like it here because the water is deep even close to shore, and these conditions attract more capelin. More capelin, more whales. Nature being nature, you can't be promised that you'll see the whales feeding, but they've been doing so with some regularity the past few years, so if you're patient the chances are good. To help you pass the time while you wait for the whales, a food stand sells souvenirs and serves fish and chips right on the beach.

You can also spend an hour at the **Fisherman's Museum,** on Route 90 across from the visitor center ((℃ **709/525-2798**). Housed in the early 1900s home of a local fishing family, you will see an example of the **Newfoundland Thermos**—a bottle wrapped in a sock that would contain the fisherman's special blend of hot tea mixed with hooch. You can examine all sorts of artifacts from a traditional fisherman's home. Upstairs is an interesting collection of handmade carpentry tools. The museum is open July and August daily 10am to 4:30pm.

SALMONIER

This little village, 57km (36 miles) north of St. Vincent's on Route 90, is just a dot on the map, but nearby is a resort-style golf course and the province's only wildlife park.

WHERE TO STAY & DINE

Salmonier Country Manor Also known as the Convent Inn in tribute to its former occupants (the Presentation sisters, a holy order), this beautifully renovated convent melds understated luxury with meditative serenity. The guest rooms are tastefully decorated in a warm country style (solid wood furnishings, toe-curling area rugs) and have elegantly appointed en-suite bathrooms. The best room in the house is the Florence Room: picture yourself sipping on champagne by candlelight in the double-jetted tub, then basking in the warmth from your in-room fireplace—all the while being serenaded by the bubble of the Salmonier River as it flows below your window.

Reservations are a must if you want to dine at the inn's licensed dining room (it's a fixed menu, so you'll want to inquire in advance about what's being served), in what was once the convent chapel. I'd highly recommend a dinner performance here of

"Christmas and the Mummers." It's a fun and informal "time," or party, that includes a traditional Newfoundland Christmas dinner, local entertainment, recitations, and a visit from wildly costumed characters known as mummers. It's scheduled Wednesday nights June through August.

7km (4⅓ miles) southwest of Salmonier on Rte. 93, Mount Carmel. ℭ **866/521-2778** or 709/521-2778. http:// manor.infotechcanada.com. 7 units. C$89–C$119 (US$77–US$103). MC, V. Open May–Dec. No small children. **Amenities:** Dining room; nonsmoking rooms (smoking permitted on front deck). *In room:* TV, en-suite bathrooms.

The Wilds at Salmonier River   Ample accommodations choices await you at a resort geared more to golf enthusiasts than luxury-seeking travelers. You can choose from one of 40 standard hotel-style rooms, or one of 19 two-bedroom, self-contained cabins. I recommend the cabins, which provide more privacy and are a better choice for families or small groups wanting to be together. Ever try to entertain a couple of young children in a hotel room? You can only hide in the bathroom for so long. Plus, a shared barbecue area is available where you can cook when it's nice outdoors. *Hint:* The cabins book up early, so try to reserve well in advance, especially for summer weekends.

The Wilds is set on the beautiful Salmonier River, and nestled in a hilly, wooded area. Among the swimming pool, the golf course, and nearby Salmonier Nature Park, you'll have plenty of opportunity to enjoy the great outdoors. And the complimentary supervised kids' program (for ages 5–14) means you'll be able to have some time to yourself.

Season's Restaurant, overlooking the golf course and river, is open daily for breakfast, lunch, and dinner. The menu is as predictable as you'd expect at a family-oriented resort, with something to please everyone and prices to please whoever's paying. The weekend breakfast buffet (C$8/US$7) is especially good value.

Rte. 90, Salmonier Line (Hwy. 1 to Exit 35). ℭ **866/888-9453** or 709/229-5444. www.thewilds.ca. C$92–C$140 (US$79–US$121) hotel room double; C$110 (US$95) cabin. AE, DC, MC, V. **Amenities:** Restaurant; lounge; outdoor heated pool; 18-hole golf course; golf academy; children's program; playground; babysitting. *In room:* TV, coffeemaker.

EXPLORING SALMONIER

Salmonier Nature Park ⋆⋆ *(Kids)* *(Finds)*   This peaceful and calming nature reserve is operated by the provincial government. Because it's a rehabilitation facility for injured and orphaned birds and animals you'll find the guest list to be constantly changing—the goal of the park is to release as many of the creatures as possible back into the wild. For those who will never be able to survive the wild again, the park

---

Avalon Wilderness Reserve

A large chunk of the interior between routes 10 and 90 is protected as Avalon Wilderness Reserve, home to the most southerly herd of woodland caribou in the world. Numbering less than 50, the herd was almost extinct in the 1960s, but numbers have rebounded and today around 2,000 animals inhabit the remote region. The reserve is total wilderness, with no services and only a few old service roads passing through. An overnight hiking trail beginning from Salmonier Nature Park is for experienced backcountry hikers only. Luckily for the less adventurous, the caribou are occasionally seen along the surrounding highways, most often along Route 90. For more information, visit www.env. gov.nl.ca/parks/wer/r_aw.

serves as a comfortable hospital or retirement home. As you stroll along the park's 3k (almost 2 miles) of wheelchair- and stroller-friendly boardwalk, you'll see moose, lynx, owls, bald eagles, and arctic fox in specially developed enclosures that represent their natural habitat. In addition to the resident mammals, approximately 100 species of birds and 175 species of plant have been recorded in the park—including the pitcher plant, Newfoundland and Labrador's provincial flower. Benches are strategically situated along the way so you can rest, enjoy a snack, or just marvel at nature. Some of the residents are shy, so call ahead for feeding times, knowing that a small bribe will coax the animals out of hiding. Allow at least an hour for your visit.

Rte. 90 (12km/7½ miles north of Salmonier). ✆ **709/229-7888**. www.env.gov.nl.ca/snp. Admission C$3 (US$2.60) adults, free for under 18. June–Aug daily 10am–5pm; Sept daily 10am–3pm.

The Wilds An 18-hole golf course that has made the greatest of efforts to preserve the native woodlands, here long before we decided it was fun to whack a small white ball around with a shiny club. You'll find waterfalls and small creeks running throughout the course, and if you're lucky you just may see a moose crossing a fairway (the big brown fellows have been known to hang around the 16th green and the woods around the 7th hole).

Because it's only minutes from Salmonier Nature Park, one parent can take the kids to the park while the other has a round of golf. Better yet, if you're staying overnight at The Wilds at Salmonier River you can avail of the child-care program so that everyone gets to play.

The Wilds at Salmonier River, Rte. 90 (Hwy. 1 to Exit 35). ✆ **709/229-9453**. www.thewilds.ca. C$42–C$47 (US$36–US$41) for 18 holes; C$29 (US$25) for a power cart. Restaurant; pro shop; club rentals; driving range.

3 Cape Shore

Circling the extreme southwest corner of the Avalon Peninsula, the Cape Shore provides access to **Cape St. Mary's Ecological Reserve,** the province's best bird-watching spot. Even if you're not an avid birder, you'll be awed by the number of gannets that inhabit Bird Rock. In fact, the symbol for the Cape Shore Route is one of our fine feathered friends, because this region is a birder's paradise. Also along the way is Argentia, were ferries from North Sydney (Nova Scotia) dock. Argentia is the site of a now-deserted U.S. naval base.

ESSENTIALS
GETTING THERE AND AROUND

The Cape Shore driving route branches off Route 90 near Salmonier. It loops south past Cape St. Mary's to St. Brides then parallels the eastern side of Placentia Bay to Argentia. From St. John's, the entire loop is a little over 400km (250 miles). Taking the winding road into consideration, it's a full day trip from the capital.

Note: The provincial travel literature tells you it will take only 2 hours to get to Cape St. Mary's from St. John's, but allow 3 hours. The road is narrow with lots of hairpin curves through gorgeous hilly countryside. It's not just difficult driving—you won't *want* to rush! If you've just come off the ferry at Argentia and your first destination is Cape St. Mary's, head south 75km (47 miles) along Route 100. It's a lovely coastal drive, and you'll be there in about an hour. If you're heading from Argentia to St. John's, take Route 100 north to the Trans-Canada Highway (Rte. 1), which will take you directly into the heart of the city in a little more than 90 minutes.

Tips **Navigating Newfoundland**

It can be confusing driving around Newfoundland, as you'll often find that a street or highway starts out with one name or number, and then changes without notice. That's why it's critical you have a detailed highway map before heading out on any road trip in the province.

VISITOR INFORMATION

If you arrive in this region by way of ferry from Nova Scotia, plan on stopping at the visitor center in Argentia (② **709/227-5272**). It is open hours that coincide with the ferry's arrivals and departures. You can also pick up brochures and information about the region at the Cape St. Mary's Visitor Centre (② **709/277-1666**). Information about the region is also available by calling the **Cape Shore Loop Tourism Association** at ② **709/227-5456.**

WHERE TO STAY & DINE

Tourist accommodations and services are not as developed along the Cape Shore Route as you'll find in neighboring regions, mainly because fewer communities are along the way, with virtually nothing along Route 92 from North Harbour to Branch. The community of **St. Bride's** is the largest one nearest to Cape St. Mary's and it is still very small.

Bird Island Resort ☆ *Kids*   This is an award-winning family resort with spectacular oceanfront property that's as easy on your eyes as your pocketbook. The two-bedroom efficiency units offer full kitchen facilities equipped with all the dishes, glasses, and appliances you could need—so you don't have to worry about the expense of a restaurant. There's a fitness center to help you stay in shape for your day at the on-site beach while a convenience store is within walking distance. The Mannings, who own and operate the place, are a considerate family who pay attention to the details that make Bird Island Resort such a popular establishment. This is the closest accommodations to Cape St. Mary's.

Rte. 100 (Main Rd.), St. Bride's. ② **888/337-2450** or 709/337-2450. www.birdislandresort.com. 20 units. C$59 (US$50) double; C$99 (US$84) efficiency units. AE, MC, V. **Amenities:** Barbecue and horseshoe pits; minigolf; fitness center; laundry facilities; sunset deck. *In room:* TV, some have kitchenettes.

Seaside Bed & Breakfast ☆   This is not your standard B&B. Along with the expected amenities of private bathrooms, cable TV, and hot breakfasts, there's an outdoor pool with a 15m (50-ft.) waterslide, as well as an indoor game room where you can play pool, table tennis, darts, or even pinball. And here's welcome news for people whose digestive systems don't react favorably to different kinds of water (a lot of rural areas have well water that isn't chlorinated): Seaside uses bottled spring water in its cooking and for drinking. The guest rooms have a sparsely furnished rustic charm that is offset by a postcard-perfect waterfront view overlooking the Southeast Arm. Rates include full breakfast.

Rte. 91, Southeast Placentia. ② **709-227-2825.** www.angelfire.com/nf/seasidebandb. 5 units. C$60–C$70 (US$52–US$60) double. V. **Amenities:** Outdoor covered swimming pool with waterslide; game room with pool table, table tennis, darts, and pinball machine; exercise equipment. *In room:* TV, no phone.

EXPLORING THE CAPE SHORE

Cape St. Mary's Ecological Reserve 𝕣𝕣𝕣 Even if you're not a keen birder, visiting Cape St. Mary's is a must. The reserve protects the breeding ground of 24,000 northern gannets, 20,000 common murres, 2,000 thick-billed murres, 20,000 kittiwakes, and 300 northern razorbills. The birds are only part of the attraction—the cliff-top setting is also spectacular. Just east of St. Bride's and a 3-hour drive from St. John's, upon arriving at the cape, your first stop should be the Interpretive Centre, where you can familiarize yourself with the types of birds you'll be seeing.

From the center, it's a 1km (.6-mile) walk across a grassy meadow to the lookout point. It will take you 15 minutes if you're a fast walker, 30 minutes if you take the time to appreciate the sights along the way. At the heart of the reserve is **Bird Rock,** a 100m-high (330-ft.) sandstone sea stack separated from the mainland by only a few meters. You'll be standing high atop a rock roughly equivalent in height to Bird Rock itself, and close enough to touch many of its feathered inhabitants.

Tip: Be sure to bring a weatherproof jacket and non-slip footwear for the walk. And remember that this is a site to protect wildlife—not humans—so be sure to hang on to small children when you are hiking near the edge of the cliff. You'll also want to be extra cautious when the fog rolls in, which happens over 200 days each year (May and June are particularly foggy).

15km/9 miles east then south off Rte. 100 from St. Bride's. ℭ **709/277-1666.** www.env.gov.nl.ca/parks/wer/r_csme. The trail to Bird Rock is open year-round and access is free. Admission to the Interpretive Centre is C$5 (US$4.30) adults, C$2 (US$1.75) children, C$10 (US$8.50) families. The Interpretive Centre is open mid-May to mid-Oct daily 9am–5pm.

Castle Hill National Historic Site This barren, oceanfront site between Placentia and Argentia protects the foundations of French fortifications dating to 1662. The site, overlooking Placentia Bay, was chosen for its strategic location above rich fishing grounds, but the land itself was poor, and self-sufficiency impossible. By 1713, when sovereignty to Newfoundland was handed over to Great Britain, the fort's usefulness waned. Unless you happen to be in the area, or arrived in the province via Argentia, I wouldn't recommend making the journey specifically to visit Castle Hill. It's a long drive and the attraction isn't as impressive as some other more readily accessed sites—Signal Hill in St. John's, for instance.

Rte. 100, between Placentia and Argentia. ℭ **709/227-2401.** www.pc.gc.ca/lhn-nhs/nl/castlehill. Admission C$4 (US$3.50) adults, C$3.50 (US$3) seniors, C$2 (US$1.75) children, C$10 (US$8.50) families. Mid-May to mid-Oct 10am–6pm daily.

4 Baccalieu Trail

Baccalieu may seem an odd word to find in Newfoundland. However, it's actually a derivation of an old Portuguese word for salted cod, and once you've spent any time in the province you realize the historical importance of cod.

The Baccalieu Trail extends up an arm of the Avalon Peninsula, one that separates Conception and Trinity bays.

Brigus, not far from the Trans-Canada Highway, is a scenic highlight. Except for the pavement, you'll think you've stepped back in time. You'll walk beneath the arching branches of aging trees gracefully overhanging the narrow streets. You'll explore the gentle paths meandering over stony escarpments and nod to the locals as they go about their daily business around immaculately maintained old-style homes, some flanked by the ordered rows of vegetable gardens. If you're driving out to Brigus from St. John's, allow 45 minutes via the Trans-Canada Highway (Rte. 1).

Beyond Brigus are a multitude of fishing villages with enchanting names such as Heart's Content, Harbour Grace, Heart's Desire, Heart's Delight, Cupids, and Blow Me Down. Each bend of the coastline brings with it a different personality.

ESSENTIALS
GETTING THERE

The gateway to the Baccalieu Trail is Exit 31 of the Trans-Canada Highway, 70km (44 miles) west of St. John's. From this point, it's 16km (10 miles) north to Brigus and 44km (28 miles) north to **Carbonear,** the largest town along the trail. The western access is near **Whitbourne,** at Route 80, which follows the coast of Trinity Bay, and extends north at **Grates Cove** before continuing south along the coast of Conception Bay as Route 70 and ending back at the aforementioned Exit 31. The entire loop is 214km (134 miles), or if you cut across the peninsula at Carbonear on Route 74, the distance is 140km (88 miles).

INFORMATION

Although there are no official visitor centers along the Baccalieu Trail, the accommodations and attractions detailed below are a good source of information. Another contact is the **Baccalieu Trail Tourism Association** (© **709/596-3474;** www.baccalieu trail.com).

WHERE TO STAY

The Brittoner √value   This beautifully restored 160-year-old saltbox-style home in the heart of Brigus is not flush with amenities, but its central location makes it perfect for sightseeing. As a bonus, there are hiking trails nearby, tennis courts across the street, and a deck that's the perfect setting for a delicious outdoor breakfast. It overlooks a lovely pond that's home to a playful family of ducks.

12 Water St., Brigus. © 709/528-3412. www.bbcanada.com/4385.html. 3 units. C$50–C$60 (US$43–US$52) double. No credit cards. Open May–Oct. Pets allowed. **Amenities:** Picnic area; playground; laundry facilities; nonsmoking rooms.

Fong's Motel   If you prefer the anonymity of a motel room as opposed to a bed-and-breakfast, Fong's is a decent choice while touring the Baccalieu Trail. Fong's has it all—a motel, restaurant, banquet room, and lounge all wrapped up into one very nice facility. Guest rooms are simple and sparse, but spacious with large windows and full bathrooms. It's conveniently located right off the highway, near the edge of town.

143 Columbus Dr., Carbonear. © 709/596-5114. 15 units. C$65–C$75 (US$56–US$65) double. AE, DC, MC, V. **Amenities:** Restaurant; lounge; outdoor swimming pool. In room: TV.

Inn By The Bay 🐟🐟   This is an exquisite waterfront lodging overlooks Dildo Bay from the historical fishing village of Dildo, named one of Canada's 10 prettiest towns. Dating to 1888, the inn is operated by Todd Warren, an enterprising young man with extensive experience in the hospitality industry. It shows, because Todd doesn't miss a beat. The finest of feather duvets and pillows adorn the tastefully furnished rooms. And each room has a private bathroom as well as its own decorative personality.

Todd's abilities as a chef make the meals at Inn By The Bay a real treat. In addition to the full breakfast, specialties such as mussels served in a caramelized sauce are an example of the gourmet dinners guests can enjoy for an additional C$30 (US$26) per person. You'll dine on those gourmet goodies (and afternoon tea or cocktails, if you prefer) in the sumptuously Victorian sunroom. Rates include a full breakfast and evening cocktails.

78 Front Rd. (Rte. 80 to Exit 28 and then 12km/7 miles to Dildo), Dildo. ✆ **888/339-7829** or 709/582-3170. www.innbythebaydildo.com. 6 en-suite units. C$79–C$149 (US$68–US$128) double. Ask about seasonal discounts. AE, DC, MC, V. Open May to mid-Dec. **Amenities:** Nonsmoking facility; laundry facilities. *In room:* TV/VCR, dataport.

NaGeira House Inn 🐾 Just over an hour's drive from St. John's (via the Trans-Canada Hwy. to Rte. 70), you'll find the full-service community of Carbonear and this welcoming bed-and-breakfast, a registered heritage structure. NaGeira's gives you a wide choice of distinctively decorated rooms. One room has an in-room whirlpool bath; another has a mahogany four-poster bed. And all rooms have down duvets and en-suite bathrooms. The exquisite woodwork sets the tone for a quiet and relaxing stay, complemented by the inn's fireplaces and library. The quiet location and exemplary service make this a great place to stay while in the area.

7 Musgrave St. (off Rte. 70 and also accessible from Rte. 74 if coming across the peninsula from Heart's Content), Carbonear. ✆ **800/600-7757** or 709/596-1888. www.nageirahouse.com. 4 units. C$99–C$149 (US$85–C$128) double. AE, MC, V. **Amenities:** Restaurant; lounge. *In room:* TV.

WHERE TO DINE

You'll get wonderful meals at the locations listed above, but if you're looking for a snack, light meal, or picnic lunch, here are a couple of reasonably priced options that are worth checking out.

Country Corner Eatery LUNCH While exploring Brigus, drop in to the Country Corner for lunch. The chowder combo gets you a delicious bowl of cod chowder and a serving of baked blueberry crisp, along with a beverage and a tea biscuit. They also sell a nice assortment of souvenirs and gifts.

14 Water St., Brigus. ✆ **709/528-1099.** C$5–C$11 (US$4.30–US$9). AE, MC, V. Call for hours.

Kountry Kravins 'n' Krafts LUNCH This is a quaint little cafe serving reasonably priced lunches at a few indoor tables or outside on the small deck overlooking Dildo Bay. Alternatively, the friendly staff will make a picnic lunch to enjoy along the road. They have a fairly limited light lunch menu and the offerings (particularly the sandwiches) aren't great, but the setting is picturesque, and it's worth stopping in at least to see the terrific selection of local crafts they have for sale.

Front Rd., Dildo (across the street from the Interpretive Centre). ✆ **709/582-3888.** Lunches for around C$6 (US$5.15). MC, V. Mid-May to mid-Sept daily 9:30am–9:30pm; mid-Sept to mid-May 11am–8pm daily.

EXPLORING THE BACCALIEU TRAIL

Avondale Railway Station (Kids) Just south of Brigus on Route 60 you'll find a gem of a museum located in Newfoundland's oldest railway station (ca. 1864). It features five static railway cars, including a snowplow, CN A913, diesel locomotive, baggage/kitchen car, a working dining car, and a caboose. What excites most rail fans about Avondale is that it is the site of the last remaining mainline track of the Newfoundland Railway and a prime example of the old narrow-gauge track. The museum runs a few small railcars on the track for kids and their parents over the 3km (almost 2 miles) of narrow gauge.

Rte. 60, Avondale Access Rd. ✆ **709/229-2288.** www.manl.nf.ca/avonrail.htm. July–Aug daily 8am–8pm. Free admission.

Baccalieu Island Ecological Reserve   This remote seabird reserve is largely inaccessible due to its steep, high cliffs and treacherous shoreline. The reserve itself contains Baccalieu Island, located off the tip of the northwest Avalon Peninsula near the tiny outport of **Bay de Verde.** It's the largest seabird island in Newfoundland and Labrador, measuring approximately 6km (3¾ miles) long and 1km (⅔ mile) wide. Between June and August, the island is home to 3.4 million pairs of Leach's storm petrels, the world's largest such colony. Eleven seabird species breed on Baccalieu Island.

You can learn more about the birds and the reserve by visiting the **Bay de Verde Heritage House Museum,** in Bay de Verde.

Museum is on Rte. 70, Bay de Verde. ⓒ **709/596-3474.** www.env.gov.nl.ca/parks/wer/r_bie. Admission by donation. June–Sept Mon–Sat 11am–5pm, Sun 1–6pm.

Dildo Interpretation Centre   A surprisingly impressive heritage site, considering the diminutive size of both the facility and its host community. Inside a restored waterfront building, you'll find a historical account of Dildo Island and people such as the Maritime Archaic Indians who called it home. There's also a display on the history of the local cod fishery and a touch tank filled with ocean critters. Outside is a replica of a giant 8.5m-long (28-ft.) squid that was caught in local waters in 1933. It has seen better days, but is still interesting for its sheer size. Most of the items on display have been donated by members of the community. A half-hour should be sufficient to tour this facility.

Front Rd., Dildo. ⓒ **709/582-3339.** Admission C$2 (US$1.75) adults, C$1 (US85¢) children, C$5 (US$4.30) families. June–Sept daily 10am–6pm.

Grates Cove   The tiny outport of Grates Cove (pop. 250) is at the very northern tip of the land finger separating Trinity Bay from Conception Bay. Here you will find examples of the old rock walls once used to separate and protect small private gardens. Hundreds of these rock walls are still intact and are plainly visible to anyone walking through the community.

Note: Grates Cove has no restaurant—or even a place to get a cup of tea (unless you're lucky enough to be invited to the home of one of the locals). Apart from the rock walls and a small art studio on Main Road, there is really very little to see or do here. There is no signage to provide an interpretation of the rock walls, nor are there guided tours. They are, however, an interesting (and free) viewing spectacle.

Rte. 70, 12km (7½ miles) north of Bay de Verde. ⓒ **709/587-2326.** Free admission.

Hawthorne Cottage National Historic Site   Built in 1830, Hawthorne Cottage in the lovely community of Brigus is one of the few remaining examples of the picturesque cottage *orné*—translated from French, this means it's nicely decorated. But it's more than that. The home once belonged to Captain Bob Bartlett (the world-famous Newfoundland-born Arctic explorer) and contains interesting artifacts from Bartlett's journeys to the Arctic during the early 20th century. As you walk through the house, you'll listen to recordings that explain the historic importance of fishing and sealing to Brigus residents. You'll also see local period artifacts and textiles in their original setting, including the various upstairs bedrooms and kitchen. Be sure to visit the lovely commemorative sculpture in the shape of a ship's sails that has been erected in honor of Bartlett on the harbor near the Brigus Tunnel.

Irishtown Rd., Brigus. ⓒ **709/753-9262.** www.pc.gc.ca/lhn-nhs/nl/hawthorne. Admission C$3.75 (US$3.25) adults, C$3.25 (US$2.75) seniors, C$2.25 (US$1.95) children, C$8.25 (US$7.15) families. Mid-May to mid-Oct daily 10am–6pm. Wheelchair accessible.

Heart's Content Cable Station   A provincial historical site commemorating the importance of the transatlantic cable that made communications between Europe and North America near-instantaneous. After the failure of two earlier attempts, a permanent transatlantic telegraph cable was landed here in 1866. The station houses equipment and interpretive displays that explain the role Heart's Content has played in the world of communications for nearly 100 years. I was fascinated by the replica of the original Victorian cable office, as well as the storyboards describing how engineers of the day were able to overcome the many difficulties associated with laying a sub-sea electrical cable between the two continents.

Rte. 80, Heart's Content. ℂ **709/583-2160.** Admission C$2.50 (US$2.15) for ages 13 and up. June–Oct daily 10am–5:30pm.

Princess Sheila NaGeira Theatre ⚹ *Value*   If you like informal, outdoor theater, you'll really enjoy the beautiful seaside setting of **Carbonear's** summer performances, held each July and August. They use a number of different venues; some are indoors and some are outdoors, but all present a perfect backdrop to the variously comic, dramatic, and satirical offerings of the day.

265 Water St., Carbonear. ℂ **877/696-7453** or 709/596-7529. www.princesssheilatheatre.com. Tickets C$14 (US$12) adults, C$11 (US$9.50) seniors and children, C$35 (US$30) for the dinner theater. MC, V.

Rodrigues Winery   If you've looped around the Baccalieu Trail, and find yourself back on the Trans-Canada Highway with some extra time, this is an interesting stop. Located near the village of **Markland** (south of Whitbourne), Rodrigues was established in 1993 as Newfoundland and Labrador's first winery. It's surprising to find that there are indeed wineries in Newfoundland, and even more impressive to learn that it has won several awards with its fine vintages.

A variety of wines are made from local berries such as bakeapple, partridgeberry, blueberry, and other special blends. I especially liked the bakeapple and partridgeberry wines for their tartness. They also distill a super-sweet pear brandy, as well as fruit-flavored vodka. Take a free tour, sample the different varieties, and take some home as a tasty souvenir.

Rte. 81, Markland. ℂ **709/759-3003.** www.rodrigueswinery.com. July–Aug daily 9am–4:30pm; Sept–June Mon–Fri 9am–4:30pm.

5 Conception Bay

Conception Bay is on the back doorstep of St. John's, and if you've been following the order of this chapter, will complete your tour of the Avalon Peninsula. If you're in St. John's and want a break from city sightseeing, a drive to Conception Bay makes a great day trip, rich in maritime history and spectacular scenery. I recommend you make the journey to **Bell Island,** an enjoyable 20-minute ferry ride from the community of Portugal Cove.

Conception Bay (the actual body of water) was named by the Spanish in the 1700s in honor of a religious holiday relating to the Immaculate Conception. The Bay has a colorful history, and was home to pirates during the 17th and 18th centuries. **Kelly's Island,** just offshore from Conception Bay South, was a popular stopover for pirates and is the rumored hideaway of buried treasure.

ESSENTIALS
GETTING THERE AND AROUND

If you take Route 40 (Portugal Cove Rd.) from downtown St. John's you'll pass the airport, and quickly find yourself in **Portugal Cove.** Portugal Cove Ferry Terminal is where you catch the Bell Island Ferry. The ferry, which carries passengers and vehicles, can't be booked in advance—it's filled on a first-come, first-served basis. **Conception Bay South** is a much larger, full-service community of about 20,000 people, accessible by taking Route 2 off the Trans-Canada Highway.

Just a bit farther south you'll come to **Holyrood,** a picturesque community at the junctions of routes 90, 62, and 60. Its location makes it a convenient place to lay your head while touring around the Avalon.

WHERE TO STAY & DINE

Beachside B&B ✿   Sunny Conception Bay South is said to have the best weather on the Avalon, so if you're affected by the weather, you might like to choose this location. Beachside is also a great location if you don't have a vehicle but would still like to stay outside the city, as guests are offered free pickup from St. John's Airport.

All guest rooms are modern, have en-suite bathrooms, and are tastefully furnished. The spacious Oceanview Celebration Suite has a double Jacuzzi and private deck overlooking the ocean. In addition to the standard breakfast fare, you'll also be treated to local specialties that include toutons, moose or caribou sausages, and salt fish (when available). Don't be surprised if your hosts, Pat and Jerdon Reid, ask you to join in a friendly Newfoundland singalong—it's a happy and musical household.

77 Gully Pond Rd., Kelligrews, Conception Bay South. ✆ 866-834-0077 or 709/834-0077. www.beachside-bb.nf.ca. 4 units. C$69–C$169 (US$59–US$145). MC, V. **Amenities:** Full traditional breakfasts; laundry facilities; nonsmoking rooms; Internet access; fireplace on beach. *In room:* TV, dataport.

Dogberry Hill ✿✿✿   Haute ambience and breathtaking vistas combine with impeccable service and distinctive decor for an unforgettable experience. This inn is the epitome of graciousness, with a friendly bilingual staff and a private country setting close to the city. Situated on an incredible 2-hectare (5-acre) property with beautifully landscaped gardens, Dogberry Hill has sweeping views of Bell Island and Kelly's Island. Each guest room has a distinctively different personality featuring tasteful custom furnishings. I recommend you take the virtual tour to ensure you choose the room that best suits your style.

The culinary experience at the Dogberry can be just as satisfying as the visual. One of the owners is from Newfoundland and the other from France, so you'll be offered the best in local and European cuisine. Dogberry Inn is highly recommended for those willing to pay a little more than expected but eager to receive the absolutely best accommodations and food in the area.

Alfred's Drung off Dogberry Hill Rd., St. Phillip's. ✆ 709-895-6353. www.dogberryhill.com. 4 units. C$95–C$175 (US$82–US$150). AE, MC, V. **Amenities:** Authentic regional and French cuisine prepared on request. *In room:* En-suite bathrooms, Jacuzzi and soaker tubs available, ocean view, antique furnishings, high-quality French linens.

Villa Nova Bed & Breakfast ✿Value   Pat and Marie Hynes have created a haven of hospitality at this inviting bed-and-breakfast. These friendly hosts enjoy making conversation and are pleased to share their wealth of local history, culture, and folklore. The peaceful seaside location along with the very comfortable mattresses and pillows are sure to help you sleep like a baby. The rooms are spacious, reasonably priced, and

---

> **(Tips   Money-Saving Tip on Accommodations**
>
> Staying close to but outside the city limits can save you—not only on the basic rates, but also on taxes. Smaller facilities with three rooms or fewer are not required to charge tax, so you save yourself an additional 18% off rates that are (in some cases) already lower than within the city.

---

only 15 minutes from the city of St. John's. This is an ideal location if you have a vehicle and are more interested in touring the Avalon Peninsula than staying in the city.

31 Baird's Lane, Long Pond. ✆ **888/315-3141** or 709/834-1659. 2 units. C$65–C$85 (US$56–US$73). V. **Amenities:** Full breakfast; nonsmoking rooms; walking distance to sea kayaking. *In room:* Shared bathrooms and en suite.

EXPLORING CONCEPTION BAY

You'll find the Conception Bay area to be a splendid outdoor retreat, offering spectacular scenery, photographic sunsets, an abundance of marine life, and even the odd iceberg. With three shipwrecks piled on top of one another in shallow water offshore, Conception Harbour offers terrific diving opportunities. Just be aware that the clarity of the water changes when the algae are in bloom.

BELL ISLAND

The largest of several islands in Conception Bay, Bell Island measures about 9km (5½ miles) by 3.5km (2 miles). There's quite a bit to see and do on the island, including diving, bird-watching, hiking, and touring. Be sure to take note of the mining murals that adorn many of the town's buildings.

At the island's south end is Lance Cove, where you can see firsthand evidence of World War II. It was here on September 5, 1942, that German U-boats sank two Canadian ships, the *Lord Strathcona* and the *Rose Castle*, along with many other British and French ships during the war. Two of these were the British *Saganaga* and the French *PLM 27,* where 69 lives were lost. Efforts are being made to protect the wreck sites.

Visit www.bellisland.net for detailed information about services on Bell Island.

GETTING TO BELL ISLAND

To get to Bell Island, take Portugal Cove Road west from downtown St. John's. This road ends at Portugal Cove Ferry Terminal. From here, the round-trip fare is C$6 (US$5.15) per vehicle and driver. Seniors pay C$5.25 (US$4.50). Additional adult passengers are C$3.50 (US$3) and seniors C$2.50 (US$2.15). The trip takes only 20 minutes, and the ferries run frequently during the summer from as early as 6am until midnight, less often at other times of the year. There are permanent residents of Bell Island who regularly commute to St. John's to work—so the service is dependable, but it can still be influenced by the weather. It's recommended not to travel from the island to Portugal Cove in the morning or try to get to the island during the late afternoon rush hours in order to avoid lineups. You can reach the Bell Island Terminal at ✆ **709/488-2842** and the Portugal Cove Terminal at ✆ **709/895-3541.** See www. bellisland.net for the online ferry schedule.

No. 2 Mine & Museum   The most popular attraction on Bell Island is this mine, located a short drive along Main Road from the ferry terminal. From 1895 until 1966, more than 78 million tons of iron ore were mined here, the world's largest submarine (underground) iron-ore mine. The mine's museum contains interesting artifacts as well as masterful photos taken by world-famous photographer Yousuf Karsh. Karsh, who is known for his uncanny ability to portray the inner character of his subjects, has captured on film the grit and determination of Bell Island's iron-ore miners. You can also take a 1-hour walking tour of the underground mine, but dress warmly.

Main Rd., Bell Island. (C) **709/488-2880**. www.bellisland.net/no2mine. Admission and tour C$7 (US$6) adults, C$6 (US$5.15) seniors, C$3 (US$2.60) children under 12. C$2 (US$1.75) for museum entry only. June–Sept daily 11am–7pm.

Scuba Diving   Conception Bay, and the water around Bell Island in particular, is an excellent place for divers to explore shipwrecks and take a closer look at torpedoed ore carriers. You'll also discover the abundance of native marine life. **Ocean Quest,** based at Conception Bay South, leads the way as a charter operator. They run full day trips aboard the M/V *Ocean Quest,* with the cost of C$135 (US$116) per person including two dives, rental equipment, and a hot lunch. If you think the water may be a little chilly for your liking, a dry suit rental is an additional C$15 (US$13). The boat itself is modern and well-equipped with amenities such as hot showers, restrooms, a barbecue, a dive platform for easy access to the ocean, a flying bridge for sightseeing, and even an inflatable tender for exploring shallow coves.

Back on shore, Ocean Quest has a dive shop, a certified learning facility complete with indoor pool, and comfortable accommodations (C$120–C$145/US$104–US$125 double including breakfast).

17 Stanley's Rd., Conception Bay South. (C) **866/623-2664** or 709/834-7234. www.oceanquestcharters.com.

6

Eastern Region

The Eastern Region of Newfoundland and Labrador is the smallest region of the province, but it would be a mistake to equate the depth of its attractiveness to its diminutive size.

On the **Bonavista Peninsula,** you'll find the twin communities of **Trinity** and **Bonavista.** Bonavista is the fabled landing spot of old-world explorer John Cabot, while Trinity is renowned for its historically accurate architectural restorations.

Turning to the region's polar opposite, the **Burin Peninsula,** you'll discover a seemingly barren area that is really a treasure-trove of glacial deposits and the favored stamping grounds of 16th-century privates and privateers. Their modern-day equivalents can be found in the rum-runners who still smuggle bootleg hooch from the French colonies offshore.

Yes, France's border actually extends this far across the Atlantic, to the tiny islands off the south coast of Newfoundland—**St. Pierre** and **Miquelon.** You can get there by plane, or via passenger ferry from the town of **Fortune** at the foot of the Burin Peninsula.

Clarenville is the region's figurative center of gravity. It's roughly halfway between the Bonavista and Burin peninsulas, and is the main service center for the area. For that reason, it's not so much a destination as it is a base for exploring the rest of the region.

Although we've said elsewhere that we're generally following the same regional divisions as the provincial tourism guide, that's not entirely true in this section. The provincial tourism guide stops the Eastern Region boundary at Port Blandford, but we're stretching it as far west as Glovertown. Why? Because you're more likely to tour this area from a Clarenville base than from the doubly distant town of Grand Falls–Windsor. Between the two towns is **Terra Nova National Park.** Not as well known as Gros Morne, this park also presents a more subdued landscape than its western cousin. Its sandy freshwater pond, children's interpretive programs, less strenuous walking trails, and nearby urban attractions make it more appropriate as a family vacation destination. That said, it still has backcountry appeal for the more adventurous souls.

If you are lodging in any of the communities just outside the park, a full-day tour of Terra Nova will give you a very good idea of what the park has to offer. But if you're camping, the scenery and terrific outdoor facilities can keep you occupied for a full week and more.

1 Bonavista Peninsula

From the picture-perfect village of Trinity, to roadside vendors of hand-picked seasonal berries, to a singularly unique railway loop (the only one of its type in North America), to a replica of a 500-year-old sailing ship, exploring the Bonavista Peninsula will be a highlight of your time in Newfoundland. Although you can easily make the

return trip in a single day, you'll really need at least 2 days to enjoy the multitude of services and attractions you'll find here.

While you'll undoubtedly head to the anchor attractions of the Bonavista Peninsula, there are other, less well-known points of interest that also deserve attention. Like the enticingly named Tickle Cove (after Bonavista, it's thought to be the oldest settlement on the peninsula), or James Leo Harty House in Duntara (a prime example of a traditional outport home, built by the great-grandson of the village's founder). There's also Elliston—the root-cellar capital of the world. Although they look like fairy dwellings, root cellars are merely holes dug into the side of a hill for winter storage of dried meats and root crops. Encased as they are by the hill itself, with roofs of grass and wildflowers, you won't recognize a root cellar from any angle except front-on. That's when you see the door. Another not-so-main attraction is Port Union, the only union-built town in North America. Sir William Coaker established the town in 1916 in an attempt to ensure fishermen were paid a fair price for their catch. The moral of the story: you're on the Discovery Trail, so don't restrict yourself to the roads most traveled.

Nor should you limit yourself to summer touring. The weather of early fall (Sept to mid-Oct) is generally very favorable, requiring just a light jacket and pants. You won't want to come here after the end of October, however, as many of the attractions and even accommodations close for the winter.

ESSENTIALS
GETTING THERE
The southern gateway to the Bonavista Peninsula is Clarenville, a 2-hour drive northwest of St. John's (189km/117 miles) along the Trans-Canada Highway (Rte. 1). From the Argentia ferry terminal, Clarenville is a 1½-hour drive. From Clarenville, Route 230 winds its way 114km (71 miles) along the peninsula to the town of Bonavista. The other main attraction in the area is Trinity, which lies just off Route 230 73km (46 miles) from Clarenville.

From the west, the Trans-Canada Highway enters Terra Nova National Park 80km (50 miles) southeast of Gander. From this point it's 48km (30 miles) south through the park to Port Blandford, where Route 233 cuts across the southern end of the peninsula to join Route 230.

VISITOR INFORMATION
You'll find visitor information in Clarenville at the office of the **Discovery Trail Tourism Association,** 54 Manitoba Dr. (© **709/466-3845;** www.thediscoverytrail.org), or call the Clarenville Area Chamber of Commerce (© **866/466-5800**).

On the peninsula itself, most accommodations hand out tourist information, as does the **Trinity Interpretation Centre** in Trinity (© **800/563-6353** or 709/464-2042), open daily during the summer months 10am to 5:30pm, and the **Ryan Premises National Historic Site** in Bonavista (© **800/213-7275** or 709/468-1600), open mid-May through mid-October 10am to 6pm.

GETTING AROUND
Roads throughout this region are in comparatively good condition (not really an endorsement when you consider the potholes and their black-patch spawn that dominate so many of the province's highways).

Tip: Within the historical communities of Bonavista and Trinity, park your car and travel on foot. Not only does the diminutive size of these towns make for an enjoyable walking tour, but you'll find that the narrow breadth of the streets (paths, really, in some sections) makes driving a less-than-pleasurable experience. *Warning:* Be aware that children may be playing on or very near the highway: extra caution is advised when traveling along the smaller routes. You may be startled to find kids playing basketball—complete with a portable hoop—right on the highway!

CLARENVILLE

For those preferring to stay in a full-service community, Clarenville is a large (by Newfoundland standards) center and the home of roughly 5,000 residents. It has full-service hotels, a hospital, banks, a couple of fair-size shopping malls, and other major services.

Clarenville itself has little of interest in the way of attractions. About 5 minutes along the Trans-Canada northwest of Clarenville, you'll find **White Hills Resort** (*©* **709/466-4555;** www.discoverwhitehills.com), with a triple chairlift accessing 12 downhill trails, 30km (19 miles) of groomed cross-country trails, and on-hill lodging.

WHERE TO STAY & DINE

Clarenville Inn ☆☆ *Kids*   This is a family-oriented hotel easily recognized by the larger-than-life inflatable crustacean flanking the front lawn (except during the winter months, when Larry the Lobster goes into hibernation). Mom and Dad can relax in the reclining chairs poolside while kids frolic in the water, shoot a few hoops, or romp over the adjacent playground equipment (all enclosed by a privacy fence). Then, after a busy day of doing as little as possible (you're on vacation, remember), retire to the cozy comfort of your room. Here you'll find all the standard features of a well-appointed hotel.

Gaffer's Restaurant ☆, the Clarenville Inn's on-site restaurant, is above average for a hotel dining room, with elegant surroundings and well-presented food. Lunch prices average C$10 (US$8.50), dinner mains C$15 (US$13). Specialties of the house include seafood and prime rib.

134 Trans-Canada Hwy., Clarenville. *©* 877/466-7911 or 709/466-7911. Fax 709/466-3854. www.clarenvilleinn.ca. 63 units, including 1 suite. C$85–C$145 (US$73–US$125) double. AE, DC, MC, V. **Amenities:** Restaurant; lounge; outdoor heated pool; video rentals; ATM; nonsmoking rooms; custom golf packages; kids stay and eat free (subject to certain conditions). *In room:* TV, coffeemaker, hair dryer, and curling iron.

St. Jude Hotel ☆☆   Almost directly across the blacktop from the Clarenville Inn is the low-slung, three-story St. Jude Hotel. While the former is ideal for the traveling family, this hotel caters to those with disabilities and to business travelers. Not only is the entire hotel wheelchair friendly (all doors and corridors are wide enough for a wheelchair, the second and third floors are accessible by elevator, and a guest wheelchair is available at the front desk if needed), but there's also a specially designed room for people with physical disabilities. Located on the first floor, it's larger than the standard guest rooms, and has hand rails in the bathroom and next to the taller-than-normal toilet. For the corporate traveler, the in-room Internet jacks as well as the front-desk photocopy and fax services are de rigueur, but the on-site audiovisual equipment (overhead projector, television, and VCR) is a bonus. That said, it's not all work and no play at the St. Jude either. You can kick back with your favorite beverage in the warm surroundings of the Republican Lounge, or pick something from the all-ages recreational reading material in the decently stocked guest library. The single

Calling All Grease Monkeys

If you can't resist the roar of high performance, plan to spend a Saturday or Sunday afternoon at the Clarenville Dragway. Every second weekend from early June to early September, performance-vehicle enthusiasts congregate on this paved airstrip 14km (8½ miles) north of Clarenville along Route 230. You'll see dragsters racing pro street cars, and the emerging sport compact class going head-to-head with Harleys. There's even something called a racing sled; it's a snowmobile on wheels. Only in Newfoundland!

Tip: On-site facilities are limited to wooden bleachers and portable washroom cubicles, so plan accordingly. For the latest racing schedule, call ℂ **709/ 749-6831** or go online to www.clarenvilledragway.com.

guest rooms at the St. Jude are cheery, but average in every way: small worktable with chair, color TV, plain but solid furnishings, and color-matched Wal-Mart prints on the wall. For double your money, you can have the best suite in the house (complete with separate sitting room, and whirlpool built for two).

Rte. 1, Clarenville. ℂ **800/563-7800** or 709/466-1717. Fax 709/466-1714. www.stjudehotel.nf.ca. 63 units, including 3 suites. C$85–C$150 (US$73–US$129) double. AE, DC, MC, V. **Amenities:** Restaurant and sports bar; banquet facilities; ATM; business center; guest library; laundry facilities; concession stand; nonsmoking rooms. *In room:* A/C, TV, coffeemaker, hair dryer.

TRINITY ✸✸✸
It's sure to be love at first sight in Trinity (pop. 350), a famously picturesque village overlooking Trinity Bight 73km (46 miles) east of Clarenville along Route 230.
 Here you'll find a passionate regard for the past embodied in an almost unanimous community-wide celebration of historically accurate home restoration. From the picket fences, vertical slider windows, vegetable gardens, and distinctive signage, it's obvious that Trinity takes pride in its history. And why not? It was a crucial pioneer settlement in the province, with some of the first clergy, doctors, and professional tradesmen in Newfoundland.

WHERE TO STAY & DINE IN TRINITY
Lodging in Trinity is limited to a number of small inns and bed-and-breakfasts. In summer especially, make reservations well in advance.

Campbell House ✸✸   A first-class hospitality home that epitomizes traditional styling and old-world refinement. Campbell House was built more than 150 years ago in conventional saltbox form (a popular Newfoundland house design, the saltbox features a main rectangle-shaped front section with gabled roof, sloping down to a single-story appendage out back). Its roadside appeal is further enhanced by the expert horticultural skills of owner Tineke Gow, a microbiologist originally from Holland.
    Once inside, you'll love the exposed brickwork in the dining area and be drawn to touch the crockery displayed in the open-face cupboard (back away from the blue-patterned serving tray—it's a hand-painted antique). Moving to the upstairs bedrooms (each has its own private bathroom, but not all are en suite), you'll delight in the low-by-today's-standards ceilings and the romance of old-fashioned washbasins. With the

four-poster bed, fireplace, bureau, and cheval mirror, some people might think the rooms crowded, but I prefer the term "cozy."

If you like the atmosphere at Campbell House but require more privacy, you'll want to stay at one of Gow's other Trinity properties: **Dover House** and **Kelly House.** Both are heritage-style vacation homes with similar amenities to those you'll find at the main house. Dover is the more "feminine" of the two properties, with dainty floral-patterned wallpaper and comforters. Kelly House has a more dominant color scheme, and a sleeker, Euro-design kitchen. Also affiliated with the same owner is the Artisan Inn, a waterfront property with dedicated studio space for arty types.

High St., Trinity. © **877/464-7700** or 709/464-3377. www.trinityvacations.com. C$99–C$225 (US$85–US$193). Open May–Oct. AE, DC, MC, V. **Amenities:** Gourmet breakfast; laundry service; book and video library; Dutch and French spoken. *In room:* Amenities and rates vary considerably, depending on whether you're taking a B&B room, suite, or one of the vacation homes. Packed lunches available on request for C$12 (US$11); 3-course dinners for C$35 (US$30) per person.

Eriksen Properties 🎔🎔

An haute-atmosphere establishment that couldn't decide if it wanted to be a high-class B&B or a gourmet restaurant, so it became both. Originally the home of a 19th-century merchant, Eriksen Properties shows what it was like to live in outport high society 200 years ago. Furnished with authentic period pieces, including Victrolas and handmade washbasins, this Mansard-style home deliberately evokes Victorian charm. But the real extravagance is in the fine-dining room, where gourmet treats are served with classical flair (think of succulent scallops in a white-wine sauce and a piano concerto softly filling the background). No reservations; seating is on a first-come, first-served basis. Also at the inn is Polly's Pantry, open daily through the summer season for light lunches.

Rte. 230, Trinity. © **877/464-3698** or 709/464-3698. www.trinityexperience.com. 7 units. C$85–C$125 (US$73–US$108). Each additional person or rollaway cot C$15 (US$13). AE, MC, V, Interac. Open May–Oct. **Amenities:** Full complimentary breakfast; restaurant; TV, VCR, and phone in common area; nonsmoking rooms (smoking allowed on patios). Restaurant: Lunches C$4–C$8 (US$3.50–US$7), dinners C$14–C$20 (US$12–US$17). May–Oct daily 8am–9pm.

Fishers' Loft Inn 🎔🎔🎔

It's a 5-minute road trip outside Trinity proper to the favored destination of visiting movie stars. Both Dame Judi Dench and Kevin Spacey stayed at Fishers' Loft during filming of *The Shipping News.* With good reason: on the exterior it fits in well with the local architecture, but inside it has the world-class flavor you'd expect from its cosmopolitan owners. John and Peggy Fisher are from England and Ottawa, Ontario, respectively. The former professional restorers (they were involved in the reconstruction of Toronto's Adelaide Court Theatre) brought their talents to Port Rexton in 1990, when they decided to turn their summer home into a year-round residence. Their handiwork is evident in each of the distinctive guest

---

Tips Best Seat in the House

For the best possible view of Trinity, stroll over to Courthouse Road, behind the Royal Bank. Climb the hill, following the hiking trail to the top, where you'll be rewarded with an incredible view of Trinity Bay. Do it just before sunset, when the soft pre-dusk lighting produces picture-perfect colors leaving you with a visual memory to last a lifetime.

Camping on the Bonavista Peninsula

If you prefer natural over man-made history, pitch your tent at **Lockston Path Provincial Park**—a provincially run campground with 36 semi-serviced and 20 fully serviced sheltered campsites, as well as a lakefront beach for swimming (© **709/464-3553**; www.gov.nf.ca/parks&reserves). The lower-numbered campsites are closest to the water, while nos. 41 to 56 have the advantage of being beside a wheelchair-accessible comfort station with laundry and shower facilities as well as a dumping station.

Lockston Path Provincial Park is 6km (less than 4 miles) from Port Rexton on Route 236—about a 15-minute drive from Trinity. The woods grow close to the road on this unpaved route, so keep a sharp eye out for four-legged pedestrians.

rooms, all of which have a big-screen view of the mini-islands scattered along the shore of Trinity Bay. The quilts and simply styled furnishings hint at old-world austerity, but the down-filled duvets are pure luxury where it counts the most.

The royal treatment becomes even more evident in the dining room, where the in-house cooks work under the tutelage of consulting chef Todd Perrin. (Perrin is a free-lance chef; his culinary artistry has graced the tables of dining rooms as far away as Switzerland.) Together, they create unique menus that are several steps ahead of the fare you'll find in most inns this size: carrot-ginger soup with fresh French bread, grilled chicken with lime mayonnaise and roasted vegetables, and frozen meringue cream with a partridgeberry coulis. *Tip:* Plan on splurging on the meal package—this is the place you've been saving for. *Hint:* Daily menus are fixed, so call ahead to see what's being served.

Mill Rd., Port Rexton. © **877/464-3240** or 709/464-3240. www.fishersloft.com. 21 units. Room only: C$110–C$194 (US$95–US$167) double. Rates with breakfast and dinner: C$224–C$308 (US$192–US$265) double. Discounts for multi-night stays in May and Oct. AE, DC, MC, V. Open May 15–Oct 31. **Amenities:** Gourmet dining; bar. *In room:* TV w/VCR available on request, dataport, en-suite bathrooms, down duvets.

Village Inn ☜   Village Inn offers a traditional inn atmosphere where guests are encouraged to socialize with their hosts rather than hide away in their rooms. If, after a busy day of touring and a satisfying meal, you're ready to relax but not quite ready for bed, head down to the living room. That's where you'll find owners Dr. Peter Beamish and wife Christine, along with other guests and any friends who happen to visit, engaged in lively conversation. Whales tend to be a popular item for discussion, and no wonder. Beamish is a biologist who has been studying whales for 30 years. If you're really keen on the oceanic behemoths, you can listen to his lectures on communications research with the whales or watch a film or slide show. From June through October, you can take it a step further by going out in Beamish's boat for an experience you'll never forget. (See the "Outdoor Pursuits" section below for details on the Ocean Contact whale experience.)

Guest rooms at the Village Inn have old-style beds, handcrafted Newfoundland quilts, folk furniture, and hardwood floors. All rooms have en-suite or private bathrooms. It's a kid-friendly environment without the abundance of breakables you'll find in so many other establishments. Ask about special deals for their 3-, 5-, and 7-night packages that include activities such as whale-watching. The small dining room (open to the public for dinner) serves traditional Newfoundland favorites at reasonable prices.

Taverner's Path, Trinity. © **709/464-3269.** www.oceancontact.com. 7 units in inn and 4 in adjacent guesthouse. C$75–C$100 (US$65–US$86). MC, V, Interac. **Amenities:** Dining room; library with collections on whales and whale research; nonsmoking; Internet access, fax machine; piano, games, TV/VCR in common room; children welcome; ample parking. *In room:* AM/FM radios, private bathrooms.

EXPLORING TRINITY

Begin your Trinity Village visit at the **Trinity Interpretation Centre** (© **709/729-0592**). Here you'll get a one-page map naming each of the significant sites (convenient in a town where so many of the buildings look like heritage structures). From there, your next stop should be the Lester-Garland Premises, located in the former general store. Take a look at the original 1896 ledger to see the names and purchases made by residents of the time. Hiscock House, a 1910 restoration, represents a typical merchant's household, complete with fancy furnishings. Next door to that is a craft shop that closes at 5:30pm, so try not to arrive too late in the day or you may be disappointed.

The various historical sites are open 10am to 5:30pm during the summer months. *Tip:* Some are Provincial Historic Sites and others are managed by the Trinity Historical Society and Trinity Trust, so you can't buy one pass to get into everything. The Interpretation Centre, Lester-Garland Premises, and Hiscock House are run by the province and can be seen under one package price of C$2.50 (US$2.15) per person. The Trinity Museum, Green Family Forge, Court House, and Lester-Garland House (built in 1819, this was Newfoundland's first brick home) are run by the Trinity Historical Society and Trust and will cost you another C$2 (US$1.75) per person. Unless you're staying in the area for several days and have lots of time, or are really interested in the details of local history, I think you'll get enough out of the three provincial sites—allow a couple of hours for all three.

Note: The historical experience is so well integrated within the community it's easy to forget that people really live here. When you see someone hanging out clothes or eating supper, remember they're not historical interpreters—they're residents. Say hello, but respect their privacy.

(Kids All Aboard!

For a trip on the longest mini–train ride in North America, head to **Trinity Loop.** It runs along one of the last remaining pieces of line from the Newfoundland Railway, which provided service from coast to coast until services stopped in 1984. This section of track, a spur from the main line, makes a wide loop around a pond on a 2,000m-long (1¼-mile) track that drops 10m (34 ft.) from beginning to end. The 10-minute trip is the highlight of a low-key amusement park, especially as you look out over the pond as you cross the bridge. In addition to the train, you'll also find aqua water trikes, rowboats, pedal boats, kayaks, bumper boats, a Ferris wheel, minigolf, and a railway museum built in—what else?(railway cars. Trinity Loop is on Route 239; follow the signs south of the Trinity Village turnoff. Visa and MasterCard accepted, Interac available. There is no day pass: you pay as you ride. Both the train and the Ferris wheel are C$4 (US$3.50) adult, C$3 (US$2.60) child. Water rides range from C$5–C$6 (US$4.30–US$5.15) per half-hour.

Random Passage

If you're a movie buff, you've probably already seen the movie *The Shipping News* and know that it was filmed in Trinity Harbour. But *Random Passage*, based on the novels *Random Passage* and *Waiting for Time* by Bernice Morgan, was filmed 14km (less than 9 miles) from Trinity, south along Route 239 in **New Bonaventure.**

Travelers can still visit the **film set** (© 709/464-2233; www.random passagefilmset.com), which includes a number of early-1800s houses, a church, school, and fishing stages and flakes (wooden structures upon which fish was traditionally dried and salted). With its weathered gray dwellings and denuded spruce trees for fencing, this re-created settlement depicts the hardships of living in a world without running water or electric heat, physically cut off from the world, dependent on a merciless sea for its people's livelihood. Set tours run mid-June through September 9am to 7:30pm and cost C$7 (US$6) for adults, C$5 (US$4.30) for seniors, C$3.50 (US$3) for children 5 to 16, and C$14 (US$12) for families.

NIGHTLIFE

A trip to Trinity wouldn't be complete without treating yourself to a performance of the **Rising Tide Theatre** (© 888/464-3377; www.risingtidetheatre.com), a professional theater company since 1978. Between June and October each year, the company puts on a number of performances in an outdoor seaside venue. It costs C$16 (US$14) for one of the regular plays in the program, and C$31 (US$27) for the dinner theater. You'll find the Rising Tide box office in the Rising Tide Arts Centre, near the waterfront.

Rising Tide's prime offering is the **Trinity Pageant** ✸, the anchor event of Trinity's Summer in the Bight Theatre Festival. Actors move from one historical site to another throughout the town, telling a story as they go. There are times when the wind and passing traffic overwhelm the actors' voices, but these impressive improv artists usually find a way to integrate such minor technicalities into the script. The pageant is held from early July until Labour Day on Wednesday, Saturday, and Sunday. Tickets are just C$12 (US$11).

If you're not into live theater but love live music, put on your dancing shoes and shuffle over to the only bar in town: **Rocky's Place** (© 709/464-3400), just up the road from Campbell House. On Wednesday evenings during the summer, fiddler Kelly Russell and folklorist Tonya Kearley get together here for Dance Up (a lively mélange of folk music and step-dancing). While you're welcome to sit back and enjoy the show, audience participation is a given. Don't worry about not knowing the steps—the music itself has a way of telling you how to move.

OUTDOOR PURSUITS

If you're looking for a more active adventure than you'll find at the local museum, invigorating outdoor activities are easy to find in and around Trinity. You can charter a yacht, go sea kayaking, or watch whales with one of Newfoundland's foremost whale experts.

If you're into hiking, you'll really enjoy the network of hiking trails developed by the local community association. Known as the Discovery Trail (not to be confused with the peninsula's driving route of the same name), the 10 trails retrace the footpaths traditionally used by early European and aboriginal settlers. You can hike along rocky outcrops 30m (100 ft.) above sea level, visit the abandoned communities of Kerley's Harbour and British Harbour, or listen to the music of a water-caressed sea stack. Several of the trails are less than 5km (3 miles) in length, to a maximum of 17km (10.5 miles). All trails are well signposted. Ask your local lodging for a map, or go to www.thediscoverytrail.org/english/hikediscovery/index.html.

Atlantic Adventures Boat Charters & Tours   Set sail for an all-in-one yachting adventure, whale-watching tour, dinner theater, and port explorer. Your host Art Andrews (former CBC radio personality) invites you for a 3-hour nature cruise aboard his 14m (46-ft.) ketch-rigged sailing boat *Atlantic Adventure*. It's a glorious feeling to be standing on the forward deck, feet braced on the plank floor, hands gripping the railing, and all 60 sq. m (642 sq. ft.) of sail stretching to catch the wind. With each graceful dip of her prow, you feel the salty sting of pure freedom. You may even find yourself in the company of a curious humpback or minke as you head into one of the narrow harbors leading to an abandoned fishing port. The 1-hour dinner cruise is limited to 12 people, but should really be no more than 8 in order to comfortably accommodate elbow room and the characters who entertain you while you dine.

Departures from Trinity Wharf. ✆ 709/464-2133. www.atlanticadventures.com. May–Oct. 3-hour nature cruise C$40–C$50 (US$35–US$43) per person; 8-hr. outport cruise C$80 (US$69) per person. MC, V.

Mag-Ami Kayaking   No-frills kayaking at its best. You won't be treated to fancy feasts or trained entertainers at Mag-Ami—just the opportunity of a lifetime to get eye-to-eye with whales, water, and seabirds. Nick and Wanda Donovan are expert instructors with a talent for making even the most apprehensive beginner comfortable with a paddle. You'll soon find yourself gliding across the ocean, changing direction with a shift of your weight or a turn of your shoulder. Sure, you can rent the kayak and go out on your own, but for just a bit more money you can go on an excursion with an expert guide. They'll show you the best places for sea caves, whale feeding grounds, and icebergs (in season), as well as abandoned settlements. If you head out on the full-day excursion, you'll be treated to an authentic Newfoundland "boil-up." *Tip:* Bring along extra footwear (as your feet tend to get wet in the kayak) as well as a warm jacket and sunscreen. Even when the air is chilly, the sun reflected off the water can give you a painful burn.

Tours depart from Trinity Wharf. ✆ 709/466-2451 or 709/464-7538. http://magamikayaking.tripod.com. Half-day tour C$50 (US$43); full-day tour C$90 (US$78). Rentals: C$10/hour (US$8.50); C$40/day (US$35); C$100/weekend (US$86). C$10 (US$8.50) extra for wet suit rental. Mid-May to Sept. No credit cards.

Enjoying a Newfoundland Boil-up

Boil-ups are a traditional Newfoundland way to enjoy a sunny summer afternoon—the equivalent of the North American picnic with sandwiches and lemonade or iced tea. But in Newfoundland, the beach boil-up generally includes boiling the kettle for a cup of tea and having a bun or slice of homemade bread with it.

"O Buena Vista!"

These were the words uttered by Italian explorer Giovanni Caboto (aka John Cabot) on his first sight of Cape Bonavista on June 24, 1497. He and his 20-man crew had been sailing into the unknown for 5 tense weeks, wondering if at any minute they were going to fall off the edge of the Earth. They were on a mission, funded by King Henry VII of England, to investigate whatever lands they might find by sailing west from Europe across the Atlantic. The underlying hope was that they would discover a shorter passage to the Far East. Instead, Cabot found a new-founde-lande teeming with fish reportedly so plentiful they filled a net at a single dip. Whether Cabot's cry of "O buena vista!" (Oh beautiful sight!) expressed his appreciation for the view, or relief that he and his near-mutiny crew had finally found land, remains shrouded in history.

Ocean Contact ✸✸✸ If you're looking for the best possible interactive whale experience in Trinity Bay, you'll find it through Dr. Peter Beamish. His "Ocean Contact" concept offers unique opportunities in human–whale interaction as you take part in active research. The whales come so close to Beamish's 8m (26-ft.) rigid hull inflatable you'll practically be able to touch them. This is a tad scary when you're in a Zodiac, but you can trust that the man knows what he's doing, as he hasn't lost a passenger yet!

One thing I especially like about Ocean Contact is that they don't overfill the Zodiacs like some other tour operators I've been with. The boats hold 24 people, but Beamish generally doesn't put more than 12 onboard at a time—and he'll go out with a minimum of just two people. This gives you room to maneuver if you're trying to get that perfect picture of a nearby whale. There are four sailings daily, but I'd recommend the early-morning cruise, when the water is generally the calmest and the wildlife most active. Beamish and his wife, Christine, also own and operate the **Village Inn** in Trinity; check the website for packages.

Trinity. ✆ **709/464-3269.** www.oceancontact.com. C$55 (US$48) adult; C$45 (US$39) ages13–15; C$35 (US$30) ages 4–12. MC, V, Interac. June–Oct daily departures.

BONAVISTA ✸✸

At the tip of the Bonavista Peninsula and the site where *continental* Europeans first touched North American soil more than 500 years ago (the Vikings were here first; you can read about that in chapter 8), Bonavista is an almost full-service community. It has a hospital, pharmacy, gas station, and banking services, but little in the way of accommodations (apart from a couple of B&Bs and a small motel). That being the case, it's best to think of Bonavista as a half-day excursion from Trinity, or Trinity–Bonavista as a full-day trip from Clarenville.

WHERE TO STAY AND DINE

Elizabeth J. Cottages ✸✸ An unexpected slice of luxury at the end of the road. No expense has been spared in the construction and interior design of these two spacious two-bedroom cottages that enjoy an absolute oceanfront setting on the edge of town. Styled on the Newfoundland saltbox style of home, the cottages are anything but traditional. The units fill with natural light, and come with unexpected niceties such as sleigh beds fitted with Egyptian cotton sheets, plush bathrobes, and baskets of breakfast provisions. Other highlights are a modern entertainment system, polished hardwood flooring, a private deck and barbecue, and a well-equipped kitchen.

Harris St., Bonavista. ℂ 866/468-5035 or 709/468-5035. www.elizabethjcottages.com. 2 units. C$250 (US$215) double. Off-season discounts. MC, V. *In room:* TV w/DVD, dataport, luxurious bathroom, kitchen, laundry facility, fireplace, barbecue.

Skipper's Café *Value* LOCAL FARE   Beside Ryan Premises, this dining room is as close to the water as you can be without getting wet. It offers a lovely, unobstructed view of Bonavista Harbour, coupled with a traditional food menu at reasonable prices. The seafood chowder may seem a tad expensive, but it's well worth it—with hearty chunks of salmon, cod, scallops, and shrimp. The cod au gratin is similarly noteworthy. The cod is caught locally, giving you an unbeatable fresh flavor topped with plenty of bubbling cheddar. Skipper's has a full liquor license, and boasts local Newfoundland wines as well as friendly service.

42 Campbell St., Bonavista ℂ 709/468-7150. Reservations not necessary. Main courses C$7–C$14 (US$6–US$12). MC, V. June–Sept 10am–9pm daily.

EXPLORING BONAVISTA

Cape Bonavista Lighthouse *⚲⚲*   A leisurely 3km (less than 2 miles) through the town of Bonavista is Cape Bonavista, site of a photogenic red-and-white-striped lighthouse. Interpreters dressed in 1870s costume will guide you through this beautifully restored facility, with its 9m-high (30-ft.) central stone tower (housed inside the building). The attention to historical detail is exquisite, from the warmth of the kitchen woodstove to the toys in the children's bedroom. After viewing the living quarters of the former lighthouse keeper, his assistant, and the assistant's family, you head up the steps to the top of the tower. From here, you can see puffins flitting around nests burrowed into various granite cliffs. Allow your eyes to trace the rust-tinted rock as it lowers to meet the sea, then follow the vast expanse of ocean until it fades into the horizon. The view is magnificent, but you may still be disappointed—it's all just for looks these days; an automated light is mounted atop a metal tower constructed alongside the lighthouse.

When you're finished the inside tour, take an hour or two to explore the marshy grounds around the site itself. Climb to the hill above the parking lot, where you'll discover a miniature pond and sandpipers searching for insects in the mud while bluebells tinkle in a light breeze and a whale snorts in the distance. Turn to the left and walk across the barrens to the municipal park, where you'll find a statue of John Cabot. Along the way, you may be lucky enough to sight the low-growing orange-red berry known as the bakeapple. Also called a cloudberry, it grows only in this province and Norway.

Cape Shore Rd., Cape Bonavista. ℂ 709/468-7444. C$3 (US$2.60) for age 13 and over. Same admission gets you into the Mockbeggar Plantation. Mid-June to Sept daily 10am–5:30pm.

⸂Fun Fact⸃ **Getting to Know the Puffin**

The official feathered mascot of Newfoundland and Labrador is the puffin, a penguin-size bird roughly 30 centimeters (12 in.) tall with a large white face and prominent, colorfully striped beak. Also known as the "sea parrot," puffins are excellent swimmers and divers. Their flying, however, is decidedly less graceful.

Dungeon Provincial Park   Located on the tip of the Bonavista Peninsula near the Cape Bonavista Lighthouse is Dungeon Provincial Park, a natural scenic wonder. The Dungeon is a collapsed sea cave with a natural archway carved out by ocean movement. It looks like someone—or something—literally sucked the land down into the ocean through the dual "straws" formed by the arches. Situated on what is locally known as "Backside," on a scenic but bumpy gravel road (approximately 2km/1 mile off Rte. 235), complete with pasture land for horses, cows, and sheep, a trip to the Dungeon makes for a nice diversion.

Cape Shore Rd., Cape Bonavista. ℭ 709-635-4520. June 1–Sept 30. Picnic sites and pit toilets are available for day users. No camping.

Matthew   Down at the harbor, you can board but you can't sail on a 20th-century reconstruction of John Cabot's 15th-century ship. The 30-minute tour, led by costumed interpreters, provides a fascinating insight into the trials faced by Cabot and his crew as they sailed the wild waters of the Atlantic in the very close quarters of a 19m (63-ft.), three-masted, wooden caravel. Imagine yourself as one of the 21 people who lived and worked on just such a ship for the 5-week crossing—manually pumping the bilge, struggling for sleep, surrounded by caged livestock, living on salt fish and ale—and you'll come a lot closer to understanding why Cabot was so grateful to make landfall at Bonavista.

Roper St., Bonavista. ℭ 877/468-1497 or 709/468-1493. www.matthewlegacy.com. C$6.50 (US$5.60) adults, C$6 (US$5.15) seniors, C$2.25 (US$1.95) ages 6–16, free for under 6, C$16 (US$14) family. May–Oct daily 10am–6:30pm. Give yourself at least an hour to tour the Visitor Interpretation Centre, ship, and gift shop.

Mockbeggar Plantation Provincial Historic Site   Although it's 300 years old, this waterfront property has a more recent event to thank for its Provincial Historic Site status. In March 1946, two of the most important political figures of the day met here to plot strategy for the upcoming referendum that would decide whether Newfoundland joined the Canadian Confederation. Gordon Bradley and Joseph R. "Joey" Smallwood agreed that, if successful in getting a majority vote in favor of Confederation, Smallwood would become premier and Bradley would become Newfoundland's first cabinet minister in Canada's federal government. Aside from being silent listeners to secret political machinations, the walls of Mockbeggar show how the upper class of the time lived, offering quite a contrast from the very basic lifestyle common to most residents of the fishing villages. Highlights include a stained-glass window inside the main house that depicts the *Matthew,* as well as an old-fashioned carpentry shop and cod-liver oil factory.

Mockbeggar Rd., Bonavista. ℭ 709/468-7300. www.tcr.gov.nl.ca/tcr/historicsites/Mockbeggar.htm. C$3 (US$2.60) admission for 13 and over. This admission also gets you into the Bonavista Lighthouse. June–Sept daily 10am–5:30pm.

Ryan Premises National Historic Site ⍟   There's nothing grand or ostentatious about this cluster of five white, red-trimmed, wooden structures with sharply angled roofs on the Bonavista waterfront. And that's exactly why you should include them on your itinerary! The understated drama of their purpose-built design gives new life to the daily interactions of 19th-century fishermen and merchants. When you walk through the former offices, look at the figures logged on the old ledger. Fishermen would sell their fish to the merchant and get paid in goods from the company store, owned by the same merchant to whom they had sold their fish. Rarely did this barter system work to the fishermen's advantage, with more than one of them going to an uneasy grave because they died indebted to the merchant.

Wonderful Woodwork

While at the Ryan Premises, check out the unique wooden furnishings and collectibles handcrafted by Mike Paterson of **Paterson Woodworking** ⟨⟩, a company based in nearby Upper Amherst Cove. If you're intrigued by Paterson's display of period reproductions at the Ryan Premises, drive down Route 235 to his shop and see his range of products from C$25 to C$3,000 (US$22–US$2,577). Call ⟨⟩ **709/445-4341** or go to www.patersonwoodworking.com for showroom hours or to request a copy of their catalog.

As you wander around the site, you'll encounter plank floors and sawdust, thick-beamed building supports, and the unmistakable scent of salt fish. You'll watch videos, read storyboards, and speak to costumed re-enactors demonstrating how the fishery brought Newfoundland and Labrador into the global economy hundreds of years before e-commerce, NAFTA, or the WTO.

Rte. 235, Bonavista Harbour. ⟨⟩ **709/468-1600.** www.pc.gc.ca/lhn-nhs/nl/ryan. C$4 (US$3.50) adults, C$3.50 (US$3) seniors, C$2 (US$1.75) children, and C$10 (US$8.50) family. May 15–Oct 15 10am–6pm. Gift shop on-site; restaurant next door. Ask about the live performances put on by the Rising Tide Theatre. Theater tickets should be reserved in advance.

2 Burin Peninsula

It's a long and lonely drive for most of the 198km (124 miles) from the time you turn off the Trans-Canada Highway at Goobies to Grand Bank near the tip of the Burin Peninsula. Approximately 60% of the peninsula's 28,000 residents live in one of the five major communities of Burin, Fortune, Grand Bank, St. Lawrence, and Marystown, the communities discussed in this chapter.

The drive down the Burin Peninsula may seem like a tedious journey over relatively flat land, with a sameness of scenery underwhelmingly punctuated by gray-brown boulders. But wait—move in for a closer look. Those aren't just rocks. They're glacial erratics, 10,000-year-old footprints of the last ice age. That's the way it is in much of Newfoundland and Labrador: even the most ordinary detail can take on new significance if you know how to look at it. You could allow yourself to be bored because it doesn't have the bustle of New York City or the architectural treasures of Italy. Or you can open your eyes to the natural understated glamour of the place, thrilling in the simple things. Like the line of birch mirrored in a ripple-free pond. Or the circling flight of a bald eagle on the hunt. And a people who'll smilingly acknowledge your presence, often stopping in the middle of whatever they're doing to say hello and help you on your way. The Burin Peninsula throbs with under-acknowledged beauty. Whether or not you see it is up to you.

ESSENTIALS
GETTING THERE

Route 210 (also referred to as the Burin Peninsula Hwy. or Heritage Run) spurs south of the Trans-Canada Highway at Goobies, 162km (100 miles) west of St. John's. If you're traveling east to west across the island, take the left turn onto Route 210 just past the Irving gas station (watch for the giant statue of Morris the Moose out front). Route 210 will take you all the way to Marystown, the largest community on the

Burin Peninsula. Past Marystown, there's a looped highway that takes you to the coastal communities around the foot of the Burin Peninsula (see the map on p. 125).

VISITOR INFORMATION

Information about sites along the Heritage Run is available from the **Heritage Run Tourism Association,** which has an office in Marystown at 1 Centennial Rd. in the lighthouse-shaped building located at the entrance to town (© **709/279-1887;** www. theheritagerun.com). The office is open from mid-June to mid-September daily 9am to 9pm. You'll also find visitor information centers in Goobies at the Irving gas station, at the intersection of routes 210 and 1 (© **709/542-3239**), and in Fortune (© **709/832-3031**) near the waterfront Customs Office. Hours at this location coincide with the arrival and departure of the St.-Pierre ferry.

Visitor information for the French islands of St. Pierre and Miquelon is available from **St. Pierre Tours Ltd** and **Lake's Travel Ltd.,** which share an office at 5 Bayview

---

Moments   **Ghosts of Days Gone By** ✮✮✮

A common theme in Newfoundland and Labrador culture is the dreaded necessity of having to leave someone or something you love (usually for economic reasons). In certain cases, entire towns have been abandoned. Such is the case with Woody Island. Except for a handful of seasonal fishing families, this once-prosperous community of 400 became a ghost town after the provincial government's resettlement programs of the 1960s.

A 40-minute sail across the waters of Placentia Bay to **Woody Island Resort** (© **800/504-1066** or 709/364-3701; fax 709/745-4937; www.woodyi.com) will bring you as close as a visitor could possibly come to understanding the indestructible connection that ties Newfoundlanders to their anchor, the Rock. While you'll stay in a fully equipped tourist lodge (open from late Apr to late October), the furnishings (ca. 1950s), tufted bedspreads, and aging linoleum make the experience as authentic as possible. Rooms range from C$139 to C$149 (US$120–US$128).

You may at first marvel that anyone would want to live so far away from the rest of the world, but you'll soon come to understand the Newfoundlander's love of place. Your first stirrings of empathy come to life with resort owner Loyola Pomroy's stories of days gone by (Pomroy was born on another resettled island—Merasheen—38km/24 miles south of Woody Island). Then, standing beside the cracked stone monuments and simple wooden crosses of uncles, parents, children, and sisters long gone but not forgotten, you feel the magnetic pull of this land. You smell it in the smoke of your beachside bonfire. It seeps into your bones as you hike in the footsteps of families and friends who will never again tend to their sheep or vegetable gardens. It becomes part of you with every breath of salt air and every glimpse of naked foundation. By the end of your 2-day tour, you may well find yourself on the upper deck of the *Merasheen*, fixated on that final glimpse of departing land, unexpected tears of bereavement mingling with the ocean spray.

St. in Fortune (𝄞 **800/563-2006** or 709/832-0429). St. Pierre Tours Ltd. also has an office in St. John's at 116 Duckworth St. (𝄞 **888/959-8214**). *Note:* When visiting the islands, you must have a passport and the same documentation as though you were visiting France (which means visa for the citizens of many non-European and North American countries).

GETTING AROUND

You'll find far fewer services for visitors in this region than on the Avalon or Bonavista Peninsulas. Be sure to plan ahead and pack snacks or a lunch, especially if you're traveling in the evening or on a Sunday, when services may be closed. The same advice goes for filling up your gas tank. Don't assume that just because you'll soon be arriving at a village that there is a gas station there, or that it will be open if you're arriving outside of daytime business hours.

The tourist brochures divide the Burin Peninsula into four regions, each traversed by a different numbered highway, beginning with Route 210, which extends all the way to Marystown, the region's major center on the east coast of the Burin Peninsula. This part of the route is known as **Mariner Drive.** The connecting route from Marystown south through routes 222, 221, and 220 to the community of Epworth, near Burin, is known as **Captain Cook Drive.** The portion of Route 220 that takes you around the bottom of the peninsula is **Captain Clarke Drive.**

The segment of Route 220 that takes you to Fortune (where you catch the ferry to the French islands of St. Pierre and Miquelon) and nearby Grand Bank is appropriately known as the **French Islands Drive.** It's all a bit confusing—with the route changing its name and number with nearly every bend in the road—but apart from a couple of very short side routes that branch off from Route 210–220 it's all one road and you can't get lost.

GOOBIES TO MARYSTOWN

As you begin your journey along Route 210, you'll leave the fast pace of the Trans-Canada Highway at Goobies, a small community of 250 residents 162km (100 miles) northwest of St. John's. Goobies is your gateway to the Burin Peninsula.

Marystown, the major regional commercial center of the Burin Peninsula with nearly 7,000 residents, is 144km (90 miles) southwest of Goobies. It doesn't sound that far, but if you look at the map you'll see it isn't a straight drive.

A little over halfway between Goobies and Marystown along Route 210, Route 212 spurs west to the community of **Bay L'Argent.** This is the departure point for a passenger-only ferry to **Rencontre East** and **Pool's Cove,** two isolated outports of Central Newfoundland. While Pool's Cove is accessible by road, the 1-hour and 45-minute passenger ferry is the only way into or out of Rencontre East, home to 200 people. It's a land of lush green hills, gravel roads, fishing boats, wooden wharves, and a single B&B. For just C$50 (US$43) per night double, you can stay in the home of Margaret and Fred Mullins, a 5-minute walk from the ferry (𝄞 **709/848-3226**). The ferry travels back and forth between Bay L'Argent–Rencontre East–Pool's Cove several times per day. One-way fare is C$4.25 (US$3.65) per adult and C$2.25 (US$1.95) per child or senior. For more information, call 𝄞 **709/891-1050** or visit the ferry schedule website at www.gov.nf.ca/FerryServices/schedules/O-rencontr.stm.

WHERE TO STAY & DINE

You aren't going to find much in the way of accommodations or restaurants between Goobies and Marystown. Which means you either eat at the Irving Restaurant in

Goobies (it's typical Irving, with clean bathroom, booth seating, slow service, and filling food at a reasonable price), or you wait for the bigger selection in Marystown. *Tip:* While you can function on low fuel for a few hours, your car can't. It's a good idea to fill your tank in Goobies before beginning the next 144km (90 miles) to Marystown.

Hotel Marystown ⚔   Part of Atlantic Canada's City Hotels chain, the best thing about the Hotel Marystown is its location—you're just 70km/43 miles (about 40 min.) from the St. Pierre ferry, and Marystown is a central point for exploring the Burin Peninsula. Bilingual service is offered and the hotel has a pretty good restaurant (see below). Although thoroughly revamped in 2005, the guest rooms themselves are standard for the brand (bland decor, comfortable beds, desk)—if you've seen one, you've seen them all.

76 Ville Marie Dr., Marystown. ⓒ **866/612-6800** or 709/279-1600. www.cityhotels.ca. 131 units. C$79–C$129 (US$68–US$111). AE, DC, MC, V, Interac. **Amenities:** Banquet/meeting facilities; P.J. Billington's Restaurant; lobby bar, lounge; saloon; room service; air-conditioned public areas; business services; laundry/valet services; pets allowed; walking distance to mall. *In room:* Private, 3-piece bathrooms, Internet access, kitchen facilities in efficiency units.

Kilmory Resort ⚔⚔⚔   You'll pay more here than for the standard rent-a-cabin, but it's worth it. Kilmory Resort is the absolute, unequivocal, best cottage getaway in the province. Private decks, a well-maintained modern playground, overstuffed furnishings, and floor-to-ceiling pine interiors all contribute to the perfection of your stay. It's a pastoral idyll of cozy log chalets and camping in a quiet, private setting overlooking Piper's Hole River and the Bear's Folly Mountains. Be sure to take a stroll to the top of the hill overlooking Swift Current as the view is spectacular—especially in the fall, when the foliage turns intense shades of reds and oranges. If you enjoy winter sports, Kilmory Resort is a great place for snowmobiling as well as cross-country skiing—making it the most beautiful resort to stay at on the Burin Peninsula, any time of year.

Rte. 210, Swift Current. ⓒ **888/884-2410** or 709/549-2410. www.kilmoryresort.com. 21 units. C$89–C$159 (US$77–US$137) double; additional person C$8 (US$7). 10 campsites C$20 (US$17). AE, MC, V, Interac. Cabins open year-round. Camping from May 20–Oct 15. **Amenities:** Boat and canoe rentals; dumping station; electrical hookup (15 and 30 amp); sewer hookup; shower/washroom facilities; water hookup; heated pool in summer; snowmobile and ski rentals in winter.

P.J. Billington's Restaurant FAMILY   Decorated with a theme corresponding to the colorful rum-running history of the Burin Peninsula area, Billington's has a casual, relaxed, and friendly atmosphere. The best value of the day is at breakfast: you can have a complete breakfast with toast, hash browns, scrambled eggs, bacon, sausage, juice, and tea or coffee for C$5 (US$4.30).

Hotel Marystown, 76 Ville Marie Dr., Marystown. ⓒ **709/279-1600**. Reservations not required, but appreciated. Main courses C$8–C$20 (US$7–US$17). AE, DC, MC, V, Interac. Mon–Sat 7am–11pm; Sun 8am–9pm.

Trailside Motel   If you've made your way as far as Goobies (about a 1½-hr. drive from St. John's) and would like to stay for the night before you head down the Burin Peninsula, there is a small, full-service lodge that might fit the bill. Trailside Motel will give you a comfortable place to lay your head and get a good home-cooked meal in a casual, friendly, and rustic atmosphere. The guest rooms—although clean, with comfortable beds and private, three-piece bathrooms—are best suited for a brief stopover. If you're looking for something fancier, you're best off continuing down the Burin Peninsula.

Rte. 1, Goobies. ⓒ **709/542-3444**. Fax 709/542-3445. 13 units. C$60–C$70 (US$52–US$60). AE, MC, V, Interac. **Amenities:** Restaurant; pub; pool table; video lottery machines. *In room:* Private bathroom, satellite TV, telephone.

Wong's Palace Restaurant CHINESE   It's like a fish out of water: a genuinely authentic Chinese restaurant in the Newfoundland heartland. It doesn't look the part, but just wait until you taste the chow mein—you'll think you're in the middle of Chinatown. Wong's is a fully licensed restaurant offering both Canadian and Chinese (primarily Cantonese) fare. Prices are very reasonable, with traditional Chinese dishes like their highly recommended chow mein starting at C$7 (US$6) and a la carte dishes such as steaks, chicken, and seafood going for around C$16 (US$14).

McGettigan Blvd., Marystown. (℃ 709/279-3773. Reservations not required. C$7–C$16 (US$6–US$14). MC, V, Interac. Sun–Thurs 11am–10:30pm; Fri–Sat 11am–11:30pm.

EXPLORING MARYSTOWN

One of the most prominent features of Marystown is Kiewit Offshore Services, the largest marine fabrication and outfitting facility in the province. Mortier Bay, which leads into Marystown Harbour, is one of the largest natural harbors in the world, at 2,300×250m (7,544×820 ft.).

Moving farther down the road, you'll find there are two shopping malls in Marystown, complete with banks, supermarkets, a liquor store, pharmacy, and department store. The town's recreational facilities include an indoor swimming pool, a municipal park, track and field facilities, and a stadium.

Marystown Museum (℃ **709/279-1462**), on Ville Marie Drive, is open from early June to early October. The displays include numerous local artifacts (for example, glass floats, ship models, and a "gob stick"—you'll have to visit to find out what that is!) and provide an interesting interpretation of the area's history.

BURIN

Detouring off Route 210 onto secondary Route 221, you'll arrive in **Burin,** a community of about 3,000 residents. This stretch of coast boasts quite a colorful seafaring history. The famous navigator and cartographer Captain James Cook spent five summers navigating the coast of Newfoundland between 1763 and 1767. His goal was to create the first accurate maps of the area, complete with sailing directions and advice on safe anchorage. Captain Cook used one of the best vantage points in the Burin area to keep an eye out for smugglers, illegal French fishing boats, and French and American mercenaries called privateers. The **Captain Cook Lookout** in Burin bears the explorer's name.

In town, **Burin Heritage Museum** is an impressive facility, with 15 display rooms that pay tribute to the community's seafaring past. It has a gallery for art and traveling exhibits, a craft shop and tearoom, and is open from the May 24 (Victoria Day) weekend through early October, 10am until 6pm, with extended hours during July and August to 8pm (℃ **709/891-2217**).

FRENCHMAN'S COVE

This tiny village, 25km (16 miles) west of Marystown along Route 213, is home to a 9-hole golf course, a small provincial park, and a couple of recommended accommodations.

Frenchman's Cove Provincial Park   is a quiet, picturesque, family-oriented facility with a golf course, boat rentals, a long geological history, a pebble beach, quiet pond, marsh and stream, and excellent bird-watching. Facilities include a campground and picnic tables.

Frenchman's Cove. (℃ **709/826-2753**. www.env.gov.nl.ca/parks/parks/p_fc. 76 sites. C$13 (US$11) Open May 15–Sept 16. **Amenities:** Day-use facilities; drinking water; picnic sites; pit privies; outdoor swimming; playground; fishing; boat and cabin rentals.

⟨Finds⟩ A Little Bit of France, Just Off the Coast of Newfoundland

The islands of **St. Pierre and Miquelon** provide a tantalizing tidbit of France—242 sq. km (93 sq. miles) to be exact—just 75 minutes away by ferry from Fortune, or a short flight from St. John's.

Roughly 7,000 French-speaking citizens live in the French territory, which is made up of three islands. Most of the population is centered on the town of St-Pierre, on an island of the same name. Here, the narrow streets are lined with colorful houses, and you'll find the assorted boutiques, the French pastry shops (*Ah, les croissants! Les baguettes! C'est magnifique!*), and the wonderful restaurants worth the trip. You'll need to be on full alert as you walk through the shopping district, as the Minis seem to race along at a speed out of proportion to their size.

You can take day trips to St.-Pierre by ferry, or you can plan for a longer stay so as to better soak up the French *joie de vivre*. Just make sure you confirm and re-confirm, as the hotels have been know to overbook and then cancel reservations at the last minute.

Call St. Pierre Tours at ⟨©⟩ **800/563-2006** or 709/832-0429 to arrange ferry and accommodations reservations (expect to pay C$85/US$73 for the round-trip ferry fare). Air Saint Pierre (⟨©⟩ **902/873-3566;** www.airsaintpierre.com) charges C$260 (US$224) round-trip from St. John's. Once on the island, there are many touring options, including bus, minitrain, bicycle, and horseback. For independent travel, call St. Pierre Tourism ⟨©⟩ **800/565-5118** (English service) or 011/508-41 23 84 for French service. The website, www.st-pierre-et-miquelon.com, is fully bilingual and will provide you with interesting current affairs as well as the history of how the islands finished in French hands.

Note: St. Pierre time is 30 minutes ahead of Newfoundland time. This is important when you're returning from the island to Fortune. You'll also find getting around on the islands expensive. Think France. Canadian money is accepted, but all prices will be quoted in euros. At press time, C$1 = 0.71€.

WHERE TO STAY

Grand Fairways Resort   From the golf course, it's just a 5-minute walk to Grand Fairways' fully equipped 2-bedroom chalets with tasteful, rustic styling and handcrafted furniture. You'll also find a pullout couch for additional sleeping quarters. Each cabin has a gas barbecue and private lot with a large grassed backyard. There is one fully accessible wheelchair unit. Be sure to bring all the supplies you'll need, as there is no local grocery store.

Rte. 210. Frenchmen's Cove. ⟨©⟩ **866/826-2400** or 709/826-2400. www.geocities.com/grandfairwaysresort. 6 units. C$95 (US$82). AE, DC, MC, V. **Amenities:** TV w/VCR; fully equipped kitchen; private bathroom.

Long Ridge Cottages   If you can't get into the Long Ridge Cottages, try the Grand Fairways Resort and vice versa: accommodations-wise they are quite similar. Like Grand Fairways, these are fully equipped 2-bedroom housekeeping units. The main difference is the view. Grand Fairways has a more private, wooded setting, while Long Ridge offers spectacular ocean views from less-private cabins. The cottages are fully winterized and open year-round, making them an excellent four-season retreat. Accommodations are spacious and very modern, with pine log interiors.

Rte. 210 to 213. Long Ridge Place, Garnish. © 709/826-2626. www.longridgecottages.com. 4 units. C$89 (US$77). AE, MC, V. **Amenities:** Color cable TV; electric heat; full bathroom; patio, barbecue; play area.

GRAND BANK

Continuing southwest from Frenchman's Cove is Grand Bank, home to around 3,000 residents. The community is most noteworthy because of its connection to the Grand Banks fishery, excellently depicted in the murals that adorn the Provincial Seamen's Museum.

WHERE TO STAY

The Thorndyke ✿✿ Historical character comes to life on the walls of this old sea captain's home. Built in 1917 by Captain John Thornhill, the home is named after one of Thornhill's fishing schooners. When completed, the Captain didn't host a house-warming party—he hosted a wall-signing party. To this day, you'll find the signatures of early-20th-century sea captains scribbled on the Thorndyke's wall. The house is an excellent example of Queen Anne architecture, with a "widow's walk," or belvedere, on the roof that guests are allowed to use. Back in the seafaring days, wives of the fishing captains would stand on the roof to watch for the flags of the incoming schooners. While the kitchen is thoroughly modern, the rest of the house is maintained in its original condition. You'll find evidence of that early-1900s character in the antique furnishings and four-poster beds gracing most of the five guest rooms, and especially in the bridal suite with its canopy bed and brass-fitted claw-foot tub. And being served with genuine crystal glasses really brings home the elegance of a more refined time. Don't take that the wrong way: this isn't a stiffly formal establishment. You can come and go as you please at the Thorndyke, even make yourself a late-night snack in the kitchen. The catch is that you might have to share with Rover and Fido, the Thorndyke's golden retriever mascots.

33 Water St., Grand Bank. www.thethorndyke.com. © 709/832-0820. 5 units. C$65–C$85 (US$56–US$73). V. Open May to mid-Sept. **Amenities:** Full breakfast; satellite TV, DVD; nonsmoking.

EXPLORING GRAND BANK

Provincial Seamen's Museum In a striking building originally used as a pavilion for the 1967 World Expo in Montreal, you'll find a large collection of models and

---

Cod Fishing and the Grand Banks

You may have heard of the "Grand Banks" off the southeast coast of Newfoundland, once considered the richest cod fishing grounds in the world. The town of Grand Bank on the west coast of the Burin Peninsula was named in honor of the region's fishing heritage, much of which is well explained in the Provincial Seamen's Museum.

If you'd like to see just how dangerous fishing on the Grand Banks can be, watch the George Clooney movie *The Perfect Storm*. The film depicts the tragedy faced by so many longliner fishing boats that never made it back from a trip to the fish-filled waters. It's based on the book *The Perfect Storm: A True Story of Men Against the Sea,* by Sebastian Junger, about Grand Banks fishermen from Gloucester, Massachusetts.

paintings of the schooners so important to the heritage and settlement of the peninsula. It will take you at least an hour to see all the exhibits—more if you're really into fishing and seafaring history. On the building you'll find the largest mural in Atlantic Canada, depicting a 1930s Newfoundland fishing village.

54 Marine Dr., Grand Bank. (*C*) **709/832-1484.** C$3 (US$2.60) for age 13 and over. May–mid-Oct daily 10am–6pm.

3 Terra Nova National Park ✦✦

Terra Nova ("new land") is Newfoundland's first and more accessible national park. The main visitor center is 240km (149 miles), or about a 3-hour drive, northwest of St. John's, and about 76km (47 miles) southeast of Gander.

If you were to give the province's two national parks human personalities, Gros Morne would be an extreme sports enthusiast while Terra Nova would be the family guy driving a minivan. But while Terra Nova doesn't possess the striking scenery you'll find in Gros Morne, it is still a beautiful park with great camping and some excellent naturalist programs. If you have just 2 weeks in Newfoundland, you can probably see Terra Nova, the Avalon Region (including St. John's), and the Eastern Region (ends just outside Terra Nova) without feeling rushed.

ESSENTIALS
GETTING THERE
Terra Nova National Park is conveniently located along the Trans-Canada Highway (Rte. 1), so if you're driving across the province you'll go straight through it. It's located in the Eastern Region about 80km (50 miles) northwest of Clarenville. Along the 48km (30-mile) stretch of the Trans-Canada Highway within the park are numerous side roads leading into the park, including to small lakes, the main information center, and two campgrounds.

VISITOR INFORMATION
You can obtain visitor information for the park at the **Marine Interpretation Centre** ((*C*) **709/533-2801**). Set on Newman Sound, this facility is the hub of Terra Nova National Park. The center is generally open from mid-May until (Canadian) Thanksgiving in early October. Hours are 9am until 9pm in summer, and 10am until 5pm in spring and fall.

There is no visitor information available at the Charlottetown or Traytown entrances to the park, and it will take you 15 minutes to drive to the Marine Interpretation Centre from the Charlottetown entrance. Visitor information is also available at a kiosk at Square Pond (the northern entrance off Rte. 1), open July and August, daily 9am until 5pm.

For general information about Terra Nova, visit Parks Canada's website at www.pc.gc.ca/pn-np/nl/terranova.

If you're planning to tour the park, you'll need to purchase a pass. A day pass, valid until 4pm following the day of purchase, costs C$5 (US$4.30) for adults; C$4.25 (US$3.65) for seniors 65 and over; C$2.50 (US$2.15) for youth 6 to 16; free for children under 6. The family rate is C$13 (US$11). If you plan on visiting many national parks, the National Parks of Canada Pass might be best for you: C$55 (US$48) for adults; C$47 (US$41) seniors 65 and over; C$27 (US$23) youth 6 to 16; and free for children under 6. There is a family rate of C$109 (US$94). This pass is valid for one year from the date of purchase. **_Note:_** You don't need a Parks Canada vehicle pass if you're just driving through the park and do not stop.

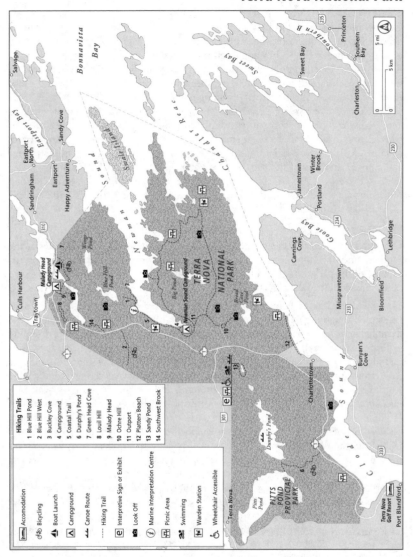

The park's visitor's guide, *Terra Nova Sounds*, will be quite useful in planning your visit and choosing which trails and campgrounds are best suited to you.

You can obtain general information about most communities near the park and private services available in and around the park from the Kittiwake Coast Tourism Association. Call them at ℂ **709/256-5070** and ask for a copy of the *Kittiwake Visitors' Guide.*

GETTING AROUND

Getting around Terra Nova by vehicle is easy, as the Trans-Canada Highway (Rte. 1) dissects the park from north to south. The road is good, also making it relatively easy traveling for the cyclist. In July and August, this road has heavy traffic with quite a few RVs that may slow things down a bit. But that's okay, as you should be watching your speed and looking out for wildlife. There are quite a few moose in the park, so take extra precautions at dusk or dawn, avoiding night travel if possible.

Over the past few years, Terra Nova National Park has made many of its facilities and programs accessible to visitors with physical disabilities. A heavy-duty all-terrain wheelchair is available at no charge from the park's Activity Centre. It's not motorized, so someone still has to push it, but this amenity allows visitors with disabilities to tour and enjoy many areas of the park that may otherwise be inaccessible to them.

Pocket-size FM "Easy Listener" receivers are available for those with a hearing impairment. Closed-captioned audiovisuals are shown at the Activity Centre and the Twin Rivers Visitor Centre.

WHERE TO STAY

Other than park-administered campgrounds and the sites near the park gates at the southern and northern access points, there are no visitor accommodations within the expanse of the park, but as it's only 50km (31 miles) from one end of the park to the other this shouldn't be a problem.

Clode Sound Motel & Restaurant ★ *Value*   You're bound to feel at home once you step through the door of this family-run establishment. Nellie Cunningham, the friendly hands-on manager, ensures you have a quality visit—whether you're dropping in for lunch, or staying with them for a week. Many small touches make the Clode Sound special. The smell of fresh bread (baked three times daily) and the apple pies made from apples grown on their property, the fresh-cut flowers on each dining table from the flower gardens that adorn the grounds, and the smiling staff—all will help make you glad you found this tiny haven just off the Trans-Canada Highway 16km (10 miles) north of the southern entrance to the park. The accommodations are aging, but well maintained. Each of the fully equipped housekeeping units has access to a picnic table and barbecue pit. The peaceful, yet convenient, location is what makes this property stand out. You're surrounded by the wilderness of Terra Nova National Park, whale- and bird-watching, sea kayaking, hiking, and golf.

Part of the complex is Clode Sound Restaurant, open May to Oct daily 7am–9pm. It serves up the usual array of cooked breakfasts, while the rest of the day cod tongues and scruncheon provide local flavor.

Rte. 1, Charlottetown. ✆ **709/664-3146** or 709/664-3411 for off-season bookings. www.clodesound.com. 19 units. C$65–C$80 (US$56–US$69) double. AE, MC, V, Interac. Open May–Oct. **Amenities:** Licensed restaurant; bakery; heated swimming pool; tennis; hot tub; playground; nonsmoking. *In room:* TV, kitchen, phone.

Terra Nova Golf Resort ★★ *Kids*   If you love to golf and you have kids, the Terra Nova Golf Resort is a wonderful vacation destination. Twin Rivers, the resort's 18-hole golf course, has been voted one of the top 30 in Canada. Its challenging layout and water views make the midweek greens fees of C$50 (US$43) excellent value. The lodge's Children's Recreation Program (included with the room rates) is so good, the kids won't want to leave! The program includes games, supervised swimming, treasure hunts, and craft-making as well as supervised lunches. Other facilities include an outdoor heated pool, walking trails, a playground, tennis courts, a basketball court, and minigolf. *Tip:* Unless you're in a ground-floor room with outdoor access, don't forget to bring a wrap. Guests aren't permitted to walk around the lodge in just their swimsuit.

Guest rooms are nicely furnished in a solid, rustic style, and notably soundproof, considering the number of children you'll find scurrying about.

Since none of the guest rooms comes with cooking facilities (even the efficiency units have just a fridge and microwave, no stove), you'll probably eat at least one meal in the on-site Clode Sound Restaurant. But don't worry, they don't take advantage of their culinary monopoly. The surroundings are business-casual elegant, with an easy-on-the-eye golf-course view and thick wooden beams running overhead to remind you you're in a lodge. The reasonably priced food is tasty and well portioned.

Rte. 1, 3rd exit to Port Blandford if you're arriving from the south. © 709/543-2525. Fax 709/543-2201. www.terranova golf.com. 83 units, including 5 suites. C$108–C$135 (US$93–US$116) double; C$155–C$219 (US$134–US$188) suite; C$109–C$209 (US$94–US$180) efficiency. AE, DC, DISC, MC, V. 18 holes of golf cost C$50–C$70 (US$43–US$60) without a cart. Open May–Oct. **Amenities:** Full-service dining room and pub; outdoor heated swimming pool; 2 golf courses; golf school; minigolf; tennis courts; fitness room; complimentary children's recreation program; babysitting; guest laundry; playground, basketball, volleyball, soccer; nature trails; nonsmoking rooms. *In room:* A/C, TV, alarm/clock radio, room service, coffeemaker, iron. Efficiency units have microwave, but no stove.

Terra Nova Hospitality Home 🖈 (Value   Located beyond the south end of the park, this is the place to make reservations if you're looking for genuine Newfoundland hospitality. There are accents so thick and so studded with motherly endearments, you'd almost think you were staying in a private outport home—especially when you smell the fresh-baked bread (to heck with Atkins!) and oven-roasted turkey. As homespun as it is, it's also a very professional, full-service resort with three distinct accommodations options. You can choose from the economical B&B, luxurious suites, or self-contained cottages (all three are located on the same property, right on the highway as you turn in to Port Blandford).

The winterized (no drafts!) 2-bedroom cabins are excellently maintained and spotlessly clean, completely lacking the musty odor that comes with so many resort cottages. With a little squeezing, two families could share one of the cottages by using the sofa bed. The main feature of the B&B has nothing to do with its six guest rooms, Master Suite, or bathroom facilities. It's the sauna—small, yes, but still a sauna. And you can use it no matter which room you rent. For just C$60 (US$52) a night, you can sweat the small stuff, then retire to your private bathtub to soak your cares away (standard size—not Jacuzzi—tubs, unless you book the Master Suite).

The resort is the suite-est of the three, containing three double-bed suites, one king-size and one queen-size. Both of the latter have their own en-suite Jacuzzi.

Rte. 1, Port Blandford. © 888/267-2333 or 709/543-2260. Fax 709/543-2241. www.terranova.nfld.net. 19 units. B&B: C$50 (US$43) single, shared bathroom. C$60 (US$52) double, private bathroom. Cabins: C$95 (US$82). Inn: C$110–C$125 (US$95–US$108). C$8 (US$7) additional for cot in room. AE, DC, MC, V. **Amenities:** Restaurant; nonsmoking rooms; wheelchair accessible. *In room:* Inn rooms have satellite TV, telephone. Some have air-conditioning, fireplaces, and Jacuzzis. Cabins have full kitchen, one with microwave and hot tub.

WHERE TO DINE

Each of the accommodations detailed above has food services, but for setting and casual ambience, my pick for a meal is the Starfish Eatery, the only place to eat within the park boundary.

Starfish Eatery CAFE   When you've finished learning about the park at the Marine Interpretation Centre, grab a free map and take a seat at this adjacent cafe and start planning your itinerary. Perfectly located overlooking Newman Sound, this homely cafe even has a few outdoor tables. The simple cooking includes pan-fried scallops and hearty chowders.

Marine Interpretation Centre. ✆ **709/664-3146**. Reservations not required. C$5–C$10 (US$4.30–US$8.50). MC, V, Interac. May to mid-Oct daily 10am–6pm.

CAMPING IN TERRA NOVA

Camping is really the way to go in Terra Nova. They have an excellent Campfire Concert Program, with weekly summer concerts at the beachside campfire circle built from natural logs. And the **Junior Naturalist Club** and **Teenage Naturalist Program** ⊛ have really made the park a hit with families. The junior program is geared toward kids ages 8 to 12 and the teenage program is for ages 13 to 17. Children get a chance to learn about nature in a fun, hands-on way. Visit the Activity Centre at Newman Sound Campground for more info.

To be assured a site, consider reserving a spot through the **Parks Canada Campground Reservation Service** (✆ **877/737-3783**; www.pccamping.ca). In addition to the two campgrounds listed here, there are also several small backcountry campgrounds (C$8/US$7 per person, per night) that you can access from hiking trails or by canoe. Find out more in the *Terra Nova Sounds* user's guide to the park.

Malady Head Campground   If you're looking for a secluded campground, this one provides a quiet, natural setting for campers wishing to experience nature without human frills. There are numerous hiking trails in the area and sightseeing is good on the "Road to the Beaches." One other great thing about this campground is that it doesn't book up like Newman Sound does, so if you arrive without a reservation chances are you'll still get into Malady Head. A national parks pass is required to enter the campground.

Rte. 1 to Rte. 310. ✆ **709-533-2801**. 99 sites. C$17 (US$15). AE, MC, V, Interac. Open July to early Sept. **Amenities:** Wooded sites; heated washrooms with flush toilets; wheelchair accessible; playground; individual site firepits; kitchen shelters; hiking trails; saltwater beach nearby.

Newman Sound Campground ⊛   This is by far the largest campground in the park, with 356 campsites, and it's my recommended destination as it's fully serviced and has treed lots. Only 66 of the sites are fully serviced with electricity, so if this is a requirement be sure to book as far in advance as possible. A national parks pass is required to enter the campground. Check-in time is 1pm. Checkout time is 11am. Quiet hours are enforced beginning at 11pm. You can camp here year-round, but the electricity is turned on only from May through October.

Newman Sound is ideally located near the Marine Interpretive Centre and just 30km (19 miles) from the south entrance of the park. The camping reservation system (✆ **877/737-3783**; www.pccamping.ca) allows you to reserve your site ahead of time, but there is an additional charge of C$11 (US$9.50) for this service.

Rte. 1 to Newman Sound. ✆ **709/533-2801**. 356 sites. C$21–C$26 (US$18–US$23). AE, MC, V, Interac. **Amenities:** Heated washrooms with showers and flush toilets; wheelchair accessible; grocery store; snack bar; laundromat; dumping station; playground; community firepits; kitchen shelter; hiking trails; interpretive programs; kids' activity center; outdoor theater; campfire programs.

EXPLORING TERRA NOVA

The landscape of the park varies from the rugged cliffs and sheltered inlets of its coastal region (which takes in Clode Sound and Newman Sound, fjords that are extensions of Bonavista Bay), to the rolling hills of the boreal forest and the bogs and ponds that jointly make up the park's inland region. Terra Nova's "Fingers of the Sea" provide many scenic vistas and give the park about 200km (124 miles) of shoreline.

As with other parts of Newfoundland, much of your Terra Nova visit will be determined by your interests and the weather. As Newfoundland has "weather with an attitude," your plans may have to be altered without choice and with little advance notice.

Blue Hill If you're not into hiking or formal tours, one of the park's highlights is Blue Hill, the highest point in the park, at 199m (653 ft.). You must take a short, somewhat washboarded, gravel road to get here, which may be difficult for RVs and low-riding vehicles. But once at the top, you'll get a lovely view of the finger fjords. If you're feeling energetic, take the short drive to Ochre Hill, the site of an ancient volcano, and climb the lookout tower for another great view of the finger peninsulas and the Marine Interpretation Centre.

Coastal Trail ⋇ If you like hiking, you're in luck. Terra Nova has 100km (62 miles) of hiking trails with various levels of difficulty, as well as three mountain biking trails. One of the nicest hiking trails is the 9km (5.5-mile) Coastal Trail that runs from the Marine Interpretation Centre to Newman Sound Campground and will take you about 3 hours. About halfway along, you'll pass by Pissing Mare Falls—not spectacular by any means, but a soothing place to listen to the water trickling down the rocks as you relax on a bench and smell the fresh air. Depending on the time of your visit, you may see the dogberry in bloom and the "old man's beard" lichen hanging from the trees. Old man's beard is also called "traveler's joy"—it's an indication of clean air in the areas where it grows. It's edible, but beware—it acts as a natural laxative!

Edible Trail You can actually take an "edible trail" hike with a park interpreter, where poisonous plants are pointed out and edible ones are sampled. You'll learn that the leaves of the corn lily taste like cucumber, but that the plant's blue-colored berries are poisonous and were once used to dye blue jeans. Register for the hike at the Marine Interpretation Centre.

Marine Interpretation Centre ⋇ An impressive facility overlooking Newman Sound just off Route 1. This is worthy not only as a stand-alone attraction, but also as the place from which you'll take a boat or kayak tour, and from where you can access the Coastal Trail.

The facility has three display areas: the wet lab, the theater, and the marine exhibit. The marine exhibit is great for children, as they can learn about and touch various live marine creatures in the touch tank. They can even conduct an experiment in the Wet Lab with guidance from an interpreter. There is also a children's activity center, gift shop, and cafe (with outdoor patio). Give yourself about 1½ hours to tour the complex before you head out and explore.

ⓒ **709/533-2801.** Admission is free once you have purchased a park pass. Mid-May to end of June and Sept 1 to early Oct 10am–5pm daily; July–Aug 9am–8pm.

Sandy Pond This is the place to be on a hot sunny day. Here you'll find a sandy beach safe for swimming and watersports. The water is shallow, so it's great for small children. And you can rent boats and surf bikes—a surfboard that you bicycle on. Boat rentals cost C$5 (US$4.30) for a half-hour and C$28 (US$24) for a full day. You can pay with Visa or cash. There are also ice-cream sales and a small concession at the beach that's open mid-June to Labor Day daily 10am to 6pm.

Kids   Splashtacular! ⋒⋒

Before you say goodbye to the Eastern region, give the kids a treat by spending a day at the largest water park in the province. **Splash-n-Putt Resort** borders the Trans-Canada Highway just outside Terra Nova National Park's northern boundary in Glovertown. And except for some overly aggressive go-kart drivers (they must think they're at the Clarenville Dragway), it makes for great family fun. There's a 91m (300-ft.) waterslide, 18-hole minigolf, half-kilometer go-kart track, miniature go-kart track, electric bumper cars, bumper boats, swimming pools, and a kiddies' recreation complex. A Splash Pass day pass (including 2 go-kart rides, 3 bumper car rides, 2 bumper boat rides, and unlimited use of all other park activities) costs C$31 (US$27). *Tip:* Try going to the park after 5pm, when you can buy an evening pass for C$16 (US$14). For more information, call ⓒ **709/533-2541** or go online to www.splashnputt.com.

TOURS

If you don't feel comfortable heading out into the wilderness by yourself, consider joining a guided tour.

Ocean Watch Tours ⋒   This company provides an easy way to leave the land behind and take to the waters of Newman Sound. But be aware that sailings are occasionally canceled due inclement weather or high winds. The captain is Ian Stroughair, whose motto is "It's better for you to be onshore wishing you could have gone out, than to be out there wishing you were onshore." It's nice to be in good hands, and Stroughair is certainly knowledgeable about the area.

The tours provide an educational experience that enables you to see parts of the park you can't see from shore. Depending on the time of your visit, you will be able to spot and learn about icebergs, whales, bald eagles, and other wildlife. The 9am tour concentrates on searching out humpback and minke whales; 1 and 4pm departures are for those interesting in soaking up the pristine scenery; and the 7pm tour provides the opportunity to visit an abandoned "outport" village. Ocean Watch's boat, the M/V *Northern Fulmar,* is a stable 11m (35-ft.) fiberglass Cape Island–style passenger vessel with a covered area and a washroom.

Marine Interpretation Centre. ⓒ 709/533-6024. www3.nf.sympatico.ca/oceanwatch. C$32–C$45 (US$28–$39) for adults, C$16–C$25 (US$14–US$22) for children 11 and under. MC, V, or traveler's checks. Tours mid-May to Oct. Daily tours mid-June to Labor Day; off season by reservation only.

Terra Nova Adventures ⋒   If you prefer a more active tour of the park, join a guided sea kayaking tour with this company, which also operates from the wharf adjacent to the Marine Interpretation Centre. The sheltered waters of Terra Nova are an excellent place to kayak, as conditions are generally quite calm. Guided single and double kayak tours are offered, with all necessary equipment and instruction included. Options range from a 2-hour paddle for C$45 (US$39) to an overnight camping trip for C$299 (US$257). If you're experienced and prefer to go out on your own, the company will also rent you a kayak to use as you wish.

Marine Interpretation Centre. ⓒ 888/533-8687 or 709/533-9797. www.terranovaadventures.ca. From C$45 (US$39) adults, C$35 (US$30) youth. Daily rentals with full gear provided for C$45 (US$39) for a single kayak and C$55 (US$48) for a double kayak. Tours operate May–June and Sept–Oct by reservation only. 2 tours daily during July and Aug 10am and 1:30pm.

7

Central Region

If all you see of the massive landmass between Terra Nova National Park and Deer Lake is what you glimpse from behind your windshield on the Trans-Canada Highway, you're going to be disappointed. For 4 hours, it's nothing but spruce, birch, pine, scattered ponds, and boreal bog. So if you're planning to just drive straight through, pack a pillow and designate another driver. But consider yourself warned: you'll miss the best of Central Newfoundland if you don't detour from the main highway.

The airport town of **Gander** made world news following September 11, 2001. With significant help from its neighbors, this community of 10,000 played host to almost 7,000 stranded air passengers—the greatest number at one time on Canadian soil.

An hour's drive west of Gander is **Grand Falls–Windsor,** population 20,000. This tidy town is best known for two things: its pulp and paper mill, and the excellent salmon fishing. The **Salmonid Interpretation Centre** explains the life cycle of a salmon, and if you time your visit for mid-July you'll catch the fabulous 5-day **Exploits Valley Salmon Festival.**

But while these two main service centers are bigger, they aren't necessarily better than what you'll find along the coastline north of the Trans-Canada Highway.

The **Kittiwake Coast,** accessed from Gambo in the east, and especially the town of **Twillingate,** is known for the numerous icebergs that can be seen just offshore—most frequently in May and June. The thrill of kayaking among these great castles of the sea provides an outdoor experience that's hard to duplicate. There are also white-sand beaches, perfect away-from-it-all picnic spots, a town cobbled together by inter-island bridges, and even an ancient aboriginal campsite. Along the road into Twillingate, **Boyd's Cove Beothuk Interpretation Centre** illustrates the daily life of the semi-nomadic Beothuk people who inhabited this region until the early 1700s.

If you'd like to meet the island's modern-day native population, visit the **Miawpukek Mi'Kamawey Mawi'omi (Conne River Tribal Nation).** The reserve is about 160km (100 miles) south of Bishop's Falls, at the mouth of one of the best salmon rivers in the province.

Finally, of note in the Central Region are the isolated fishing communities that make up its **South Coast.** Communities like **Harbour Breton, Hermitage, Francois** (pronounced "Franceway"), and **Grey River.** The first two are accessible by road if you travel south off Route 1 at Bishop's Falls onto the **Coast of Bays** (Rte. 360, which branches into routes 361, 362, and 364). To reach the latter two more remote communities (Francois and Grey River), you have to travel from town to town along the South Coast by passenger ferry.

1 Gander

The story of Gander's founding is a classic tale of putting the cart before the horse. A world-class international airport was built here in 1938—before anyone lived here! Residents, services, and accommodations came later. Even though the town has since expanded in size and raison d'être (it's now one of the main service centers in the region), much of its history and cultural character remains entwined with the transportation industry.

American Jim DeFede has written an excellent book *(The Day the World Came to Town: 9/11 in Gander, Newfoundland)* that follows Gander residents and stranded passengers through the heartwarming experiences immediately following the terrorist attacks of September 11, 2001. In stark contrast to the tumult affecting the U.S., a uniquely Newfoundland-style act of kindness was put forth through the collective effort of local service organizations, church groups, and countless individuals who opened their homes to complete strangers. This inherent generosity of spirit is what makes Newfoundland such a uniquely attractive destination.

ESSENTIALS
GETTING THERE

Outside of St. John's, Gander is the transportation hub of the province. You'll need to travel Route 1 and pass through Gander whether you've come off the ferry at Port-aux-Basques in the Western Region and are heading toward St. John's, or are making your way west toward Gros Morne from Argentia or St. John's. It's a straightforward drive from either direction, so you couldn't get lost unless you tried. You can also fly to Gander International Airport with Air Canada from St. John's or Provincial Airlines from St. John's, Halifax, and Goose Bay. The oversized airport has a cafe, gift shop, information desk, and car rentals (Avis, Budget, Hertz, National). See www.gander airport.com for information.

VISITOR INFORMATION

Gander Visitor Information Centre is on the south side of the Trans-Canada Highway as it whizzes through town. It is open late May through September daily 8:30am to 9pm. Call ⓒ **709/256-7110** or visit the community's website at www.gandercanada.com.

A limited amount of visitor information is also available at Gander International Airport. Call ⓒ **709/256-6677** to reach the Information Desk.

GETTING AROUND

It'll cost C$10 (US$8.50) for a taxi to take you the 5km (3 miles) from the airport to downtown, where you'll find most of the hotels and services. If you plan on driving yourself around town, ask for a municipal road map at the information desk. There are only five main thoroughfares in Gander (plus the Trans-Canada, which borders the town), with side streets intersecting one or more of them—you'll be navigating like a pro in no time.

WHERE TO STAY

Next to St. John's, Gander has the highest density of hotel rooms in the province. In addition, you'll find a good selection of restaurants and other services for travelers. That said, you won't come across the assortment of charming historical properties that are in St. John's or some of the smaller heritage communities.

BlueWater Lodge & Retreat ★★ *Finds*   It's like finding the pot of gold at the end of a rainbow. This wilderness retreat west of town pays homage to four-season outdoor

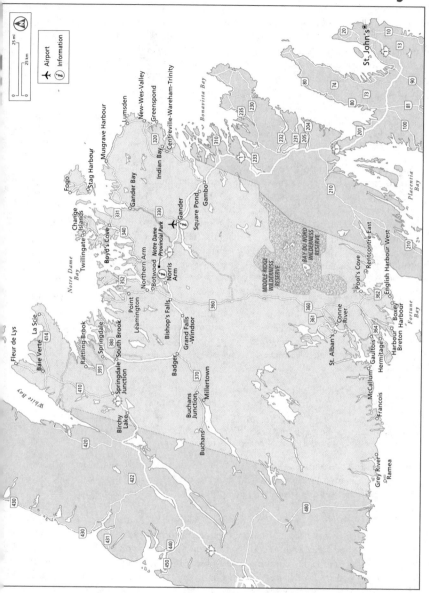

enjoyment. In winter, spring, summer, or fall, BlueWater Lodge can arrange activities for it all—like canoeing and scuba diving, kayaking and hiking, or snowshoeing and snowmobiling.

After a busy day of roaming, retire to the coziness of the lodge's dining room for a satisfyingly simple feast made from fresh produce and seasonal berries (included with your room rate). Toast your day with a glass of wine while watching the crimson farewell of a fading sun magnified in the still waters of the nearby lake. Before turning in for the night, sit by the magnificent stone hearth in the common area, where you'll also find a piano in case you're in the mood for a singalong. Finally, snuggle into a fluffy duvet for the most stress-free sleep you'll ever have. *Tip:* This is not a family vacation destination; BlueWater caters to adult visitors. *Note:* BlueWater Lodge is about an hour's drive from Twillingate; it's 3km (2 miles) east of the Notre Dame Junction on the Trans-Canada Highway.

Rte. 1, 30km (19 miles) west of Gander and 3km (nearly 2 miles) east of the Rte. 340 Notre Dame Junction. ℰ **709/535-3004.** www.relax-at-bluewater.ca. 10 units. C$125 (US$108) double. AE, MC, V. **Amenities:** Dining room; lounge. *In room:* En-suite bathroom.

Comfort Inn The units may be somewhat sterile, but you can always count on the chain to provide clean, comfortable guest rooms at reasonable prices. After a 2005 renovation, this location is no exception. It's a modern two-story building, offering drive-up rooms and some very spacious kitchenette units. A continental breakfast (hot drinks, toast, cereal, muffins, bagels, and more) is included in the rates. Plus, the Comfort Inn is home to Jungle Jim's restaurant (review below).

112 Trans-Canada Hwy., Gander. ℰ **877/424-6423** or 709-256-3535. www.comfortinn.com. 64 units. C$109–C$129 (US$94–US$111) double. Extra person C$15 (US$13). Senior's discount of 20%. AE, DC, MC, V, Interac. **Amenities:** Restaurant; exercise facility; guest laundry; nonsmoking rooms. *In room:* A/C, TV, dataport, coffeemaker, free local calls.

Country Inn Motel If you have wheels, this is a tidy, inexpensive motel offering unremarkable rooms in a quiet country setting. On the downside, unless you really like walking you'll be stranded about a 10-minute drive from downtown Gander.

303 Magee Rd., Gander. ℰ **877/956-4005** or 709/256-4005. 9 units. C$54–C$64 (US$47–US$55) double. Cots additional C$5 (US$4.30). MC, V. 10% discount for seniors. **Amenities:** Complimentary continental breakfast; nonsmoking rooms. *In room:* TV.

Country Inn Trailer Park A 5-minute drive north of town is this 60-site trailer park, where a few sites are reserved for out-of-town visitors.

325 Magee Rd., Gander. ℰ **888/256-7755** or 709/256-7755. country@nl.rogers.com. 60 campsites. C$18 (US$16). Mid-May to mid-Oct. **Amenities:** Dumping station; electrical/sewer/water hookup; shower/washroom facilities; picnic area; playground; pets allowed (on leash); barbecues on request.

Hotel Gander Catering to the convention crowd, this is the biggest accommodations in town, with a location that begs a trip to the two nearby shopping malls. Not that the malls are teeming with designer clothing, but it is a welcome panacea for desperate shopaholics.

The guest rooms are comfortably appointed, with bedside sitting areas that can be either convenient work spaces or cozy conversation corners. Among their 152 rooms they have just one Jacuzzi suite, and I advise you to get it if you can. Ascending the trio of pyramid steps is like climbing to paradise. And when you're fully immersed in the pulsating streams, you'll feel like you have your own personal hydro-masseuse. Afterward, you can get dressed up in your nicest traveling clothes and head down to Alcock & Brown's, the on-site eatery. It has a split personality: simultaneously fun and formal (see review under "Where to Dine," below). *Tip:* The Superior Rooms are worth the extra C$10 (US$8.50) for the contemporary look and brighter decor.

100 Trans-Canada Hwy. (Rte. 1). ℰ **800/563-2988** or 709/256-3931. www.hotelgander.com. 152 units. C$85–C$135 (US$73–US$120) double. AE, DC, DISC, MC, V. **Amenities:** Indoor swimming pool; spa; fitness center; limited room service; laundry facilities; nonsmoking rooms. *In room:* A/C, TV w/pay movies, coffeemaker, hair dryer, iron.

WHERE TO DINE

Alcock & Brown's Eatery CANADIAN   Named after the two airmen who made the first nonstop aerial crossing of the Atlantic, Alcock & Brown's is appropriately decorated with caricatures of the famous duo. The funky cartoon-character wall hangings signal an informal bonhomie that's made even more evident by the brown-paper table coverings and complimentary crayons. But wait, there's more here than meets the eye: there's also a quieter, more upscale eating area custom-made for intimate dining. The menu reflects the restaurant's dual personality, with burgers and chips sharing space with grown-up dishes like bruschetta salmon in a creamy dill sauce. Make sure you leave room for dessert, especially the whimsically named Chocolate Moose. Not only is it a perfectly velvety smooth concoction, it comes with its own antlers! Sunday brunch, served 11:30am to 1:30pm, is a bargain at C$10 (US$8.50) per person.

Hotel Gander, 100 Trans-Canada Hwy. (Rte. 1), Gander. ℂ **709/256-3931.** www.hotelgander.com. Dinner reservations recommended. Main courses C$11–C$20 (US$9.50–US$17). AE, DC, DISC, MC, V. Sun 7am–1:30pm and 5–8pm; Mon–Thurs 7am–1:30pm and 5–9pm; Fri–Sat 7am–1:30pm and 5–10pm.

Giovanni's CAFE   A great casual place for gourmet coffees, Italian sodas, grilled panini (seven different varieties are available), pasta salads, biscotti, and other tasty treats. Giovanni's coffee shop is located in the Town Square Shopping Centre.

71 Elizabeth Dr., Gander. ℂ **709/651-3535.** Reservations not required. Main courses C$6–C$15 (US$5.15–US$13). MC, V. Mon–Wed 7:15am–6pm; Thurs–Fri 7:15am–10pm; Sat 9am–10pm; Sun noon–5pm.

Jungle Jim's CONTEMPORARY   Swing on in for a tasty treat—it's a jungle out there! Part of a 22-strong homegrown restaurant chain, Jungle Jim's is a great choice for casual family dining. The safari-style bamboo decor, patio lights, and stuffed jungle animals provide plenty of distractions for energetic youngsters. The extensive menu includes a variety of Mexican-style dishes (nachos, burritos, fajitas, tacos) as well as steaks, hamburgers, pasta, and salad. Try the ribs—they've been simmered in a zesty sauce to a melt-in-your-mouth tenderness and seared on the grill for a final flavor kick. You'll find Jungle Jim's on the same lot as the Comfort Inn.

112A Trans-Canada Hwy., Gander. ℂ **709/651-3444.** www.junglejims.ca. Reservations not required. Lunches about C$8 (US$7); most dinners about C$12 (US$11). AE, DC, MC, V. Daily 11am–11pm.

EXPLORING GANDER

Let your spirits soar in Gander. It's as easy as checking out one of these aviation attractions:

AeroSmith Inc.   You've heard of boat tours, bus tours, and even walking tours. Why not an airplane tour? It's not cheap (their Cessna 185 floatplane charters for C$260/US$224 per flight hour), but since the plane can hold three passengers you can share the cost with fellow travelers. Allow a couple of hours for a decent tour—not just the Gander area, but the entire Central region.

ℂ **888/999-2376** or 709/651-3222. www.aerosmithinc.com.

Festival of Flight   Gander's biggest annual brouhaha is held annually through the week of August. It's a full week of family entertainment, much of it centered on the namesake theme. The schedule includes community breakfasts, suppers, and barbecues, as well as model airplane demonstrations, kite-flying, and fireworks. There are even professional buskers, pub nights, craft sales, a demolition derby, and a parade. Some events are free; others charge a nominal entrance fee.

ℂ **877/919-9979** or 709/651-5927. www.gandercanada.com/tour/t_flight.htm.

North Atlantic Aviation Museum ✿ This museum, Gander's main attraction, is on the south side of the Trans-Canada Highway as it passes through town. You shouldn't have any problem finding it: the front of the building has an airplane tail sticking out of it! The museum is both a record of Gander's growth and a timeline for aeronautical evolution. Aircraft on display include a 1938 Lockheed Hudson Mk III, which was used for coastal reconnaissance; an F101 Voodoo Canso fighter plane; a DeHavilland Tiger Moth biplane; a Beech 18-S, which was one of the world's first corporate airplanes; a 1933 Montreal-built PBY-5A flying boat, which was one of the most common aircraft that refueled at Gander during the airport's heyday; and a homemade Rutan Quickie, with a cockpit so small that the pilot had to fly lying down (no wonder he donated it to the museum!).

Rte. 1 (between the Tourist Chalet and the James Paton Memorial Hospital). ✆ **709/256-2923**. http://naam1. tripod.com. Admission C$3 (US$2.60) adults, C$2 (US$1.75) seniors and youth ages 6–17, free for children under 6. July–Aug daily 9am–9pm; the rest of the year Mon–Fri 9am–5pm.

Silent Witness Memorial On the east side of town, a side road winds down to this memorial, which marks the site of Canada's worst air disaster. On 12 December, 1985, Gander Airport was a scheduled refueling stop for a DC-8 flight carrying the U.S. 101st Airborne Division (best known as the Screaming Eagles), who were returning home from a United Nations peacekeeping mission in the Sinai. The plane, with 248 soldiers and an eight-member crew, crashed shortly after takeoff between the Trans-Canada Highway and Gander Lake. A group of statues, of an American soldier and two children, backed by Canadian, U.S., and Newfoundland flags, overlooks the lake.

4km (2½ miles) east of Gander (signposted to the south). No phone but information at www.airforce.gc.ca/9wing/about_us/general2_e.asp.

2 Kittiwake Coast

Many communities along this stretch of coast were isolated until as recently as the 1960s, when causeways were constructed between the Twillingate, Change, Chapel, and New World islands to the mainland.

The best-known community along the north coast is **Twillingate**, a picturesque haven for viewing the many icebergs that float into Notre Dame Bay. It has about 5,000 residents and numerous services, including a regional hospital.

En route to Twillingate you'll come to the village of **Musgrave Harbour** and the coastal stretch to **Lumsden,** where you'll find Newfoundland's best beach. A few kilometers farther along, you'll arrive in **Newtown.** It's known as the "Venice of Newfoundland" because it's built on a series of tiny islands joined by bridges.

ESSENTIALS
GETTING THERE
Several routes run north of the Trans-Canada Highway (Rte. 1) to the communities along the Kittiwake Coast. If you leave the Trans-Canada at Gambo for Route 320, you're in for a leisurely coastal drive that'll take you past Newtown and the Barbour Living Heritage Village, as well as the beach at Lumsden and other assorted outport settlements. If you continue west along Route 320, it becomes Route 330 at Cape Freels. Keep going until you reach the intersection at Gander Bay South, and you'll have a choice between heading south to Gander along Route 330 or continuing north to Twillingate. On the return trip, take Route 340 back to the Trans-Canada Highway, from where it's 46km (29 miles) east to Gander and 50km (31 miles) west to Grand Falls–Windsor.

VISITOR INFORMATION

Information about the entire Central Region can be obtained from the Central New-foundland Tourism Association (call ℭ **888/491-9453** or see www.centralnewfoundland.com). The Kittiwake Coast Tourism Association is another useful resource that can provide information about the northeastern part of the Central Region, including the Notre Dame Bay area. Call ℭ **709/256-5070** or visit their website at www.kittiwake coast.com.

For information specific to the Twillingate area, click through the links at www.twillingate.com.

GAMBO TO TWILLINGATE

Turning off the Trans-Canada Highway at Gambo, you pass the following attractions on the 260km (163-mile) run to Twillingate. Accommodations are few and far between, so plan on continuing to Twillingate for the night or traveling this route as a day trip from Gander.

The following sights are listed from east to west.

Barbour Living Heritage Village ⍟ *Finds*   Perched along the weathered shore of Newtown (listed as New-Wes-Valley on the map) is a re-created fishing village (ca. 1900). The sights and sounds as well as the look and feel of the Barbour Living Her-itage Village proclaim its historical authenticity. The buildings represent the prosper-ous mercantile premises owned by the Barbour family, which played an important role in the local sealing industry. In addition to the Barbour family buildings, the Village includes a Methodist schoolhouse, craft shop, restaurant, visitor information center, sealing interpretation center, theater, art gallery, stage with fish flakes, liver factory, and other smaller buildings.

Live theatrical performances are held during July and August. The actors' accents tend to be exaggerated Newfoundland, so you may have some problem understand-ing the dialogue. Dinner, which approximates a traditional potluck meal, is a serve-yourself affair featuring such items as cod au gratin, fish-n-brewis, beet salad, mustard salad, potato salad, ham, turkey, caramel tart, partridgeberry pie, and jello. The the-ater, restaurant, and craft shop are wheelchair accessible.

Rte. 330 to Newtown. ℭ **709/536-3220.** C$7 (US$6) adults, C$6 (US$5.15) seniors, C$3.50 (US$3) ages 6–18, free for children under 6, C$16 (US$14) family rate. Theater performances are an additional C$9 (US$7.75) adults, C$7.50 (US$6.50) seniors, C$3.50 (US$3) ages 6–18, free for children under 6, C$22 (US$19) family rate. June 15–Oct 15 daily 10am–6pm.

Boyd's Cove Beothuk Interpretation Centre   Little is known about the Beothuk people, because—unlike other native groups—they avoided Europeans. Boyd's Cove has particular significance because it offers more evidence about their way of life than any other site on the island. Among the items recovered at the archaeolog-ical dig are iron nails that have been refashioned into arrowheads and other tools. The nails weren't the result of trade, but of Beothuks scavenging through the debris left behind by seasonal European fishers. The life of these now-extinct people (the last known Beothuk died in 1829) is depicted in the construction and contents of the wig-wam-shaped Interpretation Centre, as well as along the 1.5km (less than 1 mile) groomed trail leading you past the excavation site of several Beothuk houses that date between 1650 and 1720.

Rte. 340, 70km (44 miles) north of Gander and 40km (25 miles) south of Twillingate. ℭ **709/656-3114.** www. heritage.nf.ca/aboriginal/beo_boydscove.html. C$3 (US$2.60) age 13 and up, free for children 12 and under. June–Sept daily 10am–5:30pm.

Fun Fact **Nightingale of the North**

Born in Twillingate in 1867, Georgina Ann Stirling was the daughter of Ann Peyton and Twillingate's first doctor, William Stirling. The clarity of her powerful soprano voice was apparent at a young age and her wealthy father sent her first to Toronto and later to Paris to train as an opera singer. Under the stage name Marie Toulinguet, she became one of the most famous singers of her time, performing in Italy, Washington, and New York. Tragedy struck at the peak of her career in the form of a serious throat ailment, thus ending her operatic dreams. She returned to Twillingate, where she lived until she died of cancer in 1935. A 2m (6-ft.) stone monument near St. Peter's Church marks her burial spot.

Fishermen's Museum   A short distance past Newtown is Musgrave Harbour and its Fishermen's Museum. You'll find this location especially interesting if you've been to Port Union (on the Bonavista Peninsula). This two-story, oversize fishing shed was built in 1910 by Sir William Coaker, founder of the Fishermen's Protective Union. The Fishermen's Museum has an interesting collection of artifacts related to the fishery (like a fish-splitting table and weighing machine). Outside, you'll see a fascinating mural depicting the way fishing traditions have progressed from past to present.

Rte. 330, Musgrave Harbour. ✆ 709/655-2119. Free admission. Late June to Aug daily 11am–7pm.

TWILLINGATE ★★

During the 1800s, Twillingate was the most active and prosperous seaport on the North Coast. Even today, you'll find a broader range of services here than in many of its neighboring communities.

If you're keen on seeing icebergs, the best time to come is late spring, early summer. If you're most interested in whales, the summer months provide your best chances. So if you come in late June or early July, you just may catch a glimpse of both these natural wonders floating about in Notre Dame Bay.

Twillingate is an Anglicized version of the community's original French name, "Toulinguet," which is also the name of a group of islands off the French coast near Brest. The French fishermen evidently saw a similarity between their homeland and this lovely Newfoundland community.

WHERE TO STAY & DINE

Cabins by the Sea *Value*   The price is definitely right for these simple but adequate 2-bedroom family getaways. The location is fantastic, with picnic tables outside each cabin and recreational facilities just a short walk away. By foot, you're 2 minutes from a playground, and 3 minutes from the indoor swimming pool in the Twillingate Recreation Centre. One of the cabins is wheelchair accessible. No pets allowed. *Warning:* Watch children closely, you're just 30m (100 ft.) from the ocean.

11 Hugh Lane, Twillingate. ✆ 709/884-2158. www.cabinsbythesea.com. 7 units. C$70–C$80 (US$60–US$68) per unit. AE, MC, V. **Amenities:** Housekeeping units; barbecues available on request. *In room:* TV.

Dildo Run Provincial Park Campground   The amenities are typical of provincial parks throughout Newfoundland and Labrador: Each of the 55 campsites comes with picnic tables and fire pits. A newer washroom complex has showers and flush toilets.

Drinking-water taps are conveniently located throughout the park, as are some less-than-fresh pit toilets. *Tip:* Ask for a campsite that's away from a pit toilet. You don't want to be caught downwind.

Facilities aside, it's the location that gives every provincial park its character. In this instance, the lovely seacoast setting offers the opportunity to see growlers and "bergy bits" (iceberg chunks that might float ashore), as well as whales. You can also see quite a few of the 365 islands in Dildo Run from the lookout point. This is a wonderful location for kayaking and canoeing.

Rte. 340, Virgin Arm. © **709/629-3350.** www.env.gov.nl.ca/parks/parks/p_dr/index.html. 55 sites. C$18 (US$16). MC, V. Open May 31–Sept 16. **Amenities:** Day-use facilities; showers; drinking water (taps); kitchen shelters; dumping station; laundry facilities; picnic sites.

Harbour Lights Inn   Located across the road from the water, this three-story home was built in the 1820s and has been beautifully restored to offer guest accommodations in nine rooms. Two rooms have jetted tubs, but all are comfortable and filled with old-fashioned charm. Out front is a covered veranda from where you can watch fishing boats making their way back to port, or relax in the sitting room with a book from the collection of local literature. Rates include a cooked breakfast.

189 Main St., Twillingate. © **877/884-2763** or 709/884-2763. www.harbourlightsinn.com. 9 units. C$99–C$119 (US$85–US$103) double. MC, V, Interac. Open May–Sept. **Amenities:** Sitting room; nonsmoking rooms. *In room:* TV, ceiling fan, hair dryer.

Long Point Lighthouse   Another must-see in the Twillingate area is one of the last manned lighthouses in the province—the Long Point Lighthouse, built in 1876. The lighthouse is not open to the public, but is still worth the drive because of its dramatic setting, especially if you arrive around sunset when its red-and-white stripes take on new, softer shades. Across the parking lot from the lighthouse is the **Long Point Interpretation Centre,** home to an exhibit explaining the connection between the area's natural and human history, as well as a small gift shop and tearoom.

Rte. 340, north of Twillingate. © **709/884-5755.** Mid-May to mid-Oct daily 9am–9pm.

Toulinguet Inn Bed & Breakfast   Location! Location! Location! Beautifully located overlooking the ocean, Toulinguet Inn is also a short distance from a coin laundry, bank, restaurants, walking trails, and the departure point for boat tours. Inside this traditional 1920s Newfoundland home you'll find a kitchen replete with antique collectibles; my personal favorite is an old-fashioned cast-iron stove. There are two spacious queen-size units and one smaller room with twin beds; all three have private bathrooms.

Toulinguet's welcoming character also deserves attention. From the minute you pull into the driveway, it's like you're a long-lost friend or favorite cousin. You feel it in the radiant greeting at check-in, you smell it in the just-washed sheets upon the bed, and you taste it with every bite of your homemade breakfast muffin. Smoking is permitted outside, on the porch, in the garden, or on the second-story balcony. This is a popular location, so be sure to book ahead as far as possible.

56 Main St., Twillingate. © **877-684-2080** or 709/884-2080. www.toulinguetinn.ca. 3 units. C$70 (US$60) double. Open May 1–Sept 30. **Amenities:** Continental-plus breakfast; laundry facilities for small fee; nonsmoking rooms. *In room:* Private bathroom/shower.

OUTDOOR PURSUITS & EVENTS
The Fish, Fun & Folk Festival ✸   Folk-music enthusiasts will want to mark their calendars for the last full weekend in July, when Twillingate is home to one of the

largest and best established folk festivals in the province. Activities include a parade, beach bonfire, helicopter rides, craft sale, and of course lots of great music and fellowship. Unlike many other folk festivals, this one's musical entertainment takes place indoors—meaning it won't be affected by inclement weather. Prices vary per activity.

C 709/884-2678. www.fishfunfolkfestival.com.

Red Indian Adventures *⋒* This adventure operator combines first-class guides and dazzling scenery in an unforgettable day and overnight trip. Experience the thrill of white-water rafting as you battle the surging waters of the Exploits River, or of paddling a sea kayak around an iceberg in Notre Dame Bay. Plus, it's full family fun—the ultimate antidote for teenage ennui. *Note:* The company is based out of Grand Falls–Windsor, so book your Twillingate adventure in advance.

Tours take place at various locations throughout the Exploits Valley. *C* 709/486-0892. www.redindianadventures. com. Sea kayaking C$100 (US$86) per person for a day tour and C$225 (US$193) per person for an overnight camping tour. Rafting and canoeing C$70 (US$60) for a day tour.

Twillingate Island Boat Tours *⋒⋒⋒* Set sail with Cecil Stockley, the self-appointed "Iceberg Man of Twillingate." Stockley has been chasing bergs for 20 years and says he has a sixth sense that enables him to track the sometimes-elusive sea castles. This is a smaller vessel than you'll find used by the competition, but "Cec" takes a more educational approach to his tours, making this the best choice for anyone who wants an in-depth interpretation of what they are seeing. The 2-hour boat tours run three times daily. Also allow time for visiting the Iceberg Shop (which is also the tour departure point) for its collection of stunning berg photography.

50 Main St., Twillingate. *C* 800/611-2374 or 709/884-2242. www.icebergtours.ca. C$40 (US$35) adults, C$20 (US$17) children 15 and under. MC, V. Departures May 1–Sept 30 daily 9:30am, 1pm, and 4pm.

3 Grand Falls–Windsor

There's always been an unofficial rivalry between Gander and Grand Falls–Windsor. Both communities are service centers, but they have very different personalities. Grand Falls–Windsor has fewer services for travelers, but it has a longer, stronger history as evidenced by its numerous heritage properties.

Grand Falls–Windsor is the home of Canadian actor Gordon Pinsent, who starred with Kevin Spacey in *The Shipping News*. But that's not all the town has to brag about. *Chatelaine* magazine, a popular Canadian publication, once named Grand Falls–Windsor one of the top places to live in North America because of its community spirit, natural beauty, and friendly residents (obviously climate was not a factor).

ESSENTIALS
GETTING THERE
Grand Falls–Windsor is the approximate halfway point between St. John's and Port-aux-Basques. To be exact, it's 428km (265 miles) west of St. John's, 476km (295 miles) east of the ferry terminal at Port-Aux-Basques, and 91km (56 miles) west of Gander International Airport.

VISITOR INFORMATION
There's a Visitor Information Centre along Route 1 on the west side of Grand Falls–Windsor that is open May 1 to October 15, daily 9am to 9pm. Call *C* 888/491-9453 or 709/489-6332, or see www.grandfallswindsor.com for more information.

WHERE TO STAY & DINE

Carriage House Inn 🐾   All it needs are a few climbing vines and you'd swear it was straight from a Norman Rockwell painting. Even without the encircling greenery, Carriage House Inn is pretty as a picture. The covered veranda, gabled roof, and 2.4-hectare (6-acre) wooded property give it the presence of a cozy country retreat. Which is exactly what it is. You'll want to relax in the porch swing with a book from the library, or soak in the sun on the spacious patio deck. Inside, you can't go wrong with any of the nine nicely furnished guest rooms with varying bed sizes and amenities—all are impressively clean, with freshly scented linens and private bathrooms. The rooms aren't air-conditioned, but they do have ceiling fans to keep you cool on a sultry evening.

181 Grenfell Heights, Grand Falls–Windsor. ℂ **800/563-7133** or 709/489-7185. www.carriagehouseinn.ca. 4 units. C$75–C$125 (US$65–US$108). V. **Amenities:** Complimentary breakfast; nonsmoking rooms. *In room:* TV, hair dryer, no phone.

Mount Peyton Hotel   It's not the only game in town, but it is the largest. The Mount Peyton is a Central Newfoundland institution that gives new meaning to "full service." Looking for a standard hotel, motel, or housekeeping unit? They have all that. In the mood for steak? They can fill that order, too. You'd rather tuck into steak and kidney pie at a British-style pub? Once again, the Mount Peyton has what you're looking for, and more. Everything, that is, except the opulence of the Royal York. But then, do you really want to pay C$300/night for a place to sleep?

Trans-Canada Hwy. (Rte. 1) to 214 Lincoln Rd., Grand Falls–Windsor. ℂ **800/563-4894** or 709/489-2251. www. mountpeyton.com. 102 hotel units, 32 motel units, and 16 housekeeping units. C$88–C$128 (US$76–US$110) double. MC, V. Hotel and housekeeping units operate year-round, motel Apr–Oct. **Amenities:** Dining room; steakhouse; lounge; laundry/valet service; nonsmoking rooms. *In room:* A/C, TV w/movies and PlayStation, coffeemaker, hair dryer, iron.

Sanger Memorial RV Park   Some people call it camping, but purists will scoff as they turn over in their sleeping bags. Why? Because it's a campground where no tents are allowed, only RVs and trailers. Sanger Memorial has a good range of amenities, including private showers and washrooms, accessible facilities, and 24-hour security. The camping lots are large and full-service, with 15- to 50-amp hookups. It's right on the river and just minutes from downtown Grand Falls–Windsor.

Trans-Canada Hwy. (Rte. 1) Exit 20 to Scott Ave., Grand Falls–Windsor. ℂ **709/489-8780**, or 709/489-7350 for off-season bookings. fred.parsons@nf.sympatico.ca. 38 sites. C$22 (US$19). MC, V. Open June 15–Sept 6.

EXPLORING GRAND FALLS–WINDSOR

There are a number of activities and events to please visitors to the Grand Falls–Windsor area: everything from hiking and fishing to snowmobiling and cross-country skiing. For information about any of the events call ℂ **709/489-0450.**

A.N.D. Company's Summer Theatre Festival   Bravo! Amateur theater so good, you'll be picturing the actors' names up in lights on Broadway. Running from early July to the end of August, the Summer Theatre Festival features a number of enthusiastic local performers. Don't let their youthful appearance fool you: their stage presence has a maturity far beyond their years. There are both evening and daytime performances. The daytime shows are considerably cheaper than the evening dinner shows and offer an economical option to see a great performance for less cash.

Royal Canadian Legion, Queen St. ℂ **877/822-7469** or 709/489-6560. www.andco.nf.ca. Reservations definitely recommended. Tickets from C$12 (US$11) for adults and C$10 (US$8.50) for students and seniors, to C$35 (US$30) for adults and C$21 (US$18) for youths (18 and under) for the dinner theater performances.

Exploits Valley Salmon Festival   During this 5-day, mid-July event, the resident population triples to approximately 60,000 (keep this in mind when booking accommodations). The festival lineup includes a salmon dinner, "Newfie Night," live music, a craft fair, and lots of family fun. The highlight of the festival is the Splash Concert, which features well-known Canadian artists of contemporary and traditional music. Tickets for the concert are usually about C$35 (US$30) and are available in advance or at the gate. Call ✆ **709/489-0450** or see www.salmonfestival.com for more information.

Salmonid Interpretation Centre   Look out—there goes a flying fish! Okay, they're not really flying—but they are jumping from rung to rung on the "salmon ladder" as they try to make their way upstream to their spawning grounds. You won't want to miss this interesting facility, located on the Exploits River 4km (2½ miles) from downtown Grand Falls–Windsor. Highlights are the underwater viewing windows, where you can see salmon in their natural habitat, and the live exhibits of brook trout, sticklebacks, and eels. The center is fully wheelchair accessible.

Cross the bridge over the Exploits River to reach the Salmonid Interpretation Centre. ✆ **709/489-7350.** C$4 (US$3.50) adults, C$2.50 (US$2.15) youth. Mid-June to mid-Sept daily 8am–dusk.

4 Baie Verte Peninsula

It doesn't have an abundance of services or attractions, but what it does have is worth seeing—especially the **Baie Verte Miner's Museum,** in the village of Baie Verte, and the **Dorset Soapstone Quarry,** 28km (17 miles) up the road in Fleur de Lys. Because it's a 2-hour trip from Grand Falls–Windsor to Baie Verte, you should plan to stay the night in the area so you can take in the two main attractions as well as spend a few hours cruising along the coast.

ESSENTIALS
GETTING THERE
From Grand Falls–Windsor, continue west on the Trans-Canada Highway for 92km (58 miles) to Route 410, the main highway up the **Baie Verte Peninsula.** From the Trans-Canada, it's 62km (39 miles) to the community of Baie Verte. Continuing north for 29km (18 miles), you reach Fleur de Lys, at the northern tip of the peninsula.

VISITOR INFORMATION
The local Visitor Information Centre in Baie Verte (✆ **709/532-8090**) is right on Route 410 at the junction of Route 412 as you enter town. This is the same building that houses the Miner's Museum. It is open daily during July and August, from 9am to 9pm.

WHERE TO STAY
Dorset Country Inn   Located in the center of Baie Verte, this welcoming inn has eight rooms, each with a private bathroom, and a delightfully homespun atmosphere. Your host, Teri Boterman, will do everything she can to make you feel comfortable— so you'd better not come here if you don't like being pampered. The common area lounge has a TV.

3 Hoskins Terrace, Baie Verte. ✆ **877/532-8095** or 709/532-8075. 8 units. C$58–C$72 (US$50–US$62) double. AE, MC, V. **Amenities:** Full complimentary breakfast; laundry facilities; nonsmoking rooms. *In room:* TV, en-suite bathrooms.

EXPLORING BAIE VERTE PENINSULA
Baie Verte Miner's Museum ✦   You won't have to dig too deep to find this goldmine of information about the region's rich mining heritage. The building is immediately

evident because of its distinctive double A-frame shape. Inside, there's a simulated mining tunnel leading to the museum, which contains an interesting collection of artifacts that date back to the first European mine built here in 1860. Among the things you'll see outside the museum is the first train in the province, used for the now-defunct Terra Nova mine.

Rte. 410 to Baie Verte. ℂ **709/532-8090.** Museum C$3 (US$2.60) for adults, C$1.50 (US$1.25) for children 6–17. June 15–Aug 31 daily 9am–8pm.

Dorset Soapstone Quarry ⟨ℱ⟩   At the northernmost tip of the northernmost community on the Baie Verte Peninsula, you'll find a little-known Provincial and National Historic Site. But don't mistake its obscurity as a measure of its worth: the Dorset Soapstone Quarry is an incomparable link to the people who lived here more than 1,000 years ago. Inside the Interpretation Centre you'll see examples of the soft-stone cooking pots used by the Dorset natives.

There are four hiking trails around the site. If your time is limited, choose the one to the main quarry. This well-marked walking trail is flanked by waving wildflowers, and along the way you can see where the Middle Dorset people carved out pots and lamps. Here you'll see archaeologists at work as they continue to uncover artifacts. *Note:* Look, but don't touch. Rather than accidentally destroy archaeological evidence, watch from the designated viewing platform.

Tip: The Interpretation Centre/Museum doubles as a community computer center, where you can check your e-mail.

Rte. 410, Fleur de Lys. ℂ **709/253-2126.** Computer hourly rates C$2 (US$1.75). Mid-May to mid-Oct daily 6am–8pm.

5 South Coast

The southern coastline of Central Newfoundland—also known as the **"Coast of Bays"**—is unknown to most visitors because of its remoteness. Route 360 will take you into the area, but you have to take a small ferry if you want to visit many of the tiny outport communities, as they are not accessible by road. It's isolated, primitive, beautiful, and totally unspoiled by commerce and tourism.

ESSENTIALS
GETTING THERE
From 19km (12 miles) east of Grand Falls–Windsor, Route 360 begins its long and lonely trek south, dead-ending after 208km (128 miles) at the town of Harbour Breton. Around 40km (25 miles) before Harbour Breton, Route 364 branches southwest to Hermitage, from where ferries depart for all points west.

VISITOR INFORMATION
The website of Central Newfoundland Tourism (www.centralnewfoundland.com) has information that will help plan a trip to the South Coast. Another handy website is www.harbourbreton.com.

GETTING AROUND
Passenger-only ferries provide the only link to the outside world for a string of communities between Hermitage in the east and Rose Blanche in the west. The service operates year-round, although the schedules change with the seasons. Per sector, the 1½-to-2-hour ride between communities costs up to C$7 (US$6) for adults and C$3.50 (US$3) for seniors, children, and students. Call ℂ **709/551-1446** or see

www.gov.nf.ca/ferryservices/schedules.stm for more information. The adventure begins in the village of **Hermitage.** The first ferry stop is **McCallum**—a community married to land and sea by both livelihood and geography. You'll have half an hour in this picturesque place, which is barely enough time to capture it on film. But never mind, you'll have a 75-minute stopover on the return trip. Next up is **Francois** (www.francoisnf.com). It's a breathtakingly rugged village (pop. 120) tucked into the shadow of 207m-high (680-ft.) hills. There are no roads in Francois: the main street is an extra-wide wooden boardwalk. Houses are built in ascending order, with the most congested area around the waterfront and increasingly fewer dwellings as you move uphill. You'll have to spend the night here, as the ferry doesn't move down the line until 7:30 the next morning. Then you're off on a 2-hour sail to **Grey River,** another fishing village of fewer than 150 residents. You won't have any problem getting to meet the locals, as many of them have a habit of coming to greet the boat. From Grey River, you'll have to decide whether to turn back or continue on to Ramea and Burgeo on a different ferry, one that sails from Rose Blanche to Grey River via Burgeo.

HARBOUR BRETON

Harbour Breton (pop. 2,000) is the largest and one of the oldest communities along the South Coast. It has a hospital, a bank, and a beautiful beach at Deadman's Cove, where on a clear day you can see the French islands of St. Pierre and Miquelon in the distance. Since the late 1700s, the folks of Harbour Breton have depended on the local fishery as a source of work and money, but in 2005, the local fish processing plant closed, and as a result the community lost its fish quota.

Conne River Mi'kmaq Reserve

For an experience unlike any other on the island, visit the Miawpukek Band in Conne River—180km (113 miles) from Grand Falls–Windsor on Route 360. They are a proud, independent, visionary people, reveling in their native heritage while simultaneously embracing modern society. You may be surprised—even disappointed—by the modern bungalows, retail stores, cars, trucks, and ATVs. Don't be. Underlying these 21st-century appendages is a deeply rooted respect for the land and each other. You see it in the design of their native crafts, and you hear it in the tales of their unique customs (like planting trees in lieu of headstones as a way to remember a lost loved one).

Time your visit to coincide with the annual **Powwow,** a 4-day event usually held early in July. It combines sacred ritual with tribal dance as well as communal feasting and elder wisdom. Non-natives are allowed to participate in most ceremonies. Free camping and trailer sites are available on the Powwow site on a first-come, first-served basis. There is no entry fee to the Powwow, but participants are asked to contribute to the daily potluck feasts. For more, visit Conne River online at www.geocities.com/pilip.

WHERE TO STAY

Southern Port Hotel ☞ This facility is so flawlessly organized and charmingly operated, you'll think you've walked into a fairy tale. And in a way, you have. The hotel is a newer (2002), single-story, fully accessible facility overlooking the town. Each of the clean, comfortable, and spacious guest rooms comes with its own private bathroom.

Rte. 360, Harbour Breton. ☏ **709-885-2283**. www.southernporthotel.com. 15 units. C$79–C$85 (US$68–US$73) double. Additional person C$5 (US$4.30), cots C$8 (US$7). MC, V. **Amenities:** Breakfast available for C$3 (US$2.60); lounge; limited room service; laundry service. *In room:* TV, dataport.

WHAT TO SEE & DO

Sunny Cottage The grandest building in town is a wonderful 1909 Queen Anne–style home that houses displays on fishing, resettlement, and the home's original merchant residents. Guides dressed in period costumes will take you on a guided tour; in the kitchen, you'll be able to sample freshly made traditional delicacies. The harborfront setting and lovely gardens add to the charm of this attraction. Sunny Cottage currently serves as the area's tourist information center.

Rte. 360 to Harbour Breton. ☏ **709/885-2425**. Free admission. Late May to early Sept Mon–Fri 9am–5pm, Sat–Sun 1–5pm.

Tradition by the Sea In mid-July, Harbour Breton hosts this lively celebration of traditional life along the South Coast. The annual festival begins with a beach party at Deadman's Cove and continues with a variety of activities—such as dory races—that demonstrate the distinct culture of this area. Other highlights include traditional music, dancing, and food, games of chance, cotton candy, and festivities for the kids. Prices vary per activity.

Activities staged at various locations throughout Harbour Breton. ☏ **709/885-2354**. www.harbourbreton.com/tbts.htm.

8

Western Newfoundland

If you're traveling in an east-west direction across the island, Western Newfoundland is the grand finale to a wondrous adventure. If, however, this is your entry point to Newfoundland, it's an enticing prelude to an unforgettable vacation. Either way, it's a memory in the making.

Just over 200km (125 miles) west of Grand Falls–Windsor is **Deer Lake.** Aside from being the first noteworthy community you'll find as you enter the Western Region, it's also the point of decision. You either leave the Trans-Canada to follow Route 430 along the **Northern Peninsula,** or you stay on the Trans-Canada and head south toward **Corner Brook** and the Marine Atlantic ferry terminal at **Channel–Port aux Basques.** Before you head in either direction, delight the kids with a visit to the **Newfoundland Insectarium & Butterfly Pavilion,** the only facility of its type east of Montreal.

North of Deer Lake is **Gros Morne National Park,** a UNESCO World Heritage Site and the undisputed highlight of the Western Region. Its cloud-shrouded mountains, glacial fjords, endangered species, and granite upheaval make it an outdoor adventurer's delight. Try to give yourself at least 2 days in Gros Morne—more if you're camping or backpacking.

It's almost 400km (248 miles) from Gros Morne to the northern end of the Northern Peninsula, but it's well worth the journey. This is where you'll find **Port au Choix National Historic Site,** the known home of four distinct ancient cultures, and **L'Anse aux Meadows,** where Vikings settled more than 1,000 years ago.

Along the way, you're likely to see moose—lots of moose. The peninsula is home to the largest percentage of the province's plentiful and impressively racked creatures. The area around St. Anthony is also a good place to see icebergs if you're visiting later in the summer.

If at Deer Lake you decide to continue south along the Trans-Canada Highway, you'll follow a mostly straight two-lane highway entwined with slumbering rivers and pastoral prettiness. You'll see places where the rising sun lends a morning glow to misty mountains and feel nature's gale-force power at the aptly named **Wreckhouse.** You'll encounter champion salmon fishing on the world-renowned **Humber River,** the best downhill skiing east of the Rockies at **Marble Mountain,** and the last francophone stronghold on the island on the **Port au Port Peninsula.** You'll see denuded trees and mountain-top ponds, thrilling theater, and international-class triathlon.

Allow at least a week if you want to enjoy everything between the northernmost tip of the Northern Peninsula and the southwesterly coastal communities of the Cabot Strait.

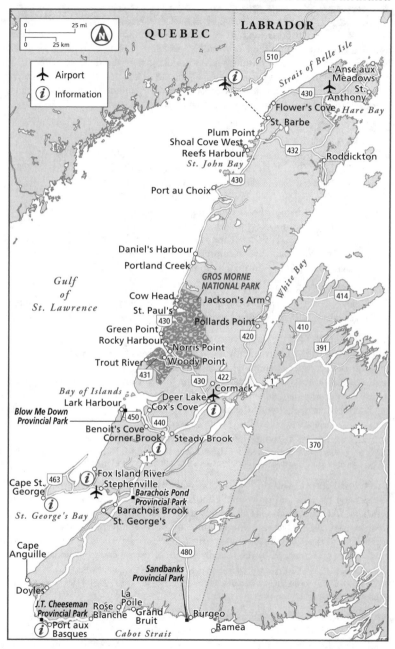

Western Newfoundland

QUEBEC

LABRADOR

Airport

Information

0   25 mi

0   25 km

Strait of Belle Isle

510

430

L'Anse aux Meadows

St. Anthony

Flower's Cove

Hare Bay

St. Barbe

Plum Point

Shoal Cove West

Reefs Harbour

432

Roddickton

St. John Bay

430

Port au Choix

Daniel's Harbour

Portland Creek

GROS MORNE NATIONAL PARK

White Bay

Cow Head

Jackson's Arm

414

St. Paul's

Green Point

430

Pollards Point

420

410

391

Rocky Harbour

Norris Point

Trout River

Woody Point

431

430

422

Cormack

Bay of Islands

Lark Harbour

Deer Lake

Cox's Cove

1

Blow Me Down Provincial Park

450

440

Benoit's Cove

Corner Brook

Steady Brook

370

1

Gulf of St. Lawrence

1

Fox Island River

Cape St. George

463

Stephenville

Barachois Pond Provincial Park

Barachois Brook

St. George's

St. George's Bay

Cape Anguille

480

Doyles

J.T. Cheeseman Provincial Park

Rose Blanche

La Poile

Grand Bruit

Sandbanks Provincial Park

Burgeo

Port aux Basques

Cabot Strait

Ramea

167

1 Deer Lake

Deer Lake is the transportation hub of Western Newfoundland. Here, you head either north to Gros Morne and the Northern Peninsula or south to Corner Brook and the Nova Scotia ferry. The community has a population of about 5,000 residents and offers a good range of services including an airport. The airport is especially convenient if you fly into St. John's, drive across the province, and don't want to drive all the way back to St. John's to catch a return flight.

ESSENTIALS
GETTING THERE
If you're coming from Channel–Port aux Basques and traveling north along the Trans-Canada Highway (Rte. 1), it's a 3-hour drive to Deer Lake. From the east, it's 637km (395 miles) between Deer Lake and St. John's. And, if you're heading south from St. Anthony on Route 430, it's a 443km (275-mile) drive to Deer Lake.

Or you can just bypass the driving altogether, and fly directly into Deer Lake airport (3km/2 miles northeast of town). The airport is serviced by Air Canada, CanJet, and Provincial Airlines. Four car-rental agencies have outlets at the airport (Avis, Budget, Hertz, and National), and in summer a temporary information desk is set up by the baggage carousel. For information go to www.deerlakeairport.com.

VISITOR INFORMATION
The Deer Lake Tourist Chalet is along the Trans-Canada Highway (Rte. 1), beside the Irving gas station. It's open June to September, daily 8am to 8pm (© **709/635-2202**).

WHERE TO STAY
Deer Lake Motel   Conveniently located on the Trans-Canada Highway, this handy motel is nothing special, although a 2004 renovation was yet to show the wear and tear of previous guests when I checked in for this edition. The on-site restaurant has a pleasant decor, quiet ambience, and predictable food at reasonable prices. The dining room is thankfully free of the most common restaurant mistake: tables are spaced sufficiently far apart to allow for private conversations.

13 Trans-Canada Hwy. (Rte. 1), Deer Lake. © **800/563-2144** or 709/635-2108. www.deerlakemotel.com. 56 units. C$85–C$129 (US$73–US$111) double; suites C$175 (US$150) double. AE, DC, MC, V. **Amenities:** Restaurant; cafe; lounge; nonsmoking rooms. *In room:* A/C, TV, coffeemaker; some with minibars; free local calls; dataport; hair dryer; iron.

Driftwood Inn *(Value*   It's affiliation with Backcountry Adventures, a company specializing in ATV and snowmobile tours, makes this a good base for adventurous travelers. You can snowmobile all the way from Deer Lake to St. Anthony, or take part in an extreme ATV adventure through some of the wildest territory on Earth. The inn itself dates to the 1950s and has a vaguely Tudor exterior. The cozy atmosphere with rustic styling is enhanced by the friendly service of the super-accommodating staff.

3 Upper Nicholsville Rd., Deer Lake. © **888/635-5115** or 709/635-5115. www.driftwoodinn.net. 25 units. C$74–C$89 (US$64–US$77) double. MC, V. **Amenities:** Restaurant; lounge. *In room:* TV, AM/FM radio, 4-piece bathroom, telephone, dataport.

Humberview Bed & Breakfast *(Finds*   This is the kind of palatial home most people can only dream about: a modern, executive-style castle in an upscale neighborhood. It's a showpiece of opulent comfort topped with crown molding and chandelier lighting. The aptly named Grand Room is 76 sq. m (820 sq. ft.) of elegant intimacy with its own sitting area and four-poster bed. Not only does the en-suite bathroom have a Grecian-style Jacuzzi flanked by twin columns, it also has a bidet! The other three rooms are named according to their color schemes. The Green Room is the most basic and compact, and it still comfortably accommodates two double beds. Rounding out the stylish setting is a sitting room complete with piano. It would be easy to be intimidated if not for the warm hospitality of owners Bronson and Irene Short. Still, you can't help but feel you have to be on your best behavior (this is, after all, a private home—not an impersonal hotel). Rates include a full home-cooked breakfast. No pets allowed.

11 Humberview Dr., Deer Lake. ✆ 888/635-4818 or 709-635-4818. www.thehumberview.com. 4 units. C$80–C$150 (US$69–US$129) double; C$10 (US$8.50) additional person. MC, V, Interac. **Amenities:** Full breakfast; laundry services available; nonsmoking rooms. *In room:* Private bathroom/shower, TV, telephone/fax service on request.

WHERE TO DINE
Irving Big Stop Family Restaurant *Value*   It offers good food at reasonable prices and attentive service. They have special offerings such as a "Jiggs Dinner" (corned beef and cabbage) served every Thursday for C$8 (US$6.85). The kids will likely be thrilled at the sight of Howley, Newfoundland's Biggest Moose—a huge moose statue located in the front of the building.

Trans-Canada Hwy. (Rte. 1), Deer Lake. ✆ 709/635-2129. Main courses C$8–C$17 (US$7–US$15). AE, DC, MC, V. Daily 24 hr. No alcoholic beverages or smoking.

Jungle Jim's *Kids*   This casual, safari-style restaurant is located at the Driftwood Inn but is independently run. Because of their hours, this is a great place to eat if you're looking for a late-night meal. Specialties include stir-fry, barbecue ribs, and spicy chicken wings. The funky surroundings and children's menu make this an ideal family restaurant (a welcome change in a sea of ultra-fast-food choices).

3 Upper Nicholsville Rd., Deer Lake. ✆ 709/635-5054. www.junglejims.ca. Reservations not required. Lunches about C$8 (US$7); most dinners about C$14 (US$12). AE, DC, MC, V. Sun–Tues 11am–11pm; Wed–Sat 11am–11:30pm.

EXPLORING DEER LAKE
Deer Lake (the lake) has one of the nicest sandy beaches in Newfoundland. To get there, take the Nicholsville Road exit from the Trans-Canada Highway; behind the beach you'll find a lovely park and scenic walking trail. The town also serves as a base for salmon fishing on the Humber River. Some of the best fishing holes are within **Sir Richard Squires Provincial Park,** 8km (5 miles) northwest on Route 430 and then 47km (29 miles) north on Route 422. Even if you don't want to dangle a line, it's worth driving out to this park to see **Big Falls,** where you can see the salmon jumping right out of the water. The best time to witness this natural wonder is in late June and early July.

Newfoundland Insectarium *⋆* *Kids*   The highlight of Deer Lake is the Insectarium & Butterfly Pavilion, just north of town on Bonne Bay Road. If you like butterflies this place is a must-see, with many specimens, including the impressive Blue Morpho. There's also an observation hive where you can watch thousands of honeybees going about their busy day—and be a breath away from live scorpions and tarantulas (safely enclosed by thick glass). If you're one of those people who like to get up close and personal with creepy crawlies, the staff will be happy to oblige by putting a live tropical leaf insect in your hand. This is one of only two such facilities in Canada (similar to sections of the American Museum of Natural History). It comes with a nice walking trail, an ice-cream shop, and a rather unique bug-themed gift shop. An elevator facilitates wheelchair access to all three levels.

Rte. 430 to Bonne Bay Rd., Reidville. ⟨℘⟩ 709/635-4545. www.nfinsectarium.com. C$6.50 (US$5.60) adults, C$5.50 (US$4.75) seniors, C$4.50 (US$4) kids 5–14, C$22 (US$19) family rate. July 1–Aug 31 daily 9am–8pm; mid-May to June 30 and Sept to mid-Oct daily 9am–5pm. Wheelchair accessible.

2 Gros Morne National Park ★★★

Gros Morne is larger than life, bordered by the Long Range Mountains and tapering to 90m (300-ft.) oceanic depths mere meters from shore. In between is an unbelievable biotic richness: old-growth forests, coastal lowlands, glacier-scarred landscapes, and a place where continents collided. The best way to really appreciate it is via a boat tour, hiking, rock climbing, skiing, or snowmobiling. In short, you have to get out there!

Unless you're the hardy type, the weather may hamper your enjoyment of the park. Between the prevailing southwest winds and the proximity of the Gulf of St. Lawrence, there is, on average, precipitation every 2 days during the summer months. From late September (for the higher elevations) on through the winter months, that dripping wetness translates into an impressive snowfall—up to 1,000 centimeters (394 in., or 33 ft.) in some areas, making Gros Morne ideal for backcountry skiing.

The weather in Gros Morne can be quite unpredictable, so be prepared with clothing for all types, and be sure to get a pre-trip orientation from a park warden before you head off into the backcountry. You'll find hiking trails for every experience level, with the most difficult being the 16km (10-mile) trail to the summit of Gros Morne Mountain, the highest peak in the park at 850m (2,788 ft.). *Warning:* Pay special attention to prudent food handling when picnicking, camping, or hiking the backcountry so that you're not surprised by a hungry black bear.

ESSENTIALS
GETTING THERE
The park entrance is 30km (19 miles) northwest of Deer Lake along Route 430. From this point, it's an additional 40km (25 miles) to Rocky Harbour, the park's main service center. From farther afield, it's 340km (212 miles) to Rocky Harbour from the ferry terminal at Port-aux-Basques and 640km (400 miles) to the park from St. John's. Alternatively, you can fly into Deer Lake from Halifax or St. John's and rent a car. (See section above for information about Deer Lake.)

VISITOR INFORMATION
The most comprehensive information on Gros Morne is available in the park's **Discovery Centre** (⟨℘⟩ 709/458-2417; www.pc.gc.ca/pn-np/nl/grosmorne/natcul/natcul12_E.asp), along Route 431 near the community of Woody Point. It's open June daily 9am to 5pm, July to August daily 9am to 6pm, September to the middle of October daily 9am to 5pm. The main **Park Visitor Centre** (⟨℘⟩ 709/458-2066), near Rocky Harbour, is open mid-May to late June 20, daily 9am to 5pm; late June to early September, daily 9am to 9pm; and the last two weeks of September, Monday to Friday 9am to 4pm. You can also get information at the **park entrance kiosk,** located on Route 430 near the southeastern entrance to the park at Wiltondale. The kiosk does not have a telephone and is open mid-May to mid-October daily 10am until 6pm.

Parks Canada publishes a wonderful visitor's guide called the *Tuckamore* that will provide you with detailed information about services in and around the park. Request

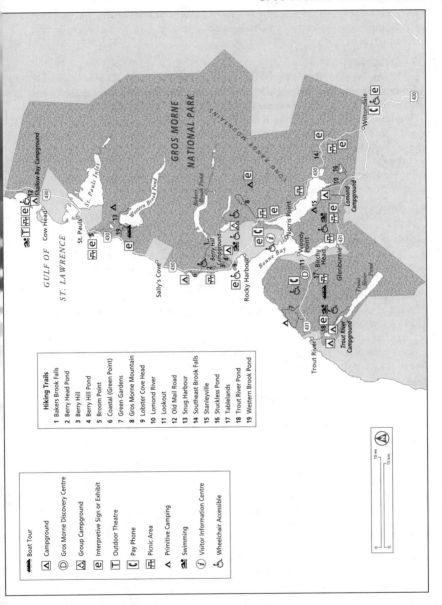

Hiking Trails

1 Bakers Brook Falls
2 Berry Head Pond
3 Berry Hill
4 Berry Hill Pond
5 Broom Point
6 Coastal (Green Point)
7 Green Gardens
8 Gros Morne Mountain
9 Lobster Cove Head
10 Lomond River
11 Lookout
12 Old Mail Road
13 Snug Harbour
14 Southeast Brook Falls
15 Stanleyville
16 Stuckless Pond
17 Tablelands
18 Trout River Pond
19 Western Brook Pond

⛴ Boat Tour
△ Campground
Ⓓ Gros Morne Discovery Centre
⊠ Group Campground
e Interpretive Sign or Exhibit
Ⓣ Outdoor Theatre
☏ Pay Phone
⊞ Picnic Area
▲ Primitive Camping
🏊 Swimming
ⓘ Visitor Information Centre
♿ Wheelchair Accessible

a copy by writing Gros Morne National Park at P.O. Box 130, Rocky Harbour, New-foundland, A0K 4N0 (e-mail: grosmorne.info@pc.gc.ca).

For information about privately run services in the communities bordering the park (a number of towns, like Rocky Harbour, are fully encompassed by the park), contact Newfoundland & Labrador Tourism (☎ **800/563-6353** or 709/729-2830;

www.gov.nf.ca/tourism). There is also a useful website at www.grosmorne.com that provides information about commercial services in the area, such as tour operators and accommodations.

GETTING AROUND

Gros Morne National Park is almost divided in two by Bonne Bay. The community of Wiltondale (gas station, lodging), 30km (19 miles) northwest of Deer Lake, is at the head of the bay, at the fork of the road where Route 431 branches out from Route 430.

Route 430 takes you north to Rocky Harbour and along the park's western coast, while Route 431 branches in an easterly direction to the southern side of Bonne Bay and ends at the picturesque fishing village of Trout River. You'll need to take Route 431 if your destination is the Tablelands and camping or hiking at Lomond or Trout River Pond. Route 431 is also the location of the park's Discovery Centre, an absolute must-see if you are to make the most of your visit to Gros Morne.

WHERE TO STAY & DINE

You'll be pleased by the wealth of motel, inn, and B&B accommodations choices located in communities encircled by the park but outside park boundaries. If, however, you're hoping to stay in a luxury hotel, you're going to be disappointed—there aren't any, though there is always ample room at the best lodgings of all, where amenities include pine-needle carpets and starlight canopies.

During July and August, accommodations in Gros Morne—both campsites and motel rooms—can be difficult to come by. It's best to make your reservations as soon as you know you'll be coming.

There are several decent restaurants in the area, but not as many as you might think given the size of the park. It's the nature of the destination; most people aren't here for fine dining. They prefer to picnic or barbecue.

Frontier Cottages　Located at the crossroads of Gros Morne National Park, thus convenient for day trips exploring both sides of Bonne Bay, this is a good choice for families. More than just a convenient exploration base, they're custom-made for outdoor fun. Stay at these fully winterized log cabins and you'll be able to start skiing and snowmobiling from the minute you walk out the door. Want to try something a little more unconventional, like ice climbing? Talk to the owners—they'll customize an expedition you'll never forget. The cabins are nicely decorated with pine and other rustic furnishings. There is an on-site convenience store and gas bar, craft/souvenir shop, and barbecues.

Rte. 430, Wiltondale. ✆ 800/668-2520 or 709/453-7266. www.frontiercottages.com. 6 units. Summer C$109 (US$94) double; off season C$65 (US$56) double, C$10 (US$8.50) additional person. AE, DC, MC, V. **Amenities:** Restaurant; small playground; laundry facilities.

Gros Morne Cabins　A short walk around the bay from downtown Rocky Harbour, these log cabins are separated from the water by nothing more than a strip of mown grass. Each has one or two bedrooms; a sitting area with TV; and a full kitchen with a stove, oven, microwave, and all the pots and pans you'd ever need. One cabin is wheelchair accessible.

Main St., Rocky Harbour. ✆ 888/603-2020 or 709/458-2020. www.grosmornecabins.com. 22 units. C$119–C$149 (US$103–US$128) double. C$10 (US$8.50) additional person. AE, DC, MC, V. **Amenities:** Playground; laundry facilities; convenience store. *In room:* TV, full kitchen, separate bedrooms.

Middle Brook Cottages and Chalets ✦✦ *Kids*   Families love the quality and convenience of this full-service facility (especially the playground and laundromat). It's perfect for a day of on-site recreation or as a much-needed rest after hiking the nearby Tablelands. Both the cottages and the chalets get top marks for cleanliness and comfort with their tidy landscaped exteriors and pine-paneled walls. I especially like the chalets because of their bright decor, cathedral ceilings, and second-floor patio (a great place to enjoy your morning coffee and watch the sun come up).

There's a convenience store on-site as well as a gift shop. There's also a picnic area with barbecues and a firepit for an evening marshmallow roast. When you're not enjoying the sights and sounds of Gros Morne, you can explore the waterfall and walking trails that are within walking distance of Middle Brook.

Rte. 431, Glenburnie–Birchy Head. ✆ **709/453-2332.** www.middlebrookcottages.com. 3 cottages, 2 chalets, 1 deluxe unit. C$89–C$129 (US$77–US$111) double; off season C$59–C$89 (US$51–US$77) double, children under 12 free, C$10 (US$8.50) additional person. AE, MC, V. **Amenities:** Playground; laundromat; nonsmoking rooms.

Ocean View Motel   For those who prefer the anonymity of a motel over the forced intimacy of a B&B, this is the largest facility in the largest town in Gros Morne. Guest rooms are standard motel style, although the bedding is of better quality than most. There is one housekeeping unit as well as wheelchair-accessible rooms. Access to upper floor rooms is a funky old-style elevator. The ocean is so close that the gentle lullaby of the surf will help you sleep at night. You may even be drawn to have a closer look, a whim easily accommodated by simply crossing the road. Or, you can stay in the comfort of the Anchor Pub and dining room, enraptured by the fading sun as it sets over Lobster Cove Head Lighthouse. That's if you can draw your focus away from the superb dinner offerings. The pub gets busiest when local bands hit the stage.

Main St., Rocky Harbour. ✆ **800/563-9887** or 709/458-2730. www.oceanviewmotel.com. 52 units. C$65–C$125 (US$56–US$108) double, off-season and group discounts available; C$5 (US$4.30) additional person. MC, V. **Amenities:** Restaurant; pub; nonsmoking rooms. *In room:* TV.

Shallow Bay Motel & Cabins ✦ *Kids*   Located 40km (25 miles) north of Rocky Harbour, there's something for everyone at Shallow Bay: natural wonder, peaceful solitude, and a sauna for adult enjoyment; minigolf, small outdoor heated pool, and beachcombing for the younger set. One activity both young and old are guaranteed to appreciate is the Gros Morne Theatre Festival—a powerful production of Newfoundland drama, story, and song hosted here each summer.

The property offers a choice of standard motel unit or fully equipped cabin. Both are fairly modest, although enhanced by the ocean just 5m (16 ft.) away. This is a wheelchair-accessible facility. The on-site family restaurant serves a tasty assortment of pocketbook-friendly home-style meals. The specialty of the house is lobster, but you can get it only in season, from early May to early July.

Rte. 430, Cow Head. ✆ **800/563-1946** or 709/243-2471. www.shallowbaymotel.com. 52 units (35 motel units, 17 cottages). C$95–C$115 (US$82–US$99) double, off-season discounts; C$10 (US$8.50) additional person. AE, DC, MC, V, Interac. **Amenities:** Dining room; lounge; outdoor heated pool; sauna; laundromat. *In room:* TV, dataport, phone, coffeemaker.

Victorian Manor Heritage Properties   A combination of seven guest rooms in two buildings, as well as two complete homes rented on a nightly basis. In Newfoundland and Labrador, it's a traditional measure of respect and affection to refer to older, unrelated acquaintances as "Aunt" or "Uncle," which is where the name **Aunt Jane's Place** is derived. Giving the title to this 19th-century tourist home evokes that old-fashioned

Gros Morne Theatre Festival

The Gros Morne Theatre Festival is an unforgettable experience of such rich cultural diversity, you won't be satisfied until you see it all. "All" in 2005 was 8 different productions, 3 different venues, 2 shows a night, and more than 30 professional actors, musicians, technicians, writers, directors, and front-of-house staff. Focus on the word *professional*—that's your first indication of the superior quality of these dramatic events. That, and the consistently sold-out shows.

A superb example of the intensely personable plays performed during the Gros Morne Theatre Festival is *Tempting Providence*. Written by Robert Chafe, it's the haunting story of Nurse Myra Bennett, Newfoundland's own Florence Nightingale. For more than 50 years, Bennett was the only medical person on the Great Northern Peninsula. During that time she delivered more than 700 babies, extracted at least 5,000 teeth, and performed kitchen-table surgeries by lamplight. For information on the latest shows and to make a reservation, call © **877/243-2899** or 709/639-7238, or go to www.theatrenewfoundland.com/gmtf.html.

charm just as much as does its period furnishings and simple square construction. Only one of the five guest rooms has one bed in the room and a private bathroom; there are two beds in each of the other four rooms, sharing two bathrooms between them. If you aren't interested in watching TV in the common room, you can still mingle with your hosts and other guests in the upstairs sitting room while enjoying its view of Bonne Bay. Alternatively, visit the main-floor **Sample Room**'s antiques display and gift shop, where you can browse through merchandise typical of what was sold here more than 100 years ago. Within walking distance is **Uncle Steve's Place,** a fully equipped 3-bedroom traditional-style home, great for a small group or family.

1 Water St., Woody Point. © **866/453-2485** or 709/453-2485. www.grosmorne.com/victorianmanor. 7 units, 2 holiday homes. Units C$50–C$70 (US$43–US$60) double. Holiday homes C$150–C$225 (US$129–US$193) for up to 6 people. MC, V.

Sugar Hill Inn *Finds*   One of the more luxurious places to stay while in Gros Morne (and one of the only places to have air-conditioning) is Sugar Hill Inn. Most impressive is the King Suite. It features a king-size bed, private Jacuzzi for two, and gorgeous leather couch. This room is popular (especially with honeymooners) so be sure to book early. There is also a nice cottage with queen-size bed, Jacuzzi tub, and a private deck. Every room has hardwood floors, and most have private entrances.

The Sugar Hill Inn offers gourmet dining in its full-service restaurant. Specialties of the house include fresh local seafood—halibut, cod, salmon, shrimp, scallops, and shark. It's one of the very few restaurants in the province where *nothing* is deep-fried. Service is by reservation only—primarily for guests of the inn. But call anyway—they may have an opening for the single 7:30pm dinner sitting.

Rte. 430 to Norris Pt. Rd. © **888/299-2147** or 709/458-2147. www.sugarhillinn.nf.ca. 6 units. C$89–C$215 (US$77–US$185) double. Off-season discounts apply. C$15 (US$13) additional person. AE, MC, V. Closed Nov–Dec. **Amenities:** Licensed dining room; bar; hot tub; sauna; laundry facilities; nonsmoking rooms. *In room:* A/C, TV.

CAMPING IN GROS MORNE

A good number of visitors come to Gros Morne to camp and thus to fully appreciate the great outdoors. The campgrounds are justifiably popular, so reservations are wise. Contact the **Parks Canada Campground Reservation Service** (📞 877/737-3783; www.pccamping.ca).

Berry Hill Campground 🎣   With 150 wooded campsites, including 4 walk-in sites especially for tent campers, this is the park's largest campground. It also has the most facilities, as well as a hiking trail. It is also close to Rocky Harbour, where grocery stores and restaurants can be found. If you want to combine culture with camping, you'll be pleased to know that the shuttle for the Gros Morne Theatre Festival makes a campground pickup.

Rte. 430, Rocky Harbour. 📞 **709/458-2417.** www2.parkscanada.gc.ca/pn-np/nl/grosmorne/index_E.asp. 150 sites. C$23 (US$20) for unserviced sites; C$6 (US$5.15) for firewood bundle. AE, MC, V, Interac. Open mid-June to mid-Sept. **Amenities:** Shower and washroom facilities; water; kitchen shelter; dump station; picnic tables; fireplace; playground; hiking.

Lomond Campground   Just down Route 431, 17km (11 miles) south from Wiltondale at Lomond, you'll find a full-service campground, the closest one to the main park entrance. This campground is ideal for people interested in fishing and boating and is popular with local residents. The area was once a logging community, and two groomed trails follow old logging roads. The campsites have lots of open, grassy spaces, and offer outstanding views of Bonne Bay, the Lomond River, and Long Range Mountains.

Rte. 431, Lomond. 📞 **709/458-2417,** or off season 709/458-2059. www2.parkscanada.gc.ca/pn-np/nl/grosmorne/index_E.asp. 29 sites. C$23 (US$20); C$6 (US$5.15) per firewood bundle. AE, MC, V, Interac. Open mid-May to mid-Oct. **Amenities:** Running water; dumping station; washrooms w/showers; swimming; boat launching/docking facilities; fireplaces; kitchen shelters; picnic tables; fishing; hiking; playground.

Shallow Bay Campground   Located near Cow Head (home of the Gros Morne Theatre Festival), this is the northernmost campground along Route 430, just before the northern entrance/exit to the park. The grassy campsites, sheltered from northwesterly winds by a protective stand of tuckamore, are a hop, skip, and jump from a 4km-long (2½-mile) white-sand beach—ideal for swimming and building sand castles. There is a trail that links the campground to the day-use area and a small outdoor theater for campfire programs.

Rte. 430 to Cow Head. 📞 **709/458-2417,** or off season 709/458-2162. www2.parkscanada.gc.ca/pn-np/nl/grosmorne/index_E.asp. 62 sites. C$23 (US$20) for unserviced sites; C$6 (US$5.15) for firewood bundle. AE, MC, V, Interac. Open mid-June to mid-Sept. **Amenities:** Dumping station; running water; showers; fireplace; kitchen shelter; picnic tables; playground; swimming; outdoor theater; fishing; hiking.

Trout River Campground 🎣   Campsites at Trout River are larger and more sheltered than in some other parts of the park and provide awesome views of the Tablelands and Trout River Pond. The drinking water is good, but it's still not a bad idea to filter it. This is a popular spot because of the nearby beach, boat tour, and boat launch. Although the most isolated campground in the park (excluding the primitive campsites), it's also the best base for exploring the Tablelands, the Green Gardens area, and the community of Trout River.

Rte. 431, Trout River. 📞 **709/458-2417,** or off season 709/458-2162. www2.parkscanada.gc.ca/pn-np/nl/grosmorne/index_E.asp. 33 sites. C$23 (US$20) for unserviced sites; C$6 (US$5.15) for firewood bundle. AE, MC, V, Interac. Open mid-June to mid-Sept. **Amenities:** Shower and washroom facilities; water; kitchen shelter; picnic tables; fireplace; playground; fishing; hiking; swimming.

EXPLORING GROS MORNE

Entrance to the park can be obtained with a seasonal, 4-day, or daily pass. The daily pass costs C$8 (US$7) for adults, C$7 (US$6) for seniors 65 and over, C$4 (US$3.50) for youth 6 to 16 years, free for children under 6. Family passes are C$16 (US$14). If you're continuing up the Northern Peninsula from Gros Morne, consider the Viking Trail Pass, which covers park entrance for 1 week, as well as admission to four national historic sites along the Northern Peninsula. The cost is C$37 (US$32) for adults, C$32 (US$27) for seniors 65 years and over, C$19 (US$16) for youth 6 to 16, free for children under 6, C$80 (US$69) for families. Your park entrance fee gives you access to park services including the wonderful Discovery Centre.

Discovery Centre 🕊🕊 Your first step to exploring Gros Morne should be a visit to the Discovery Centre. This ultra-modern and spacious facility with comfortable lounge area and huge panoramic windows offers a spectacular view of Bonne Bay.

The Discovery Centre is the best place to begin exploration of the south side of the park, which includes the Tablelands (the geological feature that helped make Gros Morne a UNESCO World Heritage Site in 1987), the beautiful Green Gardens Trail (excellent for viewing wildflowers), and Trout River Pond. You'll find some incredible interpretive exhibits about Gros Morne's geology on the first floor of the center and an art exhibit that changes regularly on the lower level.

Run collaboratively by the park and the Art Gallery of Newfoundland and Labrador, an artists-in-residence program offers lectures and workshops by artists whose work is displayed at the Discovery Centre. You can also watch the artists at work, and maybe even purchase a permanent remembrance to hang on your wall at home. In addition to the indoor displays, ask about the park's interpretive program, which includes a summer schedule of talks and guided walks. Plan to spend a couple of hours at the Discovery Centre before heading out on the 5km (3-mile) Lookout Hills Trail, which begins at the Discovery Centre. This moderately difficult trail offers the best view of Bonne Bay and the Tablelands; allow 3 to 4 hours to complete.

Rte. 431 near Woody Point. 📞 709/458-2417. June daily 9am–5pm; July–Aug daily 9am–6pm; Sept to mid-Oct daily 9am–5pm. Your park pass gets you into the Discovery Centre.

Lobster Cove Head Lighthouse 🕊 This dramatic lighthouse has marked the marine approach to Rocky Harbour since 1897. What's unique is the cast-iron structure of this lighthouse, one of the first of its kind to be built by Victoria Iron Works of St. John's. The setting of the lighthouse against a rocky backdrop has made it a photo favorite for visitors to the area.

The Canadian Coast Guard now operates an automated light from the lighthouse. The former keeper's house is open to the public as an interpretive historical exhibit about the various peoples who have inhabited this coast over the past 4,000 years. It also explains the seasonal fishery's importance to the region. The road to the lighthouse is marked and the lighthouse itself is visible from the highway. A 2km (1.25-mile) trail leads from the lighthouse to a rocky beach that's best explored at low tide.

Rte. 430, Lobster Cove Head, near Rocky Harbour. No telephone. Guided tours on the half-hour mid-May to mid-Oct daily 10am–6pm. Your admission to the park also gets you into the interpretive exhibit and on the tour.

Tablelands 🕊 This geological wonder south of Woody Point on Route 431 has gained worldwide recognition for its contribution to the understanding of plate tectonics. For this barren orange-yellow moonscape, Gros Morne National Park was declared a UNESCO World Heritage Site.

The Tablelands are an excellent example of plate tectonics, in which 470-million-year-old ultramafic rock was brought to the Earth's surface as a result of faulting. In plain English, it means that this is what the world would look like if you turned it inside out (the Tablelands were once several kilometers below an ancient ocean). Route 431 passes through the middle of the Tablelands, but to really appreciate the unique setting, plan on walking at least a part of the 4km (2.5-mile) hiking trail off Route 431. It takes about 1½ hours to get to the end of the trail. *Note:* All rocks, minerals, and fossils found within national parks are protected and must be left as found. The collection of specimens for research or educational purposes requires a permit, which you must apply for well in advance. *Tip: The Tablelands can get very hot, so bring plenty of drinking water.*

Rte. 431, 6km (3¾ miles) west of Woody Point.

Tableland Boat Tours   If you're not able to hike but would still like to see the Tablelands, at Trout River you can take a 2½-hour boat tour and view this natural wonder from the comfort of a wheelchair-accessible boat. Unlike Western Brook Pond, the boat dock is very close to the parking lot. There are three departures daily, but—like everything in Newfoundland—departures are always weather dependent.

Rte. 431, Trout River Pond day-use area. (C) **866/751-7500** or 709/451-7500. C$30 (US$26) adults, C$15 (US$13) youth 12–16, C$10 (US$8.50) children under 12. June 15–Sept 15. June and Sept, 1pm sailing. July and Aug, 3 daily sailings: 10am, 1pm, 4pm.

Western Brook Pond Boat Tours ✸✸✸   If you have only one day in the park, you'll probably want to visit the Discovery Centre in the morning and take a boat tour of Western Brook Pond in the afternoon—a 2½-hour narrated cruise through some of the most spectacular scenery you've ever seen.

Western Brook Pond isn't what we traditionally think of as a pond. It's a 16km-long (10-mile), 165m-deep (541-ft.) inland fjord created during the Glacial Epoch. There's one point in the tour when the captain pauses 1m (3 ft.) from the base of a waterfall to declare that you are floating on water 91m deep (300 ft.). *Warning:* This is not a tour to take if you have mobility problems. You must park your car at the Western Brook Pond trail head, and then embark on a 3km (nearly 2-mile) hike along the boardwalk to where you catch the boat. It's not a difficult hike, but it will take you approximately 40 minutes each way, and longer if you walk at a leisurely pace.

Access to departure point is along a 3km (1.9-mile) trail beginning 27km (17 miles) north of Rocky Harbour. (C) **800/563-9887** or 709/458-2730. www.bontours.ca. C$38 (US$33) adults; C$16 (US$14) youth 12–16; C$11 (US$9.50) children under 12. During June and Sept, there is only a 1pm sailing. In July and Aug, there are 3 daily sailings: 10am, 1pm, 4pm. If you pay at the **Ocean View Motel** in Rocky Harbour, you can use AE, MC, V, Interac. If you pay at the boat dock, come prepared with cash or traveler's checks. Departures are weather dependent. Bring rain gear.

GROS MORNE OUTDOOR ACTIVITIES
CROSS-COUNTRY SKIING

There are some pretty amazing cross-country skiing opportunities in Gros Morne. If you're a beginner, the trails around Rocky Harbour and in the north of the park will be best suited to your abilities: the terrain is more gentle, with rolling hills and no steep inclines. Skiing on the Tablelands is comparable to skiing on glaciers with steep slopes better left for the advanced skier. The alpine terrain of the Long Range Mountains is also best suited to those with advanced skills.

GUIDED PACKAGES

Whether you're looking to do some skiing, guided hiking, sea kayaking, backpacking, or snowshoeing, you should put yourself in the hands of an experienced outfitter (especially if this is your first visit to Gros Morne).

Gros Morne Adventures   This company will customize a tour for you any time of the year. If your primary focus is on hiking, try the *Gros Morne Explorer,* a combination of coastal and mountain hiking that runs June through September. Over the course of 6 days, you'll hike a number of the park's most scenic trails. Plan to cover 10 to 16km (up to 10 miles) per day, up elevations of 700m (2,300 ft.) over uneven surfaces. The cost, including transfers from Deer Lake, lodging, and meals, is C$1,895 (US$1,628).

Guided kayaking programs range from 2½ hours to a full day. You can also rent single or double kayaks and go off on your own if you're an experienced kayaker. Bonne Bay is a great place for sea kayaking because of the calm, sheltered waters. It's common to see whales, bald eagles, terns, mink, mergansers, and kingfishers throughout the summer. Winter programs include backcountry skiing and snowshoeing adventures. The scenery is awe-inspiring, the snow is plentiful, and moose and caribou are often spotted as you make your way along quiet trails.

For your overnight accommodations, Gros Morne Adventures chooses established properties to suit the individual client's preferences and pocketbook. All guides have at least 15 years' experience and are CPR and wilderness trained and certified, in addition to having avalanche awareness and safety training. The company's website will provide you with a full range of prices and options.

9 Clarke's Lane, Norris Point. ✆ **800/685-4624** or 709/458-2722. www.grosmorneadventures.com.

3 Northern Peninsula

The Bonne Bay entrance to the Northern Peninsula is a dazzling panorama of surreal extremes: you'll scale near-perpendicular mountain heights through some of the tallest trees in the province, following a twining blacktop on what seems a perpetual climb, until a sudden final crest reverses your direction into a similarly stunning descent. All the while, your vehicle is regularly overtaken by tractor-trailers, logging trucks, and speeding grannies who are obviously immune to the natural wonder.

It calms down considerably after that. As is typical elsewhere in the province, the highway follows traditional coastal settlement patterns. Virtually all settlement in the province is along the coast, a reflection of the importance of the fishery and ocean access to early settlers. From Cow Head north, the topography is mostly flat, with stands of tuckamore (trees whose growth has been stunted by wind and sea) to the right and the Atlantic Ocean to the left. Here and there you'll encounter stretches of barrens and bog, much like the scenery along the Burin Peninsula.

PORT AU CHOIX

As the approximate halfway point between Deer Lake and St. Anthony, Port au Choix is a convenient stopover on the Northern Peninsula. With a population of 1,400, it's one of the larger communities en route, and has a good number of services/facilities (for example, bank, post office, restaurants). You can either stop at Port au Choix for lunch before continuing up the coast, or stay overnight to visit the Point Riche Lighthouse and the site where archaeologists are uncovering evidence of ancient native cultures.

ESSENTIALS
GETTING THERE

Port au Choix is 13km (8 miles) off of Route 430, and 230km (143 miles) north of Deer Lake. Both the main highway and the paved access road are in good condition, but you won't find a lot of services along the way—so be sure to tank up and have a few snacks with you before heading out. It's a 2½-hour drive from Port au Choix to St. Anthony.

WHERE TO STAY & DINE

There is one motel in town as well as a B&B, a small inn, and a couple of good restaurants—making it the best place to stay while in the area. *Note:* It takes at least half a day to fully explore Port au Choix National Historic Site, so plan on an overnight stay.

Anchor Café ☆ SEAFOOD   You won't have any problem recognizing the Anchor Café—the front of the building is shaped like the bow of a boat! It's a casual, fun (albeit kitschy) establishment decorated with lobster pots, fishing nets, and a sou'western mannequin. With such an obvious fishing theme, it's no surprise this wheelchair-friendly restaurant specializes in local seafood. Of special note are any items that include coldwater shrimp (those tasty little shrimp you see on shrimp rings), which are caught in local waters and processed in the waterfront factory across the road. The

---

Moose Can Be Hazardous to Your Health

As you drive along the highway, you'll see moose silhouettes and bright-yellow signs depicting a crunched car and a moose. There's a good reason. However majestic these 450-kilogram (1,000-lb.) animals are to look at, they are a dangerous and mobile road hazard. Between 600 and 900 moose–vehicle accidents occur every year in the province, causing more than $1 million in vehicle damages as well as serious injury and even death.

You'd think it would be easy to spot and avoid these massive animals, but they are masters of camouflage—especially in low light. Their mottled brown coat blends so well into the foliage that you may not see one standing in the brush to the side of the road until it walks into your path.

How to Avoid an Accident:

- Moose are nocturnal. Reduce your speed, or avoid driving altogether, in the early morning and at night.
- Be extra cautious when you see moose warning signs. They signal high-risk areas.
- Scan the highway as far ahead as possible, paying particular attention to areas where trees and shrubbery grow close to the road. Use high beams whenever possible.
- If you see a moose on the highway, pull over and turn off your lights. Like deer, moose are transfixed by light. They have also been known to charge at lights, rather than run away.

Check out the website www.env.gov.nl.ca/env/wildlife/publications/collisions.htm for extra information.

Walking Trails

Once you've had enough of the indoor displays at the National Historic Site, head out on one of the three hiking trails in the Port au Choix area. *Note:* These are free, self-guided walking trails.

Coastal Walking Trail   At the end of the road past the National Historic Site is **Point Riche Lighthouse,** a former site of Dorset habitation. The road is paved up to the visitor center but is uneven gravel between there and the lighthouse.

Dorset Trail   Beginning from the visitor center, this 4km (2.5-mile) trail cuts across the limestone barrens to the opposite of the peninsula and Phillips Garden. Along the way, it passes Dorset burial caves and a lookout.

Phillips Garden Coastal Trail ★★   Phillips Garden is an oceanfront meadow where you can faintly discern the circular foundations of some 50 semi-subterranean houses. Every summer, teams of archaeologists can be seen working at the site—and they will be more than happy to answer your questions. On a clear day, you can see Quebec across the Gulf of St. Lawrence, some 96km (60 miles) away. This trail begins from Old Port au Choix (follow Main St. through town). It's around 1km (.6 miles) from the end of the road to Phillips Garden. From this point, you can continue to the visitor center or follow the shoreline for another 3km (1.8 miles) to the Point Riche Lighthouse.

cod and shrimp chowder can be a meal in itself, or head straight for mains like blackened halibut. The Anchor Café is on the main road through town and directly opposite the waterfront.

Main St., Port au Choix. ✆ **709/861-3665.** Reservations not required. Main courses C$6–C$18 (US$5.15–US$16). MC, V. May–June and Sept–Oct 10am–10pm daily; July–Aug 9am–11pm. daily

Sea Echo Motel   There's a wise manager in charge here: the hanging plastic seafood and lighthouse replica while charming in the adjacent restaurant are thankfully absent in the warm decor of this motel's very spacious rooms. You'll be surprised at just how much space there is: besides the bed(s), there are nightstands, a bureau, a love seat, a table with two chairs, and still ample room to move around. It's not advertised as wheelchair accessible, but I don't think maneuvering around this single-story structure will be a problem for travelers with disabilities.

Fisher St., Port au Choix. ✆ **709/861-3777.** www.seaecho.ca. 33 units. C$88–C$108 (US$76–US$93). AE, DC, MC, V, Interac. Senior and group discounts apply. **Amenities:** Restaurant; lounge w/billiard table; RV hookups to water and electricity. *In room:* TV, hair dryer.

EXPLORING PORT AU CHOIX

Port au Choix National Historic Site ★★   Archaeological findings confirm that over the last 4,500 years, five cultures inhabited the barren peninsula extending into the Gulf of St. Lawrence beyond the modern day town of Port au Choix. Although these earliest residents didn't leave a written record, from 30 years of archaeological digs, we have a good idea of the way these ancient people lived and adapted to the harsh environment. The best place to learn about the site is the **Parks Canada Visitor Centre,** which is signposted through town, on the peninsula itself. Here, you can see a wonderful assortment of displays about the Maritime Archaic Indians, Groswater, Dorset-Paleoeskimos, and more recent native cultures. Artifacts of note include stone axes, hunting tools, and bone carvings. Don't miss the life-size replica of a Dorset-Paleoeskimo dwelling from about 1,500 years ago. Whale bones were used to frame the structure, and animal skins insulated it from the region's harsh weather. The well-curated displays, such as the assortment of ancient stone and bone tools from the region's four prehistoric cultures, make for an enjoyably editying experience.

Once you've seen the indoor displays, plan on exploring the rest of the historic site on foot. The two main walks are detailed below, or check at the visitor center for scheduled guided hikes, which generally depart daily through summer at 1:30pm.

Port au Choix National Historic Site. © 709/861-3522. www.pc.gc.ca/lhn-nhs/nl/portauchoix. C$6.50 (US$5.60) adults, C$5.50 (US$4.75) seniors 65+, C$3.25 (US$2.75) youth 6 to 16, free for children under 6, C$16 (US$14) family rate. June 1–June 14 and Sept 3–Oct 14 9am–5pm, June 15–Sept 2 9am–6pm daily.

WHERE TO SHOP & STOP

Ben's Studio *Finds* If you're looking for a unique gift to bring home, stop by Ben's Studio (adjacent to the Museum of Whales & Things), run by "lath art" specialist Ben Ploughman. Don't know what lath art is? Then visit Ploughman's studio and see his 3-D wood art for yourself. His unique style depicts local life in colorful wooden squares patched together in a quilt-like fashion. The lath art is relatively expensive, at C$400 (US$345) for a small piece and up to C$2,500 (US$2,150) for a large piece.

The gallery also has unique items for the more budget-minded traveler. Take a look at the "Viking critters" that sell for C$18 (US$16) each. These comical fellows are made from a scallop shell, a mussel shell, moose hair, and a lobster claw, providing a one-of-a-kind reminder of your NL adventure.

24 Fisher St., Port au Choix. © 709/861-3280. www.bensstudio.ca. Free admission. MC, V. June 1–Sept 30 Mon–Sat 9am–5pm.

Museum of Whales & Things *⊛* It's not every day you see a 14m (46-ft.) skeleton of a sperm whale, but that's exactly what you'll find hanging from the roof of the appropriately named Museum of Whales & Things. It's not a large building or a particularly well-organized exhibit, but every nook and cranny holds something with a story to tell. This eclectic collection, at the entrance to Port au Choix, is the work of local artisan and entrepreneur Ben Ploughman.

24 Fisher St., Port au Choix. © 709/861-3280. www.bensstudio.ca. Free admission; donations accepted. MC, V. June 1–Sept 30 Mon–Sat 9am–5pm.

PORT AU CHOIX TO ST. BARBE

From Port au Choix, it's 104km (65 miles) north along Route 430 to the next town of note, St. Barbe. Along the way, the ocean is rarely out of view. You'll pass a smattering of seasonal fishing camps, but just one official attraction—an archaeological dig site at Bird Cove.

Bird Cove Archaeological Dig *⊛* At Plum Point, 18km (11 miles) before St. Barbe, a side road leads to the village of Bird Cove and a cluster of archaeological dig sites. Make your first stop Bird Cove Interpretation Centre, where displays explain the history of the sites and the Beothuk, Dorset-Paleoeskimo, and Maritime Archaic Indians that lived here up to 4,500 years ago. Other displays include local rocks, fossils, and whale bones.

It wasn't until the 1990s that archaeologists even knew of these local sites, which puts the area's remoteness in perspective. What was uncovered were several completely undisturbed village sites, including two that are now encircled by a boardwalk. Ask at the interpretive center for directions. From the center you will see a footbridge that leads across to the Dog Peninsula. More village sites were excavated here, but none are marked. Instead a network of trails leads through the coastal forest to a pebbly beach and the broken-down buildings of a farm established in the 1880s.

84 Michael's Dr., Bird Cove. (✆) **866/247-2011** or 709/247-2011. www.bigdroke.com. Admission to Interpretation Centre is C$3 (US$2.60) adults, C$2.50 (US$2.15) seniors, C$2 (US$1.75) students 6–17. Additional C$4 (US$3.50) per person for guided tour of the archaeological dig sites. MC, V, Interac. June–Oct Mon–Sat 9am–6pm.

ST. BARBE

The most noteworthy aspect of St. Barbe is that it's the departure point for the ferry to Blanc Sablon on the Quebec–Labrador border. You probably won't stay here overnight unless you're catching an early-morning ferry, but if you are you'll find a motel and dining room just up the road from the ferry terminal.

If you have time to kill while waiting for the ferry, take the short drive out to Black Duck Cove. Here interpretive panels describe the region's history.

ESSENTIALS
GETTING THERE

St. Barbe is on Route 430, 104km (65 miles) north of Port au Choix and a little under 300km (186 miles) north of Deer Lake. St. Barbe is the departure point for ferries to Labrador. The MV *Apollo* sails once or twice daily from early May to early January. The cost for the 2-hour trip is C$11 (US$9) adults, C$7.50 (US$6.50) seniors, C$5.50 (US$4.75) children, and from C$22 (US$19) for a vehicle. Even with reservations, you need to check in upon arrival at St. Barbe at the office in the Dockside

---

Creating New Money from Old Traditions

Economuseums use traditional manufacturing techniques or know-how in the production of goods and services. They provide income for skilled crafts-people while instilling cultural pride and preserving a way of life that might otherwise be forgotten. Products available might include knitted goods, quilts, and handcrafted wooden furniture. In addition to being retail out-lets, economuseums are frequently staffed by the artisans themselves—offering interested visitors the opportunity to learn about the history and process used to manufacture the products on display.

An economuseum of note on the long drive up the Northern Peninsla is **Borealis Crafts,** in Shoel Cove East, 78km (49 miles) north of Port au Choix ((✆) **709/456-2123**), which presents a wonderful opportunity to purchase handicrafts made by local artisans. Specialties include whalebone carvings, which, aside from the aesthetic value, are affordable, small, and very light-weight, making them a fabulous gift idea that won't weigh you down. The gallery and workshop is open daily 9am to 5pm.

Motel, which opens 2 hours before official departure time. For ferry information call $\mathcal{C}$ 866/535-2567 or go to www.tw.gov.nl.ca/ferryservices.

All vehicle sizes are permitted on the ferry, but if you don't want to take your RV you can leave it at St Barbe in a secured parking lot across the road from the ferry office. The parking lot has electrical hookups, laundry facilities, and a common room, so many RVers find themselves spending the night. Call $\mathcal{C}$ **709/877-2272** for details.

WHERE TO STAY & DINE
Dockside Motel & Cabins $\mathcal{R}$ The only accommodations in town is the Dockside Motel, in town and on the road down to the ferry terminal. Though white-glove clean, the motel's sparsely decorated guest rooms are obviously intended for overnight stays rather than long-term vacation ambience. You may hear truck engines running outside your window around 6:30am, when large vehicles start to line up for the ferry. The Dockside Motel has a restaurant that is tastefully decorated with linen table-cloths—something you don't see much of in these parts.

Main St., St. Barbe. $\mathcal{C}$ **709/877-2444**. www.docksidemotel.nf.ca. 15 motel units; 10 cabins. C$75–C$99 (US$65–US$85) double. AE, DC, MC, V, Interac. **Amenities:** Restaurant, pub, ferry check-in counter. *In room:* TV. Cabins are fully equipped and have private entrances. **Docker's Diner** is open daily 6am–9pm in summer, 8am–8pm the rest of the year. Dinner entrees offer generous portions and are reasonably priced at C$7.50–C$16 (US$6.50–US$14).

ST. ANTHONY
Known as Newfoundland's northern capital, St. Anthony is at the mouth of horse-shoe-shaped Hare Bay, near the tip of the Northern Peninsula. Isolated from the rest of the province by sheer distance, the community is worth visiting for its links to Sir Wilfred Thomason Grenfell, but is also a base for those wishing to explore nearby L'Anse aux Meadows. You'll also find a hospital, a small shopping mall, a pharmacy, a bank, a few nice places to stay and eat, vehicle servicing and rentals, as well as a nearby airport. A winter visit to St. Anthony allows for lots of outdoor fun—snowmobiling, cross-country skiing, and ice fishing are popular activities.

ESSENTIALS
GETTING THERE
St. Anthony is 443km (275 miles) north of Deer Lake along Route 430. If you're driving all the way from the east coast, plan on 15 hours driving time to cover the 1,090km (677 miles) from St. John's. Time wise, the town is a 2½-hour drive northeast of Port au Choix, hours from Rocky Harbour (midway through Gros Morne National Park), and 5 hours from Deer Lake.

For those who wish to investigate the multi-lineal heritage and rugged landscape of the Northern Peninsula but want to avoid the long drive from St. John's, it's an hour's flight with Air Labrador or Provincial Airlines from St. John's to St. Anthony. *Warning:* St. Anthony Regional Airport is not really *in* St. Anthony. It's 55km (34 miles) back down Route 430.

VISITOR INFORMATION
For a complete list of services in St. Anthony, visit the town's website at www.town.stanthony.nf.ca or call $\mathcal{C}$ **709/454-0061**. There is no official visitor center in St. Anthony, but information can be picked up at Grenfell Historic Properties, on West St. ($\mathcal{C}$ **709/454-4010**). The center is open mid-May to mid-June from 9am until 5pm, mid-June to September 9am to 8pm.

Roadside Peculiarities

While driving along the Northern Peninsula, you'll likely notice the garden plots alongside the highway. These are owned by private citizens who arbitrarily stake their claim and plant potatoes, beets, and other hardy crops for their own use. Occasionally a gardener will identify a plot with a flag or scarecrow, but on the whole they're not afraid of anyone pilfering their harvest.

You may also wonder why you see wood piles (most often in the shape of a tepee) standing alongside the road. This is how the local residents dry their firewood. The trees are cut and cleaned of branches and then propped together to let the sun and wind dry them out for winter burning in the woodstove.

GETTING AROUND

The only car rental company at St. Anthony Regional Airport is National. The local contact is ℂ **709/454-8522,** or call central reservations at ℂ **800/227-7368,** www.nationalcar.com.

Note: Be aware that gasoline prices are higher on the Northern Peninsula than you'll find elsewhere in the province. Expect to pay about 5¢ per liter (20¢ a gallon) more for gas here than in St. John's.

WHERE TO STAY

Personally, I prefer the lodging options in nearby L'Anse aux Meadows, but if you want the facilities of a regular motel, the following choices will suffice for a night or two—and I've included a good-value bed-and-breakfast as a bonus.

Haven Inn 🍴 Although soundproofing is almost nonexistent, the Haven Inn has good-quality standard rooms as well as premium suites with Jacuzzi and fireplace. Wheelchair-accessible rooms are available.

The Haven Inn is home to the reliable Cartier's Gallery Restaurant, named in recognition of French explorer Jacques Cartier, who visited here in 1534 and named it "St. Anthony's Haven." Basic cooked breakfasts start at a reasonable C$6 (US$5.15) while the rest of the day it's soup, salad, and seafood (and burgers).

14 Goose Cove Rd., St. Anthony. ℂ 877/428-3646 or 709/454-9100. www.haveninn.ca. 30 units. C$89–C$119 (US$77–US$103) double. AE, MC, V, Interac. **Amenities:** Full-service restaurant; lounge w/video lotto machines; non-smoking. *In room:* TV. Cartier's Galley open summer 7am–2pm and 5–9pm, rest of year 7am–2pm and 5–8pm daily.

Spruce Inn Bed & Breakfast 🔶*Value* Spruce Inn boasts exceptional prices for a professional B&B (it's not just a room in a private home). Even though all rooms are non-smoking, with private bathroom/shower and radio, you won't be attracted to the Spruce Inn for its amenities. Aside from the price, you'll enjoy the panoramic harbor view and waterfront proximity as well as the large, comfortable sitting room—custom-made for mingling with other guests. A light continental breakfast (home-baked bread with partridgeberry and bakeapple jam) is included in the room rate, but if you'd like something more substantial a full breakfast is available at a small additional charge.

1 Spruce Lane (off East St.), St. Anthony. ℂ **877/454-3402** or 709/454-3402. 4 units. C$55–C$60 (US$48–US$52) double; C$10 (US$8.50) additional person. MC, V. **Amenities:** Light breakfast, complimentary tea and coffee; laundry service available at extra charge. *In room:* no phone.

Triple Falls RV Park   Located 8km (5 miles) from St. Anthony, this fully serviced tent and RV campground offers a freshwater beach, playground, games arcade, minigolf, great salmon fishing, and lots of hot water in the showers. Campsites are nicely wooded and located along a scenic river. Facilities are wheelchair accessible.

Rte. 430, north of St. Anthony. ℂ **709/454-2599** or 709/454-2438. 105 sites. C$14–C$20 (US$12–US$17). V. Open mid-May to mid-Sept. **Amenities:** Convenience store; fully serviced sites; RV dumping station; shower and laundry facilities.

Vinland Motel   Conveniently located in the heart of town near shopping and other services, the Vinland Motel has the most extensive list of on-site amenities in St. Anthony, including a fitness center and massage therapist. The unremarkable double rooms have the bathtub and toilet separated from the sink and counter, which is convenient if you're traveling with a partner. There are some suites available as well as two fully equipped cabins. The motel is accessible to travelers with disabilities.

West St., St. Anthony. ℂ **800/563-7578** or 709/454-8843. 43 units. C$86–C$139 (US$74–US$120) double. Government, corporate, group, and senior discounts available. AE, DC, MC, V, Interac. **Amenities:** Restaurant; lounge; fitness center w/sauna and hot tub; massage therapist; coin-operated guest laundry; nonsmoking rooms. *In room:* A/C, TV, coffeemaker, iron. Restaurant open summer 7am–10pm, the rest of the year 8am–2pm and 5–9pm.

WHERE TO DINE

Both the motels detailed above have dining rooms, or choose one of the following restaurants.

Leifsburdir Viking Feast VIKING FOOD   If you'd like to become an honorary Viking, make a reservation at Leifsburdir, a Viking-themed dinner theater located at the end of Fishing Point Road. The feast is served by costumed animators in a reconstructed sod hut overlooking the ocean. You'll sit on wooden benches at eight-person tables while "slaves" bring you an assortment of acquired-taste food (the menu includes salt capelin, cod tongues, moose stew, and squid-fried rice). After dinner, you can participate in a mock trial at the "Althing" (Viking court). I guarantee your stomach will hurt the next day from the innumerable belly laughs caused by the raucous Viking high jinks.

Fishing Point Rd., St. Anthony. ℂ **877/454-4900** or 709/454-4900. Reservations required. C$38 (US$33) per person. MC, V. Open July to early Sept daily at 5pm for bar service, with dinner and ceremony commencing at 7:30pm.

Lightkeeper's Café ⊕SEAFOOD   A combination of the best views and tastiest food in town make choosing to dine at this friendly cafe an easy choice. Once home to the local lightkeeper and his family, the building has been thoroughly renovated, with big windows added to make sure you don't miss the spectacle of an iceberg floating by. The traditional red-and-white lighthouse color scheme has been taken to extremes—even down to the salt and pepper shakers. Crab claws with melted garlic butter are a good choice to start, and then you'll want to get serious with mains such as the creamiest seafood linguini imaginable. Daily dessert specials and a well-priced wine list add to the appeal.

Fishing Point Rd., St. Anthony. 709/454-4900. Reservations recommended for dinner. Main courses C$14–C$25 (US$12–US$22). MC, V. Daily 11:30am–9pm; shorter hours in winter.

EXPLORING ST. ANTHONY

The historical highlight of a trip to St. Anthony is learning about **Sir Wilfred Thomason Grenfell,** a British physician who arrived here in 1892. Appalled by the desperate poverty and even more harrowing health problems (tuberculosis was rampant), Grenfell traveled the coast, healing the sick and feeding the needy.

The several Grenfell-related sites in St. Anthony come under the umbrella of Grenfell Historic Properties, of which the centerpiece is **Grenfell Interpretation Centre.** Another part of the Grenfell legacy is at the Charles S. Curtis Memorial Hospital, where you can view the thought-provoking **Jordi Bonet Murals** in its rotunda. Bonet is a Montreal artist who was commissioned in 1967 to create this tribute to Grenfell and life in northern Newfoundland and Labrador. There is no charge to see the stone murals and no specific hours of operation. Just stop in at the reception desk and pick up the brochure for your self-guided tour. The hospital is across the road from the interpretation center at 178–200 West St. (✆ **709/454-4010**).

If you're looking for a scenic spot to just hang out and look for icebergs or whales, follow the main road in town to **Fishing Point Park**, where you can climb a 91m (300-ft.) lookout to get the best view of St. Anthony Harbour. The peak iceberg viewing time is mid-June through to early August while whales are usually spotted in July and August and as early as mid-June.

Grenfell Historic Properties 🎖🎖   On the harborfront, the modern **Grenfell Interpretation Centre** displays informative panels that aptly explain Grenfell's life and his tremendous impact on area residents. It also houses a fascinating selection of his medical tools and equipment. Although there are interpreters on hand to answer questions, the center is meant to be a self-guided tour. A small cafe on the lower level serves inexpensive snacks and afternoon tea.

Exiting the interpretation center through the cafe, you'll step into **Grenfell Park**, home to a playground and a statue of the man himself. Also here is tiny **Dockhouse Museum** Originally housing the winches that hauled Grenfell's hospital ships from the water for repairs, it's now home to a display of maritime tools and artifacts. This museum is only open July and August, daily 10am to 4pm.

The final part of Grenfell Historic Properties is **Grenfell House Museum,** a 5-minute uphill walk from the waterfront. Built in 1910 as the Grenfell home, it has also been used as a mission. Exhibits here concentrate on the doctor's private life, with the vast majority of artifacts on display having been donated by the Grenfell family.

West St., St. Anthony. ✆ **709/454-4010**. www.grenfell-properties.com. C$6.50 (US$5.60) adults, C$5.50 (US$4.75) seniors, C$3.25 (US$2.75) children, C$14 (US$12) family rate. Mid-May to mid-June daily 9am–5pm; mid-June to Sept 9am–8pm.

Hero of the Northwest-Labrador Coast

Sir Wilfred T. Grenfell: "The purpose of this world is not to have and hold, but to serve." By the time Grenfell retired in 1935, at 70 years of age, the following were in operation throughout Newfoundland and Labrador as a result of his efforts: 5 hospitals; 7 nursing stations; 2 orphanages; 14 industrial centers; 4 summer schools; 3 agricultural stations; 12 clothing-distribution centers; 4 hospital ships; 1 supply schooner; 12 community centers; several cooperative stores; a cooperative lumber mill; and a haul-up slip for ship repairs.

OUTDOOR PURSUITS AND SHOPPING

Grenfell Handicrafts ✿✿ Beyond the reception desk at the Grenfell Interpretation Centre is a large space filled with locally made clothing. It was Sir Wilfred Grenfell who originally established the business, encouraging outport residents to sell their homemade clothing such as parkas and gloves to outsiders. Traditions remain, and although the printwork is done here, the actual clothing is put together by women who make their home in remote villages throughout the region.

West St., St. Anthony. ✆ **709/454-4010**. www.grenfell-properties.com. MC, V. Mid-May to mid-June daily 9am–5pm; mid-June to Sept 9am–8pm daily.

Northland Discovery Boat Tours ✿✿ This award-winning, family-run company is on a mission to provide an experience that will be the highlight of your vacation—and do they deliver! Owner Paul Alcock (a biologist and noted conservationist) will have you crossing paths with spouting humpbacks and racing dolphins as he navigates the natural wonders of Iceberg Alley. He'll explain why some icebergs are blue, and how you can tell when an iceberg is ready to roll (*Hint:* Watch the birds). He'll even scoop a few bergy bits from the sea, giving you a taste of the purest water on Earth. Tours lasting 2½ hours operate rain or shine, from late May to early October, three times daily (9am, 1pm, and 4pm).

Behind Grenfell Historic Properties, West St., St. Anthony. ✆ **877/632-3747** or 709/454-3092. www.discover northland.com. C$42 (US$36) adults, C$25 (US$22) ages 12–17, C$20 (US$17) under 12, free for children under 4. Office hours May 15–Oct 15 daily 8am–10pm.

L'ANSE AUX MEADOWS

At a barren outpost on a flat headland jutting bravely into the North Atlantic, you'll find several innocuous grassy mounds that are both a UNESCO World Heritage Site and a National Historic Site. These "mounds" are the footprints of the first European settlement in North America. Although the Viking Norsemen who first arrived on these shores more than 1,000 years ago didn't make a permanent home of what they called *Vinland,* they left evidence of their passage in the foundations of the original sod structures that once housed them.

The community of L'Anse aux Meadows and surrounding villages offer a limited number of services, including welcoming bed-and-breakfasts and one of Newfoundland's best restaurants.

ESSENTIALS
GETTING THERE

L'Anse aux Meadows is 40km (25 miles) north of St. Anthony (turn off Rte. 430 onto Rte. 436).

VISITOR INFORMATION

Visitor information is available at L'Anse aux Meadows National Historic Site. Call ✆ **709/623-2608** or check out http://parkscanada.pch.gc.ca/lhn-nhs/nl/meadows/index_e.asp. The center is open June 1 to June 14 and September 3 to October 14 daily 9am to 5pm. During the peak visitor season of June 15 to September 2, longer hours of 9am to 8pm apply.

WHERE TO STAY & DINE

Norseman Restaurant ✿✿✿ REGIONAL Without a doubt, the Norseman is one of the province's best restaurants in all regards—creative cooking, professional service, and faultless presentation. The setting alone is superb—a tastefully decorated

Escape to Quirpon Island

For splendid, majestic isolation, **Quirpon Lighthouse Inn** 应应 stands alone. The gateway to the island is the tiny fishing outpost of Quirpon (pronounced kar-*poon*), 8km (5 miles) from L'Anse aux Meadows. Now look across the harbor. Here is Quirpon Island, a half-hour boat ride farther north than any other point on the island portion of the province. Both the dock and the helideck are a striking testament to the solitude of this sanctuary. Once ashore, you'll stay at one of two sturdy dwellings located near the base of an automated lighthouse: either the 1922 lighthouse keeper's residence or the more modern adjacent house. Regardless of which building you stay in, you're guaranteed not to be bothered by cable television, clock radios, or in-room telephones. Instead, you'll spend hours contemplating the streaks and fissures of passing icebergs. Entertainment is provided by breaching, blowing humpback and minke—you may even be soaked by a spouting whale. All this, plus home-cooked meals under the hospitable care of Doris, Madonna, and Hubert Roberts. Truly a rare gem of serenity in a world of sensory overload.

room and adjacent deck, with water views from most tables. Seafood is the house specialty. For starters, the shellfish-less seafood chowder is a delight and the smoked char is a unique flavor. If you order lobster, your waitperson will invite you across the road to visit the wharf and pick out your own lobster (in season). Other mains are as creative as cod baked in a mustard and garlic crust and as local as grilled caribou brushed with redwine glaze. At least one daily dessert is a pie crammed with local berries. The drinks menu is as notable as the food, with everything from bakeapple wine to martinis.

Through July and August, there's a dinner theater (C$32/US$28) every Tuesday and Friday at 7:30pm.

Rte. 436, L'Anse aux Meadows. (C) 877/623-2018. www.valhalla-lodge.com/restaurant.htm. Main courses C$11–C$32 (US$10–US$28). MC, V. June–Sept daily 9am–10pm.

Valhalla Lodge *(Finds* Look for these Viking-themed accommodations in a friendly B&B with understated appeal 8km (5 miles) before the L'Anse aux Meadows National Historic Site. The property is situated on a hill sloping down to the ocean. From the wide deck, you can watch icebergs, whales (up to a dozen have been seen here simultaneously), and seabirds. Guest rooms are warmly furnished in Scandinavian pine with cozy quilts on the beds and exquisite reproductions from local artists on the walls. Accommodations are fairly tight: standing between the wall and the bed, chances are good that you'll bang into one or the other. But it's the memory of your gracious hostess Bella Hodge and her famously fluffy partridgeberry pancakes that will stay with you long after you've forgotten the minor discomfort of semi-cramped quarters.

Rte. 436 to Gunner's Cove, L'Anse aux Meadows. (C) 877/623-2018 or 709/623-2018 and 709/689-4825 in the off season. www.valhalla-lodge.com. 6 units. C$75–C$85 (US$65–US$73) double, C$15 (US$13) additional for cot. Off-season discounts available. MC, V. Open June–Oct. **Amenities:** Complimentary breakfast; sauna. *In room:* Some rooms have private bathrooms; 1 Jacuzzi suite.

Viking Village Bed & Breakfast *★ (Value)*   A modern home within walking distance of L'Anse aux Meadows National Historic Site, this is as close as you can get to Viking habitation without actually sleeping in a sod hut. Its proximity to the Norseman Restaurant is an added bonus. The Viking theme–named guest rooms all have patio doors and balconies, which is a lovely feature if you're visiting during summer.

A full breakfast and evening snack are included with the room rates, and the owners will cook you a Newfoundland-style dinner for an extra fee of C$12 (US$11) per person. The owners will pick you up at St. Anthony airport or at the bus stop. The same owners also run the more basic **Viking Nest B&B** with slightly lower rates, which can be reached via the same contact numbers.

Rte. 436 to Hay Cove. (*C*) **877-858-2238** or 709/623-2238. www.vikingvillage.ca. 5 units. C$58–C$62 (US$50–US$53) double, senior and weekly rates in off season. AE, MC, V, Interac. **Amenities:** Full breakfast; complimentary evening snack; limited room service; common-area satellite TV; laundry service; nonsmoking facility. *In room:* En-suite bathrooms.

EXPLORING L'ANSE AUX MEADOWS

L'Anse aux Meadows National Historic Site and Norstead are complementary must-see attractions: one is a formal archaeological introduction to a 1,000-year-old Viking habitation, the other brings the ancient Norse experience to life. *Note:* All Vikings were Norsemen, but only a small percentage of Norsemen were Vikings.

L'Anse aux Meadows National Historic Site *★★★*   Embark on your Viking journey at the visitor center, just off Route 436 and within site of the first European settlement in North America. The details of your adventure will be revealed in a 30-minute video (offered in the theater) that details the discovery of the site by Dr. Helge Ingstad and his wife, Dr. Anne Stine. As Norwegians, Ingstad and Stine had a strong interest in determining the exact location of *Vinland,* the legendary location referenced in the Norse sagas.

After watching the video, examine the many artifacts that confirm the Vikings' presence here as far back as A.D. 1000. You'll even see a model of how the settlement would have looked when it was inhabited. From there, it's on to the real thing. A short walk along a gravel path takes you to the excavated foundations of the Viking settlement, where the use of each structure is detailed. Beyond this point are reconstructions of the sod and timber buildings that the Vikings called home all those years ago. Costumed interpreters will educate and entertain you with demonstrations of their various crafts. "Gunnar" shares the secret of navigation and ship construction, "Harald" illustrates the power of forge and anvil, while "Thora" proves that Viking women are a force to be reckoned with (she plans to divorce her impractical dreamer of a husband—Bjorn, the "brains" behind the expedition—when they return to civilization).

Rte. 436, L'Anse aux Meadows. (*C*) **709/623-2608.** www.pc.gc.ca/lhn-nhs/nl/meadows. C$9 (US$7.75) adults, C$7.50 (US$6.50) seniors 65+, C$4.50 (US$4) students 6–16, free for children under 6, C$23 (US$20) family rate. MC, V. June 1 to mid-June and early Sept to mid-Oct 9am–5pm; mid-June to early Sept 9am–6pm daily.

Norstead *★★ (Kids)*   If you want to walk like the Norse, talk like the Norse, eat like the Norse, in fact become a Norseman or -woman, then you *must* come to Norstead. Located 2km (1¼ miles) from the L'Anse aux Meadows National Historic Site, Norstead is a re-created Norse trading post. Enthusiastic and knowledgeable re-enactors walk you through every aspect of early Norse life, including religion, weaponry, blacksmithing, activities in the "Trading House," the scalley (kitchen/cooking area), handicrafts such as pottery and the carding of wool, and the sleeping quarters. You'll also get a chance to climb aboard a replica of a Viking *knarr,* the type of boat Leif Eriksson used to sail across the North Atlantic back in A.D. 1000. Visitors are encouraged to participate hands-on in activities carried on in the settlement, including baking (and tasting) flatbread, carding wool, and watching the blacksmith forging tools from bog iron.

Rte. 436, L'Anse aux Meadows. ✆ **709/623-2828.** www.norstead.com. C$7 (US$6) adults, C$6 (US$5.15) seniors, C$3.75 (US$3.25) children 6–15. Family rate of C$15 (US$13). MC, V. June–Sept daily 10am–6pm.

Viking Boat Tours ✶ (Kids)   This company gives you the chance to ride in a Viking *knarr,* an open longboat like the one Leif Eriksson may have sailed in when he landed in Newfoundland more than 1,000 years ago. The tours are 2½ hours long and let you have Viking-style fun while searching for icebergs, birds, and whales. To make the experience even more authentic, you can wear a traditional Viking costume and take a turn at the oar. But remember that there's no pillaging allowed in this Viking crowd—just good clean fun.

Weather permitting, there are three sailings daily: 10am, 1pm, and 4pm. Special full-day adventure tours are also available, where you have the chance to climb ashore and have a Newfoundland-style boil-up.

Rte. 436 to Noddy Bay, 2km south of L'Anse aux Meadows. ✆ **709/623-2100.** www.nfld.net/vikingboattours. Reservations preferred. C$40 (US$35) adults, C$25 (US$22) children 5–12, C$10 (US$8.50) children 4 and under. June–Aug.

BEYOND L'ANSE AUX MEADOWS
Burnt Cape Ecological Reserve ✶✶ (Finds)   Around 35km (22 miles) from L'Anse aux Meadows is Burnt Cape, so named for its barren expanse of limestone outcrops. While the site is renowned for rare flora, including the Burnt Cape Cinquefoil, it is the starkly beautiful scenery that draws most visitors. You can drive onto the cape via a rough gravel road, but I recommend joining a guided tour. Not only will you save your vehicle from the rough road, the interpreter will be able to show you things that the casual visitor is prone to miss, such as sea caves and geological formations of stone rings created by heavy frosts.

Rte. 437, Raleigh. ✆ **709/454-7795.** C$5 (US$4.30) per person. Check-in at Pisolet Bay Provincial Park, along Rte. 437 just before Raleigh. Guided tours depart June–Sept daily at 9:30am and 2pm.

WHERE TO SHOP
Dark Tickle Company   A delicious solution to the problem of wild-berry lovers everywhere: you can pick 'em, but you can't take 'em with you (they'd perish on the way home). The Dark Tickle Company uses only wild berries (bakeapple, partridgeberry, blueberry, crowberry, and squashberry) in their lip-smacking jams, preserves, and syrups. They even have something called Drinkable Berries: natural nectar in bakeapple and partridgeberry varieties. The result is just-picked freshness in a portable package. The Dark Tickle Company also sells products worldwide via its website.

Rte. 436, St. Lunaire–Griquet (between St. Anthony and L'Anse aux Meadows). ✆ **709/623-2354.** www.dark tickle.com. MC, V. Mid-May to mid-June Mon–Fri 9am–6pm; mid-June to early Sept daily 9am–6pm; early Sept–end of Sept Mon–Fri 9am–6pm; Oct to mid-May Mon–Fri 9am–5pm. Guided tours available on request.

Stagehead Carving Shop   Expert carver Norman Young creates interesting pieces out of whalebone, soapstone, and antler at prices ranging from C$45 (US$38) for smaller, simpler pieces to C$250 (US$215) for the larger or more intricate works of art. There are also some unique jewelry pieces for sale. All pieces, regardless of size, show a masterful blending of modern, traditional, and native influence.

Rte. 436, Griquet (between St. Anthony and L'Anse aux Meadows). ✆ **709/623-2407.**

4 Corner Brook

Its proximity to the open waters of the Gulf of St. Lawrence makes Corner Brook a favorite destination for cruise ships sailing Canada's east coast. That's just one of many appealing aspects to Corner Brook's spectacular location. The community is in a hilly lowland region surrounded by the Long Range Mountains—a continuation of the Appalachian belt stretching up from the New England states—so the natural beauty is stunning.

Corner Brook has been called the "Forest Capital of Canada," so it's no surprise to find one of the world's largest integrated pulp and paper mills here. Too bad it spoils the view of the Humber Arm, but the mill provides a very important and much-needed source of employment to the community's 24,000 residents. You'll find a full range of services in Corner Brook, including a good selection of churches and the Western Region's largest hospital.

ESSENTIALS

GETTING THERE

Corner Brook is 53km (33 miles) southwest of Deer Lake along the Trans-Canada Highway (Rte. 1) and 218km (135 miles) north of the Port aux Basques Ferry Terminal. It's 687km (426 miles) west of St. John's.

VISITOR INFORMATION

Corner Brook Tourist Chalet, located at 11 Confederation Dr. (© **709/639-9792;** www.cornerbrook.com) can provide you with information on all of the west. The center is open year-round, from June 15 to September 15 daily from 9am until 9pm, and the rest of the year Monday to Friday from 9am until 5pm.

WHERE TO STAY & DINE

There are quite a few places to stay and eat in Corner Brook, but I always prefer spending the night at one of the appealing Steady Brook lodgings, 12km (7½ miles) north of town at the base of Marble Mountain.

Glynmill Inn ⭐   The professional confidence of the staff and the understated dignity of the foyer tell you that this is the most prestigious property in Corner Brook. This traditional Tudor-style hotel overlooking its namesake pond is within a 10-minute walk of downtown Corner Brook. Built as a guesthouse for executives of the pulp mill back in 1924, the Glynmill Inn has been thoroughly modernized. The inn carries an Olde-English theme throughout (think dark wood furnishings and gilded picture frames), and offers a variety of standard guest rooms as well as several styles of more spacious suites. It's also home to two good restaurants. The elegant Wine Cellar dining room specializes in steak and seafood and is one of the finer restaurants in Corner Brook. The casual and moderately priced Carriage Room restaurant specializes in traditional Newfoundland favorites such as cod tongues with scruncheons (save room for a generous slice of partridgeberry pie). The inn has an elevator and a wheelchair ramp.

1 Cobb Lane, Corner Brook. © **800/563-4400** or 709/634-5181. www.glynmillinn.ca. 81 units. C$90–C$180 (US$78–US$155) double. AE, DC, MC, V. **Amenities:** 2 restaurants; pub; fitness room; business center. *In room:* A/C, TV, coffeemaker, hair dryer, iron, ironing board, some fridges. Carriage Room restaurant open daily 7am–9:30pm. Wine Cellar dining room open evenings only.

Holiday Inn Corner Brook   Located right downtown, this hostelry has a little more style than the average Holiday Inn. Elegant tile floors, leather furnishings, and a dramatically curving staircase are among the features that grace the open reception areas of the hotel. Amenities include an oversize whirlpool, fitness facility, underground heated parking, and the only hotel swimming pool in town. Guest rooms are midsize and regularly renovated, with beautifully solid furnishings. There are also executive and king suites to choose from, as well as a special unit for guests with disabilities. If you don't feel like splurging across the road at Thirteen West (see below), the on-site Crown and Moose Pub and Eatery is a reliable dining choice. As at all Holiday Inns, kids 12 and under eat free.

48 West St., Corner Brook. ✆ **888/465-4329** or 709/634-5381. www.holidayinncornerbrook.com. 101 units. C$92–C$120 (US$79–US$104) double. AE, DC, DISC, MC, V. **Amenities:** Restaurant; lounge w/VLTs; indoor pool, fitness center, whirlpool; room service; laundromat; nonsmoking rooms. *In room:* A/C, TV w/pay movies, dataport, coffeemaker, iron.

Marble Inn ★★ *Value*

Marble Inn is on the banks of the Humber River 12km (7½ miles) north of Corner Brook—within walking distance of the alpine resort. The maroon-colored cedar-shake cottages range in size from one to four bedrooms. Amenities and services differ from cabin to cabin, with some having full kitchens and others having kitchenettes. Several have a fireplace and Jacuzzi. *Hint:* If choosing between the Studio Cabin and the 1-Bedroom Deluxe, go for the Studio Cabin. The open-concept design is more spacious than that of the 1-Bedroom Deluxe and the bathroom is nicer, too. The Chalet Cabin is the most luxurious, with a cathedral ceiling, fireplace, and Jacuzzi.

A convenience store, gas station, takeout restaurant, and liquor store are within walking distance; more extensive services are 10 minutes away in Corner Brook.

12km (7½ miles) north of Corner Brook at Dogwood Dr., Steady Brook. ✆ **877/497-5673** or 709/634-2237. www. explorenl.com. 12 cottages plus 10 inn suites. C$99 (US$85) for a 1-bedroom up to C$199 (US$170) for a 4-bedroom unit; C$109 (US$94) for the inn suites. Midweek and off-season discounts apply. Inquire about ski-pass discounts. MC, V. **Amenities:** Dining room; den w/bar service; heated pool; sauna and exercise facilities; playground; laundry facilities. *In room:* TV, fully equipped kitchen/kitchenette, some with fireplace and Jacuzzi.

MarbleWood Village Resort ★

Here, at the foot of Marble Mountain, you'll find ultimate convenience, deluxe accommodations, and premium prices. For almost double the money you'll spend at Marble Inn, you can ski or snowboard all day from the doorstep of your very own luxury chalet. Each of the adjoining units is styled along modern, clean lines with dramatic cathedral ceiling, pine-and-marble fireplace, and private sun deck or patio. With the fully equipped kitchen (even down to the microwave and dishwasher), TV with VCR, and top-quality linens, it's like taking the comforts of home with you on vacation. *Tip:* As part of a ski resort, winter is high season, so check the resort website for summer deals (rooms were selling for C$99/US$85 midweek in July during the research for this edition). *Note:* As part of Interval International, MarbleWood Village Resort offers timeshare vacation options that are interchangeable with The Royal Caribbean resort in Cancun, Mexico, and Marriott's Cypress Harbour in Orlando, Florida.

8 Thistle Dr., Steady Brook. ✆ **888/868-7635** or 709/632-7900. www.marblemountain.com. 24 units. C$99–C$199 (US$85–US$170) for a 1-bedroom up to C$199–C$499 (US$170–US$429) for a 4-bedroom. AE, DC, MC, V, Interac. *In room:* TV w/VCR, full kitchen.

Strawberry Hill Resort ★★

Share a pillow with some of the world's most famous people. Originally built and designed by a pulp and paper magnate (Sir Eric Bowater) as a corporate retreat for visiting dignitaries, Strawberry Hill Resort has hosted former Canadian prime minister Pierre Trudeau as well as Queen Elizabeth II and Prince

Philip. This exquisite retreat has a breathtaking location on the Humber River, and even has its own boat shed, from where you can hire a guide to take you salmon fishing. Not only does the resort have a sauna, hot tub, some nice hiking trails, and horseshoes to amuse you, but the owners will also help you arrange boat tours and guided excursions. Guest rooms at Sugar Hill epitomize rustic luxury. Each has a king-size bed, cozy feather duvet, and fireplace. And there's a video library available so you can enjoy movies in your room. Guest rooms in the Manor House are nice, but the chalets are newer, larger, and more expensive.

Exit 10 off Rte. 1 to Little Rapids. ✆ **877/434-0066** or 709/634-0066. www.strawberryhill.net. 14 units (6 rooms in Manor House and 8 chalets). Manor House: C$175–C$200 (US$150–US$172) double. Chalets: C$300–C$400 (US$258–US$345). Off-season and seniors' discounts available. MC, V. **Amenities:** Gourmet dining; hot tub, sauna. *In room:* TV w/VCR.

Thirteen West 🌟🌟 CONTEMPORARY   Thirteen West is one of the best restaurants west of the capital—it has an innovative menu with a wide range of offerings. This is the high-caliber kind of restaurant you'd expect to find in a major city, and a wonderful find in a smaller city like Corner Brook. Along a rather uninspiring main street, the setting, in a renovated residence surrounded by bland buildings, is also a surprise. The emphasis is on local and seasonal produce and seafood, which is given a modern makeover and beautifully presented. The prices, however, are also higher than you'll find in most other restaurants in town.

13 West St., Corner Brook. ✆ **709/634-1300.** Reservations recommended. Dinner entrees C$16–C$28 (US$14–US$24). AE, DC, MC, V. Mon–Fri 11:30am–2:30pm and 5:30–9:30pm; Sat 5:30–10:30pm; Sun 5:30–9:30pm.

EXPLORING CORNER BROOK

Corner Brook has a couple of attractions, but it's also worth considering the coastal drive along the southern side of the Humber Arm. Route 450 begins right in town and passes a string of fishing villages en route to Lark Harbour, at the end of the road 50km (31 miles) from town. Aside from admiring the coastal panorama, allow time for a stop in delightfully named **Blow Me Down Provincial Park,** from where the Bay of Islands spreads out to the north, and to the south you can easily spot the barren rust-colored peaks of the Blow Me Down Mountains. Allow 3 hours for the round-trip.

Corner Brook Museum & Archives   A former courthouse/telegraph office/customs house now finds life as a regional museum. The collection of approximately 1,000 items highlights the town's forestry and pulp and paper industries, the lifestyle of the aboriginal people who once lived here, and leisure time as displayed through old skis and toboggans. In addition to enjoying the intriguing black-and-white photos depicting life in Corner Brook around 1900, you'll be captivated by the century-old artifacts (like the Nestlé floor-model hair-perming machine: it looks like Medusa on wheels). If nostalgia overwhelms you, compare the push-button modern clothes washer to the crank-handle wringer washer. It gives you a completely new perspective on the "good old days."

2 West St., Corner Brook. ✆ **709/634-2518.** www.cornerbrookmuseum.com. C$5 (US$4.30) adults, C$3 (US$2.60) for students age 12–17, free for children under age 12 accompanied by an adult. Mid-June to Aug daily 9am–7pm; the rest of the year by appointment.

Marble Mountain 🌟🌟🌟 *(Kids)*   Atlantic Canada's biggest and best winter resort destination. Rising steeply from the Humber River, Marble Mountain has a peak elevation of only 546m (1,790 ft.), but receives an amazing 4.8m (16 ft.) of snowfall per year (plus a man-made boost when Mother Nature needs a break). There are 34 different runs ranging from novice to expert, with 27 groomed trails and 7 mogul runs, as well as a half-pipe, terrain park, and tube park. Marble Mountain operates 4 lifts, including a high-speed detachable quad chair, 2 more quad chairs, and a beginner's platter lift. While the steepness of the slopes will catch your eye, so will the magnificent post-and-beam day lodge, where you find multiple eateries, a ski school, and rental shop.

While winter is most definitely high season, it's also worth stopping by in summer. A short but steep trail leads to photogenic Steady Brook Falls, while the super-fit who slog their way to the summit of Marble Mountain will be rewarded with sweeping mountain and river views.

Rte. 1, Steady Brook, 12km (7½ miles) north of Corner Brook. ✆ 888/462-7253 or 709/637-7601. www.skimarble.com. Lift pass C$42 (US$36) adults; C$30 (US$26) seniors and students, C$20 (US$17) children aged 12 and under. Ski lifts operate late Dec to early April.

Newfoundland Emporium *(Finds* Sophisticated junk, antique collectibles, and Newfoundland crafts make this unusual establishment the shopping highlight of a trip to Corner Brook. Shop owner Dave Le Drew originally assembled a fascinating selection of wreckage and cargo that washed ashore after one of Newfoundland's famously horrendous storms, and has since expanded the operation and filled a second building with collectibles. You can get lost in here for hours, if you've got the time. *Tip:* Unlike many island shops, absolutely everything on display is from Newfoundland.

7 Broadway Rd., Cornerbrook. ✆ 709/634-9376. http://newfoundlandemporium.com. July 1–Aug 31 daily 9am–9pm; reduced but flexible hours the remainder of the year.

5 Stephenville to Channel–Port aux Basques

South of Corner Brook is Stephenville (pop. 5,000), a good base for exploring the lovely Port au Port Peninsula or Barachois Pond Provincial Park, both just minutes away from town. Stephenville is often of interest to American visitors, as the town is home to a former U.S. air base.

Channel–Port aux Basques is at the southerly end of Route 1. The community gets its name from its French heritage, as this region was originally settled by Basques fishermen who came to Newfoundland in the 1500s. Today, Channel–Port aux Basques has around 5,000 residents and is home to a Marine Atlantic ferry terminal, which receives year-round ferry service from North Sydney (Nova Scotia). The community is usually referred to as Port aux Basques.

ESSENTIALS
GETTING THERE
Stephenville is 796km (494 miles) west of St. John's, 77km (48 miles) southwest of Corner Brook, and 166km (103 miles) north of Channel–Port aux Basques.

Channel–Port aux Basques is 218km (135 miles) south of Corner Brook. Most people who come here do so because of its ferry terminal. (See the "Getting There" section of chapter 2 for full details on the Nova Scotia to Channel–Port aux Basques ferry.) Unlike the utilitarian North Sydney terminal in Nova Scotia, the Port aux Basques docking area and terminal site features a romantically lighted harbor entrance and a dramatic blasted-rock approach. And, although significantly smaller in size, the Port aux Basques waterfront is more visitor-friendly than the one in St. John's.

VISITOR INFORMATION

Coming off Route 1, you'll reach Stephenville Visitor Centre before town, at the junction of Route 1 and Route 490. It's open June to early September daily from 7am until 10pm. Call ☎ **709/643-5854.**

The Channel–Port aux Basques Visitor Centre is on the Trans-Canada Highway 4km (2½ miles) from the ferry terminal, at the turnoff to downtown; its hours coincide with the arrival and departure of the ferry. The center is open June to August daily from 9am until 10pm. Through summer and the rest of the year, it also opens for all ferry arrivals. Call ☎ **709/695-2262.**

WHERE TO STAY

Barachois Pond Provincial Park Campground *Kids*   Beside Route 1 20km (12 miles) east of Stephenville is one of Newfoundland's most scenic and best-maintained provincial parks. Glorious natural eye-candy combines with a host of family fun for an unparalleled outdoor adventure. Activities in this 3,500-hectare (8,650-acre) park include lake swimming, water-skiing, boating, and fishing for both brook trout and salmon. There are also two sandy beaches (one is sheltered from westerly winds, the other from easterly breezes) as well as boat and canoe rentals. The most enjoyable of three hiking trails is the Erin Mountain Trail. Beginning from across the bridge spanning the lake, the trail starts out as a boardwalk. This section, to a lookout over the lake, is excellent for families. The upper half of the trail is recommended for experienced hikers because it's a tougher climb through brush and barren rock. The park also has an excellent interpretive program that includes guided walks and campfire singalongs.

Trans-Canada Hwy. (Rte. 1) to Barachois Pond Provincial Park. ☎ **800/563-6353** or 709/649-0048; off season 709/635-4520. www.env.gov.nl.ca/parks/parks/p_bp. 150 sites. C$13 (US$11). MC, V. Open mid-May to mid-Sept. **Amenities:** Convenience store; day-use facilities; dumping station; laundry facilities; showers; freshwater swimming; boat rentals.

Cape Anguille Lighthouse Inn *★★ Finds*   For a completely different experience, consider spending the night in this lightkeeper's home, which sits high atop cliffs on Cape Anguille. The adjacent lighthouse is still in operation—and your hosts are the keeper Leonard Patry and his family. The units are all clean, comfortable, and modern, and they have ocean views. A full breakfast is included in the rates. *Tip:* Birdwatchers will love the cape and adjacent Codroy Valley, with over 200 species recorded, and some such as great blue herons at the northern extent of their range.

Turn off Trans-Canada Hwy. at Doyles, 37km (23 miles) north of Channel–Port aux Basques to Cape Anguille. ☎ **877/254-6586** or 709/634-2285. www.linkumtours.com. 6 units. C$90–C$100 (US$78–US$86) double. MC, V. Open May–Oct. **Amenities:** Meals available; nonsmoking rooms.

Holiday Inn Stephenville   Stephenville's largest hotel is ideally situated for shopping (it's connected to the town's shopping plaza), golfing at Harmon Golf and Country Club's 18-hole golf course, and touring the Port au Port Peninsula. Guest rooms are big enough to dance in—should you feel a sudden urge to mambo—and have air-conditioning to help you cool off afterward. Wheelchair-accessible rooms are available.

44 Queen St., Stephenville. ☎ **888/465-4329** or 709/643-6666. www.holiday-inn.com/stephenville. 47 units. C$92–C$140 (US$79–US$121) double; family and package rates available. AE, MC, V. **Amenities:** Restaurant; lounge; nonsmoking rooms. *In room:* A/C, TV, coffeemaker, hair dryer, iron.

Hotel Port aux Basques   If you're looking for the closest accommodations to the ferry terminal in Channel–Port aux Basques, this is it. Formerly a Holiday Inn, this personable hotel is regularly renovated and modernized through the addition of

several suites as well as new paint, carpet, beds, and TVs. The on-site casual restaurant specializes in generous helpings of seafood and even has a special kids' menu. Hotel Port aux Basques is within walking distance of shopping, churches, a railway heritage site, a cinema, a hospital, and recreational facilities. You're a 20-minute drive from the St. Andrews Na Creige Golf Course. The hotel is wheelchair accessible. Pets are allowed.

2 Grand Bay Rd., Channel–Port aux Basques. ✆ 877/695-2171 or 709/695-2171. www.hotelpab.com. 50 units. Standard guest rooms: C$90–C$140 (US$78–US$121) double. Family, seniors, and off-season discounts available; kids stay free. AE, DC, MC, V. **Amenities:** Dining room; lounge; fitness center; business center; laundry; nonsmoking rooms. *In room:* TV, coffeemaker, hair dryer.

Spruce Pine Acres Country Inn ✶✶   This is a deluxe oceanfront lodge 10 minutes from Stephenville. The country comfort of the rustic furnishings—even the strategically placed balconies and pure mountain air—are deliberate stress reducers. If that isn't enough to help you put the cares of the workaday world behind you, you can avail of the on-site sauna and hot tub, then head down the stairway to the ocean before partaking of a European-style picnic complete with gourmet cheeses, pâtés, chocolate fondue, and fine wine (it's no wonder the inn's initials spell "spa"). Each of the four standard guest rooms has a private bathroom with tub and shower as well as a telephone and deck access. The chalets each have a full kitchen, deck with ocean views, hardwood floors, and separate sleeping areas. Rates include breakfast and afternoon tea.

Rte. 460 to Front Rd., Port au Port West. ✆ 877/239-7117 or 709/648-9273. www.spa.nf.ca. 4 units, 2 chalets. C$125–C$155 (US$108–US$134) standard double. C$150–C$195 (US$129–US$168) chalet. AE, MC, V. **Amenities:** Breakfast room; lounge; hot tub; sauna; fitness room, nonsmoking rooms. *In room:* TV.

St. Christopher's Hotel   On a hill overlooking the scenic harbor, this is the largest hotel in Port aux Basques. It has more amenities than its competition, but the rooms aren't as nice. The standard guest rooms are simply adequate. There are several more spacious suites to choose from, some with fully equipped kitchenettes. The hotel is wheelchair accessible, near the marine boardwalk, and just 1km (less than a mile) from the ferry terminal.

146 Caribou Rd., Channel–Port aux Basques. ✆ 800/563-4779 or 709/695-7034. www.stchrishotel.com. 57 units. Standard rooms C$105 (US$90) double. Suites C$135 (US$116). Off-season discounts available. MC, V. **Amenities:** Full-service restaurant; lounge; fitness room; nonsmoking rooms. *In room:* A/C, TV/VCR, coffeemaker.

WHERE TO DINE

Emile's Pub and Eatery CANADIAN   Located within the Holiday Inn, this is the closest thing to fine dining that Stephenville has to offer (although it's not unusual to see patrons dressed in jeans and a nice sweater). Emile's has an excellent reputation for delivering reliably good food. Some of their better offerings are their homemade soups—especially the rich and chunky seafood chowder. They also make great hot wings and cod dishes and have excellent sandwich specials. Emile's has a lounge as well as a separate section for families with children. There are smoking and nonsmoking sections.

44 Queen St., Stephenville. ✆ 709/643-6666. Reservations recommended for dinner. Prices range from C$6–C$19 (US$5.15–US$17). AE, MC, V. Mon–Thurs 7am–10pm; Fri 7am–11pm; Sat–Sun 8am–midnight.

Hartery's Family Restaurant ✶ *Value* TRADITIONAL   If you're looking for a more traditional Newfoundland atmosphere and a good meal, I recommend Hartery's. They serve a large variety of dishes and are well known for their traditional "Jiggs Dinner" (boiled beef and cabbage), served every Thursday and a steal at C$6.50 (US$5.60). They also serve a very nice seafood platter for C$19 (US$17).

109 Main St., Stephenville. © **709/643-2242.** No reservations required. C$5–C$7 (US$4.30–US$6) lunch; C$7–C$18 (US$6–US$16) dinner. MC, V, Interac. Mon–Fri 9am–9pm; Sat–Sun 11am–9pm.

Water's Edge Restaurant ✦✦   Most diners at this friendly little restaurant are guests of the affiliated Spruce Pine Acres Country Inn, but everyone is welcome with advance reservations. Appetizers range from steamed mussels to baked brie with raspberry brandy sauce. Mains include pan-fried scallops, boiled lobster, poached salmon topped with cucumber dill sauce, and, for the adventurous, moose pie. Other pluses include the raspberry cheesecake and well-priced drinks (beer from just C$3.50/US$3). There's a kid's menu as well.

Rte. 460 to Front Rd., Port au Port West. © **709/648-9273.** www.spa.nf.ca. Reservations required. Main courses C$13–C$28 (US$11–US$24). AE, MC, V. Daily from 5:30pm for dinner.

EXPLORING STEPHENVILLE & CHANNEL–PORT AUX BASQUES

St. Andrews Na Creige Golf Course   Dodge glacial boulders at this par-35, 9-hole course (slated to open with 18 holes in 2006), in the beautiful Codroy Valley. Views from most fairways extend across the Little Codroy River to the Long Range Mountains. The course has club and power-cart rentals, as well as a driving range.

Finds The Last French Stronghold

West of Stephenville along Route 460 is the **Port au Port Peninsula,** Newfoundland's only remaining French region. The original settlers were reportedly Cape Breton Acadians who moved here in the 18th century. Until the last 50 years, geographic isolation and a rural economy protected the language and customs of this small francophone population.

Each August the people of Cap Sainte-Georges and surrounding communities hold "Une Longue Veillee," a folk festival that celebrates their French heritage. In recent years this festival has attracted traditional musicians, singers, and dancers from all over the province and a host of visitors and performers from the Maritime provinces, Quebec, and the French islands of St. Pierre and Miquelon.

Things to see include **Our Lady of Mercy Church and Museum** in Port au Port West (the largest wooden structure in the province; © **709/648-9236** for more information); **Our Lady of Lourdes Grotto** in the town of Lourdes (in addition to the religious monument, the Grotto also features a beautiful flower garden and an 1800 man-of-war cannon); and **Lewis Hills** (the highest point in Newfoundland).

It takes 2½ hours to drive around the loop of the peninsula and back to Stephenville—if you don't stop. But if you take your time and enjoy the breathtaking cliff-hanging vistas, consider it a full day's outing. *Note:* There aren't a lot of services for travelers in the area. It's best to tank up before you head out, and either pack a picnic lunch or have a big breakfast that will do you until you return to your post for the night. For more information, contact the Port au Port Economic Development Association (© **709/642-5831;** www.nfld.net/paped).

Rte. 407, St. Andrews, 20 minutes from the ferry terminal at Channel–Port aux Basques. ✆ **709/955-3322.** www.golfnewfoundland.ca. Greens fees C$25 (US$22). Open May–Oct.

Stephenville Theatre Festival The Stephenville area has several festivals during the summer, the most popular of which is the professional theater festival that runs during July and August. Since its inaugural year in 1979, the festival has won several awards and has been named one of the top attractions in its category by the North American Bus Association.

Stephenville Arts and Culture Centre, 380 Massachusetts Dr., Stephenville. ✆ **709/643-4982.** www.stf.nf.ca. Tickets for main-stage productions are C$17 (US$15) adults, C$12 (US$11) seniors, and C$10 (US$8.50) students.

9

Labrador

Labrador is Canada's last undiscovered frontier and North America's most pristine wilderness. In a word association game, it would likely be coupled with "cold," "vast," and "remote." The slightly more enlightened might add "fjords," "bakeapples," and "permafrost." All of which are true, but just barely hint at the complexity that is Labrador.

Its nickname is **The Big Land**—a moniker it well deserves. Physically, it dwarfs the island of Newfoundland by a ratio of 2:1. It covers a distance of more than 1,080km (670 miles) from north to south and 839km (520 miles) from east to west, for a total landmass of **294,330 sq. km** (114,789 sq. miles). Looking at it another way, it's almost identical in size to the U.S. state of Arizona but has a population of just **30,000 people** (compared to Arizona's 4.78 million).

Within that epic terrain are natural and man-made wonders of immense proportion: the **highest mountain range** east of the Rockies; one of the **world's longest runways;** 7,800km (4,875 miles) of coastline; world-class nickel and iron-ore deposits; the **largest caribou herd** in the world; and the world's largest underground hydroelectric project at **Churchill Falls.**

It is simultaneously simple and mysterious, a place of ancient civilizations but few people, a land of glacial conditions and temperate breezes. Here, engineers have achieved numerous record-setting feats, but paved highways are few and far between.

Most visitors come to Labrador because they long for a back-to-nature experience untainted by excessive commercialism. No one comes here expecting a glitzy nightlife or Caribbean-style sun and sloth (if they do, they need to switch travel agents).

The most densely populated communities of Labrador are Happy Valley–Goose Bay and the twin towns of Labrador City and Wabush. This is where you'll find the largest quantity of services (banks, hotels, restaurants, and so on), but even here your choices are limited.

Labrador City and **Wabush** are in western Labrador, not far from the Quebec–Labrador border. They grew in response to mining operations by the Iron Ore Company of Canada. Between them, they have a combined population of 11,400 people.

The remaining 10,000 inhabitants live, for the most part, in scattered coastal communities. The largest of these are **L'Anse aux Loup** (pop. 610, across the Strait of Belle Isle from the Northern Peninsula); **Port Hope Simpson** (pop. 580, it's 200km/125 miles of gravel road north of L'Anse aux Loup); **Cartwright** (pop. 620, close to Eagle River and the best salmon fly-fishing in the world); **North West River** (pop. 600, 35km/22 miles from Goose Bay via a rare portion of paved highway); **Hopedale** (pop. 560, site of Moravian Mission Museum, accessible only by ferry and air transportation); and **Nain** (pop. 1,100, the largest Inuit community in Labrador, again accessible only by coastal boat and air transportation).

> **Fun Fact What Time Is It?**
>
> Labrador is home to two time zones. The Labrador Straits operate in the New-foundland time zone, a half-hour ahead of the rest of Labrador in the Atlantic time zone. Quebec is in the Eastern time zone, an hour behind the Atlantic time zone. So, if it's 4:30 in Red Bay, it's 4:00 in Happy Valley–Goose Bay and 3:00 in Blanc Sablon.

1 Labrador Straits ★★

In the southeastern corner of Labrador, an 80km (50-mile) paved highway extends northeast along the Strait of Belle Isle from Blanc Sablon, where ferries from St. Barbe, Newfoundland, dock. At Red Bay, the road turns to gravel and extends 325km (203 miles) north to Cartwright. The route in its entirety is known as the Labrador Coastal Drive. Most attractions are concentrated along the paved road, where approximately 2,300 people inhabit nine small coastal communities. Each of the communities is so close to the next one, you really won't know when you're leaving one and entering another until you see a sign with a different town's name! This is the section of Labrador you'll be most likely to visit if you're planning a Newfoundland *and* Labrador vacation.

Be prepared for cold, damp weather along the Labrador Straits—whichever season you're traveling. Even in summer, the average temperature is a lowly 50°F (10°C) because of the cooling effect of the iceberg-carrying Labrador Current. It flows in a southerly direction past the east coast of Labrador and Newfoundland, except that Labrador, unlike southeastern Newfoundland, doesn't receive the warming benefits of the Gulf Stream. In sheltered areas that deflect the Labrador Current's onshore breeze, summer temperatures often rise to 78° to 85°F (25°–29°C).

ESSENTIALS
GETTING THERE

You can take your car on a ferry from St. Barbe on Newfoundland's Northern Penin-sula to Blanc Sablon, Quebec, at the south end of the Labrador Straits. There are one or two daily sailings between May and early January. The one-way fare is C$11 (US$9) for adults, C$5.50 (US$4.75) for children, and C$22 (US$19) per vehicle. Reservations are recommended for the 90-minute crossing. Call **866/535-2567** or go to www.tw.gov.nl.ca/ferryservices. Until the final link of the Trans Labrador High-way is completed (scheduled for 2009), ferries also operate from Happy Valley–Goose Bay to Cartwright. The sailing departs twice weekly in each direction through a May-to-October season. The one-way fare is C$46 (US$40) for adults, C$23 (US$20) for children, and C$75 (US$65) for vehicles. Even with reservations, you need to check in before joining the line of vehicles.

Alternatively, you can fly Air Labrador or Provincial Airlines into Blanc Sablon, just a few kilometers southwest of L'Anse-au-Clair. (If you happen to fly into Blanc Sablon, take a few minutes to look at the arrowhead display, housed in a wall-mounted case. It's interesting to see the different shapes and sizes of arrowheads that have been found in the area). Air Labrador also flies to Mary's Harbour from St. John's.

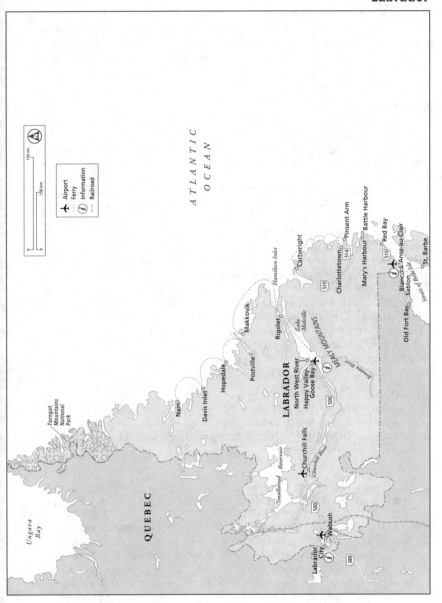

VISITOR INFORMATION

Information about the Labrador Straits can be obtained in L'Anse-au-Clair at the **Gateway to Labrador Visitor Centre** (© **709/931-2360**), located in a restored building formerly occupied by St. Andrew's Anglican Church. It's right on Route 510 and open June through September, daily 10am to 5pm. A helpful online resource for this region is www.labradorcoastaldrive.com.

GETTING AROUND

It's only 80km (50 miles) of paved highway from the ferry terminal in Blanc Sablon to Red Bay, but there's so much to see that it'll take you a full day to travel the whole road. The official highway number is Route 510, but it is promoted as the Labrador Coastal Drive. The highlight north of Red Bay is Battle Harbour (once a regional commercial center, the former community has been opened as a heritage site). To get there, you drive to Mary's Harbour, 85km (53 miles) past Red Bay (where, unfortunately, the paved highway ends) along Route 510. From Mary's Harbour, it's a 1-hour boat ride to Battle Island, home to Battle Harbour.

The coastline north of Battle Harbour has been relatively inaccessible until recently. If you continue on the gravel road past Mary's Harbour, you can drive as far north as **Cartwright,** which is now at the end of Route 510. This road was just completed in the fall of 2002, making exploration of Port Hope Simpson, Charlottetown, Paradise River, and Cartwright possible by vehicle. From Cartwright, 240km (150 miles) north of Mary's Harbour, you can catch a ferry to Happy Valley–Goose Bay (see "Getting There," above). *Warning:* Don't be surprised if you come across two cars halted side-by-side on the highway. Locals often stop in their tracks upon recognizing a neighbor, roll down their windows, and start chatting. It may take them a moment or two to finish a thought and pull aside in order for you to pass, so smile and be patient, remembering that you're now on Labrador time.

L'ANSE-AU-CLAIR

Driving northeast along Route 510 from the ferry terminal at Blanc Sablon, the first community you'll come to will be L'Anse-au-Clair. This (like all other communities on the Labrador Straits—is small (less than 300 residents), but it has the largest hotel in the area.

Understanding the Labrador Flag

The unique personality and heritage of Labrador is well depicted in the three horizontal bars of its flag. The top bar shows the twig of a spruce tree on a white background. This represents the three cultures that primarily make up the region's population—the Innu, the Inuit, and the settlers (or Europeans)—and how they have made a livelihood in harmony with the snow.

The middle bar of forest green represents the green and bountiful land, and the bottom blue bar represents the abundance of water in the region and how the many rivers, lakes, and seas have served as highways for the people and brought them a harvest of fish and wildlife.

WHERE TO STAY

Beachside Hospitality Home   You'll discover hospitality that's short on frills, long on warmth, in the welcoming home of Norm and Gloria Letto—walking distance from the L'Anse-au-Clair beach. The three guest rooms provide good value in terms of cleanliness and comfort, but only one has a private bathroom (with a Jacuzzi, no less!). For an additional C$10–C$15 (US$8.50–US$13) per person, Gloria will be pleased to cook you fish casserole or some other Labradorean dinner favorite. And if you ask nicely, Norm may get out his accordion for an after-dinner singalong. Guests have access to the telephone, the kitchen, and a private entrance.

L'Anse-au-Clair; turn at the Gateway to Labrador Visitor Centre. ℂ 877/663-8999 or 709/931-2053. www.labrador coastaldrive.com/home/99. 3 units. C$40–C$45 (US$35–US$39) double; C$10 (US$8.50) additional person. MC, V. **Amenities:** Complimentary breakfast; full dinners available on request; nonsmoking rooms. *In room:* No phone.

Northern Light Inn ☆   With 49 standard hotel rooms, 5 suites, 5 housekeeping cottages, and 10 fully serviced RV sites, the Northern Light Inn is the largest accommodations option along the Labrador Straits. This clean, cozy, and cheerful place has something to please just about everyone: laundry facilities, wake-up service, in-room phone, coffee shop, licensed lounge, craft shop, and ATM. A nearby indoor swimming pool makes it a perfect location for water recreation. It has no elevator, however, so be prepared to struggle up stairs with your suitcase to the upper-floor rooms. *Tip:* Even if you don't stay overnight at the Northern Light Inn, treat yourself to a meal in the on-site Basque Dining Room (see "Where to Dine" below for a review).

58 Main St., L'Anse-au-Clair. ℂ 800/563-3188 or 709/931-2332. www.northernlightinn.com. 69 units (including 10 serviced campsites). C$70–C$120 (US$60–$104) double. AE, DC, MC, V. Weekly rates and seniors' discounts available. **Amenities:** Dining room; *Greco Xpress* pizza service; coffee shop/lounge; laundry facilities. *In room:* A/C, TV, some fully equipped housekeeping units, limited room service.

WHERE TO DINE

Basque Dining Room ☆ CANADIAN   This casual restaurant is in the Northern Light Inn, the largest lodging along the Labrador Straits. The specialty is seafood and traditional Labrador dishes, but standard Canadian favorites are also served. I went for a combination of local delicacies in the pan-fried cod tongues and fish cakes. Both were delicious.

58 Main St., L'Anse-au-Clair. ℂ 709/931-2332. Reservations not required. Dinners C$9–C$22 (US$7.75–US$19). AE, DC, MC, V. Daily 7am–10pm.

EXPLORING L'ANSE-AU-CLAIR

Gateway to Labrador Visitor Centre ☆☆   Heading east from Blanc Sablon, the first Labrador community you'll come to is L'Anse-au-Clair, where you'll find the Gateway to the Straits Visitor Centre, operated by the Labrador Straits Historic Development Corporation. This center will provide you with information on the entire region. Because you're so close to the Quebec border, you'll also find information here about the Lower North Shore of Quebec. The center, in a restored 1919 church, has an extensive selection of visitor information. There is a complete set of menus from local restaurants, literature on attractions and other services, helpful and friendly bilingual staff, assorted historical photos, quilts depicting local history, natural treasures from the sea (including a good selection of shells), and some very impressive fossils of 500-million-year-old archaeocyathid and 1-billion-year-old Precambrian granite found in the area of the Point Amour Lighthouse.

Rte. 510, L'Anse-au-Clair. ℂ 709/927-2360. Free admission. Mid-June to Sept 30 daily 9:30am–5:30pm.

FORTEAU

Just north of L'Anse-au-Clair is Forteau, a slightly larger community that offers a couple of interesting shopping opportunities and a good restaurant.

WHERE TO STAY

Grenfell Louie A. Hall Bed & Breakfast *Kids*   A Registered Heritage Structure 1 block from the harbor, this inn is in a nursing station started by Dr. Grenfell and named after the Rochester, New York, woman who, in 1946, donated the funds to build it. Unlike some heritage sites (those with atmospheres as welcoming as a mausoleum), this is an enchantingly nostalgic building filled with curious antiques, old-fashioned radiators, and a resident dog. It's an ideal place for families, because the upstairs attic has been converted into a guest unit with two double beds and lots of playroom for the kids. All guest rooms are comfortable (they're each named for a different nurse who once worked here), but amenities vary: some have private bathrooms; others share. *Hint:* Be careful getting in and out of bed: the charmingly sloped bedroom ceilings can give you a nasty bump if you're not careful. Guests can order full breakfasts and other meals in the dining room for an additional charge.

3 Willow Lane, Forteau. ☎ **877/931-2916** or 709/931-2916. www.bbcanada.com/1345.html. 5 units. C$45–C$60 (US$39–US$52) double. Additional charge for more than 2 people; family rates available. MC, V. **Amenities:** Complimentary continental breakfast; laundry facilities. *In room:* No telephone.

WHERE TO DINE

Sea View Restaurant *✦* TRADITIONAL   A full-service dining room offering home-style meals and local specialties that include bakeapple crepes, some incredibly hearty seafood chowder, caribou rouladen, and unique desserts such as screech parfait and partridgeberry baked Alaska pie, available only by special request.

33 Main St., Forteau. ☎ 709/931-2840. www.preserves.nf.ca for information about *Labrador Preserves* made onsite. Lunch C$5.50–C$9 (US$4.75–US$7.75); dinner C$12–C$21 (US$11–US$18). AE, MC, V, Interac. The restaurant is open year-round (weather permitting) 9am–midnight daily.

EXPLORING FORTEAU

While Forteau itself has little interest, the **Overfall Brook Trail**, which is accessed from town, is one of the prettiest and most accessible walks along the Labrador Straits. Finding the trail head is easy—simply drive past the main wharf to the end of the road (it's within walking distance for guests of Grenfell Louie A. Hall Bed & Breakfast). From this point, the trail climbs gently to the headland, where you'll be rewarded with a great view of the Point Amour Lighthouse and a lovely waterfall.

Labrador Straits Museum *✦*   Heading east from town, you'll arrive at a small museum and gift shop operated by the local Women's Institute. If you're interested in purchasing local handicrafts (primarily of the knitted or crocheted variety), or in finding out how women of the area lived before the modern world was opened up to them, you'll find this an informative stop. Other highlights are the collection of reproduction tools and weapons from L'Anse Amour Burial Mound and the replica of an early outport nursing station.

Rte. 510 east of Forteau. ☎ 709/931-2067. C$2 (US$1.75) admission for adults, free for children under 12. Mid-June to Sept daily 9am–5:30pm. Wheelchair accessible. Items purchased in the craft shop are tax exempt.

SHOPPING

Forteau Bay Pottery   If you like unique handcrafted pottery, be sure to visit the small shop right on Route 510 owned and operated by Tracy Keats. Keats is extremely creative, offering original items such as pendants with implants of local leaves and themed drinking mugs such as the Viking Knarr. In addition to her personal studio, Keats's work is on display in several shops throughout the province.

69 Main St., Forteau. © **709/931-2160.** E-mail: tgkeats@yahoo.ca. Most items C$10–C$28 (US$8.50–US$24). MC, V, Interac. COD for mail orders. Mid-June to mid-Sept daily 10am–6pm.

Labrador Preserves 🎁   You can buy more than just lunch at Sea View Restaurant in Forteau: you can also purchase a selection of jams, syrups, and preserves made from locally harvested bakeapples and partridgeberries. Under the name Labrador Preserves, the products are made in the shop right behind the Sea View Restaurant, so you know you're getting them fresh and for prices lower than you may pay in gift shops throughout the area.

33 Main St., Forteau. © **709/931-2743.** www.preserves.nf.ca. C$4.50–C$7 (US$4–US$6). AE, MC, V, Interac. Year-round (weather permitting) daily 9am–midnight.

L'ANSE-AMOUR

Your next stop along the Labrador Coastal Drive is L'Anse-Amour (meaning "Cove of Love"). Through the village of just four homes is **Point Amour,** where you'll find Point Amour Lighthouse, the tallest lighthouse in Atlantic Canada and the second tallest in all of Canada. Between Route 510 and the lighthouse, a plaque marks the earliest known funeral monument in North America—a 7,500-year-old Maritime Archaic Burial Mound.

WHERE TO STAY

Lighthouse Cove Bed & Breakfast 🎁🎁   The ferry was delayed and the other guests had finished dinner by the time I knocked on the door. But welcoming owners Rita and Cecil Davis were more than happy to make sure I was well fed before turning in for the night at Lighthouse Cove, one of only four homes set around a picturesque cove. Cecil is a retired fisherman with simultaneously funny and poignant stories of how he made his living from the sea. His ancestors were granted this cove from the king of England back in 1922, so in effect L'Anse Amour is a private cove—and very special to the Davis family that today inhabits all four homes.

Rita is the shining light of the home. From the moment you enter the door, you'll feel like your visit is the highlight of her day. With a little encouragement, she'll tell you about life in L'Anse-Amour—including the story of how, in 1922, the family was able to retrieve six mahogany dining-room chairs and a piano from the HMS *Raleigh*—hung up on a sandbar just offshore—before it broke up and sank. A continental breakfast is included with your room rate. With advance notice, dinner is available at an additional charge (keep your fingers crossed that Rita makes you her delicious chocolate brownies). The three guest rooms are fairly compact, but completely spotless and very tidy. There are no private bathrooms.

L'Anse-Amour Rd., L'Anse-Amour. © **709/927-5690.** E-mail: lighthousecovebedandbreakfast@yahoo.com. 3 units. C$45 (US$39) double. MC, V. 1km from Point Amour Lighthouse; 3km/almost 2 miles off of Rte. 510 on a gravel road. **Amenities:** Complimentary continental breakfast. *In room:* No phone.

EXPLORING L'ANSE-AMOUR

L'Anse-Amour Burial Mound   Between Route 510 and the village of L'Anse-Amour, watch for a small plaque and pile of stones on the side of the road. It's the L'Anse-Amour Burial Mound, a National Historic Site documented as the oldest native ritual burial site discovered in North America. An interpretive sign explains that

Cove of Deaths

In times of heavy fog, even the strongest light can't help ships avoid the treacherous rocks at Point Amour. Eight shipwrecks have occurred here, including that of the HMS *Raleigh*, pieces of which can still be found along the nearby coastline. The original French name for this location was L'Anse-aux-Morts, meaning "Cove of Deaths."

archaeologists believe this is a 7,500-year-old Maritime Archaic Indian burial mound containing the remains of a 12-year-old child, who was wrapped in skins and birch-bark before being placed in a shallow pit and covered in stones. Ritualistic artifacts found with the boy included a walrus tusk.

L'Anse-Amour Rd., L'Anse-Amour.

Point Amour Lighthouse ⚓   Walking the 127 steep steps to the top of the tallest lighthouse in Atlantic Canada is a worthwhile journey for anyone who doesn't have bad knees or a fear of heights.

The costumed interpretive staff have a sense of humor: they've set up "Fun Factoids" at each level of the lighthouse tower to divert your thoughts from the stress of the 33m (109-ft.) vertical climb. And a chair at every second level enables you to rest if you need to. This is one of only four Imperial Towers erected by the Government of Canada to protect ships traveling between Canada and England.

It took 3 years (1854–57) to complete the 2m-thick (6½-ft.) walls of the lighthouse. The primary layer comprises locally quarried limestone covered first by brick and then wooden shingles to protect the mortar from disintegrating in the sea air. The lighthouse was first illuminated in 1858 and was manned until 1996, when it became automated. Today, the beam of light projects over 18km (11 miles).

Inside the old lighthouse keeper's house, informative panels explain the region's naval history and all aspects of early life here. There are also some fascinating maps from the National Archives of Canada.

From the top of the lighthouse, you'll be rewarded with a magnificent view of Forteau Bay and a 500-million-year-old archaeocyathid fossil bed in the rock below. Take note that Point Amour was the site of a Marconi wireless telegraph station from 1904 until 1965. Give yourself 2 or 3 hours to explore the lighthouse exhibits and hike the trail.

L'Anse-Amour Rd., L'Anse-Amour. ⓒ **709/927-5825.** Guided tours of the lighthouse cost C$3 (US$2.60) for ages 13 and up. Mid-June to early Oct daily 10:30am–5:30pm.

HIKING

The **Raleigh Trail** ⚓ begins at Point Amour Lighthouse and follows the shoreline past pieces of the HMS *Raleigh*, a 12,000-ton light cruiser that ran aground in 1922. Pieces of live ammunition and cordite can still be found being washed ashore and in fishers' nets. The Royal Canadian Navy gets the job of safely detonating any ammo found. As you hike your way along the easy 1km (.5-mile) trail, you'll pass fossil beds, small but scenic waterfalls, crowberry patches, bakeapple plants (the berries ripen in August), and tuckamore(the wind- and sea-stunted spruce providing some greenery to this otherwise treeless land. Allow 20 minutes for the round-trip.

L'ANSE-AU-LOOP

Continuing north from L'Anse-Amour is L'Anse-au-Loup, the largest community on the Straits. L'Anse-au-Loup offers a good range of services for local residents including a credit union, library, public swimming pool, sports complex, and a fish-processing plant. It's also home to the annual Bakeapple Folk Festival, the largest annual event on the Labrador Straits. You won't find many services in L'Anse-au-Loup for travelers, and are better off overnighting in one of the neighboring communities.

PINWARE RIVER

From its source in the remote interior of Labrador, the Pinware River flows southward, and drains into Labrador Straits between L'Anse-au-Loup and Red Bay.

Signposted from Route 510, **Pinware River Provincial Park** protects a spit of land at the river's mouth. Because of the shelter offered by the thick stands of spruce, fir, and birch, summer temperatures here climb considerably higher than in the more open coastal stretches. For river and ocean views, plan on taking the short trail leading to the low summit of Pinware Hill; allow 20 minutes round-trip. The park also has unsupervised swimming, beachcombing, and a picnic area. Do bring your insect repellent or clothing with mosquito netting, as you'll find there are quite a few (many more than you might expect!) airborne residents of the park anxiously awaiting your arrival.

Route 510 parallels and then crosses the river 9km (nearly 6 miles) north of the village of Pinware River. Here, you'll enjoy spectacular views of the river cascading over swift rapids 21m (70 ft.) below. In the lower gorge area near the bridge are the best salmon-fishing holes. This is where several rustic angling camps are located. The Pinware River is a scheduled salmon river. Licenses can be purchased locally and local residents

---

⌜ Fun Fact ⌝ Bakeapples

Bakeapples, also known as cloudberries, are similar in shape to raspberries and blackberries. They're red when they're green (unripe), turning a soft cloudy-orange when they ripen in mid-August. There are many bakeapple marshes alongside Route 510 and directions to them are freely given at information centers, gas stations, and local stores. Picking bakeapples is backbreaking labor: they grow close to the ground, as single berries on a short stalk. The tart but tangy flavor of these succulent northern beauties is unlike anything else you've ever tried. Then again, you're probably better off *not* developing a taste for them. There are only two places in the world where you can find bakeapples: Norway is one, Newfoundland and Labrador is the other.

Coinciding with the beginning of the picking season is the **Bakeapple Folk Festival** (✆ **709/931-2097**), hosted by various Labrador Straits communities the second weekend of August. This gathering has been running for over 25 years and offers 4 days and nights of traditional music, dancing, games, and displays, as well as great food. The Labrador Fisherman's Union Shrimp Company sponsors a delicious seafood reception on opening night. Family Day, held on the Friday, is popular with kids and always features a well-known children's entertainer. On Saturday and Sunday you can enjoy musical performances by a variety of local artists, and browse the booths for information, games, food, and crafts.

are available as guides. *Note:* It is mandatory for visitors from outside the province to be accompanied by a local fishing guide. For complete and current information on fishing regulations, licenses, fees, and outfitter information contact the Newfoundland & Labrador Department of Conservation, ✆ **709/927-5580;** www.env.gov.nl.ca.

WHERE TO STAY
Pinware River Provincial Park Campground   This small campground comes equipped with vehicle parking, picnic tables, drinking water, bathroom facilities, and firepits. A major plus is its proximity to a sandy beach, where you can enjoy unsupervised swimming (if you dare take a dip in these subarctic waters!).

Rte. 510 to Pinware. ✆ **800/563-6353** or 709/927-5516. www.env.gov.nl.ca/parks. 15 unserviced sites. C$10 (US$8.50) per night. MC, V. Open May 24 long weekend to mid-Sept. **Amenities:** Picnic table; fireplace. Pit toilets and drinking-water taps are accessible throughout the park. You can purchase firewood at the check-in point for C$5 (US$4.30) per bundle.

RED BAY
Incredibly, it wasn't until 1977 that Red Bay was identified as a historic whaling port, and today it is this history that is the major attraction. The first industry established on Canadian soil was a seasonal whale-oil factory in Red Bay and by the late 1600s Red Bay was the largest whaling port in the world, with more than 2,500 men from the Basque region of Europe (along the Spanish/French border) calling the bay home during the summer whaling season. The bloodshed was so intense that the waters of the bay would be red with whales' blood. It is thought that this scene provided the origin for the name of the village. The whalers lived aboard Spanish galleons that were moored here for the season. Through the decades, four of these vessels sunk in the bay, giving historians a unique opportunity to study these impressive ships in shallow water, where cold temperatures have helped in the preservation process.

Today, the essence and importance of that bygone whale fishery are eloquently explained through the interpretive presentations at the Red Bay National Historic Site. But don't limit your explorations to the formal site. The community itself has a story to tell through its location and topography. Picturesque rocks protrude peacefully out of the water in the harbor, and an eerie half-sunken ship lurks in the fog just offshore.

WHERE TO STAY
Basinview Bed & Breakfast   The only place to stay in Red Bay, this modern home is the residence of Wade and Blanche Earle. It's an inviting waterfront property, beside Route 510 on the south side of town. The home has a large sitting room with a great view where guests can enjoy satellite TV and have access to the telephone. Blanche will even cook you a real Labrador-style dinner such as caribou stew or pan-fried cod for an additional C$15 (US$13). The three basement rooms share a bathroom, but have the most privacy. The upstairs bedroom has a private bathroom and water views, but is directly off the living room.

145 Main Hwy. (Rte. 510), Red Bay. ✆ **866/920-2001** or 709/920-2002. 4 units. C$56–C$75 (US$49–US$65) double. MC. **Amenities:** Continental breakfast included, cooked breakfast C$6 (US$5.15); laundry facilities. *In room:* No phone.

WHERE TO DINE
Whaler's Restaurant ⭐ *Value* LIGHT FARE   A biggish restaurant with well-spaced tables, Whaler's serves some of the province's best fish and chips. The Chalupa

fish and chips is listed as a snack on the menu, but you'll get two generous filets of cod along with home fries and coleslaw. The fish is delicately coated with a light, spicy coating and not greasy at all. The fries and coleslaw are also good, making this quite a meal for C$10 (US$8.50). The seafood chowder costs C$4.50 (US$4) and is also very good. Save room for ice cream topped with local berries. A small gift shop sells an assortment of souvenirs, including some lovely Labrador jackets. Whaler's is down on the waterfront, beside the Visitor Interpretation Centre, but unfortunately doesn't have water views.

Red Bay. ✆ **709/920-2156.** Lunch C$6–C$10 (US$5.15–US$8.50); dinner C$10–C$19 (US$8.50–$16). MC, V. Daily 8am–10:30pm.

EXPLORING RED BAY
Red Bay National Historic Site ✸✸   Like Basque whalers of old, you'll be immediately drawn to Red Bay Harbour—the present-day location of the Red Bay National Historic Site. While the site consists of two separate buildings, the buildings are under the administration of Parks Canada; you'll pay a fairly hefty entrance fee, but it's well worth it. Pay at the Visitor Reception Centre at the top of the hill and watch the 30-minute video that explains the history of the Basque whalers who once populated this bay. This building also offers a remarkable display of a *chalupa,* a 400-year-old preserved and reconstructed wooden whaling boat surrounded by the mandible of a 5.3m (18-ft.) bowhead whale. The bowhead is a member of the "right whale" family, so named because they were the *right* whales to slaughter for the best oil.

The Visitor Interpretation Centre, located down the hill at the waterfront, contains artifacts from the Basque whalers and one of their ships, the *San Juan,* which was loaded with about 1,000 barrels of whale oil when it sank in Red Bay during a storm in 1565. The wreck of the *San Juan* was discovered in 1978 and subsequently dismantled by underwater archaeologists. Part of its hull is on display in the Grand Hall at the Museum of Civilization in Ottawa, Ontario. Also here you can view a replica of the *San Juan* (built to a scale of 1:10), and recovered artifacts such as pottery fragments and the broken remains of a sandglass.

If you step out the back of the Visitor Interpretation Centre, you can get a good look at the *Bernier,* a half-sunken French ship that went down in the same spot as the *San Juan.* It provides an eerie reminder that other shipwrecks are well preserved in Red Bay due to the coldness of its water.

Red Bay. ✆ **709/920-2142.** www.pc.gc.ca/lhn-nhs/nl/redbay/index_e.asp. C$7 (US$6) adults, C$5.50 (US$4.75) seniors, C$3.50 (US$3) ages 6–16, free for children under 6. There is a family rate of C$14 (US$12). Mid-June to mid-Oct daily 9am–6pm (July–Aug until 8pm).

BOAT TOURS
Gull Island Charters (✆ **709/920-2058**) offers customized boat charters and tours of Red Bay. Short, half-hour runs are possible throughout the day if there are whales or icebergs around. Longer runs are possible in the early morning (before 9am) or in the evening (after 6pm). The maximum number of passengers is six. Expect to pay around C$80 (US$69) per hour to charter the entire boat.

BATTLE HARBOUR ✸✸✸
Red Bay is formally the end of the Labrador Straits, and it's where the paved road ends. But there is one point farther up the coast that, although it takes some effort to reach, will be a highlight of your trip not just to Labrador Straits but the entire province. Located on a rocky island, Battle Harbour is the province's only intact salt

fishing village and is dutifully maintained by the a local historical trust. You can come for just the day, or stay overnight. Either way, visiting Battle Harbour is a poignant peek at history.

The mercantile salt-fish premises at Battle Harbour were originally established by the firm of John Slade & Company of Poole, England, in the early 1770s. Salt fish is cod that has been cleaned, split, salted, and dried; this is how fish was stored in the days pre-refrigeration. The population of Battle Harbour increased quickly after 1820, when fishing schooners adopted the community as their primary port of call and declared it the capital of the Labrador floater fishery. The term "floater fishery" refers to migratory Newfoundland fishermen who fished the bountiful Labrador waters each summer and returned to their permanent homes in Newfoundland each fall. A high point for the community occurred in 1892, when Dr. Wilfred Grenfell arrived in Battle Harbour. A year later he built Labrador's first hospital here. (See more about Dr. Grenfell in chapter 8's section on the Northern Peninsula.)

Like so many other remote communities through Newfoundland and Labrador, the residents were encouraged by the provincial government to move closer to civilization beginning in the late 1960s, and by the 1970s, the permanent population of Battle Harbour had been resettled on the mainland, mostly at Mary's Harbour. The fully intact town of Battle Harbour was left abandoned.

Founded in 1990 to preserve the town, the Battle Harbour Historic Trust does a wonderful job of maintaining the buildings, operating boat transfers, leading site tours (C$7/US$6 per person), running an inn, and providing other visitor services such as serving up lunch to day-trippers (C$12/US$11 per person). Around 20 buildings have been restored, including many along the harborfront, a narrow waterway facing the sheer rock cliff line of a neighboring island. Some are filled with interpretive boards telling the story of the history of the local fishery and how Battle Harbour was once the hub of Labrador. Others are simply historically important spaces, such as the low-roofed loft where in 1909 Robert Peary held a press conference to tell the world of his successful expedition to the North Pole. Beyond the restored buildings, a boardwalk leads through the residential part of village. While a small number of the homes are inhabited on a seasonal basis, the harsh northern weather has taken its toll on those that remain abandoned. The departure for many island residents was swift, and as a result, some homes remain furnished, complete with vases of now-wilted flowers left on windowsills.

An unmarked trail leads from the back of the homes through a rocky cleft to a cemetery, where the headstone engravings make for touching reading. If you're feeling spry, continue beyond the cemetery to a smaller cemetery and then scramble up to the high point of the island, where a plaque marks the spot of a 1904 Marconi wireless telegraph station.

GETTING THERE

Getting to Battle Harbour is half the fun. Boat transfers depart from Mary's Harbour, 85km (53 miles) north of Red Bay along unpaved Route 510. The boat leaves from the government wharf June through September daily at 11am and 7pm. The return trip departs Battle Harbour at 9am and 4pm. Cost for the round-trip is C$40 (US$35) per person. Guarantee a spot by making reservations at ✆ **709/921-6216.**

WHERE TO STAY

Battle Harbour Inn ✿   It's possible to make Battle Harbour a day trip from points south, but for the full effect, plan on staying on the island overnight, at the Battle Harbour

Inn or one of four associated cottages. Once the home of a merchant, you get a flavor of former glory in the antique furnishings and commanding hilltop location. Early in the season, you'll be happily distracted by the sight of passing icebergs as you contemplate the meaning of life from this historical property's wraparound porch. The nearby restored cottages each have one or more beds and kitchen facilities. On the island, everything is within walking distance of the dock and a general store is stocked with necessities. Breakfast is C$8 (US$7), lunch C$12 (US$11), and dinner C$15 (US$13). Specialties of the house are crab, salmon, trout, char, and smoked fish products produced on-site. Other extras include round-trip transportation from the mainland (C$40/US$35 per person) and site tours (C$7/US$6).

Battle Island. (**709/921-6325** or 709/921-6216. www.battleharbour.com. 5 rooms, 4 cottages. C$100–C$150 (US$86–US$129) double. V. Open June 1–Sept 30. *In room:* No phone, no TV.

2 Happy Valley–Goose Bay

Happy Valley–Goose Bay is Labrador's hub and its largest service center. The community is strategically located at the point where Labrador's coastline is naturally split by Hamilton Inlet and Lake Melville.

The town of Happy Valley–Goose Bay is a rather new entity, and was formally established only in 1973. The fur trade initially brought settlers to Central Labrador and others were attracted to the region's abundance of fish, wildlife, and timber, as well as its rich soil and longer growing season. Slow growth continued until World War II. The turning point came in 1941, when the air base at Goose Bay was built as a landing and refueling stop for the Atlantic Ferry Command. During World War II, thousands of aircraft passed through Goose Bay. The airbase continues to provide support and coordination for NATO tactical flight-training activities. Military Base "5 Wing Goose Bay" provides support to Allied, NORAD, and Canadian Forces training and operations. Today, the foreign military component at CFB Goose Bay has added a cosmopolitan flavor to the community and helped its population grow to 8,000.

The pristine Mealy Mountains, between Cartwright and Happy Valley–Goose Bay, represent the East Coast Boreal Natural Region of Canada. For this reason, they are expected to be protected as a national park by 2008.

ESSENTIALS
GETTING THERE
Happy Valley–Goose Bay has an airport served by Air Canada, Air Labrador, and Provincial Airlines. If you decide to drive to Happy Valley–Goose Bay from Labrador West, you must travel Route 500, a gravel highway with few services other than what you'll find in Churchill Falls, the halfway mark between Labrador City and Wabush and Happy Valley–Goose Bay.

A road between Cartwright and Happy Valley–Goose Bay is scheduled for completion in 2009. Until that time, a ferry operated by the provincial government is the main link between the two centers. Ferries operate from May until October, with two sailings weekly. The one-way fare is C$46 (US$40) for adults, C$23 (US$20) for children, and C$75 (US$65) for vehicles. Call (**866/535-2567** or go to www.tw.gov.nl. ca/ferryservices for details.

VISITOR INFORMATION
The Labrador–Lake Melville Tourism Association operates a visitor center at 365 Hamilton River Rd. in Happy Valley–Goose Bay ((**709/896-8787** or 709/896-3489;

www.happyvalley-goosebay.com), open June 1 to September 30, Monday to Friday from 8am to 8pm and Saturday and Sunday from 8am to 5pm. The center is open the rest of the year from Monday to Friday, 8am to 5pm. They'll provide you with maps and brochures as well as the most current information on services and events in the central Labrador region.

WHERE TO STAY & DINE

Aurora Hotel ⊛   If X marks the spot, then this hotel's location at the crossroads of town is a sure signal of quality accommodations. Opened in 1989, the Aurora offers the personal attention of a B&B and the professional service of a four-star property. Guest rooms and suites are nicely furnished and spacious (although the bathrooms are on the small side). Friendly accessories, like the checkered tablecloths in the dining room and a dramatically toned red-and-gold-trimmed front desk, lift it beyond the realm of generic hotel decor. The Aurora is conveniently situated near the visitor center and is a 5-minute drive from the airport, seaport, seaplane dock, and Trans Labrador Highway. One suite is specially designed to meet the needs of travelers with disabilities.

Rte. 500 to 382 Hamilton River Rd. ℂ 800/563-3066 or 709/896-3398. www.aurorahotel.com. 40 units. C$98–C$128 (US$84–US$110) double. MC, V. **Amenities:** Full-service restaurant; lounge; business services; limited room service. *In room:* TV.

Bradley's Bed & Breakfast *Value*   Great value and a good location in a trim bungalow with well-tended gardens. Bradley's is ideally situated for four-season fun: in summer you can walk to the nearby golf course, in winter you can snowmobile on a good trail system from right outside the door. Each guest room has a private bathroom and a telephone. The rooms here are HST-exempt, which is a nice bonus. E-mail and fax service are available. A full breakfast is included in the room rate.

13 McKenzie Dr., Hamilton Heights. (Take the 5th exit off Rte. 500.) ℂ 877/884-7378 or 709/896-8006. www.bb canada.com/bradleybb. 3 units. C$60–C$70 (US$52–US$60) double. V. **Amenities:** Complimentary full breakfast; laundry facilities; nonsmoking rooms. *In room:* TV.

Goose River Lodges *Kids*   Just a 20-minute drive northeast from Happy Valley–Goose Bay, these two-bedroom fully equipped housekeeping cabins and an RV park boast a playground, beach volleyball, and snowmobile rentals, all within walking distance of the namesake Goose River. Cabins are clean and comfortable, with electric heat, air-conditioning, and solid, albeit mismatched, furnishings. Bedrooms and eating/sitting areas are spacious, but the diminutive bathrooms come with just a shower (no bathtub). A bonus is the barbecue and picnic table out front of each cabin. There is also a wheelchair-accessible unit.

North West River Rd. ℂ 877/496-2600 or 709/896-2600. www.gooseriverlodges.ca. 19 units (including 10 RV sites). C$85 (US$73). V. **Amenities:** A/C; TV w/VCR available; children's playground area; nonsmoking units. RV sites are well-spaced and serviced with 30-amp electrical outlets.

Labrador Inn ⊛   The Labrador Inn is the largest and most modern property in Labrador, with the typical amenities you'd expect from a hotel this size (except there's no swimming pool or fitness room), including high-speed Internet access in each room. It's centrally located near the military base, just minutes from the airport and the port of Goose Bay as well as government, educational, and municipal facilities. The inn is home to Banniken's, part restaurant, part lounge. The inn is also wheelchair accessible.

380 Hamilton River Rd. (C) **800-563-2763** or 709/896-3351. www.labradorinn.nf.ca. 74 units. C$85–C$150. (US$73–US$129) double; C$10 (US$8.50) additional person. Discounts available for seniors and government. AE, DC, MC, V. **Amenities:** Dining room; military-style pub with pub menu; business center; room service. *In room:* TV, minibar.

Mulligan's Pub PUB GRUB   Because it's a club that serves food (as opposed to a restaurant that serves alcohol), you must be at least 19 years of age to enter Mulligan's. The food is as good as it gets this far north—and inexpensive. The fish and chips are superb and the Chicken Delight (grilled chicken served over a Caesar salad) is excellent. If you're looking for local flavor, Mulligan's also serves caribou burgers. The pub is open until 2am, but the kitchen closes at the hours below. You can still get light snacks after that.

368 Hamilton River Rd. (C) **709/896-3038**. Reservations not required. C$6–C$14 (US$5.15–US$12). MC, V. Mon–Sat 11am–6pm; Sun 11am–3pm.

EXPLORING HAPPY VALLEY–GOOSE BAY

Labrador Interpretation Centre   This is Labrador's provincial museum. You'll see four galleries filled with life-size dioramas, exhibits, and archaeological artifacts that interpret Labrador's history from the arrival of the first humans 9,000 years ago to today. The museum is on Portage Road in North West River, a neighborhood of Happy Valley–Goose Bay where you'll also find the Labrador Heritage Museum.

Portage Rd., North West River. (C) **709/497-8566**. C$2 (US$1.75) adults, C$1 (US85¢) children. June 1–Aug 31 Wed 1–4pm, Thurs–Fri 10am–4pm, Sat–Sun 1:30–4:30pm; closed Mon–Tues; Sept 1–May 30 Wed–Fri 1–4pm.

Northern Lights Military Museum   Check out this museum's interesting display of the region's military history, including a good collection of authentic World War II artifacts. In the same building is a display of stuffed animals.

170 Hamilton River Rd. (C) **709/896-5939**. Free admission. Tues–Sat 9am–5:30pm.

FESTIVALS AND SPECIAL EVENTS

The community hosts several fun cultural events, such as the **Sheshatshiu Innu Etiun Summer Festival** in late August. Here are some other worthwhile events.

Labrador Canoe Regatta   The 3-day paddling event features teams from all over Labrador that compete in six-person voyageur canoe races on Gosling Lake, a 20-minute drive from town. Male and female contestants paddle replicas of traditional two-person canoes in several age-specific category races. A variety of food booths will keep your tummy from growling, and bands provide traditional entertainment throughout the weekend. Held the first weekend in August, there is no entrance fee.
(C) **709/896-5817**.

North West River Beach Festival   Labrador's largest outdoor music festival takes place near Happy Valley–Goose Bay the third weekend of July. Free live entertainment can be enjoyed right on the beach (pray for a stiff breeze, or you may find yourself doing the "Black Fly Swat" dance) while the auction of local crafts spices things up a little.
(C) 709/497-3339.

Sno-Break   This event, formerly known as the Happy Goose Winter Carnival, is a weeklong family-oriented winter event held the second to third weekend of March. Sno-Break is 8 days of continuous winter activities including snowmobile races, trail rides to surrounding communities, family games, relay races, and more.
(C) **709/896-3489**. Most activities are free. There is a small registration fee to participate in the races and trail rides. Call for specifics.

3 Churchill Falls to Labrador West

Labrador City and Wabush are the major centers of Labrador West, the resource-rich region that stretches along the Quebec–Labrador border. Churchill Falls is the halfway point between Labrador City/Wabush and Happy Valley–Goose Bay.

Labrador City was established as a community in 1958 and now offers a full range of services including visitor information, a hospital, lodging, camping, hiking, sport fishing, golf, skiing, and snowmobiling. The 9,700 residents of Labrador City and Wabush happily embrace their sometimes harsh—what some call a two-season—climate. Winter can seem never-ending when the snow is on the ground for up to 8 months! And summer temperatures in July and August are that perfect balmy warmth that more southerly residents dream of in the midst of their heat waves.

But what both Labrador City and Wabush are best known for are their open-pit iron-ore mines, the largest of their kind in North America. The community of Churchill Falls on the Churchill River is best known for having the world's largest underground hydroelectric generating station.

ESSENTIALS
GETTING THERE

If you're coming from Baie Comeau, Quebec, on the Gulf of St. Lawrence, partially paved Route 389 will take you north to the twin communities of Labrador City and Wabush. Labrador City is less than 20km (12 miles) from the Quebec–Labrador border; Wabush is 3km (about 2 miles) farther along Route 500 and is home to the regional airport.

The 581km (361-mile) stretch of gravel highway from Labrador City to Happy Valley–Goose Bay is basically unserviced except for what you'll find in Churchill Falls—roughly halfway along your journey—and will take you about 8½ hours to complete. Churchill Falls is situated 238km (148 miles) from Labrador City and 288km (179 miles) from Happy Valley–Goose Bay and is pretty much the only service center you'll find along Route 500.

The communities at either end of Route 500 also have small airports, so you can fly into Wabush, rent a car, drive as far as Happy Valley–Goose Bay, and then fly to St. John's or a limited number of other destinations without having to drive the return route.

You can also travel to Labrador West by train via the Quebec North Shore & Labrador Railway, which is owned and operated by the local mining company. The train departs Sept-Îles, Quebec, on Tuesdays and Thursdays. The return trip departs Labrador City on Wednesdays and Fridays. To reach Labrador City takes 7 hours if you get on the nonstop service and 12 hours if you get the milk run that stops at several communities en route. The train eventually terminates at Schefferville, 588km (357 miles) north of Sept-Îles. Before reaching this remote mining town, there is a 58km (36-mile) spur line that will take you from Ross Bay Junction to Labrador City. The cost to Labrador City is C$56 (US$49) one-way, with discounts for seniors and children. MasterCard, Visa, and Interac are accepted. You must reserve your ticket at least one week in advance and pick up your ticket the day of your travel at Voyages Tour Monde, in Sept-Îles. Call ✆ **800/463-4123** or 418/968-1350. There is no website for this company.

Navigating the Trans Labrador Highway

Many people are surprised to discover that the majority of the Trans Labrador Highway is a two-lane, gravel road. If it's wet the road is slick and slippery; if it's dry the dust is blinding; and if it's icy or snowy driving can be lethal. Here are some tips to make the trip a bit easier:

- Try to drive on Sundays, when there are fewer tractor-trailers on the road. Even though the highway is supposedly two lanes, you don't want to be crowded onto the shoulders, which are not nearly as solid as they look.
- Never start out on the highway without a full tank of gas (an extra container in the trunk wouldn't hurt either) and a spare tire.
- Be extra cautious in winter, especially with regard to traveling close to the outer edge of the highway. What looks like snow-covered highway may just be loose snow without a solid foundation.

VISITOR INFORMATION

Regional information for Labrador West is available at the tourist chalet in Labrador City at 500 Vanier Ave. This chalet is open year-round. From mid-June to September 1 the hours are daily 9am until 5pm. The center is open the remainder of the year from Monday to Saturday, 9am to 5pm (© **709/944-7631**).

WHERE TO STAY & DINE

Carol Inn   This is a good choice if you want to do your own cooking. The Carol Inn offers 21 fully equipped efficiency units and one deluxe suite. All units are spacious and are regularly refurbished. The inn is the only Labrador City lodging to have air-conditioning. There is an on-site gift shop. The inn features fine dining, a family restaurant, and pub-style food as well as live entertainment.

215 Drake Ave., Labrador City. © **888/799-7736** or 709/944-7736. E-mail: carolinn@crrstv.net. 22 units. C$92–C$132 (US$79–US$114) double. AE, DC, MC, V. **Amenities:** Full-service restaurant; family restaurant; pub; nonsmoking rooms. *In room:* A/C, TV, kitchenette, minibar.

Churchill Falls Inn   For those in town on government business, this property is conveniently located in the town complex. There's even a swimming pool available for guest use, a real treat for this part of the world. Being in the town complex is a good thing if you're visiting during the winter, as you can get from one place to the next without having to go outdoors.

Ressigieu Dr., Churchill Falls. © **800/229-3269** or 709/925-3211. 21 units. C$82–C$112 (US$71–US$96) double. AE, MC, V. **Amenities:** Dining room; lounge; indoor swimming pool; limited room service. *In room:* TV.

PJ's Inn by the Lake ⚴   Perfectly located on the shoreline of Little Wabush Lake, this small B&B has sweeping water views (except in winter, when you're likely to see dog teams rushing across the frozen water), with a deck taking full advantage of the view. Inside, you find three midsize rooms, one with a jetted tub and all three with modern amenities like Internet access. The ambience throughout is welcoming, with guests also having use of a book-filled living area and dining room.

606 Tamarack Dr., Labrador City. ℂ **888/944-6648** or 709/944-3438. www.bbcanada.com/8517.html. 3 units. C$50 (US$43) single room; C$60 (US$52) queen-size room. **Amenities:** Complimentary continental breakfast; laundry service available. *In room:* TV, Internet, phone. Jetted tub in one room.

Wabush Hotel   A distinctive three-story chalet-style property built in 1960, this hotel is the best in the area, with spacious guest rooms, exemplary customer service, and dependable food. The hotel features two dining rooms specializing in Chinese and Canadian cuisine—the Chinese food is really good, something that is rare in NL. It is within walking distance of downtown and the recreation center. The hotel offers a complimentary shuttle service to and from the airport upon request (with sufficient notice), as well as a 24-hour reception desk.

9 Grenfell Dr., Wabush. ℂ **709/282-3221.** www.wabushhotel.com. 68 units. C$86–C$93 (US$74–US$80) double. AE, MC, V. **Amenities:** Dining room; lounge; salon; limited room service; laundry service. *In room:* A/C, TV, hair dryer.

EXPLORING LABRADOR WEST

Churchill Falls Hydroelectric Generating Station   Touring this facility, the world's largest underground hydroelectric generating station, is the highlight of a stop in Labrador West. On the tour, you'll hear some impressive facts and figures, but nothing will prepare you for the sheer size of the operation, especially the underground powerhouse, which is as high as a 15-story building and 3 football fields long. The free tours are conducted four times daily during the summer months and less frequently the rest of the year. The tours are about 3 hours long and are indoors, so you don't have to worry about wearing special clothing. Hard hats are provided. For security reasons, children under 8 are not permitted to participate in the tours. Reserve a spot by calling ℂ **709/925-3335.**

Iron Ore Company of Canada and Wabush Mine Tours   The Labrador West Tourism Association offers 1-hour bus tours of the open mine pits. Visit their booth in the Labrador Mall for further details.

Call Labrador West Tourism at ℂ **709/944-7631.** E-mail: tourism@ccrstv.net. C$10 (US$8.50) for adults. For safety reasons, children under 10 are not permitted. July 1 to early Sept Wed and Sun 1:30pm. Reservations recommended.

OUTDOOR PURSUITS

The area boasts excellent hiking trails and some of the best outdoor winter fun in the province. You can cross-country ski at the **Menihek Nordic Ski Club** from late October

---

Mush!

If your idea of fun includes being pulled more than 160km (100 miles) across frozen lakes and around mountains in –40° temperatures, guided only by fluorescent markers spaced 91m (300 ft.) apart, then you'll want to know more about the Labrador 120 Dog Sled Race. In mid-March, teams from across Canada and the United States gather in Labrador City to take part in this annual test of endurance. Teams are composed of a musher (driver), sled, survival gear, and 10 dogs (usually either Siberian or Alaskan huskies). Guided by voice commands from the musher, the dogs leave Labrador City and pull the sled nonstop 80km (50 miles) across country to Steers River, returning by the same route after a 6-hour break. Regardless of weather, the race starts at 4pm on a Saturday and usually ends around 8am Sunday.

> *Moments* **Labrador: A Spiritual Experience**
>
> It takes a big heart to appreciate the Big Land. You'll see "brown" ponds where the water is so clear the color comes from the sun reflecting off the rocks on the bottom. You'll see double and triple rainbows, their colorful clarity enhanced by the crisp, clean air. And you'll see the aurora borealis playing across the northern sky in flowing flames of golden-crimson-emerald light. Truly, a trip to Labrador is an unforgettable, life-altering journey.

to mid-May. After the snow melts, the Menihek Interpretive Trail follows the winter trail system for 5km, with information boards describing local flora and fauna. Other winter thrills include downhill skiing at **Smokey Mountain** and snowmobiling with Grande Hermine Adventures; call ℂ **709/282-5369.** If you're more into spectator sports, time your visit in March for the **Labrador 120,** a dogsled race that attracts participating teams from across Canada and the United States. Contact Labrador West Tourism at ℂ **709/944-5013** for more information about any events in the Labrador City and Wabush area.

If you're into hunting or fishing, call Newfoundland & Labrador Tourism at ℂ **800/563-6353** or 709/729-2830 for a free copy of their *Hunting & Fishing Guide.* Labrador is a great place for hunting black bear or caribou and trophy fishing for salmon, trout, and northern pike.

4 North Coast

North of Happy Valley–Goose Bay, the Labrador coast comprises tiny outport fishing communities that are accessible only via ferry or plane. The farther north you go, the more icebergs you'll see (many break up or melt as they head south toward St. John's), making Cape Chidley at Labrador's northern tip the place where you're likely to see the most and largest icebergs.

After many years of negotiations, the Inuit and Kablunangajuit people of the North Coast reached an agreement with the provincial and federal governments for a form of self-government. Beginning in 2006, Nunatsiavut (meaning "our beautiful land") came into being, with the 5,300 North Coast residents controlling matters such as health and education. Another part of the agreement saw the dedication of **Torngat Mountains National Park,** which protects the Torngat Mountains in the remote northern corner of Labrador.

ESSENTIALS
GETTING THERE
The ferry trip up the North Coast from Happy Valley–Goose Bay is an adventure in itself, and the main reason many visitors find themselves this far north. On this passengers-only boat, you'll stop at several small villages and travel as far north as Nain. Operated by the provincial government, Coastal Labrador Marine Services (ℂ **709/925-3335**) charge C$200 (US$172) per person one-way. Accommodations range from dorm beds (C$120/US$104) to private cabins (C$400/US$345). As an alternative to the ferry, you can return to Goose Bay on an Air Labrador flight from Nain.

NAIN
Established in 1771 as a mission, Nain today has a population of 1,200, most of whom are of Inuit or Kablunangajuit descent. The few visitors that do travel this far

The Inukshuk

The North Coast is inhabited by various native peoples, including the Inuit. As you travel this area, you may see unusual rock or stone figurines shaped in the rough outline of a person. They are *Inukshuk,* an Inuit word meaning "in the image of man." These lifelike figures originally served as signposts to mark the way across barren land and to offer guidance to those who followed. They are a symbol of friendship, caring, and the strong sense of community you find in the north.

north arrive on the twice-weekly ferry, while only the adventurous few continue north by chartered boat or plane to the abandoned mission at Hebron or to the wilds of Torngat Mountains National Park. While fishing is important to the local economy, a massive nickel and copper mine south of town at Voisey Bay draws the most outside business interests. Aside from simply soaking up life this far north, the only official attraction is Nain Piulimatsivik, a small museum displaying Inuit artifacts and telling the story of the Moravian settlers. It opens whenever the ferry is in town.

WHERE TO STAY

Atsanik Lodge   The only place to stay in Nain, this 25-room property is a full-service hotel, with a dining room, lounge, laundry, room service, and airport shuttle.

Sand Banks Rd., Nain. ✆ **709/922-2910**. 25 units. C$115–C$135 (US$99–US$116) double. MC, V. **Amenities:** Restaurant; laundry. *In room:* Television, phone.

Appendix: Newfoundland & Labrador in Depth

To really understand this unique province and the people who live here, it's important to delve into the history of the island of Newfoundland and its mainland region of Labrador. It is the history, and sense of place, that makes Newfoundland and Labrador such a culturally unique destination.

Despite being the oldest European settlement in North America, through the 1980s and 1990s the province was one of the least economically developed places in Canada. But, change is in the air. Since the commencement of offshore oil drilling and the development of the world's biggest nickel mine at Voisey Bay, the local economy has come ahead in leaps and bounds. So much so, that economic growth in the last decade to 2005 has been 25%, highest of all Canadian provinces.

History has taught the people of Newfoundland and Labrador a harsh lesson of exploitation. Time and again, they have seen the heartbreaking out-migration of their vast natural resources and human potential. From the earliest days of the commercial fishery through to iron ore development, hydroelectric power, and offshore petroleum reserves, the majority of royalties and profits from these resource extractions have traditionally gone elsewhere. But the people have always been fiercely determined to maximize their indigenous involvement on the labor side , and as a result, in 2005 the province began keeping 100% of oil royalties without affecting subsidies from the federal government. Overall, the future for Newfoundland looks bright. So much so that there has begun a steady flow of displaced Newfoundlanders returning to their home province.

Decades of competition for employment and development dollars have created an intra-provincial rivalry. Rural areas resent the growth of urban centers, especially the capital of St. John's. Labradorians continue to lobby for provincial autonomy, feeling the benefits they receive from the provincial government are nowhere near proportionate to the wealth that is generated by the region's hydroelectric and mining developments. After decades of receiving little recognition or recompense for the land and resources that were theirs for thousands of years before European settlement, the Inuit of Labrador scored a massive victory with a 2005 agreement reached with the federal and provincial governments for self-governance of a vast tract of land known to them as Nunatsiavut.

Through all the hardships endured, Newfoundlanders and Labradorians extend their hands in friendship. The Maritime provinces of New Brunswick, Nova Scotia, and Prince Edward Island have a well-deserved reputation for being gracious and welcoming, but there is still a noticeable difference between that gregarious threesome and Canada's easternmost province. Unlike the rest of the country, locals see themselves as Newfoundlanders who happen to be Canadian rather than the other way around. It must be the isolation. Newfoundland is an island, Labrador a remote northern locale; both are difficult to access. But instead of closing them off from the world, their remoteness makes them hungry for connections beyond their borders.

Fun Fact A Cultural Time Capsule

As you travel throughout the province, you'll marvel at the distinctive dialects. Along the Southern Shore (in the Avalon Region), it's difficult to distinguish the brogue of the Irish-born local priest from that of the local people. Similarly, there are other places where the British accent is so strong, linguists can identify the part of England from which local ancestors emigrated. Why does it sound so pure, hundreds of years after the out-migration of these early European settlers? The answer is geography—Newfoundland's island isolation protected the original cultural identity of its settlers.

They greet strangers with heartfelt smiles, warm words, and genuine curiosity. Everyone is welcomed as a person with a story to tell.

1 History 101

Early settlement patterns of Newfoundland and Labrador followed the length of the rocky shores, providing ready access to the sea. Little has changed. Fishing has been—and for the most part, continues to be—the primary activity around which the world turns for Newfoundlanders. Even for those not directly involved in the ocean harvest, the industry and its environment are a powerful social, cultural, and economic influence.

WHO DISCOVERED THE NEW FOUNDE LAND?   Newfoundland has a long and intriguing history. Evidence of a burial mound of the Maritime Archaic Indians dating back 7,500 years—the oldest discovered burial mound in the world—has been found in L'Anse Amour on the Labrador Straits. And archaeologists have determined that as far back as 5,500 years ago the Maritime Archaic Indians, followed by other native peoples, were living in the area of the Port au Choix on the Northern Peninsula.

It was also on this Northern Peninsula that Leif Eriksson and his gang of Vikings landed in A.D. 1000. Although the Vikings did not form a permanent settlement in the newfound land or officially claim what they called Vinland, they left evidence of their community in the mounds found at L'Anse aux Meadows National Historic Site.

Dateline

- **1000** Leif Eriksson and his pack of Vikings land at L'Anse aux Meadows, making them the first Europeans to unofficially discover the New-found-land.
- **1497** Explorer Giovanni Caboto (aka John Cabot) lands at Cape Bonavista aboard his ship the *Matthew,* and is recorded as the man who discovered Newfoundland.

- **1583** Sir Humphrey Gilbert officially claims Newfoundland for England, making it the first overseas Crown possession.
- **1610** John Guy establishes the first British settlement in Newfoundland. It is not successful.
- **1621** Sir George Calvert (who later became Lord Baltimore) establishes the first successful planned colony, at Ferryland.

- **1651** Oliver Cromwell of England appoints a board of commissioners to govern Newfoundland.
- **1660** The French establish the colony of Placentia and build Fort Louis to defend it.
- **1763** Labrador is annexed to Newfoundland.
- **1771** The Moravians establish the community of Nain in Labrador.

Battle of Beaumont Hamel

Two years into World War I, the Allies planned a major offensive to break through German lines, hoping to turn the tide of war in their favor. The attack was scheduled for July 1, 1916. Miscalculating the positioning of German troops, the Allied forces ran straight into heavy bombardment from machine-gun fire. Almost 20,000 British troops died that day, but hardest hit of all was the Newfoundland Regiment. The 778 members of the Regiment were among the first wave ordered to cross No Man's Land and penetrate the German front line near the village of Beaumont Hamel. The next morning, only 68 men answered the roll call—each unacknowledged name a symbol of a lost generation for the fledgling colony. There is today a permanent memorial on the battlefield of Beaumont Hamel; it is a bronze statue of a caribou, the symbol of the Newfoundland Regiment.

Next up was Giovanni Caboto, more commonly known as John Cabot, the Italian-born explorer who claimed the newfound land for England in 1497. The French and Spanish soon followed, looking for a share of the bountiful Newfoundland fisheries, and many battles ensued, with the British eventually becoming the enduring force on the Newfoundland front.

Most of the early permanent settlers to Newfoundland came from southwest England and southeast Ireland, with the majority emigrating between 1750 and 1850. And because the Newfoundland outports were so isolated and family groups kept tightly intact, contemporary Newfoundlanders continue to speak with a strong Irish accent in parts of the Avalon (particularly the Irish Loop), and a fainter British or Scottish accent in St. John's and throughout the rest of the island.

PRE-CONFEDERATION Prior to joining Confederation and becoming part of Canada in 1949, Newfoundland was an independent British colony with its own governor and government house. Loyalty to the mother country was particularly evident during the world wars, when thousands of Newfoundland youth voluntarily sailed overseas to do what they felt was their duty in the war effort.

Until 1949, Newfoundland produced its own currency and postage stamps.

- **1774** Control of Labrador is given to Quebec via *The Quebec Act*.
- **1784** Religious freedom is proclaimed and the first Roman Catholic bishop arrives in Newfoundland.
- **1802** The Treaty of Amiens gives control of the islands of St. Pierre and Miquelon to France.
- **1809** Labrador is re-annexed to Newfoundland.
- **1813** Newfoundland's first lighthouse is built at Fort Amherst.
- **1825** The coast of Labrador is annexed to Quebec.
- **1832** Cape Spear Lighthouse is built to light the way for ships arriving at the most easterly point in North America.
- **1858** The first transatlantic telegraph message is transmitted via submarine cable from Heart's Content in Newfoundland to Ireland.
- **1866** The transatlantic telegraph cable is successfully laid.
- **1871** The Newfoundland Constabulary is formed.
- **1873** Cod fishing in Newfoundland is revolutionized with the invention of the cod trap.
- **1888** Newfoundland abandons British currency and adopts the dollar.

Native Inhabitants of Newfoundland & Labrador

Palaeo-Indians (or "ancient" Indians) lived in Labrador about 9,000 years ago. Little is known about them, but based on the scant archaeological evidence, an educated guess is that they were nomadic hunters and gatherers, living along the coast in the summer and following inland caribou in the fall.

Maritime Archaic people (descendants of the Palaeo-Indians) lived throughout the entire province from 3,000 to 7,500 years ago. The first known inhabitants of the island of Newfoundland, they were coastal dwellers, dependent on the sea (mammals, birds, and fish) for their sustenance.

Palaeo-Eskimos began moving into Northern Labrador about 4,000 years ago, emigrating south from Greenland. Included within the Palaeo-Eskimo tradition were the Groswater and Dorset cultures.

Innu, who have lived in Labrador and northeastern Quebec for approximately 2,000 years, are thought to be descendants of the Maritime Archaic people. Traditionally, they are nomadic hunters like the other aboriginal groups of Newfoundland and Labrador. They differ, however, in that they are an inland people who make sporadic trips to the coast. To learn more about the modern Innu population, visit www.innu.ca.

Beothuk, the original native inhabitants of Newfoundland, are extinct. The last known Beothuk, Shanawdithit, died in 1829. It is estimated that there were fewer than 1,000 Beothuk living on the island at any one time; their population was decimated by starvation, disease, and periodic skirmishes with European settlers. Archaeological evidence seems to indicate they were of Algonkian origin (similar to Mi'Kmaq, Montagnais, and Naskaupi). They inhabited central and western Newfoundland. The website www.heritage.nf.ca/aboriginal/beothuk.html is filled with information on this almost mythical people.

- **1892** The Great Fire destroys 2,000 buildings in St. John's.
- **1892** Dr. Wilfred Grenfell arrives from England to establish the Grenfell Mission.
- **1897** First ferry service sails between North Sydney, Nova Scotia, and Port aux Basques, Newfoundland.
- **1897** Cabot Tower at Signal Hill is built.
- **1901** Sir Charles Cavendish Boyle, Governor of Newfoundland, writes the "Ode to Newfoundland."
- **1901** Marconi receives the first wireless signal from England at Signal Hill.
- **1904** France relinquishes rights to Newfoundland's "French Shore."
- **1908** William Coaker forms the Fishermen's Protective Union.
- **1912** The SS *Titantic* sinks off Cape Race after colliding with an iceberg.
- **1925** Newfoundland women get the vote by way of the Women's Suffrage Bill.
- **1927** Grenfell Mission Hospital is opened in St. Anthony and Dr. Grenfell is knighted.
- **1927** Labrador becomes an official part of Newfoundland.
- **1932** Amelia Earhart takes off from Harbour Grace on her historic flight across the Atlantic.

Thule people were the most recent aboriginal arrivals in Labrador, crossing the Bering Strait from Asia as late as 500 to 600 years ago. They lived in small family groups, and were nomadic hunters and gatherers. They were also known as whalers, hunting baleen whales using harpoons thrown from their *umiaks* (open, flat-bottomed boats) and kayaks. The Thule are the ancestors of the Inuit.

Inuit (aka "Eskimo") of Labrador are traditionally nomadic hunters and gatherers known for traveling great distances in search of food and other sustenance materials. Pre–European settlement, they ranged from Cape Chidley in northern Labrador to the island of Newfoundland. The introduction of Moravian missionaries in the mid-1700s marked a change in the Inuit's traveling lifestyle as well as the dilution of their culture through the integration of European tools and ideas. In 2005, their land claim agreement was ratified and self-governance began with elections in 2006. For more information, visit their website at www.nunatsiavut.com.

Mi'Kmaq have lived in Newfoundland for more than 200 years, with their main settlements on the island's west coast. Some anthropologists have surmised that they are of Maritimes (that is, Nova Scotian) origin and that their emigration was motivated by scarce resources. About 600 Mi'Kmaq today live in Conne River, along Newfoundland's south coast. You can visit the band on the Internet at www.mfngov.ca.

Métis people of Labrador are striving for recognition of their native status, both from acknowledged aboriginal groups and from non-natives. Métis are a combination of Innu or Inuit bloodlines mixed with European settlers. There are approximately 5,000 Métis living in Labrador, which makes them the largest aboriginal group in the province. Visit www.labmetis.org.

- **1949** Newfoundland becomes a province of Canada with Joseph Smallwood as its first premier.
- **1957** All children under 16 years of age are provided with no-cost medical care.
- **1961** Forest fires force the evacuation of 9,000 people from 300 communities. A million acres and 35 homes are destroyed.
- **1965** The Fisheries Household Resettlement Program is introduced to encourage residents of remote outport communities to move to larger centers.
- **1965** The iron-ore mine at Wabush, Labrador, is opened.
- **1965** Newfoundland's 500,000th citizen, Bernard Joseph Hynes, is born at 2:25am on July 30 in the Twillingate Cottage Hospital.
- **1965** Come Home Year is instituted as a major tourism initiative.
- **1966** Bell Island mine closes.
- **1966** The Newfoundland portion of the Trans-Canada Highway is completed.
- **1966** St. John's businessman Chesley Pippy donates the funds to establish Pippy Park.
- **1967** Construction begins on the Churchill Falls hydroelectric generating station.
- **1968** CN introduces a trans-island passenger bus service.
- **1969** Newfoundland introduces Medicare.

The Little Man from Gambo

Joseph Roberts Smallwood was born in 1900 in Gambo, a central New-foundland town of just over 2,000 residents. Although small of stature, Smallwood had a larger-than-life persona. He worked as a journalist, a farmer, and a labor organizer before striking his true vocation: politics. He was convinced that Confederation with Canada was the best option for a prosperous future for Newfoundland and Labrador; his mission was to per-suade enough of his fellow citizens to feel the same way. He traveled the province from one end to the other, using his impressive oratorical skill and staccato style of delivery to maximum effect. He achieved his desired goal in 1949, when Newfoundland and Labrador became the tenth province of Canada.

A particularly endearing Smallwood quirk (aside from his famous bow tie) was his habit of reiterating salient points three and four times so that they were imprinted on the minds of his listeners. He also had an incredible memory for both names and faces, often recognizing voters he had met years before and linking them to other family and friends throughout the province.

Smallwood served as Premier of Newfoundland and Labrador for 22 years. His leadership was marked by an intense drive for industrialization: his government supported rubber boot and chocolate factories as well as an oil refinery, linerboard mills (manufacturers of the corrugated layer found in the middle of cardboard), and a hydroelectric power development at Churchill Falls. Even though many of his initiatives were fated to fail, the lack of success never diminished his dream of prosperity. Until his death in 1991, he was often affectionately referred to as the last living Father of Confederation.

Newfoundland stamps are still relatively common, so their value isn't extremely high, but they make a wonderful souvenir for any collector. Their variety is rich and

- **1969** The first ship is con-structed at the Marystown shipyard.
- **1969** The Newfoundland Railway is closed.
- **1970** The Maritime Archaic Indian burial ground is dis-covered at Port au Choix.
- **1972** After 23 years in office, Premier Joseph Smallwood resigns.
- **1972** The Newfoundland dog is declared the province's official animal.
- **1973** The Newfoundland fishery is booming, with an estimated value of C$45 million.
- **1976** Well-known New-foundland politician John Crosbie is elected as a Mem-ber of Parliament.
- **1978** L'Anse aux Meadows is designated a UNESCO World Heritage Site.
- **1978** St. John's Day is cele-brated for the first time, with parades, steak dinners,
- fish-splitting contests, and a street dance.
- **1979** Oil is discovered on the Grand Banks and the Hibernia well established.
- **1979** Progressive Conserva-tive Brian Peckford is elected Premier.
- **1979** The Matrimonial Prop-erty Act is passed, giving women financial rights in their marriage.
- **1980** Official Newfoundland flag is unveiled.

Petroleum Power

There are three producing oil fields on the Grand Banks, offshore from New-foundland and Labrador: Hibernia, Terra Nova, and White Rose (the last began production in Nov 2005). Between them, the three fields produce about 145 million barrels of oil annually, which equates to about one-half of Canada's conventional light crude-oil production. And with the price of oil peaking in 2005, interest has been renewed in a fourth Grand Banks oilfield, Hebron-Ben Nevis, as well as more remote sites like the Orphan Basin and Labrador Shelf.

colorful, and each stamp tells a fascinating story. As well, Newfoundland produced its own coinage and bank notes from 1834 to 1949, many of which are now quite valuable to collectors. The coin denominations issued were 1¢, 5¢, 10¢, 20¢, 25¢, 50¢, $2, and gold.

CONFEDERATION   The man responsible for bringing Newfoundland—Britain's oldest colony—into Canada's Confederation was Joey Smallwood, Newfoundland's first premier. Between 1946 and 1948, Smallwood organized a number of what turned out to be very controversial and emotional debates, asking his constituents whether they were in favor of becoming a Canadian province. In 1948, the final vote was incredibly close—51% supporting and 49% opposing—which is why some Newfoundlanders still think of Smallwood as a traitor, and others see him as Newfoundland's greatest contemporary hero.

LABRADOR   What is also important to understand is that most of Labrador (other than the Labrador Straits and the coastal region) has quite a different history and persona than the island of Newfoundland. Inland Labrador is a land rich in wildlife and natural resources, but its history has been spotted with struggle about who owns these lands. Labrador became part of Newfoundland only in 1927, and the boundary following the Torngat Mountains was set to separate Labrador from the neighboring province of Quebec. In many ways, it is both physically and emotionally distant from Newfoundland, leading many in the region to argue that they should form their own provincial entity.

WHEN COD WAS KING   No matter what tangent you go off on as you research the province's natural or sociological history, everything will always

- **1982** Offshore oil drill rig the *Ocean Ranger* sinks in a winter storm. All 84 lives aboard are lost.
- **1982** The provincial unemployment rate hits 20%.
- **1983** Construction begins on the first phase of the Trans Labrador Highway.
- **1985** Arrow jet crashes at Gander, killing 256 U.S. servicemen and crew.
- **1986** Legislation puts an end to the killing of seal pups.

- **1987** Gros Morne National Park becomes a UNESCO World Heritage Site.
- **1991** Former Premier Joseph R. Smallwood dies at 90 years of age.
- **1992** Ottawa enforces the Cod Moratorium in an attempt to replenish depleted cod stocks.
- **1993** Prospectors Al Chislett and Chris Verbiski discover the world's largest nickel

deposit at Voisey Bay in northern Labrador.
- **1994** Recreational cod fishing is reintroduced to Newfoundland.
- **1998** The Royal Newfoundland Constabulary begins carrying firearms.
- **2001** First oil pumped from the Terra Nova oil field.
- **2001** Brian Tobin resigns as Premier and moves to federal politics at the request of Prime Minister Jean Chrétien.

Canine Companions

Each of Newfoundland and Labrador's distinct geographic entities has its own namesake dog. The **Newfoundland dog** is a large animal with long black fur and webbed feet. Some Newfoundland dogs have a splash of white across their chest. In spite of their imposing size (weighing up to 54kg/119 lb. at 12 months), these dogs have a gentle, patient temperament that makes them ideal family pets. The history of the breed is marked by tales of strength, courage, and loyalty to their human masters. An example of their heroism can be found during the 1919 wreck of the *S.S. Ethie*, when the ship's Newfoundland dog jumped into the roaring sea and carried in a line, which was then secured by people on shore. The line was the lifeline by which the shipwrecked passengers were able to reach safety.

For the first time in history, the Westminster Kennel Club awarded the 2004 Best In Show Trophy to "Josh," a Newfoundland, at their 128th Annual Dog Show.

The province's other canine companion is another water-loving dog known as the **Labrador retriever.** Although they are similar to the Newfoundland in temperament, they are about half the size and have short, straight hair. As their name indicates, these dogs make excellent hunting companions.

bring you back to the fishery. The abundance of fish is what undoubtedly attracted the first native inhabitants to this land of shorelines. It is also the magnet that induced European commercial interests to make an annual pilgrimage to the province's treacherous shores. The fishery is what built the province. For 300 years cod was the most numerous and valuable of all species, with halibut, haddock, and pollock processed as a side catch. As fishing techniques improved, the catch increased. The first megatrawlers appeared in local waters in the 1960s. Capable of hauling in up to 200 tons of cod within a single hour, they had the onboard facilities to also process and

The Liberal Party chooses Roger Grimes to be their new leader, effectively making him the new Premier.

- **2002** The province officially changes its name to Newfoundland and Labrador (and its postal abbreviation from NF to NL).
- **2003** Roger Grimes and the governing Liberal Party lose the provincial election to the Progressive Conservatives

under the leadership of Danny Williams.

- **2004** Premier Danny Williams orders Canadian flags removed from provincial buildings in protest of federal policies regarding oil revenues.
- **2005** The government imposes a ban on smoking in public places, including restaurants and bars.

- **2005** The Rooms—a combined provincial museum, art gallery, and archives—opens in St John's.
- **2006** As a result of a land claim agreement with the government and the Inuit of Labrador, elections are held to form a government in Nunatsiavut.

freeze the fish, and then transfer the catch to motherships. The total catch began declining after peaking at 810,000 tons annually in 1968. It took until 1977 for the Canadian government to act by extending territorial waters from 12 to 200 miles, thereby preventing the mostly foreign fleet from cod fishing. In an act of incredible shortsightedness, the government then encouraged Canadian companies to continue to fish using megatrawlers, and while it was a popular short-term policy with Newfoundlanders, the end was near. Quotas were eventually established, but it was too late. By the late 1980s fish stocks were so completely decimated that annual quotas were barely met.

By 1992, it was all over—there were no cod left to catch. The idea behind the 1992 Cod Moratorium was that if fishing were stopped completely, the fish would slowly return. What wasn't fully understood at the time was that not only were the cod gone, but the entire ecosystem had been changed forever. The effects extended well beyond the ocean. Some estimates of the resulting unemployment were as high as 60,000 people, in a provincial population of 500,000.

Today, if you order fish and chips in a local restaurant, you'll get cod. That's because a small part of the cod fishery has reopened in the Gulf of St. Lawrence. Despite the terrible effects of the moratorium, today the sun shines brightly (metaphorically speaking) on Canada's Far East as it turns its attentions to tourism and other newly discovered jewels of the sea to feed and clothe its people.

2 A Land of Bountiful Natural Resources

NATURAL RESOURCES AND THE GREAT OUTDOORS   Newfoundland and Labrador is a land rich in natural resources. To commemorate this abundance, the province has designated a tree, plant, gemstone, and bird as its official representatives of nature. The provincial tree is the black spruce, which is the most common tree in the province.

Newfoundland's official floral emblem is the pitcher plant. More than 100 years ago, Queen Victoria of England chose the pitcher plant to be engraved on a newly minted Newfoundland penny. In 1954, the Newfoundland Cabinet designated this fascinating plant as the official flower of the province. This unusual wine-and-green-colored flower can be found on bogs and marshes in Newfoundland and Labrador. You can see it growing on the hills surrounding Cape Spear and in Salmonier Nature Park. The plant gets its nourishment from insects that are trapped and then drowned in a pool of water at the base of its tubular leaves. If you stick your fingers into the death pod at the base of the plant, you're likely to pull out an insect or two. Don't worry: pitcher plants don't eat humans.

In summer, berries are everywhere. The most popular of the local berries is the bakeapple, internationally known as the cloudberry. The ripened berry is a cloudy orange-yellow color, and only one berry grows on each plant. Bakeapple plants grow approximately 7 to 10 centimeters (3–4 in.) high—so you'll have to get down pretty low to pick them, but at least they're easy to spot because of their bright color. The berries are quite unique in flavor and generally ready for picking in mid-August, when you'll see many roadside stands selling basketfuls.

Another popular Newfoundland berry is the partridgeberry, internationally known as the lingonberry and a relative of the cranberry family. Each plant produces a single dark-red tart-tasting berry that usually ripens after the first frost in September. Both the bakeapple and the

---

> ### ⌒ Fun Fact More Than Fiddles & Accordions
>
> For anyone who thinks that all Newfoundland music and musicians fall under the "traditional" banner, think again. The province is teeming with all kinds of talent, ranging from pop rock to alternative to hip-hop and blues. In April 2003, Corner Brook native Christa Borden won *Pop Star: The One* (a competition similar to *Canadian Idol* or *American Idol*). And the following year Upper Island Cove resident Jason Greeley was one of the top finalists in the *Canadian Idol* competition.

---

partridgeberry make excellent jams, spreads, and even wines that can be purchased at various shops throughout the province.

The Dark Tickle Company sells an array of local berry products from its Northern Peninsula factory outlet and online at www.darktickle.com.

ROCKS ON THE ROCK   Appropriately, Newfoundland—nicknamed the Rock—is rich in geological resources. Mistaken Point on the Avalon Peninsula has what are thought to be the world's oldest fossils, and you can find several other great places for fossil hunting throughout the province. Tourism Newfoundland and Labrador (© **800/563-6353**; www.newfoundlandandlabrador tourism.com) offers free information about places of geological interest in the *Newfoundland & Labrador Traveller's Guide to Geology*. Newfoundland's Department of Mines & Energy (© **709/729-3159**; www.nr.gov.nl.ca/mines&en) is a good resource for geology-specific maps and information.

Named the province's mineral emblem in 1975, *Labradorite* is one of about 20 semiprecious stones found in Newfoundland and Labrador. You may spot it at a number of locations on the coast of Labrador and on the island of Newfoundland. Labradorite is an igneous, iridescent crystalline mineral (also known as Labrador feldspar) that looks like a piece of the Labrador night sky, with the colors of the aurora borealis captured inside. It's used to make lovely pieces of jewelry that you can purchase at various stores throughout the province.

WILDLIFE   Some 30 to 40 million seabirds, representing many different species, visit Newfoundland and Labrador each year. The favorite among these for most travelers is likely to be the provincial bird of Newfoundland: the Atlantic puffin, also known as the sea parrot or Baccalieu bird. Puffins are quite small compared to many other seabirds, and they're striking in appearance with their black-and-white plumage and brightly colored, rounded beaks. They're exceptionally cute to watch, because their short wings seem to have difficulty supporting their chubby little bodies. Puffins need to flap their wings repeatedly to keep themselves in flight, lacking the grace or ease of flying exhibited by most birds. About 95% of all puffins in North America breed in colonies around the Newfoundland and Labrador coast.

The fertile waters of Newfoundland and Labrador are home to 22 species of whales; the more common species are the massive humpbacks and the much smaller minke whales. In fact, the waters around the province have the world's largest concentration of humpback whales. Between April and October, your chances of seeing a humpback fairly close to shore are quite good nearly anywhere in the province, with numbers peaking between June and September. The province also possesses the world's largest number of salmon rivers. The Main River near Corner Brook is the first Canadian Heritage River to be so designated in the province.

Only 14 land mammals are indigenous to the island of Newfoundland. Additional species have been introduced by humans—most notably the moose, which have taken quite nicely to the Rock and now number 150,000. Sufferers of ophidiophobia will be relieved to know that Newfoundland has no snakes.

However, certain land species are here in abundance. The province is home to one of the world's largest caribou herd, approximately 500,000 animals, at George River, Labrador. The island of Newfoundland also boasts North America's highest concentration of moose, as well as the continent's largest black bears, making the province an ideal destination for lovers of wildlife, whether you're hunting with a camera, a gun, or a fishing rod. Labrador is a great place for trophy fishing and for hunting black bear or caribou; Newfoundland offers fine moose hunting and salmon fishing. You can get a free copy of the *Hunting & Fishing Guide for Newfoundland & Labrador* by calling ✆ **800/563-6353** or 709/729-2830.

ICEBERGS Thinking back to the untimely sinking of the *Titanic,* we all know that icebergs can be dangerous and even fatal if their vastness and power are not respected. Nevertheless, they are awe-inspiringly beautiful, and Newfoundland is one of the most accessible places in the world to see icebergs. Each spring, hundreds float southward from Greenland past Baffin Island and down the coast along Iceberg Alley. The largest iceberg spotted off the coast of Newfoundland was about 13km (8 miles) long, weighed more than 9 billion metric tons, and likely took 3 years to make the journey from Greenland, where it would have calved off a gargantuan land-based glacier.

As the massive iceberg continues to float farther south into warmer waters, it weakens and begins to break apart into smaller, more manageable pieces. Bigger pieces that are comparable to the size of a large ship are called "growlers." Smaller chunks that may be the size of a car, a small house, or less are called "bergy bits." But for those of us who "come from away" it's equally exciting, whether we're fortunate enough to see a massive iceberg or just a piece of one in a lesser but still impressive form.

Newfoundlanders are respectful of icebergs. They know that one of the massive missives of compressed snow can break up or overturn at any time, taking with it a boat that has ventured too close. Seabirds seem to be able to sense when an iceberg is about to roll and will fly away just before it does its dangerous dance. Remember, only 10% of an iceberg's mass can be seen above the surface of the water, and the other 90% is submerged and cannot be seen.

When the bergs break up into growlers or bergy bits, they become more manageable and more predictable. This natural process has created some interesting opportunities for enterprising Newfoundlanders, who have begun marketing several innovative iceberg products.

Bergy bits are harvested and broken down into even smaller bits and used as ice cubes in drinks. There's something unique about iceberg ice, because of its effervescence. Your drink will pop, crackle, and fizz when the air bubbles contained in the ice make contact with the liquid.

As well, iceberg pieces are melted down and bottled into drinking water. One popular brand is Iceberg Water. Just think: you're drinking water that's more than 10,000 years old! Canadian Iceberg Vodka, bottled in St. John's, is another interesting product made from the charcoal-filtered and triple-distilled water of iceberg growlers and bergy bits and mixed with grain alcohol. The award-winning vodka has been voted the second-best vodka in the world. Leave it to those fun-loving Newfoundlanders to get a buzz out of a berg!

3 Newfoundland & Labrador Today

Despite the devastating blow dealt to them with the Cod Moratorium, Newfoundlanders continue to be proud of their heritage, and today the economy is humming along nicely. Offshore oil developments lead the way in terms of economic growth, with enough production to catapult the province ahead of all other Canadian provinces in terms of economic growth beginning in 2003.

St. John's remains an old-fashioned port city through and through, but the newfound wealth is obvious and well received by most. Less than a generation ago, thousands of young adults were fleeing the province in search of work elsewhere in Canada. Today, those finishing school are mostly choosing to remain, and many that left in the 1990s are returning, young families in tow. Unthinkable even a decade ago, today in St John's you can sip a chai latte at a sidewalk cafe, enjoy a day spa in a converted monastery, or visit one of the world's premium museums. There are boutique hotels, Thai restaurants, and even million-dollar condominium projects. Beyond city limits of the capital, the scene is a little different. The sea of change to hit St. John's is not obvious, unemployment is high, and there is little or no reason for younger generations to remain. For many towns and villages across the province, tourism is the shining light for future prosperity. Postcard-perfect villages like Trinity, which starred in the movie *Shipping News,* have embraced tourism without changing in outward appearance. South of St. John's fishing boats that once hauled in cod now take visitors on whale-watching trips, while along northern coastlines it's icebergs that the visitors come to see.

SOME THINGS WILL NEVER CHANGE Through good times and bad, Newfoundlanders have never been accused of being unsociable. George Street, in downtown St. John's, is known far and wide for its concentration of pubs. Here, beer flows freely and dancing to Celtic music comes easily. The vibe for out-of-towners is welcoming. So much so that at many bars you can become an honorary Newfoundlander by participating in a "screech-in." The tongue-in-cheek ritual varies from place to place but generally requires you to recite a silly verse, drink an ounce of the hair-raising dark rum straight up, and then kiss a piece of salt cod (or, in some establishments, a stuffed puffin), upon which you'll be presented with a certificate for a keepsake. Trapper's John's, in the capital, is a well-known place to be screeched-in.

For those who prefer their liquor with a mixer, try screech in a "Dark 'n' Dirty," the local name given to what most other places call a rum and cola.

MUSIC AND THEATER Planning a celebration seems to come easily to Newfoundlanders. In simple words, they know how to party, and they certainly know how to make fabulous music. Some of the better-known acts include The Irish Descendents, Great Big Sea, The Masterless Men, and The Ennis Sisters, all known for their Celtic sound.

As well, Newfoundlanders love their live theater, and you'll find many regional festivals occurring throughout the province during summer, including in St John's, Trinity (Eastern Region), and

Gros Morne National Park (Western Newfoundland). Contact Tourism Newfoundland and Labrador (*©* **800/563-6353;** www.newfoundlandandlabrador tourism.com) for current schedules and prices.

COME HOME CELEBRATIONS Because of the province's unstable economy, many of Newfoundland's young and educated have felt compelled to move away from the Rock in order to earn a good living for themselves and their families. The province's population has actually decreased over the last decade because of this outflow of people and the fact that Newfoundland and Labrador has a very small percentage of immigrants in comparison to the rest of Canada.

Most of those leaving the province have ended up in Ontario (because of the opportunities in commerce, science, and technology) and Alberta (for those interested in the petroleum industry, as close ties have formed between the two provinces with Newfoundland's recent involvement in offshore drilling). It is said that the population of Fort McMurray, Alberta, is now the third largest town of Newfoundlanders (after St. John's and Gander).

You may be able to take the Newfoundlander out of Newfoundland, but you can never exorcise the spirit of Newfoundland from its people. As a result, many who have left return each summer to spend time with family and friends and to visit the place they will always call home. To commemorate this spirit, many communities throughout the province have created "Come Home Year" celebrations, filled with all sorts of food, fun, and frolic.

DICTIONARY OF NEWFOUNDLAND ENGLISH This useful tool will not only help you prepare for your trip to the Rock, but provide fun reading long after you've returned home. Even though Newfoundlanders speak English, they have their own dialect that has introduced new and varied meanings for common words, and they have developed unique words of their own. These can be found in the whopping 770 pages that make up the *Dictionary of Newfoundland English,* published by the University of Toronto Press.

Any visitor to the Rock will find this book extremely useful, and any student of languages will find it extremely interesting. Some examples of what you'll discover in this bulky volume include seven different meanings for the word "cat," which includes the obvious interpretation as well as others, and some surprisingly pleasant meanings for the word "piss." The book retails for C$42.50 (US$36.50), and you can find it at St. John's booksellers such as Wordplay (www.wordplay.com). ***Note:*** Not every person in every region of Newfoundland and Labrador will use words found in the *Dictionary of Newfoundland English.* Some of the recorded words and phrases are obsolete.

Index

See also Accommodations and Restaurant indexes, below.

ACCOMMODATIONS

RESTAURANTS

FROMMER'S® COMPLETE TRAVEL GUIDES

Alaska
Amalfi Coast
American Southwest
Amsterdam
Argentina & Chile
Arizona
Atlanta
Australia
Austria
Bahamas
Barcelona
Beijing
Belgium, Holland & Luxembourg
Belize
Bermuda
Boston
Brazil
British Columbia & the Canadian
  Rockies
Brussels & Bruges
Budapest & the Best of Hungary
Buenos Aires
Calgary
California
Canada
Cancún, Cozumel & the Yucatán
Cape Cod, Nantucket & Martha's
  Vineyard
Caribbean
Caribbean Ports of Call
Carolinas & Georgia
Chicago
China
Colorado
Costa Rica
Croatia
Cuba
Denmark
Denver, Boulder & Colorado Springs
Edinburgh & Glasgow
England
Europe
Europe by Rail

Florence, Tuscany & Umbria
Florida
France
Germany
Greece
Greek Islands
Hawaii
Hong Kong
Honolulu, Waikiki & Oahu
India
Ireland
Italy
Jamaica
Japan
Kauai
Las Vegas
London
Los Angeles
Los Cabos & Baja
Madrid
Maine Coast
Maryland & Delaware
Maui
Mexico
Montana & Wyoming
Montréal & Québec City
Moscow & St. Petersburg
Munich & the Bavarian Alps
Nashville & Memphis
New England
Newfoundland & Labrador
New Mexico
New Orleans
New York City
New York State
New Zealand
Northern Italy
Norway
Nova Scotia, New Brunswick &
  Prince Edward Island
Oregon
Paris
Peru

Philadelphia & the Amish Country
Portugal
Prague & the Best of the Czech
  Republic
Provence & the Riviera
Puerto Rico
Rome
San Antonio & Austin
San Diego
San Francisco
Santa Fe, Taos & Albuquerque
Scandinavia
Scotland
Seattle
Seville, Granada & the Best of
  Andalusia
Shanghai
Sicily
Singapore & Malaysia
South Africa
South America
South Florida
South Pacific
Southeast Asia
Spain
Sweden
Switzerland
Texas
Thailand
Tokyo
Toronto
Turkey
USA
Utah
Vancouver & Victoria
Vermont, New Hampshire & Maine
Vienna & the Danube Valley
Vietnam
Virgin Islands
Virginia
Walt Disney World® & Orlando
Washington, D.C.
Washington State

FROMMER'S® DOLLAR-A-DAY GUIDES

Australia from $60 a Day
California from $70 a Day
England from $75 a Day
Europe from $85 a Day
Florida from $70 a Day

Hawaii from $80 a Day
Ireland from $90 a Day
Italy from $90 a Day
London from $95 a Day

New York City from $90 a Day
Paris from $95 a Day
San Francisco from $70 a Day
Washington, D.C. from $80 a Day

FROMMER'S® PORTABLE GUIDES

Acapulco, Ixtapa & Zihuatanejo
Amsterdam
Aruba
Australia's Great Barrier Reef
Bahamas
Berlin
Big Island of Hawaii
Boston
California Wine Country
Cancún
Cayman Islands
Charleston
Chicago

Disneyland®
Dominican Republic
Dublin
Florence
Las Vegas
Las Vegas for Non-Gamblers
London
Los Angeles
Maui
Nantucket & Martha's Vineyard
New Orleans
New York City
Paris

Portland
Puerto Rico
Puerto Vallarta, Manzanillo &
  Guadalajara
Rio de Janeiro
San Diego
San Francisco
Savannah
Vancouver
Venice
Virgin Islands
Washington, D.C.
Whistler

FROMMER'S® CRUISE GUIDES

Alaska Cruises & Ports of Call

Cruises & Ports of Call

European Cruises & Ports of Call

FROMMER'S® DAY BY DAY GUIDES

Amsterdam
Chicago
Florence & Tuscany

London
New York City
Paris

Rome
San Francisco
Venice

FROMMER'S® NATIONAL PARK GUIDES

Algonquin Provincial Park
Banff & Jasper
Grand Canyon

National Parks of the American West
Rocky Mountain
Yellowstone & Grand Teton

Yosemite and Sequoia & Kings
Canyon
Zion & Bryce Canyon

FROMMER'S® MEMORABLE WALKS

Chicago
London

New York
Paris

Rome
San Francisco

FROMMER'S® WITH KIDS GUIDES

Chicago
Hawaii
Las Vegas
London

National Parks
New York City
San Francisco

Toronto
Walt Disney World® & Orlando
Washington, D.C.

SUZY GERSHMAN'S BORN TO SHOP GUIDES

Born to Shop: France
Born to Shop: Hong Kong, Shanghai
& Beijing

Born to Shop: Italy
Born to Shop: London

Born to Shop: New York
Born to Shop: Paris

FROMMER'S® IRREVERENT GUIDES

Amsterdam
Boston
Chicago
Las Vegas
London

Los Angeles
Manhattan
New Orleans
Paris

Rome
San Francisco
Walt Disney World®
Washington, D.C.

FROMMER'S® BEST-LOVED DRIVING TOURS

Austria
Britain
California
France

Germany
Ireland
Italy
New England

Northern Italy
Scotland
Spain
Tuscany & Umbria

THE UNOFFICIAL GUIDES®

Adventure Travel in Alaska
Beyond Disney
California with Kids
Central Italy
Chicago
Cruises
Disneyland®
England
Florida
Florida with Kids

Hawaii
Ireland
Las Vegas
London
Maui
Mexico's Best Beach Resorts
Mini Las Vegas
Mini Mickey
New Orleans
New York City

Paris
San Francisco
South Florida including Miami &
the Keys
Walt Disney World®
Walt Disney World® for
Grown-ups
Walt Disney World® with Kids
Washington, D.C.

SPECIAL-INTEREST TITLES

Athens Past & Present
Cities Ranked & Rated
Frommer's Best Day Trips from London
Frommer's Best RV & Tent Campgrounds
in the U.S.A.

Frommer's Exploring America by RV
Frommer's NYC Free & Dirt Cheap
Frommer's Road Atlas Europe
Frommer's Road Atlas Ireland
Retirement Places Rated

FROMMER'S® PHRASEFINDER DICTIONARY GUIDES

French

Italian

Spanish